RUDY GIULIANI

EMPEROR OF THE CITY

RUDY GIULIANI

EMPEROR OF THE CITY

Andrew Kirtzman

WILLIAM MORROW

An Imprint of Harper Collins*Publishers*

HarperCollins books may be purchased for educational, business, or sales promotional use. For information please write: Special Markets Department, HarperCollins Publishers Inc., 10 East 53rd Street, New York, NY 10022.

FIRST EDITION

Designed by Betty Lew

Printed on acid-free paper

Library of Congress Cataloging-in-Publication Data has been applied for.

ISBN 0-688-17492-2

00 01 02 03 04   QWF   10 9 8 7 6 5 4 3 2 1

My grandfather, Irving Cohen, used to call New York City "God's Country" with just a touch of irony. He was a proud New Yorker who rarely traveled beyond the five boroughs, a newsstand dealer who was proud that his son and grandson became journalists and who boasted that they'd inherited their love of the news business from him. Neither he nor my grandmother, Mary Cohen, were widely known beyond their small circle of friends and neighbors on Grand Street on Manhattan's Lower East Side. But they were integral to the life of this city, and more than integral to my life growing up in God's Country, and it is to them that I dedicate this book.

Contents

Introduction

I t all seemed to be falling apart. As he stepped out of the 50th Precinct house into the first warm breeze of spring, everything Rudy Giuliani had done to revive New York seemed forgotten. The city was turning on him.

All the powers he'd outfoxed or bullied into submission—the liberals, the Harlem politicians, the editorial page editors, the civil liberties crowd—were rising together as one to protest the fatal police shooting of an unarmed immigrant. The daily sit-ins in front of Police Headquarters had grown exponentially and had taken on the air of a movement: several congressmen had been arrested, along with the state comptroller, a former mayor, and some movie stars. Giuliani's popularity had plummeted 21 points, to the lowest point of his five-year tenure. The man who'd solved the unsolvable, who ran the city seemingly by himself, a kind of robo-mayor immune to fatigue, fear, or self-doubt, was under siege, and the legion of officials he'd insulted, ignored, or humiliated were just sitting back and watching him suffer, alone and virtually friendless.

A few miles away, protestors filled the streets in front of the majestic Bronx County Courthouse, forcing court officials to shut down most business for the day. It was indictment time for the four officers at the center of the case, all made famous for spraying a hail of forty-one bullets at the

African immigrant, Amadou Diallo, as he tried to enter his building one early February morning in 1999. Along the Grand Concourse, it seemed like a holiday, a festival called to rally around the coming fall of Rudy Giuliani. Peddlers were hawking "Impeach Rudy" T-shirts. Signs bobbing in the air read "Impeach Rudy" and "Depose Rudy." Shortly after 2 P.M., the crowd would explode in a roar when the Reverend Al Sharpton made his entrance, accompanied by Kadiatou Diallo, Amadou's mother. The man most singularly vilified by the mayor was greeted like Mandela, fresh out of Robben Island.

It was all a bit surreal to see the person most linked to the city's rebirth dangling on the precipice of disaster. In Times Square, one and a half million tourists were flooding the streets, gawking at $4 billion worth of new towers, hotels, electronic news zippers, and theme restaurants. Internet millionaires were blooming like the tulips along Park Avenue, generating tax revenues that had city government awash with cash. Police had restored order on the streets: crime had plunged so low that FBI statistics were showing New York to be the safest large city in America. Unemployment was down, and 400,000 fewer people were on the welfare rolls. *Time* magazine, which announced the city all but dead in a 1990 cover story called "The Rotting of the Big Apple," was cheering the city's comeback. And Rudy Giuliani was the hero of the revival.

As the Diallo case unfolded, though, people had started to look at this man and all he had accomplished in a different light. Minority residents had been harassed and humiliated by his police so many times on the streets of their own neighborhoods that the department had come to be viewed as an occupying force, and the shooting of the African street peddler was the last straw. Watching for Giuliani's response to Diallo's death, the public saw a cold man, unsympathetic to the pain of black residents and so alienated from their leaders that he'd refused to meet with them for years.

As Giuliani stepped up to a microphone planted outside the Bronx precinct house this morning, he was at yet another juncture. The indictment of the four cops had offered him one more opportunity to make a gesture of conciliation to his black constituents.

The mayor had come to dedicate the street outside the 50th Precinct house to Vincent Guidice, a police officer who'd died while responding to a domestic violence dispute. As he began to address the officer's family and three lines of police officers in full funeral attire, it became clear that the demonstrations were on Giuliani's mind.

"As we ask the police department to show more respect," he said, "and we make Herculean efforts—*they* do—to show more respect, we have something that we have a right to demand.

"We have a right to demand more respect from the citizens of the city for the police officers of the City of New York. It's about time to stop carrying signs pretending that they're racist, it's about time to stop carrying signs equating them to the KKK, and it's about time to stop invocations of Adolf Hitler, about our police department."

Gazing out on the officers in their blue uniforms and white gloves, a tremble of anger entered his voice. "They have to make decisions that I don't know that I'd be capable of making," he said. "And then they're second-guessed by some of the worst in society.

"The short-sighted, and those who want to focus blame on the police, maybe for their own personal inadequacies, we're never going to convince," he said. "But I think we've convinced most of the people of this city that the aggressive, appropriate police strategies of this department have saved thousands and thousands of lives."

In private meetings about the Diallo crisis, Giuliani had rejected the idea of delivering a televised address in which he might have offered solace to the black community *and* defended his police force. That would have been too ambiguous, too political, too much like the old regime, always quick to create a moral equivalence when it should have shown the difference between right and wrong. Defying waves of politicians pleading with him to rise above the cops vs. community war, Giuliani had apparently come here today with one purpose—to side with the police.

"I'd also ask you to think about the restraint exercised by Officer Guidice," he said. "I think that reflects to a very large extent what this police department is like—not what the *bashers* of this police department would like you to believe."

His resentment hung in the air. Guidice's brother Paul looked shaken.

Eileen, the slain officer's mother, limped tentatively up the stairs to the dais, shook Giuliani's hand, then threw her arms around him and cried. The bombs were dropping all around this little makeshift island in the Bronx, but Giuliani didn't care. With his mayoralty hanging in the balance, he'd come to tell the demonstrators, the newspapers, and the rest of the critics to go to hell.

This is the story of a defiant man whose strength, resolve, and vision helped bring a city back from a state of bedlam. It's an account of how a person with no experience in municipal government outsmarted its political leaders, union chiefs, and media lords and ended up changing the face of New York. It's about a leader whose accomplishments rank among the most dramatic in urban history.

It is also a story about one of the most polarizing political figures since Richard Nixon. By the middle of his second term, Giuliani was a villain in the eyes of the black community, a fascist in the eyes of liberals, and a traitor to leaders of his own party. His likeness, grotesquely altered to look like the devil, or Hitler, was plastered on hundreds of mailboxes and lampposts around the city. "Heartless Bastard," a *Village Voice* cover once called him, and many agreed.

Giuliani's paranoia, his distrust of outsiders, his need to control everything around him and to destroy those he saw as enemies were harrowing to observe. The path of his mayoralty is pockmarked with a long list of missed opportunities, chances he refused to take because of his inherent distrust of people. As a result, the most successful mayor in fifty years spent much of his reign alone and disconnected from the public. The tragedy of his mayoralty is that he could have accomplished so much more.

But it is equally true that his flaws were key to his successes. As he demonstrated that tormented day in the Bronx, when the whole city was waiting for a sign of conciliation, Giuliani never bent to threats, and rose in anger when challenged publicly. Through force of personality and through a deliberate effort to centralize all power in his office, he intimidated the reigning powers of New York. No one wasn't afraid of Rudy Giuliani. In a fight he was resolute, unable to bluff. He crushed the barriers that had stood in the path of his predecessors.

It is hard to overstate the degree to which the culture of the city changed under his mayoralty. New Yorkers heading to work no longer encounter men urinating on the sidewalks. They no longer travel in graffiti-covered trains, in which homeless men sleep across the seats and peddlers loudly hawk ragged copies of *Street News*. They don't fear for their safety as they exit onto deserted streets. The parked cars they pass no longer sport signs addressed to car thieves taped to their windows reading "No Radio," and old ladies in the parks no longer talk exclusively about who's been mugged over the weekend. The porn stores have vanished from neighborhoods, and drug dealers no longer sell loose joints in children's parks.

The parks sport surveillance cameras, however, and are closed to the public at midnight. Many nightclubs have been busted over and over and finally shuttered. City Hall is an armed camp, closed to office workers who used to stroll past the center of government at lunchtime. Motorists caught driving drunk forfeit their cars. Times Square is back, but is disdained by New Yorkers as a tourist trap. The homeless have largely vanished from sight, but soup kitchens are overflowing. The city has sacrificed some of its anarchic spirit—and some of its heart—for the order Giuliani imposed.

The political culture has changed as well. Rudy Giuliani ended the fifty-year reign of liberalism in New York City, one of the cradles of American liberalism. He helped smash the consensus for welfare and a score of other programs held dear by the public. He dealt a blow to identity politics and put an end to a run of racial blackmail that had paralyzed a succession of regimes. His aggressive brand of police enforcement was so successful that even his Democratic rivals had to pledge their support for it.

While driven by a moralism acquired from a religious upbringing, Giuliani's tactics were often ruthless and in some cases immoral. During his first campaign, his aides distributed to the press love letters from a married rival's purported girlfriends. The reformist mayor made patronage a staple of daily life at City Hall; aides regularly terrorized commissioners into hiring hacks and cronies. He stood by as his closest aide, Cristyne Lategano, disparaged the reputations of political foes, while Giuliani himself thought little of attacking the reputations of people who stood in his way. A year after the Diallo shooting, when the controversy had faded, Giuliani smeared the reputation of Patrick Dorismond, an unarmed security guard gunned down in another police confrontation, triggering yet another wave of outrage. In the midst of a nationally watched race for the U.S. Senate, he flaunted an extramarital affair even as he lectured others on morality.

Giuliani's police force was so aggressive in pursuing minority suspects that his one black deputy mayor had to be issued an identification badge from the NYPD to stave off routine police stops—in his official car. It was no accident that the mayor's worst, most debilitating crises involved the black community.

Giuliani was often criticized for his hardball tactics, but he had a core belief in loyalty, and to those he considered loyal he was often generous and fatherly. While known for his inflammatory language in public, he was renowned throughout his administration as a calm and brilliant strategist. The vast majority of holdovers from the previous administration regarded Giuliani as smarter, more knowledgeable, better engaged, and more decisive than his predecessor, David Dinkins.

For the past eight years, as a political reporter for New York 1 News, the city's all-news television channel, I've watched Giuliani as closely as anyone and have often found myself mesmerized by the drama that has consumed City Hall since the moment he took office in 1994. In that time I've thought of him variously as a great man and as a mean-spirited one; a visionary and an opportunist; a transforming leader and an intolerant one. Somewhere in the midst of juggling the different emotions he elicited, I decided that I needed to tell the story of this extraordinary figure and his equally remarkable reign.

I set about interviewing people who worked side by side with Giuliani as well as those he battled—more than two hundred people in all. My hope was that, as controversies faded into history, the combatants would feel liberated to speak more freely, and in most cases that proved to be the case. The majority of my interviews were conducted on the record, though some people would speak only on condition of confidentiality. The latter group tended to include people who still work for the mayor, though a handful of people outside of City Hall feared retribution for talking openly about this famously vengeful man.

Giuliani himself declined to cooperate, and never offered an explanation as to why. To compensate, I interviewed dozens of his aides and confidants to learn his positions, thoughts, and feelings about the events and stories that are described in this book. I should also note that City Hall attempted to ban a handful of those aides and supporters from sitting down for interviews. But in the end I spoke with the vast majority of the people who were close to Giuliani during his mayoralty.

This is a chronicle of his rise to power in New York City. It is not a definitive history of the Giuliani administration, nor is it a comprehensive survey of every event that occurred in that period. It is, rather, an observer's account of one man's extraordinary ride, and how the city was changed, perhaps forever, because of it.

RUDY GIULIANI

EMPEROR OF THE CITY

1

The Runner Stumbles

R ain was falling on the campaign van as it wound through the streets of Manhattan toward the Metropolitan Republican Club. The trip to the Giuliani-for-Mayor kickoff ceremony should have been a joyous occasion. But as the candidate traveled through midtown traffic this dreary May morning in 1989, there was more desperation in the air than anything else.

Ray Harding had worried about the Giuliani crew from the beginning. "Smart guys, no experience," the Liberal Party chief had said. "How do I know this isn't Amateur Night at the Bijou?" The question hovered over Rudy Giuliani as he mapped strategy to contain the disaster of the day, a front-page story in the morning's *Daily News* disclosing that his law firm was registered as a foreign agent for Panama, as the U.S. government was charging General Manuel Noriega with cocaine trafficking. Giuliani wasn't the dictator's lawyer, but the distinction was lost on its way to the front page.

Harding was back at Liberal Party headquarters wondering how it could all be going so wrong. The candidate's huge lead in the polls was disintegrating. The campaign was running out of cash. Giuliani's strategists were jumping from crisis to crisis, while the candidate flailed about on the campaign trail.

When his moment came, Giuliani walked into the tiny space in which

Fiorello LaGuardia had announced his run for mayor fifty-six years earlier. Dozens of sweat-soaked reporters were already there, squeezed against banks of television cameras. Giuliani introduced his wife, Donna, and held his three-year-old son, Andrew, aloft for the cameras. Then he launched into a tirade against the forces that had overtaken New York.

"Now is the time to take back our city from the violent criminals on our streets and the white-collar criminals in their office suites," he said, "from the drug dealers in abandoned buildings and the crooked politicians who have abandoned their oath of office.

"It is time to restore the reputation of New York, so that once again our city will be known for its libraries, its universities, its culture, its industry, and its spirit—not as it is known today for crime, crack, and corruption."

It was time, he said, "to take our streets, parks, and subways back from the criminals."

"No deals for jobs, no deals for contributors," he pledged. "What you see is what you get."

When he finished his speech, the candidate stuck to the game plan and took no questions. It was a strategy that made Harding furious: How could Giuliani ignore the New York City press corps on the day he launched his campaign? It was insanity. Sure enough, reporters shouted their questions to him as he made his way out of the room: Did he know about the Noriega connection? What would he do about it? Would he quit his law firm?

Within forty-eight hours, a commercial was running on television attacking him. "Rudy Giuliani is being paid almost one million dollars by the law firm that represents Panama's drug dictator Noriega," an announcer intoned as a picture of the general appeared next to Giuliani's. It was paid for by Giuliani's opponent in the Republican primary, Ronald Lauder, a multi-millionaire propped up by Senator Al D'Amato.

Soon afterward Mayor Ed Koch, the Democratic incumbent, jumped into the fray, accusing Giuliani of taking "drug money."

"Why is it unfair, if Noriega would be arrested by some foreign marshal, to talk about the fact that he might call Rudy on the phone?" Koch asked reporters. Twisting the knife a little further, he questioned why Giuliani's firm, White & Case, had no black or Hispanic partners.

Giuliani fell into his trap. "Koch is intelligent enough to know he's lying" about his having taken drug money, he told reporters the next day. "I expect him to lie. With Lauder, who knows?" Lauder, he said, was "an incompetent" who "never had to work for a living." The front page of the next day's *Newsday* read "RUDY SNARLS."

Sensing weakness, D'Amato went in for the kill, appearing on CNBC to pronounce the Noriega question perfectly fair. "I don't believe you join a law firm like White and Case and get one million dollars and don't even know who your clients are," he said, almost doubling the size of Giuliani's salary. "Are they buying access to City Hall? That's a tough question, a fair question—they pay you one million dollars to run for mayor?"

It was a classic New York feeding frenzy, sparked by an issue that was completely meaningless. Giuliani was getting banged around by politicians far more seasoned at this kind of game than he. The rookie candidate had kept a non-story alive and revived questions about his temperament in the process. Finally, on June 5—nineteen days after he announced his candidacy for mayor—Giuliani put the Noriega story out of its misery and took a leave of absence from White & Case.

The candidate took a breath, then set out on another mission, which was to understand why his run for mayor, which had started out with so much promise, was unraveling.

On January 11, 1989, the front page of the *New York Post* featured a huge photo of New York's best-known prosecutor holding an automatic pistol with a long black silencer. "GOOD NEWS FOR BAD GUYS," the headline roared. "Crimebuster Giuliani steps down."

America's most celebrated U.S. attorney had gathered his closest aides together and announced to a room full of reporters that he was resigning. "I hope the legacy we leave," he said solemnly, "is the continued emphasis on the need to reform the way in which we do business and practice politics."

Newspapers in Missouri normally don't chronicle the comings and goings of New York prosecutors, but the *St. Louis Post-Dispatch* made an exception. "Giuliani was one of the most visible and successful federal prosecutors the country has seen in decades," it reported the next day. The sentiment was echoed in the *Boston Globe*, the *Los Angeles Times*, and across the Atlantic in the *Financial Times* of London.

The coverage was hardly unusual. Most every day was a good one for Giuliani, another opportunity for the press to bathe him in superlatives or refer to him as a historic figure. "Not since the days of Thomas E. Dewey," the *Post* gushed, "has a federal prosecutor so captured the public imagination."

Indeed, Giuliani was a hero of his times, a living antidote to the decadence of the 1980s. As prosecutor he seemed to be the only public figure in town who wasn't high on something—not the drugs or the money or the nightlife that had made New York the epicenter of a roaring decade. Far from ignoring the bacchanal around him, he took direct aim at it. His targets were on Wall Street, the source of the good times, and at City Hall, where Ed Koch was the life of the party. Busting insider-trading schemes and municipal corruption scandals, he seemed utterly unseduced by it all. There seemed to be a moral power about the devout Catholic that made him something more than just a prosecutor. He was a cause unto himself.

He *looked* like a religious figure, cut out from some stained-glass window. He had a monkish intensity about him: his large face was pale, his eyes beady and dark, his tone of voice solemn. He spoke with the gravity of someone who knew right from wrong.

The causes he took on were breathtaking in their audacity. He prosecuted the entire Mafia high commission in a sweeping effort to decapitate the Genovese, Gambino, Lucchese, Columbo, and Bonanno families all at once; he extracted guilty pleas from Dennis Levine, Ivan Boesky, and a legion of millionaire insider-trading suspects, and toppled junk-bond king Michael Milken and his firm, Drexel Burnham Lambert; he won the convictions of Bronx Democratic boss Stanley Friedman, Congressman Mario Biaggi, and a slew of others in the vast municipal corruption scandals of the Koch era.

But as the new year began, his crusade to rid the city of evil had started to backfire. His conspiracy case against Koch confidante Bess Myerson and Judge Hortense Gabel ended in acquittals, and Giuliani took a bath of bad publicity for putting Gabel's daughter on the stand to testify against her. A tide of resentment had also begun to swell over his tactics in the insider-trading crusade, particularly the 1987 arrest of three Wall Street traders, one of whom had been led across the trading floor of Kidder Peabody in handcuffs. The prosecutor was increasingly being seen as an overzealous, even reckless man, lacking the judgment and compassion necessary for someone in a position to ruin lives. Giuliani's certainty about right and wrong and good and evil, ingrained in him at a young age, struck many as a dangerous thing.

A tavern owner's son, he had been groomed at all-male Catholic schools, serious places like Bishop Loughlin Memorial High School in Brooklyn, where students were taught to respect authority and teachers were Christian Brothers who'd taken vows of poverty. He'd thought for a time about becoming a priest himself but opted instead to enroll at Manhattan College, where students began each class with a prayer to remind them of God's presence, a prayer that ended with the invocation *"Live, Jesus, in our hearts. Forever!"*

For Giuliani, Catholicism was never just a convenience available to those who needed occasional spiritual direction; it was a code by which to judge the intentions and conduct of others. Those found wanting deserved condemnation. In his column in the *Manhattan Quadrangle*, the college newspaper, Giuliani damned a long line of politicians as hypocrites, liars, or worse. "Our glorious political history abounds with payoffs, bribes and bought state legislatures," he thundered. Then-mayor Robert Wagner was a "selfish, self-centered, power-hungry" man who'd sacrificed the good of the people for his own ends. Barry Goldwater was an "incompetend [sic], confused and sometimes idiotic man." Even as a young student, Giuliani had held people to high, perhaps impossibly high, standards and judged them harshly when they failed to live up to them.

Giuliani's ambitions had always driven him toward politics. At Loughlin, he'd been voted "Class Politician," even though he'd never run for student government. But as he grew older he found his calling in the law. Like religion, it prescribed codes of behavior and spelled out punishments for those who violated them. As he rose through the ranks of the Justice Department into the most high-profile U.S. attorney's job in America, Giuliani used the law to determine right and wrong, crime and punishment, a priest in a pinstriped suit.

With the Reagan administration coming to an end and criticism of his prosecutions rising, January 1989 was a good time, and perhaps a last chance, for Giuliani to exit the U.S. Attorney's Office a hero. It also offered him his opportunity to finally run for office.

As early as the previous September, he had started conversations about a run for mayor with the small group of lawyers who constituted his inner circle. The crowd was always the same: Peter Powers, his best friend since Bishop Loughlin; his wife, Donna Hanover, a television news reporter for WPIX-TV; Justice Department pals like Arnie Burns, Randy Levine, and Ken Caruso; subordinates at the U.S. Attorney's Office like Denny Young, his discreet second-in-command. The circle of white male attorneys were enthusiastic participants in a cult of personality revolving around the chief. His deputies at the U.S. Attorney's Office were known as the "Yesrudy's"—pronounced "Yes, Rudy," with an exaggerated slave accent. Loyalty was the sine qua non for admission to the club.

Again and again, in restaurants and midtown law firms, they went over the numbers, the names of political players, anything to get a handle on a subject they knew little about. They were making it up as they went along: at one meeting the group decided to name attorney John Gross the campaign treasurer because no one else wanted the job—and he'd gone to the bathroom.

The city seemed primed for the emergence of a fresh face. The Reagan boom had ended with a crash on Wall Street a year and a half earlier. The public had long grown used to decaying city services, from trains that didn't run on time to public schools that were turning out semiliterate graduates. But there was a sense of menace in the air that was new—and growing.

In a stupefying act of government negligence, the state had emptied thousands of patients from mental institutions and set them free onto the streets with barely any support. They were joined by families and single men displaced by the demolition of single-room occupancy hotels—a product of the construction boom. Grand Central Terminal and the Port Authority Bus Terminal seemed like mental wards, with armies of lost souls roaming their lobbies, protected only by vigilant civil liberties lawyers concerned about their rights.

The fear of crime was palpable. Commuters tried to avoid eye contact when gangs of teenagers rampaged through graffiti-covered subway cars. When a lanky engineer named Bernhard Goetz rose from his subway seat in December 1984 and opened fire on a gang of rowdy young men, much of the city applauded. Racial conflicts seemed to sprout up every month, from the death of a young black man named Michael Griffith in Howard Beach, Queens, to the alleged rape and abduction of Tawana Brawley, a young black woman in upstate Wappingers Falls. In response, Reverend Al Sharpton was leading "days of outrage" around the city, large and angry demonstrations that struck fear in the hearts of the white middle class.

The political leadership was in a tailspin. Queens Borough President Donald Manes plunged a kitchen knife into his chest in 1986, a suicide sparked by the unraveling of the worst corruption scandal in a generation. Although Koch was never implicated, the cascade of revelations showed that a cabal of corrupt Democratic bosses had grabbed pieces of City Hall, with the mayor an oblivious bystander.

Mayor Koch was an exuberant figure, a leader of boundless energy and uncommon wisdom who seemed less a politician than a professional kibitzer. Tall and balding, with a hearty laugh, he offered the public a running commentary on everything from balanced budgets to the cost of movie tickets. Mixing moderate politics with a borscht belt delivery, he'd dominated the city stage for a decade. But the act had started to wear thin: the public was growing tired of his ego and weary of his battles, especially with minority leaders, and he seemed helpless in the face of the corruption scandals and deteriorating living conditions. As the 1989 election year dawned, his popularity was plummeting. After twelve largely successful years, it seemed his moment had passed.

The promise of Giuliani's candidacy did not elude the political class. The power brokers who had been locked out of City Hall during Koch's hegemony were eyeing Giuliani as a potential ticket back from the wilderness. And no one was more eager to meet with him than Ray Harding.

The head of the New York State Liberal Party was an enormous man, with a mane of silver hair and a voice so syrupy slow that every word he uttered sounded conspiratorial. A proud immigrant who'd fled Yugoslavia to escape the Nazis, he was a master tactician, once described by a *New York Times* columnist as a one-man smoke-filled room. One grunt from him could mean the difference between victory and defeat for a candidate.

Sitting at his desk at Liberal Party headquarters, a cigarette burning between his fingers, Harding had twice taken it upon himself to dial up the U.S. Attorney's Office to speak with Giuliani, only to receive some bland thank-yous from the prosecutor's right-hand man, Denny Young. Giuliani couldn't, or wouldn't, talk politics with outsiders until he left his job.

Harding was thus beginning the campaign season with one eye on a candidate who would not speak to him. On December 16, two Fridays before Christmas, he set out to meet another candidate who was courting him aggressively.

Manhattan Borough President David Dinkins had toiled in the vineyards of New York politics for decades, handed out palm cards in Harlem as a young lawyer, served a term as an assemblyman, and risen to the city clerk's job before attaining the highest elected position of any black man in New York City. It was finally the black community's moment to conquer City Hall, just as the Irish and the Italians and the Jews had done several times already.

The Borough President's Office had called Harding to request his presence downtown at the Municipal Building at 4:30 P.M. this Friday afternoon, which didn't sit well with the Liberal Party leader. When Harding met with politicians trying to sell him on their dreams of higher office, the conversations would take place on neutral ground, usually a midtown restaurant. If a meeting had to be kept secret, someone would rent a hotel room. That's the way things were done. But out of respect for the borough president's wishes, the baron of the New York State Liberal Party agreed, reluctantly, to head downtown.

Dinkins was slim and athletic for a sixty-two-year-old, though his gray hair and double-breasted suits gave him the mien of a grandfather. Like a grandfather, he could be warm on some occasions and prickly on others. The son of a housekeeper and an ex-Marine, he carried himself with a kind of regal bearing, and he was easily irritated when challenged. Political types considered him a man who needed to be handled.

Two men, one trim and fastidious, the other large and rumpled, sat down in Dinkins's office.

"I know from conversations with Barry Feinstein that Barry's talked to you about coming on board," the borough president said. (The head of the local Teamsters Union, Feinstein had been serving as a cheerleader for Dinkins, singing his praises to Harding at a series of breakfasts. The Liberal Party chief had eventually put an end to the courting over a recent meal at the Plaza, telling him the emissary b.s. had to stop.)

Dinkins continued: Labor was rallying to his side. The black community was energized. Koch was in deep trouble. The Liberal Party could be the next cog in the Dinkins campaign machine. Besides, he said, he was a natural choice for Harding's party: he was the most liberal candidate in the race.

Harding didn't nod and didn't smile. He felt that Dinkins had reached his full potential in the relatively harmless post he currently held. Diplomacy called for a more polite response, though, so Harding invoked Dinkins's famous embarrassment, his failure to pay income taxes for four years in the 1970s, a revelation dug up in a background check when Dinkins was offered a deputy mayor's job.

"You'll get hurt by the rehashing of the tax situation," Harding said. "It'll come back to haunt you. Why do you need the headache?" The Liberals would give Dinkins due consideration if he ran, of course, but Harding's message was clear: Don't do it.

Things went downhill from there. Dinkins tried to make his case, as Harding sat stone-faced. Before long there was nothing left to talk about. Harding had simply come to deliver his verdict. He thanked the borough president and left for his long drive to Riverdale, grumbling all the way home that he'd been dragged so far downtown on a Friday evening. A fuming Dinkins was left behind to ponder the blow-off.

There was much that Harding had left unsaid. He was giving polite consideration to a stream of Democrats: He ate breakfast once every month or so with the city comptroller, Jay Goldin, and was on good terms with businessman Richard Ravitch. But endorsing a Democrat for mayor would relegate him and his party to a footnote in the campaign. To endorse a Republican, on the other hand, could make him a kingmaker.

The Republican-Liberal fusion concept had worked for LaGuardia and Lindsay, and Harding felt the city was in the mood for a reprise. And that had him thinking a great deal about Rudy Giuliani.

On Tuesday, January 31, 1989, the U.S. attorney stepped out of his office in Foley Square for the last time and set out to begin his life as a politician. It was Ray Harding's birthday.

Denny Young had called Harding and told him Giuliani was finally ready to meet with him. The two arranged for the prosecutor and the party boss to have lunch that Friday. At 12:30 P.M., Giuliani walked into Romeo Salta, a venerable midtown Italian restaurant down the block from Harding's party headquarters. If the party boss needed a reminder that Giuliani was from a different world, it showed up alongside the career prosecutor in the form of three U.S. marshals in dark suits who shadowed him from dawn to dusk. They sat a discreet distance away as Giuliani and Harding exchanged pleasantries and pored over the basics of running for mayor.

Giuliani was smart, to the point, and very curious. What were his chances? How much money would he need? How would he put together a team? What consultants had to be hired? As Harding listened to the prosecutor talk about his plans, it dawned on him that Giuliani had little sense of New York City politics and the role the Liberal Party had played. No Republican since the Depression had won the mayoralty without the backing of the Liberal Party. In a Democratic town like New York, where voting Republican is a foreign concept, Republicans try to lure Democratic votes by running on the more palatable Liberal line. Harding's party had just 25,000 members, but the ballot line that it came with was worth the world to Republicans in search of the mayor's job.

The meeting led to another one, and then to more. The two dined together four times in the span of a week. Harding and Giuliani met at luncheonette counters and restaurant tables, alone and with Giuliani's inner circle, each side warily sizing up the other.

The Giuliani group viewed Harding as something of a throwback to another era—which he was—while Harding viewed the prosecutor and his followers as novices. His concerns grew when he asked Giuliani if he'd be willing to speak at the Liberal Party's annual fund-raising dinner if the party nominated him. "Sure," Giuliani said. "If it's legal, I'll be happy to consider it."

Wow, Harding thought. This man has a long way to go.

Eleven days after Giuliani and Harding had their first meal, thirty reporters traveled to the city's ornate Municipal Building to watch Dinkins announce his candidacy for the Democratic nomination for mayor. Harding may have held a low opinion of the borough president, but Dinkins felt it was his time.

"I am running because our city has become sharply polarized," Dinkins told the overflow audience. "We need a mayor who can transcend differences so we can work together to solve our problems."

His style was defiantly bland. He was terrible at producing sound bites and spoke in a kind of King's English, a style so stodgy it provoked puzzled looks from unfamiliar reporters. Asked repeatedly whether he was tough enough to survive a punishing campaign, he replied, "The fact that I don't pound on the table or call somebody a name does not suggest I am less than intense and sincere with that which I am advocating." It was odd, to be sure. Somewhere down the line, he had dealt with a racist world by deciding to act civilly, dress impeccably, and speak precisely. To outsiders, they were affectations. To him, it seemed, they were armor.

In setting out to battle the famously belligerent incumbent, Ed Koch, Dinkins's lack of charisma was starting to look like an asset. The media sensed that something important was happening: the day after his announcement, the front page of the *Daily News* featured a large picture of a smiling borough president. "DINKINS: I'M IN," it read. "Vows new direction for city in bid for mayor." The dailies could smell Koch's downfall and the rise of the first black candidate in history with the potential to win.

Jay Goldin and Richard Ravitch were also running in the Democratic primary and still seeking Harding's endorsement. But the Liberal Party chief had already fallen in love with a candidate.

Both Harding and Giuliani were NYU Law School graduates, and the party boss was developing the impression that of all the lawyers he'd known who were public officials, this was the best of them, better even than the governor, Mario Cuomo, a law professor. Giuliani was politically naive; he was stiff around people; his knowledge of the issues ranged from skin deep to passable. But Harding was coming to see in his new pupil a born leader with enormous potential. Who better to step into the LaGuardia role—the angry reformer—than the prosecutor who'd busted open the municipal corruption scandals? The party boss knew his critics would complain that Giuliani was a Reagan appointee who favored the death penalty and opposed abortion, that it would be the ultimate illustration to some that Harding had sold out his party's principles at the smell of a deal. But from his perspective, the critics were ideological purists. The city was in trouble: it needed a savior, not the status quo.

Besides, Giuliani's political philosophy was anyone's guess.

As a kid attending school in Brooklyn, Giuliani was enchanted by John F. Kennedy's campaign to become America's first Catholic president, and he led the JFK-for-President committee at Loughlin. His devotion to the Kennedys continued in college, where he supported Bobby Kennedy's campaign for the Senate and vilified the conservatives in the GOP. "The Republicans," he scolded in his column, "must find men who will adequately address themselves to the problems of discrimination, of poverty, of education, of public housing and the many more problems that Senator Goldwater and company throw aside in the name of small laissez-faire government.

"Strong, large government is necessary," Giuliani concluded, "to deal with industries that are national and international and with problems that cities and states have ignored for too long a time."

As an NYU law student, he admired Hubert Humphrey—a terrific man, he felt, a man with a vision for America. He opposed the war in Vietnam, though never enough to join the antiwar effort on campus. In 1972, two years after he became an assistant U.S. attorney in Manhattan, he voted for George McGovern.

When Richard Nixon crushed McGovern in a landslide, heralding years of Republican rule in Washington, Giuliani switched his party affiliation and registered as an independent, explaining years later that McGovern's left-leaning politics had bothered him (though evidently not enough to stop him from voting for him). When Ronald Reagan was elected in 1980 and Giuliani was courted as an associate attorney general, the young lawyer's philosophy shifted conveniently to parallel his political master's, and he registered as a Republican.

Now, stepping into the mayor's race, he was expected to have opinions about the whole gamut of ailments plaguing New York, and it was clear he hadn't yet thought them all through. In a wide-ranging interview with *New York* magazine's Joe Klein, Giuliani exuded infectious energy. "New York City needs a change in attitude," he told the writer. "This is a pivotal year, the sort of year that doesn't come around often. This year, there's a chance to make a real change." The changes he proposed, though, weren't as sweeping as his rhetoric. Asked how to combat the growth of the welfare class and the explosion of single-parent families, he proposed forcing young unwed mothers to attend parenting classes. But when asked whether he'd deny benefits to a mother who refused to show up for her class, his one small tough-love proposal melted. "Well, I believe in incentives and disincentives up to a point—the point at which they call your bluff," he explained. "I mean, we're not going to let them starve."

His economic plan for a city reeling from recession revolved around trying to lure small businesses to the boroughs outside of Manhattan. He called for "dramatic action" in the homeless crisis but didn't say what it should be. Even his crime-fighting proposals were cautious, derived from moderate Democratic theology: expand jail facilities for drug dealers; increase treatment slots for drug addicts; expand drug education programs for schoolchildren.

The fledgling candidate seemed to grasp the urgency of the moment. "I think the city is at a crisis point," he said. The problem was that he didn't seem to know what to do about it.

If Giuliani barely survived scrutiny of his philosophy, that wasn't the worst of his problems. As he prepared to take the leap into political life, he found himself paying the price for triggering a feud two years earlier with his fellow Republican, Senator Al D'Amato.

A product of the Nassau County, Long Island, Republican machine, D'Amato was an old-school fixer, an exuberant, wild-eyed man who seemed at once the village romantic, high on the joy of life, and the neighborhood thug, capable of breaking someone's kneecaps at the hint of betrayal. The senator was cunningly smart, with a first-rate antenna for fools and liars, yet also buffoonishly inappropriate. Together with his longtime campaign guru, Arthur Finkelstein, the senator had made an art form of the low blow. It was D'Amato who had recommended Giuliani for the U.S. attorney's job in the first place. But the prosecutor soon let the public know that he didn't think much of his political patron.

In 1987 Giuliani flirted with the idea of leaving the U.S. attorney's job to run for senator against Pat Moynihan, the Democratic incumbent, who was up for reelection the following year. D'Amato was intrigued. Yet Giuliani let it be known that he didn't trust D'Amato to name his successor, a senatorial prerogative. Giuliani wanted to name his *own* successor and wouldn't run for the Senate unless he could do so. An outsider, he complained, someone with Wall Street connections, might have to disqualify himself from the host of insider-trading cases Giuliani would leave behind. "This is not a political type of situation that is subject to negotiating," Giuliani told a reporter. "It is a question of what is right and what is wrong."

Giuliani's righteousness proved disastrous. In casting himself as a hero defending the integrity of his office, he effectively portrayed D'Amato as a meddler, even though D'Amato was just invoking a routine privilege. "Anyone who knows me and wants to get something," D'Amato fumed to a friend, "knows not to threaten me." Giuliani eventually passed on the Senate race, having made a lifelong enemy of the most powerful man in New York Republican politics.

Now, two years later, D'Amato found his vehicle to punish Giuliani in Ronald Lauder, a forty-four-year-old heir to the Estée Lauder cosmetics fortune, a multimillionaire with a bottomless appetite for spending money on a campaign he couldn't win. Lauder's generosity to the Republican Party had earned him what some viewed as a ceremonial job as a deputy assistant secretary of defense in the Reagan administration, followed by a stint as ambassador to Austria. He was an awkward candidate who spoke with a stammer and was so ill at ease that he rarely appeared in public or spoke with reporters. But Lauder embarked on a kamikaze mission to take out Giuliani, and by mid-February he had assembled a twelve-person staff, plus at least five political consultants—most tied to D'Amato.

Giuliani, by comparison, had yet to find a headquarters, raise any money, or hire a single employee.

R ich Bond was at home on Shelter Island when the phone rang. His new house was a hundred miles and a world away from Manhattan, a hideaway accessible mainly by ferry. It was his refuge from the cacophony of the campaign trail, from which he'd emerged after George Bush's forty-state rout of Michael Dukakis in the '88 presidential race. After eleven years of strategizing, glad-handing, and spinning for his boss, Bond was hoping Bush would reward him with the chairmanship of the Republican National Committee. Instead the new president handed the job to Lee Atwater, just as he'd bypassed Bond for Atwater a year earlier in the jockeying for the campaign chairman's job. Bond agreed to serve as a senior adviser to Atwater while setting up shop as an independent political consultant.

It was Guy Molinari on the line. The congressman was close to Giuliani—he'd been the first Republican politician to urge him to make a run for mayor, and like Harding he'd been educating him on the rules of the game since then. As state chairman for Bush, Molinari had come to know Bond well. "How would you like to come head the Giuliani campaign?" he asked. It would be a high-profile assignment for Bond's fledgling consulting business, a chance to run the campaign of America's best-known prosecutor for the most prominent office in the media capital of the world. Bond was delighted. "I'd die and go to heaven to do that," he said.

Bond still had responsibilities at the RNC in Washington, so he installed a day-to-day campaign manager, a former Bush campaign staffer and former Molinari aide named Russ Schriefer.

With Bond away most of the time, it fell upon thirty-one-year-old Schriefer to put together an organization from scratch—all under the watchful eyes of a campaign high command that seemed like a star chamber culled from

New York's top law firms. There were Ken Caruso from Shearman & Sterling, Denny Young from White & Case, Arnie Burns and Randy Levine from Proskauer Rose Goetz & Mendelsohn, and John Gross from Anderson Kill. It was an intimidating group, one that questioned every decision, and there wasn't a man among them with a day's worth of campaign experience.

Giuliani was in first place in the polls, still enjoying a honeymoon in the press. But the campaign was already in trouble. Harding was appalled by the emerging campaign organization, located in an office building next door to Radio City Music Hall. The new headquarters, formerly the corporate home of Chiquita Banana, was huge, with long hallways and offices for each of the campaign's top commanders. It was sterile, like a law firm. There weren't enough coffee cups on the floor. The lease called for the campaign to pay all rent money through November up front. New employees were being added to the payroll every day, it seemed. Where was the money for all this? The candidate had ventured out of Foley Square in search of New York's biggest prize without so much as an index card with the name of a contributor on it.

The Liberal Party leader was suspicious of the two groups running the campaign. Schriefer seemed in over his head, and Bond was never around. As for the lawyers, Harding thought of them as "thin Republicans"—patricians short on political know-how but long on confidence.

Giuliani was having his own problems. Out on the streets, he was shy and awkward. Advisers tried different ways to warm up his public persona, sending reporters with the candidate on visits to baseball games and the opera. An advance man, Todd Ciaravino, tried without success to get him to take his jacket off and roll up his sleeves. But Giuliani's lack of charm was obvious: people he'd approach on the street seemed afraid of him.

He didn't do much better with the press. Toward the end of March, State Senator Roy Goodman, leader of the Manhattan Republicans, informed the campaign that he was ready to support Giuliani. It was a gutsy move because D'Amato was storming around the city trying to strong-arm Republicans into supporting Lauder. Goodman and Giuliani called a news conference at the Roosevelt Hotel to hail the good news.

It wasn't long before Giuliani strayed off the subject, unleashing a furious attack on Koch. The mayor was playing "Ping-Pong" with drug-treatment programs and "beating up on homeless people," he charged. For good measure he threw in criticism of the *governor*: "Thousands and thousands of lives were destroyed and hundreds of thousands of crimes committed in the time they were dillydallying," he said. Giuliani wasn't even an announced candidate, and he was firing serious artillery. His comments were "harsh," the *Times* reported the next day. News of the endorsement was lost.

Giuliani floundered from one misstep to the next. His position on abortion proved dumbfounding to people on every side of the issue. The candidate initially said he personally opposed abortion and opposed the landmark abortion ruling in *Roe* v. *Wade*—though for legal reasons. When the Supreme Court curtailed certain abortion rights in the middle of the campaign, however, he took two weeks to respond, then issued a "clarification" adamantly opposing any efforts to outlaw abortion. His poll numbers plummeted. By the time the Noriega story broke on Giuliani's campaign kickoff day in May, he was still ahead of Koch and Dinkins, but his campaign was in deep trouble.*

The finger of blame was pointing to Bond and Schriefer. Ray Harding lobbied the candidate to reassess their status, and after weeks of gaffes and controversies Giuliani agreed.

The members of Giuliani's small world of advisers gathered at Arnie Burns's apartment on Sutton Place. Everyone was there but Bond and Schriefer: Peter Powers, the candidate's genial sidekick and oldest friend; Denny Young, his slight, impeccably dressed confidential aide; Randy Levine, the boyish, curly-haired attorney who'd worked under Burns at the Justice Department; and Ray Harding, the barrel-chested fixer with the perpetually burning cigarette.

Harding made his case: the campaign was in free-fall; the candidate was off-message; the bloated payroll was devouring huge sums of money. In truth, much of the problem lay in Giuliani's inexperience as a candidate, but Harding fixed the blame on the strategists.

---

*The press the next day was kinder than Giuliani's allies had feared. *Daily News* columnist Bob Herbert was enchanted with him. "He is offering New Yorkers a sense of energy and a sense of hope, and those are things that have been in short supply in recent years," he wrote. The column's headline was "KENNEDY TONE & N.Y. ACCENT."

There was little argument. By now most everyone agreed with Harding, including the candidate. As the meeting progressed downstairs to some park benches outside Burns's house, the group made the decision. Bond and Schriefer had to go.

Molinari was summoned to HQ for a meeting with the candidate and Bond. The three of them sat down in Giuliani's office. Bond began by releasing some pent-up anger of his own. "You're paying me a lot of money and you're not listening to me," he said. "If you're not going to listen to me, why don't you let me walk out the door?" Giuliani thought for a moment. "Okay," he said. Bond shook his hand, said good-bye, walked out the door, and was gone. Molinari was left speechless.

A few days later Giuliani and Peter Powers were on a train to Philadelphia when the subject of campaign managers came up. Giuliani had turned to his best friend to compile a list of replacements for Bond, and the two went over the names for about an hour. As the train neared its destination, Giuliani looked Powers in the eye. "You left a name off the list that I want," he said.

"Who?" Powers asked.

"You."

Peter Powers had never worked on, much less run, a professional campaign. But he had Giuliani's confidence. He had been his friend for thirty years: they'd gone to the same high school, college, and law school. They'd double-dated together, even named each other the godfather of their children. They were inseparable.

If Giuliani was a firebrand, Powers was a diplomat. Giuliani was brash and impatient; Powers was reserved and cautious. Both were lawyers, but only one was a star. When Giuliani confided to him a year earlier that he was thinking of running for mayor, Powers characteristically focused on the risks. "Let's look at the résumés of every former mayor," he said, "and let's look at their next job after being mayor." None of them had ever gone on to higher office. Giuliani didn't care.

"I've never run a campaign before," Powers said now. And once again, his impetuous friend didn't care. "I think you can do it. I trust you, and I really need your help right now," Giuliani said. "I wish you would do it."

Giuliani's other priority was to find a media consultant. Harding had decided the campaign needed a superstar—"Joe Namath," he said—someone who could throw the long ball and save the team from disaster. Harding found him in Roger Ailes, President Bush's media adviser and a venerated player in Republican circles since the '68 Nixon campaign. If Bond was a bit of a Milquetoast, Ailes was all color: he was a cigar smoker, paunchy and bald, with a goatee. Ailes and Harding immediately hit it off, two men of the old school whose opposing politics didn't matter.

Powers and Ailes started work the same day. Powers was painfully aware that some in the organization had been wondering not so privately about the wisdom of having a novice take the helm of the campaign, so he called a 7:30 A.M. staff meeting to try to allay their fears. He and Ailes sat down at the far end of a long conference table. "Excuse me, I'm new here," Ailes shouted out. "I just want to introduce myself. My name is Roger Ailes, and I report to Peter Powers." His new partner smiled.

Powers went to work. The campaign was down to $400,000. The polls were running the wrong way. Thanks to Lauder's attack ads, Giuliani's changing position on abortion, and his wayward performance on the campaign trail, 20 percent of the public now had a negative opinion of him, up from just 4 percent at the start of the year. The ax had to fall on the bulging payroll, and the candidate had to stop lashing out at his opponents. Powers started on the first problem, Ailes on the second.

The consensus at Giuliani headquarters was that Mayor Koch would be his opponent in the general election. The mayor had started the year trailing Dinkins in Democratic primary polls, only to see his fortunes rise as he ratcheted up his criticism of Giuliani. Dinkins was also seen as the candidate who lost the most from a highly publicized April incident that conjured up the worst nightmares of black-on-white crime: the savage assault and rape of a white female jogger in Central Park by a large gang of fourteen- and fifteen-year-olds, all of them black or Hispanic. As the summer of '89 began, Koch seemed well on his way to a political comeback. But the chemistry of the mayor's race was about to be altered because of a lover's quarrel on a darkened street in Brooklyn.

L et's club the niggers!" The shouts rose up from a mob of neighborhood tough guys who thought they were protecting their turf. Yusuf Hawkins, a high school kid from East New York, Brooklyn, had come to Bensonhurst a few miles away with three friends to check out a used 1982 Pontiac advertised for sale in the classifieds. Four black kids in an Italian neighborhood, wrong place, wrong time.

Gina Feliciano had been telling her pals about her new black boyfriend and about her new gang in East New York, where poor black kids lived. Keith Mondello, her ex-boyfriend, wasn't happy about it. Tonight was Gina's eighteenth birthday party, and Mondello and his friends were hanging outside her house, on guard in case her new flame and his crew decided to crash the party. At nine-twenty they spotted Hawkins and his friends. Mondello's gang ran to a schoolyard, picked up a bunch of baseball bats, and went after their prey. Mondello took a bat. Joey Fama grabbed a gun. Hawkins and his friends ran for their lives. When they turned the corner of Bay Ridge Avenue, they found themselves surrounded by thirty-two avengers shouting racist slurs. Fama didn't wait long to squeeze the trigger. He got off four shots, two of which blew right through Hawkins's chest. Then he ran away.

For two weeks at the end of the summer of 1989, the explosion of hatred between the races that followed the killing would rivet the attention of the public and throw the race for mayor into the balance. It was a spasm that confirmed the worst fears of blacks and made whites fear for the established order. Koch, who was already loathed by many black New Yorkers, immediately sensed the threat the incident posed to him and called for the appointment of a special prosecutor. He had rallied in the polls and was running neck and neck with Dinkins with less than three weeks to primary day. But Bensonhurst had the potential to finish him off: if Dinkins played it correctly, he could become the peacemaker in this crisis.

The Reverend Al Sharpton was sitting in the Hawkins family living room in East New York when Dinkins came to pay his respects. The minister was a unique New York creation. Wild-haired and heavyset, with a big gold Martin Luther King Jr. peace medallion hanging from his neck, he'd been a minister since the age of ten and a community activist since he was sixteen. Like a lawyer, he took up the cases of poor people who had grievances with the government, yet made his arguments in front of cameras, not courts.

The law was secondary to Sharpton: his battles were waged for public opinion. He was an activist-for-hire who didn't charge a fee.

Many whites viewed Sharpton as a racial arsonist, always on hand to pour gasoline on a flaming situation. Defending Tawana Brawley, the young black teenager who charged she'd been raped by a white man and smeared with excrement, Sharpton and his associates hurled accusations of racism at every public official in sight and tried to incriminate everyone from the Mafia to the Irish Republican Army. After an inquiry, a grand jury found that Brawley had fabricated the whole story. Sharpton just moved on to the next case.

Yet the minister's adoption by the Hawkins family was a tribute to his reputation in poor communities as one who could force the power structure to listen. He'd been anointed the family spokesman within a day of the murder.

The Reverend ushered Dinkins and his campaign manager, Bill Lynch, into the living room and introduced them to Yusuf's father, Moses Stewart, Stewart's wife, Diane, and a cousin of Yusuf's named Geraldine Bryant. Dominic Carter, a reporter from WLIB Radio, was also in the room, having made a deal with Sharpton to secure an exclusive interview with Stewart. After offering his condolences, Dinkins sat down.

"What can you do for us?" said Yusuf's mother.

"Well, if I become mayor of New York, those type of killings will hopefully cease, because I know how to bring the city together," Dinkins said.

Bryant jumped to her feet.

"You Tom son of a bitch, this has nothing to do with being mayor! It's because of politicians like you that we're in this position in the first place! You need to get the hell out of here, because we called Reverend Sharpton—that's the man that we were interested in telling us what to do. We don't need a bunch of people around here trying to use this family and just showboating and taking pictures!"

The room fell silent. No one rose to defend Dinkins. The borough president was just paying his respects, and now he was facing an accusation by a family member that he was exploiting the young man's murder—as reporters waited outside the house.

"Listen," Sharpton said. "The man is running for mayor. Let's not hurt him. Let him go out and make his statement, and we'll stay inside and let it alone."

Dinkins got up to leave, the future of his campaign hanging in the balance. He made a short statement to the press and drove away.

Events seemed to be spinning out of control. Whites in Bensonhurst yelled, "Get out, niggers!" and brandished watermelons when Sharpton led a peaceful march through the neighborhood. Radical black activist Sonny Carson led a violent demonstration of blacks chanting, "War! War!" that injured twenty-four cops and shut down the Brooklyn Bridge. Koch, meanwhile, was floundering. Saying that the marches through Bensonhurst were inflaming tensions, he implored black activists to call them off—earning him widespread condemnation for his insensitivity to the black community. When he went to Hawkins's funeral, hundreds of mourners jeered him, hounded him as he left the funeral home at the end of the service, and threw bottles in the path of his departing car.

It all worked to Dinkins's advantage. "The tone and the climate of this city does get set at City Hall," he said sternly, referring to the Hawkins murder as a "lynching." But he also called for unity. "We must now come together and stop the violence and start the healing—to touch and reawaken what is best in New York and in ourselves." With his sonorous voice and instinctive cautiousness, he seemed the embodiment of the statesman while all around him was falling apart. Koch was on television being pelted with bottles; Dinkins was playing the role of leader.

When primary day came, Dinkins cruised by Koch, beating him 50 to 42 percent and leaving Jay Goldin and Richard Ravitch in the dust. The borough president put an end to the Koch era and became the first African American candidate for mayor of New York nominated by a major party. Rudy Giuliani easily dispatched Lauder in the Republican primary. He and Dinkins had eight weeks to fight it out.

It did not occur to either of the candidates running for mayor in 1989 that an era was ending. The city had always been a wondrous place, a center of extraordinary sophistication and breathtaking energy. Yet as long as anyone could remember, the rest of the country had hated it for its excesses: its filth, its noise, its crime, its chaos. It was a metropolis that almost went under in the 1970s, only to see the rest of the country turn its back on the place. "FORD TO CITY: DROP DEAD" was the famous *Daily News* headline, and it doubtlessly reflected the opinion of much of America at the time.

No one loved New York except New Yorkers, who wore its maddening problems like a badge of honor. It was perpetually running short of money, spending what it didn't have, but its leaders would scoff at anyone who dared raise the subject. "Human needs are greater than budgetary needs," Mayor Robert Wagner announced in 1961, when he took the city budget out of balance for the first time since the Great Depression, and he proved it by building more than three hundred new schools, hundreds of new playgrounds, and five new hospitals.

The city borrowed and taxed to close its widening budget gaps, and its leaders glossed over the troubles with balms similar to Wagner's. The great center of Democratic liberalism was more generous to its poor, more caring to its hungry than any city in America. Long after Roosevelt passed away, his ideals lived in the hearts and minds of New York's citizens, who kept the Republican Party and the conservatives at bay even as Ronald Reagan was changing the political landscape everywhere else.

It was a full three years before Bill Clinton would wrest the Democratic Party away from the liberals and force his new brand of moderate politics upon the old cities. So it was hard to know that the 1989 mayoral race would turn out to be the last hurrah of New York liberal Democratic politics as it had been practiced since the 1930s. It was hard to see that a backlash against the indignities of daily life was brewing; that the waves of vagrants and petty thieves who filled the streets would cause citizens for the first time to think of themselves as victims and the less fortunate as the victimizers. Its citizens did not see it, and to be sure, the men running for mayor did not see it either.

All were blinded by the color of one candidate's skin. The growing problems of the underclass, the structural imbalance of the city's finances, even the explosion of violent crime were clouded, and mostly forgotten, under the question of race. Did David Dinkins represent all the people? Could he manage the city as well as heal it? What was his agenda? The final eight weeks of the race were defined by the public's effort to take the measure of this man and by Rudy Giuliani's efforts to undermine its newfound admiration of him.

The Republican had a long way to go. He had squandered a huge lead in the polls and now was trailing the Democrat by 23 points. The public had gotten a look at the prosecutor and seen a snarling, unfocused neophyte who'd flip-flopped on abortion rights. He had blown his moment. Now the benefit of the doubt belonged to Dinkins.

At campaign HQ, Powers and Ailes had gotten their organization into shape. Salaries were cut across the board. Harding, no longer viewed suspiciously by the candidate's friends, assumed a central place in the operation. The candidate's message was sharpened. Having wasted an inordinate amount of energy preparing for Koch, the team focused its sights on Dinkins.

A key was recapturing Jewish voters, who had abandoned Giuliani in part because of his wavering on abortion. A desperate and uncoordinated effort to turn them off of Dinkins commenced. Without telling his advisers, Giuliani had named comedian Jackie Mason, a supporter of his, as honorary campaign chairman. The old borscht belt fixture had made a recent comeback, with a sellout one-man show on Broadway and a starring role in his own ABC sitcom, *Chicken Soup*. As a New Yorker, he told the *Village Voice*, he was amazed that Jews preferred Dinkins to Giuliani. "There is a sick Jewish problem of voting for a black man no matter how unfit he is for the job," he told an interviewer. "Jews are sick with complexes. They feel guilty for the black predicament as if the Jews have caused it. The Jews are constantly giving millions of dollars to the black people—have you ever heard of a black person giving a quarter to a Jew?" Dinkins, he said, "looks like a black model without a job."

This is bad, Ray Harding thought. Mason had campaigned with Giuliani. He'd taped a TV commercial for him. The only option was to cut the controversy short by kicking Mason off the team quickly. He and Powers brought divorce lawyer and Mason sidekick Raoul Felder up to headquarters the next day—when the *Voice* hit the stands—along with Mason's manager Jyll Rosenfeld. They insisted Mason resign from the campaign by 3 P.M. The comedian held a farewell press conference later that day to deny he was a bigot. "I hate bigots of any kind," he said, then added, "Jews fought ten times harder for blacks than blacks for Jews."

The next week—as *Newsweek* reported that Mason had called Dinkins "a fancy shvartze with a mustache" at a luncheon attended by Giuliani—the candidate was on the defensive again. His campaign placed a full-page ad in an Orthodox Jewish newspaper, showing Giuliani with George Bush and Dinkins with Jesse Jackson. "LET THE PEOPLE OF NEW YORK CHOOSE THEIR OWN DESTINY," its ominous headline read. Giuliani held yet another angry press conference to answer charges that he was inflaming Jewish-black tensions.

The effort to convert the city's Jews was not going well. But it was far from over.

One of the legacies of the Bond-Schriefer team was their opposition research man, Christopher Lyon. He was a college intern when he first walked through the doors of the Republican National Committee in 1984 and was lucky enough to be discovered by Bond and RNC chief Atwater, who at the time was raising negative campaigning to an art form. Atwater's campaign philosophy was simple: if you keep your candidate's positive ratings high and drive up your opponent's negatives, your side wins. Lyon spent years learning how to accomplish the latter. He was a twenty-three-year-old researcher for the Bush campaign when he hit on the Rosetta Stone of opposition politics, the case of Willie Horton, a black convict released from prison under Michael Dukakis's prison-furlough program who went on to rape a woman and stab her fiancé. The mother lode provided the basis for perhaps the most infamous political advertisement in American history, widely denounced as racist, and advanced Lyon's name in the flowering op-research trade. Lyon was back in Washington at the RNC, fresh off the Bush campaign, when Rich Bond called to ask him to come to New York to work for Giuliani.

For a man who claimed the moral high ground, Giuliani kept in close proximity to people who practiced the art of the smear. At the U.S. Attorney's Office, he employed a former IRS agent named Tony Lombardi, who spent a fair amount of time trying to discredit Giuliani's political enemies. Writer and AIDS activist Larry Kramer says he was at home in 1983 when he got a call from Lombardi seeking information on Mayor Koch's sex life.

Kramer was furious at Koch for his lack of interest in the early AIDS crisis and was seeking a way to spur him into taking action, even if it meant outing him as a homosexual. Koch had always denied being gay, but Kramer had run into a man at a Los Angeles fund-raiser who claimed to have been the mayor's lover. Kramer says he gladly agreed to cooperate with Lombardi. "I was willing to do this because things were still pretty awful in terms of the relationship with Koch and AIDS," Kramer says. "I was in essence talking with the enemy in an attempt to out Ed Koch, and I cooperated."

He says he spent an hour being interviewed by Lombardi at the U.S. Attorney's Office about Koch's alleged homosexual affair. Lombardi's pretext was that Koch could have used government funds—perhaps contracts for the ex-lover's consulting business—to buy his alleged paramour's silence, but Kramer figured it was just Giuliani trying to get the goods on a potential political foe. "He asked me all sorts of questions," Kramer recalls. "We spoke several times on the phone after that." Giuliani has denied knowledge of Lombardi's activities.

Lyon was a more respectable practitioner—every candidate had an op-research guy. Hired to dig up what he could about Koch, Lyon now turned his sights on Dinkins.

An anonymous tipster had called the campaign with some advice: "Watch out for the scary-crazies in the Dinkins campaign." The advice stuck in Lyon's mind as he pulled a flyer off his wall that a volunteer had brought back from a City College panel discussion filled with Dinkins supporters. "Always hold on to lists of names," Atwater had once told him. "You never know who'll end up in the news." He ran the names of the panelists through a newspaper database and struck gold.

Jitu Weusi was cochair of African-Americans United for David Dinkins, a group of grass-roots organizations around the city. In the old days, he had been a high school teacher in Brooklyn known as Leslie Campbell. In 1968, during the Ocean Hill–Brownsville school decentralization wars, he read a poem one of his high school students had written on WBAI Radio. *"Hey Jew boy, with that yarmulke on your head/you pale-faced Jew boy, I wish you were dead."*

Just the thing to put Jewish voters at ease with the first black Democratic mayoral candidate.

There was more. Dinkins's campaign filings revealed a $9,500 payment to the Committee to Elect Black Heroes, a group run by Robert "Sonny" Carson, a convicted kidnapper and racial agitator who had led the violent Brooklyn Bridge protest after the Hawkins shooting. Lyon says he passed the information to the high command, which fed it to receptive reporters at the *New York Post*.

Dinkins was incensed that Giuliani had jumped on the information, but Carson didn't help matters when he held a press conference to announce that he and Weusi were resigning from the Dinkins camp to spare the candidate further problems. Asked by reporters if he was anti-Semitic, Carson waxed indignant. "I'm anti-*white*," he corrected them. "Don't limit my anti to just one group of people." He thereafter swore off elected politics, which may have come as a relief to the Dinkins camp.

Lyon wasn't finished.

He took a look at the personal disclosure reports Dinkins had filed as city clerk and borough president. The forms are meant to disclose an official's employers, investments—anyone or anything that could benefit from a public official's actions. A group of Giuliani volunteers started to comb through Dinkins's votes on the old Board of Estimate.

What they found was "nuclear fusion," in Lyon's term: conflict of interest.

It looked as if Dinkins had disregarded a ruling from the city's Board of Ethics and voted on a matter involving a company in which he held stock, Inner City Broadcasting. Lyon passed the information upstairs, and the matter shortly found its way into the headlines.

Dinkins's explanation was worse than the sin itself. He produced documents showing he had sold the stock to his son for $58,000 the day he was sworn in as Manhattan borough president in 1985. But a state document he'd filed two years earlier placed the value of the stock at $1 million. Giuliani demanded to know whether his opponent had evaded paying taxes on the difference.

As Dinkins fumbled for days with the issue, Giuliani and company effectively linked the issue to Dinkins's failure to file income taxes from 1969 through 1972. It all made for a nifty campaign commercial: "David Dinkins," the announcer intoned. "Why does he always wait until he's caught?"

All hell was breaking loose as the two campaigns unleashed a fury of

charges and countercharges. Stories materialized about Giuliani's first marriage: Giuliani avoided divorce, which is forbidden by the Catholic church,
by obtaining a 1982 annulment on the grounds that he thought his wife of
fourteen years, Regina, had been his third cousin when, in fact, she was his
second cousin.

It almost got a lot worse. On a quiet Saturday afternoon in October, a volunteer walked up to Lyon at his desk at Giuliani HQ and handed him a
shoebox. "Here. It's personally damaging to Dinkins—it's about his illicit
relationships," she said. "Please protect my identity."

Lyon says he walked back to his desk, opened up the box, and pulled out
a handful of letters and postcards addressed to Dinkins. "You are constantly
in my thoughts," read one note in careful handwriting. "Can't wait to steal
some time alone with you . . . Misses and Kisses, 'Cupcake.' "

Many were from foreign countries and came with return addresses,
names, and phone numbers. One was postmarked Los Angeles. Another,
postmarked Washington, was a poem that ended *All I can do is pray/Stay
with Me/Stay with Me.* There were dozens of them, on postcards and sta-
tionery, neatly typed and scrawled in flowery handwriting. One, postmarked
Columbia, South Carolina, was stamped "RECEIVED—OFFICE OF THE CITY
CLERK." There were photographs enclosed of Dinkins in tropical settings
posing with younger women and on countless tennis courts standing with
male and female friends.

Dinkins had been married for over thirty-five years. This was bombshell
material. Lyon's heart was pounding. We're going to win this race, he
thought. We're going to drive up his negatives.

Lyon says he brought the box over to his boss, Jennifer Raab, Giuliani's
issues director. "I've got this research issue you should be aware of," he
recalls telling her. "I think, in the best interests of this campaign, this should
be shown on a limited, need-to-know basis. You want the candidate to have
genuine deniability."

She didn't listen. Instead, he says, she took the shoebox and walked it into
a senior staff meeting. A half-hour later, she called him into it, he says. Harding, Young, Powers—the high command were all there, passing around the
love letters with happy grins on their faces, laughing as they read quotes to

one another ("my heart thumped like a bouncing ball"). Then they started talking like lawyers. Is the person who gave it to you credible? Can we trace whether city funds were used in Dinkins's pursuit of these women? The decision was made to sit on the issue for the moment.

Weeks went by. Lyon says he decided to speak to Powers about the letters the week before Election Day. "I haven't seen anything about the Dinkins information," he recalls saying.

"We have shopped it all over town," Powers replied, according to Lyon. "No one will print it."

"What if I plant them myself," Lyon suggested, "maybe in the *Washington Times*? I've got a friend—"

Powers cut him off. "If it shows up somewhere else, we'll be blamed and ultimately it'll come back to hurt us," Powers allegedly said. "If it appears, our fingerprints are all over it." Lyon walked away, convinced Giuliani was going to lose. Powers says the conversations with Lyon never happened, and Harding denies being in the meeting.

A member of the Giuliani team in '89 says the Giuliani high command gave the letters to Fred Dicker, a famously unmerciful reporter at the *New York Post*. "They used the excuse that their action was justified because the Dinkins people were talking to the press about Rudy's marrying his cousin," the Giuliani aide says of the high-command members.

Dicker won't say who handed him the letters but adds, "They were given to me with the intent to harm David Dinkins. It doesn't take a genius to figure out who'd want to do that."

Dicker was convinced the letters were authentic, but his editors told him to drop the story. "I felt I'd come up with a terrific story and all of a sudden I became a pariah," he recalls. "They treated me like I was a criminal, when I was just doing my job as a reporter." Rumors abounded about a supposed deal that *Post* publisher and big-time developer Peter Kalikow made with Dinkins to keep the letters out of the paper. The editor at the time, Jerry Nachman, says Dicker simply couldn't prove their veracity. Dicker says they wouldn't let him try.

The closer to Election Day the Giuliani camp got, the more ferocious the prosecutor became. He was hammering away at Dinkins's ethics, his finances, anything to tarnish his image. The polls tightened. On the week-end before Election Day, the two candidates debated twice. But the most telling moment came on Sunday night. Giuliani, prosecuting to the bitter end, accused Dinkins of accepting free trips, including one to the south of France, without disclosing them on ethics forms. "If I had done that," Giuliani told an American Legion crowd, "they'd try to put me in prison."

It was a characteristically harsh way to end his race. Dinkins ended it in character as well. Aware that reporters were waiting to ask him about the trip, he left the dais at the Human Rights Campaign Fund's annual dinner at the Waldorf Astoria and spent thirty-five minutes on the telephone in the hotel men's room, as reporters waited for him outside. When he emerged, he had a fairly lame excuse for the France trip. "I think what must have happened is the staff fellow who filled out those forms for me usually just copies the information from the year before," he began. "By and large there are no changes. I guess he didn't ask me."

It was not an impressive image. Just as Giuliani had hoped, it caused people to further doubt Dinkins's competence. Pollsters watched Dinkins's large lead over Giuliani erode precipitously on the final day of the race.

In the end, though, voters looked at the Republican and saw a man who wasn't ready for prime time. The race had come down to a referendum on Dinkins with no real alternative. All Giuliani could do was scare people away from his opponent.

On election night, Dinkins beat Giuliani by less than 3 percentage points, the slimmest margin in a New York City mayoral race since 1905. "Granted the margin is not 5 or 10 points," the new mayor said. "But it is a winning margin."

Years later Dinkins would be less philosophical. He had won the '89 primary overwhelmingly, without the need for a runoff, in a city with an overwhelming Democratic enrollment, he pointed out. "Giuliani," he says, "was at that point just a hard-nosed prosecutor who carried some guys out in handcuffs."

"And so the real question is how come I won by such a small margin?" Dinkins says.

The answer? "I think it's racism, pure and simple."

Some New Yorkers may have shied away from electing a black man mayor, just as others may have voted for him solely because he was black. But Dinkins was mayor now, the first African American to reach the office in New York City history. And the question was whether he was prepared to be more than just a symbol. Giuliani, battered by the race, would watch closely, determined to learn from his mistakes.

2

"We Have a City to Save"

The knife was five inches long. With better aim, Michael Riccardi might have hit a lung and ripped a gash that could have collapsed Al Sharpton's respiratory system. As luck would have it, his kitchen knife just grazed past the arteries near the lung and tore through the left clavicle. Riccardi was in jail—the cops had gotten to him after the crowd had a chance to pummel him a bit—and the Reverend was going to live.

Sharpton was somewhere between consciousness and never-never land when he opened his eyes. He had just been wheeled out of surgery into the recovery room and was beginning to recognize the four men leaning over him with masks on their faces. He'd later joke that when they lifted their masks he thought he'd died and gone to hell. It was the mayor, David Dinkins; his deputy mayor, Bill Lynch; the police commissioner, Lee Brown; and old Judge Mollen, deputy mayor for public safety.

"Al, call for peace," the mayor said. He was holding Sharpton's hand.

Sharpton didn't know what he was talking about. Were the demonstrators in Bensonhurst threatening to burn down the city? He hadn't heard anything after Riccardi lunged at him from out of nowhere, as a few hundred followers lined up to stage their twenty-ninth protest at the scene of Yusuf Hawkins's murder. "Call for peace, Al!" "Okay," he said. "Of course I'll call for peace." Before long, Dinkins was outside with the press, deploring the violence and announcing that the Reverend Al Sharpton was calling for peace in the city.

David Dinkins must have felt like a racial fireman in 1991, dashing to contain one flare-up after another between the races. The city's first black mayor was determined to keep the peace among the hundred warring tribes, each of them harboring age-old grudges against the other. On the Lower East Side it was the Jews and the Puerto Ricans. In Bensonhurst it was the Italians and the blacks. In East Harlem it was the blacks and the Puerto Ricans. In Crown Heights it was the blacks and the Jews. The city was "a gorgeous mosaic," said Dinkins, but it seemed more like a boiling stew, ready to spill over at any second. City Hall was always on patrol for a potential calamity. "We may not learn to love one another, but we damn well better learn to respect one another," he said again and again.

But the courtly mayor was no match for the forces of grievance and revenge swirling through the neighborhoods, and his status as first black mayor created pressures that his predecessors hadn't faced. When Giselaine Felissaint, a Haitian immigrant, left the Red Apple Grocery in Flatbush, Brooklyn, in an ambulance on January 18, 1990, black activists shouting anti-Korean slurs set up a boycott outside the store, ignoring the owners' assertion that the customer had dropped to the floor claiming to be hurt after refusing to pay the full price for some limes.

The city watched as Dinkins and his team tried in vain to negotiate a solution, disregarding a court order to move the demonstrators fifty feet away from the store. As weeks turned into months, the mayor convened a commission to study the matter and delivered a speech to the public urging racial understanding. Meanwhile, agitators like Sonny Carson stood outside the grocery vowing "funerals, not boycotts," and the store's business dried up. Eight months after the boycott began, Dinkins finally visited the grocery to show solidarity with the owners. Carson repaid the mayor for his failed peacemaking efforts by branding him "a so-called black man" who was "a traitor to his people."

A sense of thanklessness wafted over City Hall throughout Dinkins's mayoralty. Instead of the joy and excitement that should have come with the advent of this pioneering administration, the air was often filled with dread, as the cautious and reactive mayor waited to be hit with one smack of bad news after another. He never had to wait very long. The economy was listing, and his dreams of expanding social programs for the poor were stymied before he'd served his first day in office. The welfare rolls were hovering at one million, the highest level since the Great Depression. Since 1969, more than 100 of the city's 131 Fortune 500 companies had either left New York or merged or would do so in the next two years. Half a million jobs would vanish with them.

These were structural problems whose solutions were beyond the mayor's interests or abilities. Every instinct he had was focused on helping people, not cutting back their services or rethinking the government's responsibilities. In the face of a deteriorating economy, Dinkins raised taxes by a billion dollars—most of which went simply to keeping up with the expenses he'd inherited. Hapless in the face of overwhelming adversity, he waited for a national economic turnaround to lift New York above its problems. And in truth, he could have succeeded in postponing the hard choices, as so many mayors before him had done, if the streets had not fallen into a state of chaos.

The sounds of havoc varied depending on the neighborhood. In the middle-class black communities of southeast Queens, they were the screams of children killed in drive-by shootings, innocent victims of the explosion of the crack trade. Drug-dealing gangs with childish names like the Supreme Team and the Fat Cats were fighting for control of strategic corners, and bodies were turning up all over the place. The Reverend Floyd Flake, the local congressman, was attending a stream of funerals for little kids. Walking down Sutphin Boulevard, he didn't know whether the teenagers hanging out near his Allen African Methodist Episcopal Church were killing time or dealing drugs. All he knew was that he was afraid to go near them.

In Park Slope, Richard Schrader was worried about his family's safety. He was the first deputy commissioner at Dinkins's Consumer Affairs Department, one of the bright young liberals who came to power with the new administration, and he had watched his beloved neighborhood deteriorate. Park Slope was a kind of vanishing species: a community that was racially integrated, where white yuppie watering holes and Puerto Rican bodegas shared the same streets, and neighbors strolling down tree-lined sidewalks actually knew one another's names. Toward the end of the Koch era, the number of murders there started to climb, almost tripling during Dinkins's first two years. Kids with guns started turning up on street corners. Each morning as Schrader walked to the subway station, he passed by people urinating against the buildings. On the train to City Hall, homeless people armed with copies of *Street News* would take their positions and sound the morning reveille: "Good morning, ladies and gentlemen, I'm sorry to bother you, but I'm homeless and have no way to feed myself and my children. . . ." Commuters would bunch together at one end of a subway car if a homeless man, reeking of urine, lay down to take a nap at the other.

On the streets of Manhattan, psychotics talking to themselves or screaming at imaginary enemies mixed with a legion of beggars. The competition for a handout was so intense that some intrepid panhandlers developed comedy routines to catch the attention of jaded commuters. Stories of atrocities abounded, like that of twenty-four-year-old Jeffrey Rose, a homeless man who grabbed a woman's twenty-two-month-old son from her arms on Manhattan's Upper East Side and started stabbing his head with a pen. New Yorkers didn't expect great things from their municipal government—most assumed the city was unmanageable—but it was an outrage that its leaders couldn't keep order on the streets.

The morale of the city, which rose in the boom years under Koch, plummeted under Dinkins. *Time* magazine angered the mayor and his citizens in September 1990 with a cover story entitled "The Rotting of the Big Apple," a glossy litany of gloom and doom replete with polls showing, among other things, that 59 percent of New Yorkers would move out of the city if they could. It struck New Yorkers as obnoxious, but who could argue? The week before, a twenty-two-year-old tourist from Provo, Utah, named Brian Watkins was stabbed to death on a subway platform after a gang of eight youths attacked his parents. It was the kind of crime that frightened people in and out of the city: the teens attacked the Watkins family as a gang initiation rite and then went dancing, leaving Brian dying on the subway platform. The mayor's subsequent vow to get tough on crime was a classic of the genre: "I say that if two nations are in dispute and one diplomat says to the representative of another government, 'Her Majesty's government is exceedingly distressed,' everybody knows that means we're mad as hell. Now, however, I'm prepared to say I'm mad as hell, not simply, 'We're exceedingly distressed.' " As for his citizens, most of them weren't so much distressed as resigned.

The pressure on Dinkins to act grew so intense ("DAVE, DO SOMETHING!" urged a *Post* front page) that he ordered up a $1.8 billion crime-fighting package even as he was decimating other city services. With great fanfare, Dinkins debuted the Safe Streets, Safe City program in October 1990. Its centerpiece was the proposed hiring of nearly 8,000 police officers, which would swell the size of the New York Police Department to nearly 32,000, the largest figure in its history. The new taxes he proposed for Safe Streets would also fund youth and education programs that, theoretically, would address crime at its roots. "Our war against fear will return peace to our communities," Dinkins announced in a televised speech.

Eight months later, the sound of gunfire exploding at a Brooklyn housing project interrupted Dinkins as he delivered a speech about gun control. It would be a long time before the new troops would graduate from the Police Academy, and even longer before they'd begin to make a dent in the crime problem. When the crime rate actually started to fall in the last two years of Dinkins's term, the public seemed too demoralized to care.

R ay Harding's morning began like any other. Just another ride to work down the dilapidated remnants of the West Side Highway. Another stop at the intersection at 56th Street, world headquarters of the window-washing brigade. *"Hey, hey, don't worry, don't worry, no problem."* The soapy water splashed across the windshield, and for an instant the city was obliterated from sight. A moment in a forced car wash. Two wipes of the squeegee and the world became visible again. Then the hand would come out, and Harding would either slap a dollar in the open palm or not, depending on his mood. As he made the turn toward midtown, away from the pier on which he'd arrived forty-nine years earlier as a refugee, someone had already messed with his day.

Harding was in the midst of planning Rudy Giuliani's second run for the mayoralty this April morning in 1993, the last year of Dinkins's term. The candidate had spent the years since the '89 loss in private law practice preparing for a rematch. Giuliani was making the transition, finally, from prosecutor to politician, memorizing the names of Brooklyn activists and Manhattan fund-raisers, learning about issues he'd never had the time to explore the first time around. His pillars in '89, Harding and Peter Powers, were also at work, rebuilding the campaign machinery for the fall race. The candidate was already doing some light campaigning.

Not far away from Harding's office, Senator Daniel Patrick Moynihan was striding to the podium at the Sheraton New York Hotel before an audience that included Dinkins and several hundred businessmen. It was a breakfast sponsored by a city cheerleading outfit, the Association for a Better New York. But Moynihan was not going to be a cheerleader for the city or for his friend the mayor this morning. He had just marked the fiftieth anniversary of his high school graduation—class of '43—and he was in a reflective mood.

"I find myself at this half-century mark asking how much more difficult a city we have now. And wondering where so much went wrong," the former professor began. "We were a city that had a social structure, an infrastructure, the best subway system in the world, the finest housing stock in the world, the best urban school system in the world, and in many ways the best behaved citizens."

The New York of 1993, he said, was a city that had stopped functioning, its social ills so vast that politicians and citizens alike had grown numb to deviant conditions like violent crime and the disintegration of the family.

"In 1943 the illegitimacy rate in New York City was 3 percent. Last year it was 45 percent," he said. "There are parts of the city today where families have disappeared, and the social chaos that comes in the aftermath of the inability to socialize young males is all around us and growing worse."

A society overwhelmed by its problems was "defining deviancy down," he said. "You are getting used to behavior that's not good for you at all."

Dinkins was in the audience, but that didn't stop the senator from illustrating his point with a quote from the city's police commissioner. In a speech before an FBI symposium on violent crime, Ray Kelly had decried

the "No Radio" signs that New Yorkers were placing on their car wind-
shields. "The translation of 'No Radio' is 'Please break into someone else's
car, there's nothing in mine,'" Moynihan quoted Kelly as saying. "These
'No Radio' signs are flags of urban surrender."

Moynihan produced a blizzard of harrowing statistics. In 1943, he said,
seventy-four abandoned children were brought to the New York Foundling
Hospital. In 1993, "we have 74,000 people sleeping in the street."

Dinkins was outraged. Moynihan had come to talk about how Washington could help the city out of its fiscal problems, he thought, not lecture its
civic leaders about the good old days. "In the good old days, I wore the uniform of a U.S. Marine, and I had to sit in the back," Dinkins later fumed.

But the political world took away another message: New York's respected
senior senator, a member of Dinkins's own party, was condemning the state
of the city—in the midst of a mayoral race.

Calls about the speech started coming into Harding's office at noontime.
Intrigued, he called Moynihan's office and got hold of the text, along with
an article Moynihan had authored in the winter edition of the *American
Scholar*, "Defining Deviancy Down." True to his character, the Harvard
professor had penned a groundbreaking treatise on urban policy for an academic journal. Harding was elated: Moynihan was arguing that New Yorkers
had become desensitized to a vast breakdown of the societal compact, something New Yorkers felt intuitively each time they were menaced by, say, a
squeegee cleaner on the West Side Highway.

Harding brought news of the speech to a meeting of the Giuliani high
command later in the day. As it happened, Giuliani had heard radio reports
about the speech inside his campaign van. He, Harding, and just about
everyone else realized that Moynihan had handed the campaign a major
gift.

Fred Siegel stared out his widow. Outside the college professor's first floor
office at Cooper Union in Manhattan's East Village, the carnival was in
full bloom. Kids were buying dime bags of pot from dealers. Peddlers were
hawking stolen books. People were urinating against buildings. Now and

then a vandal would break into a car. Everyone griped about the problem, but Siegel was convinced it was an urgent public policy matter. The city's streets, parks, and subway stations were the precious arteries of city life. As they became increasingly unusable, the very reason people lived here in the first place was undermined. Siegel concluded that an evacuation mentality had taken hold in the city: people were talking over their dinner tables about leaving New York before their property values or their safety could erode any further. An increasing number of New Yorkers had come to see the situation as hopeless. Looking out his window, he understood why.

In the spring of 1992 the *City Journal*, published by the Manhattan Institute, a conservative think tank, devoted its entire issue to "The Quality of Urban Life." Siegel, then a senior editor, let loose a screed against the forces that had allowed the city's public spaces to deteriorate. "Our shame is that we've allowed fear and filth to subvert one of our most important assets," he stated. "The slow subversion of civility in New York's public spaces has caused even die-hard New York loyalists, black and white, to think about what was once unthinkable—leaving."

Siegel was called in by the Giuliani campaign. Together with Richard Schwartz, Giuliani's policy adviser, he designed a curriculum for Giuliani. A file of policy experts made their way through the conference room of Anderson Kill, Giuliani's new law firm, holding tutorials as the candidate took notes. They were experts on homeless policy, like the governor's son Andrew Cuomo, and education, like former Yale president Benno Schmidt. Most influential was the Harvard academic George Kelling, who was brought in to teach his theory of crime-fighting. He and James Q. Wilson had published an *Atlantic Monthly* article ten years earlier entitled "Broken Windows," which argued that police strategy in big cities like New York had failed because departments had turned their sights away from street-level criminals and toward high-level drug dealers and big-time criminals.

Disorder and crime are inextricably linked, they maintained: Once a vandal throws a rock through a window, others will do the same until all the building's windows are broken. Allow small crimes to go unchecked and they'll lead to bigger crimes. "The citizen who fears the ill-smelling drunk, the rowdy teenager, or the importuning beggar is not merely expressing his distaste for unseemly behavior," they stated. "He is also giving voice to a bit of folk wisdom that happens to be a correct generalization— namely, that serious street crime flourishes in areas in which disorderly behavior goes unchecked. The unchecked panhandler is, in effect, the first broken window."

Siegel carefully watched Giuliani in these sessions. Clearly intrigued by Kelling's theories, he was enormously attentive, took voluminous notes, and asked sharp questions. What was legal and what wasn't? How could the laws be used in creative ways to accomplish these goals?

For a beginning pupil, Giuliani was hard to intimidate. Lawrence Kudlow, chief economist at Bear Stearns, the investment house, and a top economist under Reagan, advised Giuliani to cut taxes significantly immediately after assuming office. It would spur the economy and send a signal to corporations that were thinking about leaving the city, he argued. Siegel thought Kudlow, who was a force in a room, was pushing Giuliani around. But the candidate refused to be steamrolled. "You can't do it," Giuliani said. "You have to get control of the government first, establish your credibility. Tax cuts are important, but so are other things—like law enforcement." As Siegel saw it, Giuliani not only refused to back down, but forced the famous economist into a retreat. Siegel felt he hadn't seen a politician with such a sophisticated grasp of the issues since Bill Clinton.

As Dinkins fended off budget crises and race riots, Giuliani read about privatized garbage collections in Indianapolis and workfare programs in Westchester. Having never had much of a political ideology to begin with, he had few ideological convictions standing in the way of these new concepts. As a Republican, he wasn't threatened by the urban strategies he was learning about from authors like David Osborne and Ted Gaebler, whose *Reinventing Government* challenged liberal orthodoxy by advocating the privatization of such union strongholds as garbage collection and health care. Giuliani identified with a new breed of moderate mayors across America, like Philadelphia's Ed Rendell and Los Angeles' Richard Riordan, who were paring the size of their governments and introducing competition in their budgeting practices.

New York got its first good look at the new Giuliani early in 1993 when he appeared on New York 1, the city's new twenty-four-hour television news station. Sam Roberts of the *New York Times* interviewed him on *New York Close-Up* about Dinkins's State of the City speech the previous day.

"New York State accounted for 20 percent of the job loss in America," Giuliani said. "I would have begun the speech with how we're going to create more private jobs in the city.

"The Cuomo commission report was a challenge to the city administration to privatize, in the sense of not-for-profit organizations, the way we deal with the homeless, to make it not only less expensive but more humane.

"In Phoenix, the result of privatization was actually to have the city sanitation workers get their jobs back because they were allowed to compete."

Giuliani was a student showing off all he'd learned. Only when the subject turned to a recent rally at City Hall did he fall out of the policy wonk's role and display some emotion.

If New Yorkers needed evidence that the Rudy Giuliani who spewed vitriol so prodigiously in '89 hadn't disappeared, they had it splashed across their television screens on September 16, 1992. Ten thousand police officers in plain clothes converged on City Hall to protest Mayor Dinkins's call for an all-civilian Civilian Complaint Review Board. The anger in the air was palpable: the cops hated Dinkins for failing to back them up in tough moments. When police officer Michael O'Keefe killed a young Washington Heights resident named Kiko Garcia, sparking neighborhood riots, Dinkins comforted Garcia's family. It turned out that Garcia was a drug dealer who'd been armed with a gun during the scuffle.

At the invitation of the police union, Giuliani mounted a flatbed truck a block from City Hall and set off a deafening roar from the crowd of cops by decrying Dinkins's policies as "bullshit."

Only when Giuliani sat down to watch the evening news in his office later in the day did his smile fade. The reports interposed his comments with shots of drunken protestors a block away carrying racist signs, jumping up and down on cars, and storming the front steps of City Hall until they had basically captured the building. It wasn't a rally as much as a riot. Giuliani was depicted as the foul-mouthed, intolerant guiding force. He complained later that he had never witnessed the rowdiest elements, but the city

that day saw Giuliani in a light that made him resemble Mussolini com-
manding the troops of a fascist nation. He locked himself in his office while
staffers stood around a television set, amazed that the boss had exercised
such bad judgment.

Now, trying to get off the defensive on the issue, Giuliani told his New
York 1 interviewer that it was better to support the police too much than not
to support them at all. "I believe that what the mayor is doing to the police
department of this city is pretty close to criminal," he said. "He is destroying
the morale of one of the great institutions in America, not just in this city.
It's a police department that doesn't want to make arrests, it's a police department that doesn't want to intervene to help, because they feel they'll be
second-guessed by an administration that wants to scapegoat the police for
all the problems of New York City."

As the campaign of 1993 began, Giuliani was determined to stay focused,
disciplined, and unemotional. People watched him closely, wondering once
again whether he was a good man or a dangerous one.

Another lesson Giuliani had learned from the '89 defeat was to hire a
strategist who was better attuned to the chaotic rhythms of New York than
the Washington Republicans he'd hired in '89. Harding was convinced that
only David Garth, New York's preeminent strategist for more than two
decades, fit the description. Garth was a pioneer, a pudgy, foul-mouthed
bulldog of a man who'd trained a generation of top strategists in the art of
manipulating public opinion. He was a New York institution, the one who'd
gotten John Lindsay to apologize for bungling the cleanup of The Great
Snowstorm of '69 and Ed Koch to rein in his sense of humor in 1977. Harding felt there was no one in Garth's league as a political master.

Others were looking for Mr. Right in Dick Morris, a scrappy New Yorker
who'd advised Bill Clinton as governor of Arkansas. Members of Giuliani's
inner circle met with Morris at Anderson Kill and were impressed by his
instinctive feel for how to run a campaign and focus on important issues.
But he proceeded to talk his way out of contention when he started to speak
about the Clintons, particularly the president. "He was really trashing him,"

one participant recalls. Peter Powers was disturbed. "If this is what he says about Clinton, is this what he'll say about us someday?" he asked the group. "Can we trust him?"

Harding made the decision easier. He wouldn't meet with Morris. Harding had been a rival of his when Hugh Carey beat Howard Samuels in the 1974 Democratic gubernatorial primary. In the end, the Liberal Party chief prevailed and Garth signed on, with the goal of re-creating Rudy Giuliani in the public's mind.

Dinkins was facing a primary challenge from City Council President Andrew Stein, and the focus was just as well kept off Giuliani while the Republican's organization bloomed. A new high command was forming, consisting of Garth, Powers, Harding, and Giuliani. From the beginning of the campaign until the end, the four set strategy at late-night sessions in Garth's apartment at the Des Artistes building on West 67th Street. It was a collegial group, though Giuliani had taken some advice about dealing with Garth from Bobby Wagner Jr., a longtime Koch confidant. "He'll drive you crazy, overwhelm you with advice and phone calls if you don't install a buffer between the two of you," Wagner said. That task fell to Powers. Garth resisted having to answer to someone besides the candidate himself, but Powers, easygoing as ever, won him over after a chat over coffee.

Compared with the '89 effort, the '93 organization was a model of modern management. Powers was in charge, though Garth had enormous power over strategy. There were three deputy campaign managers: Fran Reiter, a Harding protégée who handled operations; Richard Schwartz, the policy wonk; and Tamra Lhota, back from the '89 campaign to handle the money. The only adviser without a specific responsibility was Donna Hanover Giuliani, who was a fixture on the campaign trail and a key adviser to her husband.

The headquarters at 49th Street and Madison Avenue buzzed with a sense of purpose. There were all types there, Democrats, Republicans, liberals, and conservatives. Frank Luntz, a thirty-one-year-old pollster, was hired away from a stint at the *Daily News* to poll for Garth; Harding had installed another Liberal Party apparatchik, Carl Grillo, to oversee the Election Day vote-pulling operation, which had been initiated by a young staffer named

Darryl Fox. Ken Frydman, a young ex-reporter who'd met Giuliani at a cocktail party a year earlier, was handling press. Bruce Teitelbaum, a perpetually harried young aide, was the liaison to the Jewish community. Ken Johnson had the unenviable task of dealing with the black community, more than 95 percent of which had voted for Dinkins in '89.

The candidate, still awkward in his boxy suits, remained stiff on the campaign trail. But this time around he was fueled by an unmistakable sense of mission. "We have a city to save," he told a crowd, and he campaigned as if he meant it.

He was an uncommon politician. When he cracked his toothy smile, it looked like hard work for him. Other politicians could lose themselves in the moment when working a crowd, but Giuliani never lost the look in his eye that said all this was just a means to an end. There was an ascetic quality to his manner. When he spoke before a crowd he didn't romance them or flatter them or try to seduce them. Rather, he argued his case; a lawyer making his final summation. He was all prose and no poetry.

Powers and Harding worked out of one office, guiding the operation as Giuliani hit campaign stops around the city. They were both on the phone one afternoon when Giuliani tried to call them from the campaign van, only to be bounced to the new voice mail system. The candidate exploded into the phone at Harding and Powers: *"If you don't fix the fucking phones there I'm going to come up and rip up the entire phone system! Do I make myself clear?"*

Powers and Harding started to chuckle, then burst out laughing. As the candidate read them the riot act, the two roared uncontrollably. Things were gelling.

Deputy Campaign Manager Fran Reiter was a brassy, outspoken woman with the mind of a lawyer and the mouth of a truck driver. She was a bit stocky, with short brown hair and big glasses, and was partial to chinos and oxford shirts. Like her mentor, Ray Harding, she was a chain-smoker. Having tagged her as a natural political operative, the Liberal Party chief had installed her two years earlier as state chair of the party.

Sometime in the late spring, Harding called Reiter with a surprising question. What would you say, he asked in his slow, Strangelovian cadence, if Rudy Giuliani asked you to join him on his ticket as the candidate for public advocate? The newly created job, although relatively powerless, was by charter the second-highest position in city government, right under the mayor, and one of only three citywide positions. It was quite a prospect for a woman who'd never held public office and spent most of her professional life in the television syndication business.

Garth had decided that Giuliani needed to form a fusion ticket with Democrats and perhaps Liberals to make the Republican more palatable to a city of Democrats. It was a way of telegraphing that Giuliani couldn't be *too* much of a Republican after all—a strategy that helped John Lindsay win the mayoralty in 1965 and Fiorello LaGuardia win in 1933. The campaign staff was already talking to former congressman Herman Badillo about running with Giuliani for the comptroller's job. Theoretically, Badillo, a Democrat, could lure Hispanic voters to the ticket, while a Liberal woman such as Reiter could help Giuliani attract female Democrats.

Reiter was intrigued. "Don't agonize over it," Harding said. "It's still early. Just think in the back of your head that this might be something that could happen."

It didn't stay early for long. A few weeks later Harding approached her again. "Are you prepared to do this?" "Yes," she said, "I just need to get my life in order, some business stuff, some family stuff." "Go ahead and do it," he said. Days later she got a call from Denny Young, Giuliani's top aide from his U.S. attorney days and now his personal troubleshooter. Young was small and bespectacled; he spoke in whisper-quiet tones and usually disappeared into the background at public events. But he had an exalted role in Giuliani's life: he was his keeper of secrets, who operated out of the campaign chain of command, answerable only to the candidate.

"We're a go," Young told her. "Any final things you have to do, go ahead and do."

It was a riveting moment for Reiter and a tantalizing one for Harding as well. The Liberal Party leader thrived on patronage, the ability to promise and deliver a job to someone. The public advocate's office would be a hell of a stronghold for the Liberals.

Harding left for Europe for a few days, confident the deal was done.

When he returned, things started to unravel. Giuliani called him. "I have to see you," he said. The candidate traveled to Harding's home in Riverdale.

"We've concluded we need two Democrats on the ticket," he told Harding. Reiter was out. There was to be no more discussion.

The next day Harding pulled her into his office and gave her the news. "It's virtually a hundred percent sure you're not going to be the candidate," he said.

Reiter was taken aback. "Excuse me?"

The high command had found a new choice, Harding explained, a councilwoman from Brooklyn named Susan Alter. She was a Democrat, an Orthodox Jew, a pro-choice woman—all constituencies Giuliani was courting.

Reiter became very quiet. "This is no time to have a discussion about this—I'm too angry," she said. "I'm leaving." She got up and walked out.

The fusion ticket of Giuliani, Badillo, and Alter debuted on a flatbed truck in Harlem on May 28, 1993—Giuliani's forty-ninth birthday. The location was the same corner on which Fiorello LaGuardia had launched his fusion campaign against the Tammany Hall Democratic machine sixty years earlier. It was also the heart of one of the city's largest Hispanic neighborhoods.

The campaign to unseat New York's first black mayor was fraught with racial minefields. More than 95 percent of black New Yorkers had voted for Dinkins in '89 and were expected to do so again. But 60 percent of white voters—including the vast majority of white Catholics—had gone for Giuliani in '89 and would likely do the same in '93. It was left to a tiny number of people, many of them white liberals and Hispanics, to decide the election.

Dinkins made race relations a major, if not the major, focus of his reelection effort. He suggested to reporters that the city's racial climate would have been more tense if Giuliani had beaten him in '89. Bill Lynch, at the helm of Dinkins's campaign, compared Giuliani to Klan leader David Duke for his performance at the police rally. Dinkins Deputy Campaign Manager Jose Torres declared that voters with "racist tendencies" would support Giuliani.

The ex-prosecutor was a tempting target. He was clearly more comfortable among white men, and he didn't speak the language of the civil rights generation. Unlike his contemporaries, he didn't seem to regard racism as America's original sin. While Dinkins spoke endlessly about "bringing people together," Giuliani talked about the need to get beyond identity politics. "I've got to get this city to stop thinking in categories, to stop thinking of black and white and Hispanic, and gay and heterosexual, and get us to start thinking about people," he told a group of Hispanic parents in Sunset Park, Brooklyn. "I've got to get New York to stop thinking about all this symbolism."

But at the same time, Giuliani was making a bald appeal to the resentments of white New Yorkers who felt Dinkins had favored the black community. The Republican's campaign slogan was "One Standard for One City." He invoked the Korean boycott, of course. But the event around which all resentments flowered was Crown Heights—and what Giuliani termed the "pogrom."

By 1993 the folklore had grown into a virtual certainty in some quarters that Dinkins had deliberately held back the police during three days of rioting in this Brooklyn Orthodox Jewish neighborhood. The community was a throwback to the Polish ghettos, where rabbis formed a ruling council and woman wore wigs in deference to their religion. As a motorcade for Grand Rebbe Menachem Schneerson—believed by many to be the *Moshiach* himself—wound through the streets of the community one evening, a car in the entourage that had fallen behind ran through a red light, careened out of control, jumped a sidewalk, and struck and killed a black seven-year-old boy, Gavin Cato, who was riding his bicycle. When an ambulance run by a private Hasidic Jewish company took the injured driver away at a police officer's instruction, erroneous rumors raced through the community that the driver had been tended to before the critically injured black child.

Angry black onlookers—convinced that this was yet another incident of Jews receiving preferential treatment—formed a rampaging mob and raced through the streets throwing bottles and bricks. A rabbinical student from Australia, Yankel Rosenbaum, was confronted by a gang of up to twenty teenagers yelling *"Let's get a Jew"* and stabbed. He later died at a city hospital after doctors who treated him failed to notice his knife wound.

The riots continued for four days, with police officers playing an oddly passive role. Only after Dinkins made an appearance in the community and saw for himself the war-zone conditions did police move in and shut things down.

That was in August of 1991. The damage to Dinkins, though, seemed to spread instead of fade as time passed. The Rosenbaum family and the Crown Heights community leaders proved tenacious foes, relentlessly accusing the mayor of preventing the police from protecting terrified Jews from mobs of violent blacks. Nothing, from a mayoral visit to Israel to a televised address, seemed to help him.

When a jury acquitted the one man arrested in Rosenbaum's murder, Lemrick Nelson Jr., Governor Cuomo commissioned his criminal justice chief to launch an investigation of the entire affair. The resulting six-hundred-page report, released on July 20, portrayed City Hall during the riots as a study in ineptitude, its officials either unaware of what was taking place in the streets of Crown Heights or unable to process the information that it got. Police Commissioner Lee Brown was out of touch with the situation, the report stated, even as his officers were being shelled with bottles and rocks for four straight days. Dinkins and company had not held back the cops, it stated. Instead he and his aides were—as the front page of the *Post* put it the next day—"OUT TO LUNCH."

Giuliani didn't need to say a word. Three and a half months before Election Day, a report by a Democratic governor painted the mayor as a failure in a major crisis. Even a television commercial from the Giuliani campaign proved unnecessary: the local news was already saturated with images of Dinkins, looking dazed as a punch-drunk boxer, reaching to explain why things weren't as bad as they seemed.

The city was split virtually along the same lines as on election night of 1989. Garth's polls showed that almost half the electorate favored Dinkins, while close to half favored Giuliani. The undecided vote was tiny, yet those voters, maybe 100,000 of them, would decide the election. Research showed they were alarmed about the state of the city—and worried about whether Dinkins was up to the job of turning things around. The key to victory, Garth concluded, was competence. Dinkins was making his race—and Giuliani's racial sensitivity—central to the campaign. Giuliani's goal would be to plant doubts about Dinkins's competence and to establish his own. The Republican candidate would need to control his temper, his instinct to lash out at every comment or question that irked him. He would need to discipline himself, to stay on-message, to repeat the mantra of competence no matter what the question or the situation.

At the Republican Party's annual fund-raiser on February 9, 1993, Giuliani started to spread the message. "What we really have to offer is common sense, moderation, reasonableness," he told the crowd. The campaign against Dinkins would not be fought on racial lines, he pledged. "Color lines and racial lines and gender lines and ethnic lines and religious lines have nothing to do with what we're about," he said.

Garth set out to get the media on the program.

The campaign already had a press secretary in Ken Frydman, who had been with Giuliani in the lonely years between the '89 loss and the rematch. He was thirty-four years old, a bright, earnest young man who started by working for nothing but the thrill of being side by side with a larger-than-life reformer. His mother warned him that he was idolizing Giuliani, and she was right. For a few months back in '92 it had been Rudy and Ken, tooling around the city, hitting small Republican clubs, shooting the breeze at pizza parlors. The candidate brought Frydman to his uncle Rudy's house in Queens for family dinners, where the famous nephew was the sun and his relatives were the planets circling around him. There wasn't even an office or a chair for Frydman at Giuliani's law firm: he sat on the attorney's office couch.

Frydman had bounced around in his short career, starting out as a reporter before trying his hand in the restaurant consulting business. Giuliani didn't care that his young aide had no experience in politics: he was energetic and loyal. As the '93 race approached, Giuliani put him on staff as his campaign spokesman.

The two matched each other's adrenaline level, which was not always a good thing. They had both come back from the police rally on a high, thrilled with the candidate's reception, high-fiving one another on the car ride home. "It was a grand slam," Frydman told people at the time, and Giuliani agreed.

Garth was not impressed. In his eyes, Frydman was out of control. He'd get the candidate excited or anxious. He was too comfortable with Giuliani, too ready to give him his advice—to "piss in his ear," as Frydman put it.

"We've got to get Frydman out of that fucking car," Garth said. "He's getting him agitated."

Frydman had chummed it up with the city's political reporters, but in Garth's eyes that wasn't a good thing. The strategist wanted someone with no friends in the press corps and no need to make them, someone whose only constituency was Rudy Giuliani—and David Garth. He wanted someone who wasn't afraid to be an asshole. "My feeling," Garth says, "was that the press would bend over backwards for Dinkins, giving him every break because they didn't want to see a black mayor voted out." The press would need to be whipped into shape.

Richard Bryers had been an aide to Pennsylvania's Senator John Heinz and was still recovering from the senator's death in a 1991 plane crash. Garth had run Heinz's campaigns and had taken a liking to Bryers, who despite his ponytail and wire-rimmed glasses was a true-believing conservative. The boyish-looking thirty-seven-year-old had the two qualities Garth was looking for: he wasn't from New York, and he knew how to take orders. Garth hired Bryers as communications director.

In turn, Bryers began looking for a deputy who could bump Frydman aside. He interviewed twenty-five people for the job and rejected most of them quickly. "They thought that they were political strategists and geniuses," Bryers recalls. "We only had one genius on the campaign. And it wasn't me—it was David Garth." He finally came across a young woman named Cristyne Lategano, who had worked short stints on a number of campaigns. She was shy and mousy, a little intimidated by the job she was applying for, and willing to take orders. Bryers thought she understood that she'd be a cog in a machine, and a fairly small cog at that. Lategano soon took Frydman's place riding alongside the candidate. Frydman was moved to the Badillo campaign.

The phone rang at Todd Purdum's desk at the New York Times. The chief metropolitan political reporter was a young personification of the old-school Timesman, a witty, bow-tied intellectual with a history student's interest in city politics. Purdum had written a 6,000-word profile of Giuliani in the previous weekend's New York Times Magazine entitled "Rudolph Giuliani and New York's Race Race—A Wonder Bread Son of the 50's Runs, Strongly, against History." The story had examined the pitfalls of running against New York's first black mayor and questioned whether a 1950s square — "a striking throwback in New York City's anything goes atmosphere" — could pull it off. "Can a hopscotch candidate, a purebred product of the tidy world of St. Joseph's, win and govern a hip-hop city?"

David Garth was calling Purdum with his review of the story: *"You fucking asshole!"*

Purdum was jarred. "It was something along the lines of 'If you fucking people over there want to play hardball, you haven't seen anything yet,' " the reporter recalls. The Giuliani camp was trying to change the subject from race. The *Times*, Garth yelled, was setting up the election as a racial confrontation.

Purdum respected Garth and often brushed aside his cranky style as that of a crazy uncle. But he was astonished by the intensity of the abuse he received. "I've never experienced anything like that — this unhinged quality, this ranting," he says.

If Purdum personified the *Times*, Paul Schwartzman was the embodiment of the tabloid *Daily News*. No matter what the time of day, the reporter looked as if he'd just rolled out of bed. The rumpled look belied a sharp reporter's mind, though, and he took pleasure in puncturing a strategist's spin. One of the first things he noticed about the Giuliani campaign was how *white* it seemed. There were no blacks at high levels of his campaign staff. Giuliani's followers, fans, and assorted hangers-on were all white. He rarely campaigned in black neighborhoods and was poorly received when he did. Schwartzman repeatedly asked the campaign for a racial breakdown of its staff and was repeatedly turned down. So he did the next best thing and took the campaign's payroll records, which were public, and determined himself how many minorities were on Giuliani's payroll.

The answer: thirty-one of thirty-seven staffers were white, including all the senior advisers.

Giuliani's communications director, Richard Bryers, was livid. He accused Schwartzman of being a "racial arsonist." Schwartzman used the quote in his story. The fights continued for the rest of the election season.

Garth thought that the fledgling all-news channel New York 1 would play a decisive role in the mayor's race and had his staff tape it twenty-four hours a day. The channel never went off the air: its stories repeated throughout the day and night, and the half-hour *Road to City Hall* aired twice a night. The channel was always on in the mayor's office, the City Council office, the city rooms of every newspaper and wire service, and the offices of most every politician, consultant, pollster, advocate, and lobbyist in town. A story could easily run a dozen times a day, something that could drive a campaign chief into hysterics if it was unfavorable.

Garth had suspicions from the start about New York 1. The man who'd conceived the station was Time Warner executive Dick Aurelio, a prominent Democrat and a deputy mayor under John Lindsay. One of the political reporters, Dominic Carter, came to the station from WLIB, a fiercely pro-Dinkins black radio station. Each night, at the conclusion of *The Road to City Hall*, a voice mail message from Garth awaited the Giuliani campaign reporter when he returned to his desk: "*Andrew Kirtzman, this is David Garth. You claim to know something about politics. But that interview with the mayor's aide was a fucking joke. . . .*" For three minutes the gravelly voice on the phone would dissect the interview in an obscenity-laced diatribe. His insights were sometimes penetrating but usually just self-serving: every Dinkins partisan was a hypocrite, every question a failure.

Campaign staffers called New York 1 managers, producers, assignment desk editors—whoever would answer the phone—with complaints about stories, mistaken titles, erroneous facts. The station was new, and error-prone, but in the eyes of the Giuliani campaign, nothing happened by accident at New York 1.

As the weeks progressed, Garth decided to make it harder for the station to cover the news. Giuliani staffers stopped sending New York 1 his public schedule. All requests for guests for *The Road to City Hall* were refused. The campaign ceased to cooperate with New York 1's reporters. The cold war lasted right through election night.

The effect of all this pressure on the local media was subtle but unmistakable. Purdum, Schwartzman, and others heard Garth's complaints in the backs of their minds whenever they sat down to write a story. What word choice would trigger another diatribe, another fight over the phone? It was an intimidation tactic used against a press corps that the public thought was all-powerful. In truth, Garth was meaner than any reporter in Gotham. And the campaign got a double bonus out of it: Bryers felt that every time a story appeared about Giuliani's war with the press, the public saw the candidate as fighting yet one more institution that needed to be brought under control. Rudy Giuliani wasn't just intimidating the press—he was considered a hero for doing it.

It wasn't hard to notice that Giuliani was an emotional man. When aides handed him the morning papers, he'd often throw them down on his desk in disgust. Sometimes, when Dinkins appeared on the television set in the press office of his Lexington Avenue campaign headquarters, he'd kick the tube. One day an aide handed him a copy of *Heather Has Two Mommies*, the primer for third graders about lesbian couples that had roiled the public school system. After paging through the book for a few seconds, he threw it across his desk in revulsion.

Giuliani's every instinct was to attack Dinkins. He and Donna pushed Garth in vain to make what became known around the office as the A-bomb ad, an attack commercial that would finish off Dinkins by invoking Crown Heights or the Korean boycott.

The Dinkins camp was priming the press and the public for a Giuliani meltdown, a burst of temper that would expose him as unfit to lead the city. "I say he doesn't have the temperament to be the mayor of New York City," Dinkins told reporters.

Garth was determined to show the city Giuliani's warmer side, and he finally got his chance. The strategist's commercials were famous for depicting politicians as real people: the candidates would look you in the eye and tell you the truth, admit their mistakes and speak from the heart, as when John Lindsay faced the people of New York in 1969 and admitted he'd mishandled the cleanup of the snowstorm. Garth sat Giuliani on a bench near Bishop Loughlin, his alma mater, and tossed questions to him. "What are you going to do about education? . . . You say you want to give kids a chance—what do you mean?"

The candidate spoke his mind about the issues, framing them all around the theme of competence, as Garth had proscribed. After a while they had produced a good amount of tape and the shooting wrapped. "You did pretty well," Garth told Giuliani. The candidate relaxed. "I grew up around here," he said. "I feel pretty comfortable."

He launched into a story about his childhood, about his uncles, die-hard Dodgers fans, and about his friends, who bled Dodger blue. Rudy Giuliani was the only Yankees fan in Brooklyn. Garth quietly motioned to his cameraman, resting his camera on his shoulder, to start rolling again.

"When I was two years old, my father put a Yankees uniform on me and sent me downstairs to play with the kids. The first thing they did was throw me in the mud. . . ."

Days later, at campaign headquarters, Garth screened a series of commercials for the candidate—the crime spot, the education spot, the health care spot—and rolled the Yankees commercial last. "What's that?" Giuliani asked, but he caught on fast enough. It was the story of a man who could face tough odds and keep going. The commercial—which began with footage of Giuliani playing ball with his young son, Andrew—made him seem vulnerable. Garth aired the spot first.

On September 9, Giuliani walked to the front of a drab function room at the Sheraton Hotel to give a speech. A small "Rudy Giuliani for Mayor" sign was tacked to the front of his podium, which rested on a riser draped in red cloth. Behind him was a wall covered with dreary yellow wallpaper. On his right was the American flag, on his left the flag of the city. His face sported a five-o'clock shadow under the huge horn-rimmed glasses, and his hair was plastered down in almost a perfect right angle. There was no cheering crowd around him, just the usual smattering of supporters rounded up by the campaign to provide applause at the right moments. As a photo opportunity, it was as bad as it gets.

The room quieted.

"New Yorkers have always braved the hardships of life with a true flair. They did so because New York was an exciting and stunning place; to live, to work, and to visit. . . . It was a place where people came to have a dream, stayed to live their dream.

"But somehow, the city's government got the idea that the people would accept indifference to critical social problems, problems that lowered the quality of life."

He ticked off a list of problems that instilled "a sense of dread" in New Yorkers, from drug dealing on neighborhood blocks to illegal street vendors to garbage on the streets. He quoted from "Broken Windows" and from Fred Siegel's quality-of-life article. He invoked Pat Moynihan and "Defining Deviancy Down." He criticized Dinkins for "a detached reaction to the disorder that is driving the city down."

And he offered a radical promise.

"When a panhandler uses intimidation in order to ask for money and instills in the victim a reasonable fear of bodily harm, that is the crime of assault.

"The same thing is true of squeegee operators if they menace in order to extort someone into paying for their services. Every time it happens in New York City, it is a crime, and it is a crime that cannot be ignored if we want to restore a civilized city."

It seemed a self-evident equation to him, hardly worthy of discussion: a person who commits a crime must face arrest. But it was a departure from the everyday reality of life in New York, and a direct attack on the culture of the city and its leadership.

Those newspapers that bothered to report the speech buried coverage of it. The stories that did run quoted Dinkins's spokesman Lee Jones attacking Giuliani for a lack of compassion, calling his approach "arrestonomics." Jones scoffed, "His vision of New York seems comprised entirely of jails."

But little by little the message spread to the public, as Giuliani incorporated the battle cry into his stump speeches and television commercials. Dinkins, asked about the idea two weeks later, dismissed the so-called quality-of-life issue. "Killers and rapists are a city's real public enemies—not squeegee pests and homeless mothers," the mayor said.

But the Republican candidate had put his finger on the pulse of what the public was feeling, and he promised to do something about it. Dinkins was completely blind to it.

On a cold day in 1991, about a year after Dinkins became mayor, Al Sharpton, dressed in a dark wool coat, climbed up the stairs of City Hall accompanied by a small entourage. As he attempted to enter the building, he was stopped by a plainclothes police officer guarding the front door. "Do you have an appointment?"

Sharpton flew into a rage. "Who the hell do you think you are, asking me for an appointment?" Sharpton yelled. His husky voice boomed through the rotunda inside. "Do you know who I am?"

It was the sound of a VIP who'd been insulted. The guard seemed bewildered by the tongue-lashing but held his ground until a member of Dinkins's press office came racing out of his office to talk the reverend down. Apologetically the aide escorted Sharpton and his entourage past the guards and through the metal security gate leading to Dinkins's inner offices. The point was clear: Al Sharpton didn't need an appointment when he came to City Hall.

The minister's climb toward respectability had taken him from jogging outfits and gold medallions to pinstriped banker suits. Dinkins often kept him at arm's length, but he was grateful to Sharpton for helping him keep the city calm in 1992 when the Rodney King verdict set off riots in other cities. They'd had their differences, but Sharpton was a vocal supporter of Dinkins in 1993.

Curiously, though, at the same time that he was calling on black churches to ban Giuliani from speaking to their congregations, Sharpton held a private meeting with the Giuliani camp. In the summer of 1993, Giuliani's aide Denny Young approached Rudy Washington, a businessman who was one of Giuliani's few black supporters. "Sharpton wants to talk to us," Young told him. Washington was asked to accompany Ken Johnson, Giuliani's staff liaison to the black community, to meet with Sharpton at Carmichael's, a Queens diner.

Sharpton showed up with his wife and kids, according to a friend of Washington's named Vincent Roberts, who also attended. The group sat down in the back dining room, where prominent politicians from southeast Queens often conducted business. The reverend began talking about the desperate shape minority neighborhoods were in. The schools were dilapidated, crime was rampant, and Dinkins was a disappointment who had done little to change things.

What was the point? Why was one of David Dinkins's best-known supporters trashing the mayor's performance to Rudy Giuliani's black advisers? Though nothing was offered and nothing was accepted, Washington, Johnson, and Roberts all walked away from the meal with the same impression. "It was for Sharpton to get in with the campaign," Roberts says. "He was going to play both sides. He was saying, businesses contribute to both sides in an election, so why shouldn't I?"

Washington also left thinking that Sharpton wanted to do business with the Giuliani campaign — as long as it was kept secret.

They weren't surprised. Sharpton had once worn a wire for the FBI. He'd helped elect a Republican, Senator Al D'Amato, in the 1986 race. He was just looking out for himself again, they figured, keeping an in with Giuliani in case Dinkins lost.

Sharpton, who calls their interpretation "crazy," says he was asked — he doesn't remember by whom — to come to Carmichael's to help Johnson or Washington win an upcoming City Council race. But only Roberts ran in an election after that meeting — for a district leader's job at a local Republican club.

Nothing grew out of the Carmichael's meeting for the rest of the '93 campaign. But soon after the election was over, Sharpton, Washington, and Johnson would meet again.

The race was tight, and each camp was battling to outmaneuver the other. Thanks in part to Garth, Giuliani won crucial endorsements from Ed Koch and Robert Wagner Jr., giving him key stamps of approval from two Democratic party icons. A secession referendum to be held on Election Day in the largely white enclave of Staten Island promised to push Giuliani's vote totals higher in that conservative borough. And this time around the campaign had enough money.

Dinkins was also on a roll. Andy Stein's challenge to him had crashed and burned before Primary Day. The memory of the Crown Heights report was receding, and his commercials attacking Giuliani—for his past opposition to abortion, among other things—had helped the mayor reverse his fortunes.

By October 1, Dinkins had erased Giuliani's 4-point lead and was now ahead by 6 points. The poll was taken the day President Clinton arrived in New York to help out Dinkins, and it radically complicated the campaign. Flying with the mayor aboard Air Force One from Washington, the president began to wonder why a mayor who'd kept the budget balanced in a bad economy, hired more police, and seen crime decline would be locked in such a tight race, especially in a city that was five-to-one Democratic.

That night, speaking to a thousand people at a $1,000-a-plate fund-raiser, the president came up with the answer. "Too many of us are still too unwilling to vote for people who are different than we are," he mused. "It's this deep-seated reluctance we have, against all our better judgment, to reach out across these lines." A voice shouted from the crowd: "Tell 'em, Bubba!" The audience roared with approval and gave the president a standing ovation. Dinkins, overcome by it all, hugged him. Clinton had said what the mayor could not. "For me," Dinkins told the crowd, "it does not get better than this."

A lot of white New Yorkers were fed up with the condition of their city but felt guilty about deserting a black mayor for a white Republican. Now the president of the United States had come to tell them they had reason to feel guilty. Over at Giuliani headquarters, pollster Frank Luntz tracked the reaction: Giuliani's support among Jews collapsed in response to the speech.

In the final month, Dinkins played guest of honor at increasingly large, buoyant rallies. A stream of out-of-town politicians came to his aid, from the president and his wife to Jesse Jackson and Senator Howard Metzenbaum. Hollywood celebrities poured in as well, such as Danny Glover, Gregory Hines, and finally Barbara Streisand. The events had celebrity power but little relevance to the issues that would decide the race. Yet Dinkins seemed star-struck by the attention the jet set was lavishing on him.

The two candidates would not cross paths in the election. Dinkins would debate only if the Conservative Party candidate, George Marlin, was included. Giuliani insisted on a one-on-one contest, fearing that Marlin would take precious votes from him if given the exposure.

On Election Day, a smoldering problem exploded at Giuliani headquarters. Susan Alter, the candidate for public advocate, had become an irritant. While Giuliani and Badillo had bonded journeying around the city in the campaign van, Alter was alienating both the candidate and his senior advisers with her complaints about the lack of money she was receiving for her campaign. Badillo had hoped to win the Democratic primary for comptroller, but when he lost to Alan Hevesi he realized he'd never win the job in November. Alter, shellacked in the September primary by Mark Green, kept prodding the Giuliani campaign to fund her race, a lost cause if there ever was one. "The woman really took it seriously that she could beat Mark Green," says a high command member. "And so she became a menace. She started to try to blackmail the campaign that unless we threw in X dollars into her running, she would blast Giuliani. She was a walking H-bomb."

Fran Reiter, passed over for the spot on the ticket that went to Alter, had come back to the campaign after licking her wounds, only to face the indignity of having to baby-sit Alter and her husband, an Orthodox rabbi named Gilbert Klaperman. "She was just a very abrasive character," Reiter says. "She never went on television prepared. She didn't work hard. She sat back and sorted of wanted it to happen."

For her part, Alter felt the campaign high command had misled her into thinking they planned to take her candidacy for public advocate seriously, when they'd really put her on the ticket to make Giuliani more appealing to Democrats and Jews. As for Reiter, Alter says she never knew she had been scratched from the ticket to make room for her. "Now I know why Fran was so disgruntled and so angry," Alter says. "I realize now that her anger was a reflection of her own dissatisfaction that she wasn't considered as useful as I was in that campaign."

It came to a head in the final few days of the campaign. In order to create a central command room, everyone had been told to clear out the evening before Election Day so their phone lines could be extended a few hundred feet and draped across the office into the big conference room. Reiter spent election eve on her hands and knees laying gaffer's tape on the floor. She got to sleep at 4 A.M.—on Giuliani's office couch.

When the sun rose on Election Day 1993, Rabbi Klaperman showed up at campaign headquarters demanding a phone and an office.

"There isn't one, you can't have one, everybody's cleared out, there are no offices," Reiter said. But Klaperman became insistent. Reiter, raw from lack of sleep, exploded at him. *"Get out of here! Go someplace, go campaign somewhere! Enough with you guys already!"* Reiter threw the public advocate candidate's husband—a rabbi—out of campaign headquarters. *"Get out!"*

That wasn't the only Election Day drama. The previous day, David Garth had quit in a fit of pique after Powers overruled him on the strategy for a last-minute advertising blitz. It was not the first time Garth had walked out in a huff. Normally a phone call from Powers assuaging the temperamental consultant was enough to convince him to come back. This time Powers and Ray Harding sent Garth a bouquet of flowers with a sweet note. Giuliani followed that with a phone call. "I know you're angry, but this thing may be a cliffhanger, and that's when I'm going to need you the most," the candidate told him. Garth agreed to take back his resignation and come to the Hilton that night.

The *Post* poll that day had Dinkins beating Giuliani by 6 points. The *News* had Giuliani up by 1.

At the Hilton that evening, Luntz was tracking twenty-five precincts. He knew how each had voted in the '89 race, and he was getting calls from the field and comparing the numbers. At 9:38 P.M., the pollster walked into Giuliani's private suite. It wasn't yet crowded—the polls had only closed thirty-eight minutes earlier. Giuliani was sitting on a bed watching TV.

"I want to be the first to say 'Congratulations, Mister Mayor,' " Luntz said.

Giuliani laughed. "What do you got?"

Seventeen of the twenty precincts Luntz was hearing from showed Giuliani's numbers were up from the previous election. The Giuliani voters scared off by Clinton's speech had ultimately come back to him.

On the tube, the vote totals were showing Dinkins in the lead over Giuliani. Luntz started to get nervous. Garth had warned him that sometimes it's better to just shut up and let history take its course. The young pollster pulled Ray Harding aside. "I hope I didn't screw up," he said.

"Luntz, we trust you," Harding replied.

The returns from Staten Island had yet to come in.

Downstairs, a strange quiet enveloped the ballroom floor. A thousand minor players from the Giuliani campaign milled about listlessly, little plastic drink cups in hand, as the election returns dribbled inconclusive results for hours. Field-workers from a hundred neighborhood Republican clubs were there with their wives, dolled up for a night on the town. Guardian Angels in red jackets and berets mixed with Hasidic rabbis from Brooklyn swathed in black vestments. Cops, firemen—anyone with a gripe about Dinkins had come out to watch the returns.

Without warning, at a moment well past midnight, a news station on the giant TV screen flashed a graphic showing a photograph of Rudy Giuliani and the words "PROJECTED WINNER" beneath it. The hushed crowd suddenly erupted in a deafening roar, a sound that felt like a tremor and held in the air for minutes. It wasn't so much a victory cheer as a cathartic scream that seemed to emanate from the belly of the city itself. When the mayor-elect walked out onto the stage with Donna, it seemed inside this jubilant ballroom as if the city had a chance again.

A few blocks south, at the Sheraton, another crowd stood by as the city's kind and grandfatherly mayor slid into defeat, and it felt to those who witnessed it like a death. All the outsiders he'd brought into his administration were there with him, the activists and intellectuals, the advocates-turned-administrators, the blacks and Latinos, gays and lesbians, homeless advocates and AIDS activists. They stood by him weeping as the hopes that sprang from the election of the city's first black mayor came crashing down. One dream had been born at the expense of another, and the faithful who sank with David Dinkins would forever hold the moment in infamy.

Dinkins's election gave black New Yorkers a taste of extraordinary power, and Rudy Giuliani wrested it away. But where other black politicians would doubtlessly come along with a chance to regain City Hall, Dinkins's loss represented the end of an era for another reason. This was the death knell for Lindsay-era liberalism. Dinkins had believed with all his soul in a status

quo that had been calcifying for twenty years; he rhapsodized about government's promise, the generosity of its spirit, even as it barely functioned anymore. He spoke in old civil-rights-era balms and preached tolerance and
understanding while lawlessness abounded in every subway station and on
every street corner. He believed in the power of good intentions, even as his
city was slowly dying. For years afterward, Democrats would be associated
with weakness in the face of disorder. To survive, they would have to rank
public safety and the quality of life higher than the lofty liberal ideals of
equal opportunity and generosity to the poor. Dinkins had given compassion a bad name.

The city was split in half by this election: Giuliani won by almost 45,000
votes, largely because a massive number of conservative Staten Island voters
who favored him were drawn to the polls by a non-binding referendum calling for the borough to secede from New York City. But Giuliani saw the victory as a mandate, not just to govern New York City but to save it. He was
about to usher New York into a new, unromantic era.

The public never really got a chance during the '93 race to assess the prosecutor as he really was. David Garth had done too good a job of shrouding
his personality and sugarcoating his temperament. But now that he was the
city's new leader, New York was about to meet Rudy Giuliani unbound.

3

The New Order

Most New Yorkers were still asleep when Rudy Giuliani's inauguration ceremony began. It was Sunday morning on New Year's Eve weekend, and even City Hall Park, covered in a blanket of snow, seemed hushed. The chatter of five thousand guests, bundled in down jackets or long, thick coats, seemed to dissipate into the cold winter air as the mayor-elect walked to center stage outside City Hall and raised his right hand.

Seven-year-old Andrew Giuliani was standing between his father and Judge Michael Mukasey, repeating the oath of office along with the new mayor. "*I, Rudolph W. Giuliani . . .*" Behind this tableau was the reassuring backdrop of the state's political establishment. Governor Cuomo was there, and Senator Moynihan sat two chairs away from him, chatting with Mrs. Cuomo. The state's chief judge, Judith Kaye, was present, as was Cardinal O'Connor, the Pope's trusted voice in New York.

The audience of dignitaries on the stage was itself part of the changing-of-the-guard ritual, as the ruling class publicly blended the new regime into its ranks, with only David Dinkins himself remaining to remind the world of his vanquished administration. Nothing demonstrated this more clearly than when Ray Harding, a nonpresence at City Hall in the Koch and Dinkins years, slowly climbed the great steps to the center of power in the city and assumed his seat in the front row, a breath away from Giuliani.

When the new mayor finished his oath, he turned to his wife, Donna, who seemed frozen by the moment, and kissed her. Then he looked at her again, smiled, and kissed her a second time. The crowd exploded in a cheer that cut through the stillness of the winter morning. "RUDY! RUDY! RUDY!"

"The era of fear has had a long enough reign," he declared. "The period of doubt has run its course. As of this moment the expressions of cynicism— New York is not governable, New York is not manageable, New York is not worth it—all of these I declare politically incorrect.

"As we step into the future, the indomitable spirit of LaGuardia will infuse our city. The common sense of Ed Koch will echo again."

A man who'd won his job by fewer than 45,000 votes was speaking in terms of destiny, an emperor exhorting his citizens to battle. His son, Andrew, stood at his side throughout the speech, vamping for the cameras, making silly faces, echoing his father's applause lines with his own chosen fiat, "It should be so and it will be so!" Giuliani was unconcerned. "On the second day of January of 1994, I dedicate my administration to you—the people of New York City. May God bless each one of us as we prepare to give our children a stronger, healthier city. It should be so and it will be."

The crowd roared, and Giuliani took his seat between his mother, who was wearing a long fur coat, and his wife, dressed in bright red. It was 40 degrees, and he had nothing on but a suit. His intensity seemed to insulate him from the cold.

Then the boyish public advocate–elect, Mark Green, stood up to take his oath. The position had just been created out of the old City Council president's job, and no one quite knew what a public advocate was supposed to do. In his speech, Green pledged to become the city's "quality-of-life cop, patrolling the bureaucracy beat without fear or favor or flinching and no matter whose toes we have to step on."

Green was one of Nader's Raiders, a liberal with a national reputation, thanks in part to his appearances on CNN's *Crossfire*. As Dinkins's consumer affairs commissioner, Green had been just as likely to churn out position papers on domestic policy as price comparisons for milk and orange juice. The longer he spoke this day, the loftier his prose became.

"If we invested billions of dollars in the nineties in a Gulf War, isn't it time now we invest in an Operation Domestic Storm here at home?" he asked. "No foreign enemy can cause greater losses than drug addiction and failing health care and inadequate schools do right now, right here in this city.

"There's an African proverb: It takes an entire village to raise a child. By that measure, aren't we failing?"

As Green's rhetoric soared higher, Giuliani sat scowling.

"We need to hear more from the symphony of New York, a glorious city in which each of us may rehearse and practice our parts alone, but the music is sweetest only when we come and play together into a more harmonic whole. I'll do everything I personally can to help orchestrate our diversity into harmony."

He ended with a pledge. "As your first public advocate, I may wear you out, but I promise to never let you down."

A few days later Green's phone rang. It was Peter Powers, the new deputy mayor for operations. The two had already met about a month earlier, when Green paid a courtesy call to Giuliani transition headquarters. The incoming Republican mayor and the incoming Democratic public advocate had a comfortable chat, trading war stories from their campaigns, talking about joint projects they could work on together. Green came away from the meeting impressed with Giuliani's mind.

Powers came right to the point. "I want you to know that we weren't happy with your inauguration speech," he said.

Green was taken aback. "Why?"

"It sounded like you were telling the public what you'd do if you were the mayor. I thought it was a political speech."

"You thought it was too *mayoral*?"

"I thought your speech was inappropriate. I thought it sounded like a speech for a campaign for mayor. I didn't think that was appropriate to do at an inauguration."

Green thought for a moment. "I have two responses, Peter. First, I'm always interested in your editorial observations of my public remarks. And second, I don't work for you. I'm an independently elected official. I don't care whether you think my remarks were mayoral or not."

The conversation ended soon afterward. It was Green's first inkling that the new mayor did not like to share the spotlight—and would move to squash anyone who tried. Giuliani's battle for dominance over New York City had begun.

City Hall got its first look at the new regime the day after the inauguration, Monday, January 3. Flanked by a squad of aides in dark suits and detectives with walkie-talkies, the mayor and his crew bounded up the steps like G-men inspecting some criminal's captured headquarters. Giuliani took a quick tour of the building, shaking hands with staffers in the hallways. He popped into the press room, admiring the memorabilia hanging on the walls as a throng of cameramen and reporters squeezed around him. "Mister Mayor," a reporter shouted. "Do you have any message for the press corps?" He thought for a moment. "No. You ask the questions, I'll answer them." And then he and his entourage left for the mayor's wing, closing the electronic gate behind them.

They were a different breed from what City Hall was used to. They were a tight-knit group of ex-prosecutors, like Randy Mastro, the chief of staff; Denny Young, the mayor's counsel; Howard Wilson, the Department of Investigation chief; and Randy Levine, the labor commissioner. Powers, a tax attorney, was named deputy mayor for operations, the unofficial number-two spot beneath the mayor. The aides were discreet and loyal, and they didn't leak. "He surrounded himself with people who would throw themselves in front of a bus for him," a Dinkins holdover said of Giuliani. "Dinkins had people who would have pushed him in front of a bus." The "Yesrudy's" had invaded City Hall.

The new team was appalled at the conditions they found. Desks were jammed together. Boxes were piled on top of one another. Fran Reiter, rewarded for her work on the campaign with a deputy mayor's job, was alarmed when she toured the mayor's basement offices. If the fire department ever came down to do an inspection the place would be condemned, she thought. From the perspective of people more accustomed to corporate life than municipal government, the Democrats had left behind a mess.

An instant face-lift was ordered. Painters were brought in and desks were moved out. Partitions were erected between workstations. Furniture was replaced. Paths were cleared from one area to the next.

Under Dinkins, the atmosphere in the mayor's office had been chaotic, with secretaries shouting to one another or yelling to their bosses to pick up phone calls. Even the way staffers dressed startled Giuliani's team: it was too casual, not befitting a mayor's office. The new occupants swept in with work habits acquired from their law firms: they were dressed neatly in business attire and were generally better organized than their predecessors. Another Dinkins holdover was startled by the new operating style. "We would strategize long before we held a meeting," the aide said of the new team. "One of us would say, 'Okay—I'll take the lead, you can handle this question, you can handle that question.' Just like any lawyer, you don't ask a question you don't know the answer to."

The administration that had been cobbled together in the waning weeks of December was a pragmatic bunch, a contrast to the idealists—and ideologues—of the Dinkins regime. But there were exceptions, like the two deputy mayors named to serve with Powers and Reiter. John Dyson, deputy mayor for economic development, was the most conservative of the bunch. White, aristocratic, and eccentric, he seemed to operate in a bubble, clueless to the realities of the nonprivileged. "Do not worry," he wrote Giuliani after a newspaper article questioned whether two white guys like Giuliani and Powers could run a diverse city. "Two white guys have been running this city of immigrants for over 200 years." Ninfa Segarra, the new deputy mayor for health and social services, was a conservative Board of Education member who had helped thwart the efforts of a former schools chancellor to teach tolerance of gays and lesbians in elementary schools. Though widely derided as unqualified for a deputy mayorship, she was one of the most prominent Hispanics to back Giuliani—and Hispanics, unlike blacks, were part of his political base.

Giuliani's most important appointee didn't work at City Hall. Police Commissioner William Bratton was a cop's cop, a man of the working class whose Boston accent communicated loudly and clearly that an out-of-towner had come to Gotham to clean things up. "We will fight for every house in the city," he promised at his maiden press conference. "We will fight for every street. We will fight for every borough. And we will win." It had a Giuliani kind of ring to it.

The press went wild for him, but inside the mayor's camp, opinions were more mixed. Staten Island Borough President Guy Molinari had walked out of Bratton's job interview convinced he was "shallow—full of b.s." Molinari toiled to convince Giuliani to reappoint Dinkins's highly regarded police commissioner, Ray Kelly, instead, setting up a secret midtown meeting between Giuliani and Kelly to give the commissioner a chance to make his case. The mayor-elect eventually chose Bratton for his reputation as an innovator. But Molinari had clearly planted a seed of doubt about him. "He's going to be such a prima donna," Giuliani predicted at a late-night meeting at Garth's apartment, "that he won't remember who's the commissioner and who's the mayor."

The moment Bratton got off the plane from Boston on January 9, he had his first inkling that his biggest problem might not be the criminals but the mayor.

It was a snowy, bitter cold Sunday, about 4 p.m. The cops had received a 911 call reporting that two men with guns were robbing a Nation of Islam mosque two floors above a grocery store on 125th Street in Harlem. It was Muhammad's Mosque No. 7, Louis Farrakhan's outpost in New York. "It's called the Muhammad Mosque Incorporated," the anonymous caller told a police dispatcher. "It's Mr. Farrakhan, the guy on television, and they're doing it."

Two police officers pulled up to the Bravo supermarket and ran upstairs toward the third floor, only to be met by a dozen Muslim security men barreling down the other way, infuriated that police would barge into a place of worship. A fight ensued, and the cops ended up being thrown down a flight of stairs, with an officer's radio and gun taken by a security man. Cops and Muslims duked it out downstairs on the icy sidewalk. Both sides called in reinforcements. A standoff ensued, and the crowd of spectators grew.

With the potential for a riot escalating, David Scott and Joseph Leake, the

police commanders at the scene, both black men, tried to negotiate a reso-
lution with the Muslim leaders, while Bratton stayed at LaGuardia Airport
glued to his cell phone. The negotiations were frequently interrupted: An
agitated Mayor Giuliani was on the phone, urging the cops to storm the
building, according to Bratton. *"You have police injured. You have stolen
police property. Why aren't you going in?"* It was unheard of that a mayor
would be giving tactical commands to police in the field. But this was a man
with a firm belief in his own judgment, and he seemed eager to send a message this night: The days of vacillation were over. No one was going to hold
the city hostage anymore. The days of special treatment from City Hall were
history, along with Dinkins.

Bratton was astonished: Eight days into his mayoralty, with the city still
racially polarized from the campaign, Giuliani was bucking for a riot in
Harlem. *"I want arrests!"* The new police commissioner called the mayor to
talk him down while the cops at the scene negotiated.

At last a settlement was reached: The cops got their gun and radio back,
and the Muslims promised to turn in the men who had assaulted the officers—a promise they broke the next day. No arrests were made. But the
threat of a bloody ending abated.

The city's black leadership was outraged. The cops, unaware that the
reported robbery was taking place at a mosque, had violated their own regu-
lations, which required that commanders be called to the scene before
police entered certain "sensitive locations," including the Harlem mosque.
It also turned out that the robbery call was a hoax.

The mayor was outraged as well—at Bratton. Cops had been thrown
down a flight of stairs and beaten up. Eight were injured, one with a broken
nose. There should not have been negotiations, yet Bratton had sided with
the commanders on the scene. That's not what the new administration
stood for.

A classic New York racial outrage drama started to play out, with the stakes
higher than usual because a white lawman had just taken occupancy of City
Hall. The best-known players assumed their roles. "Women and children
were there," protested C. Vernon Mason, the attorney who, with Al Sharpton, had helped perpetuate the Tawana Brawley hoax. "They attacked mem-

bers of the mosque." Harlem's preeminent minister, Calvin Butts, blamed the new administration and hinted at the possibility of violence. "This says to us that, yes, we are now dealing with a police department that now feels they have an apologist in Rudolph Giuliani and Bratton," he told New York 1. "And I think it's going to lead to more trouble if we don't deal with the incident at the mosque in the proper way."

The scene was set for the inevitable entrance of Sharpton. And sure enough, on the afternoon of January 13, four days after the incident, the reverend, joined by Mason, pulled up at One Police Plaza.

Conrad Muhammad, the minister at the mosque, had called Sharpton's New Jersey home late Sunday night. The incident had just ended, the crowd had dispersed, and the mosque leaders needed a strategy. He invited Sharpton to join him the next day at Sylvia's Restaurant, a temple of old-fashioned soul food on 126th Street and Lenox Avenue. Sharpton accepted.

There were about eight people at the meeting, including Mason. Farrakhan's group was militantly antiwhite, but the group was famously insular: its leaders had little experience dealing with City Hall. Bringing Sharpton and Mason into the fold was like hiring specialists. The leaders wanted a meeting with Bratton. After all, the police were still hunting for the person who assaulted one of the cops. It was agreed that Sharpton would serve as a spokesman for the group while Mason would serve as attorney.

Bratton was enthusiastic about the meeting. His office set a date: Thursday, January 13—four days after the incident. The commissioner was happy to learn that Don Muhammad, regional minister for the Nation of Islam, would be coming along. The two had dealt frequently, and amicably, back in Boston. But when Sharpton and Mason showed up with the group at One Police Plaza, claiming they'd been invited, Bratton's tone changed. It was one thing to meet with the parties involved, another to give a forum to Sharpton and Mason. Don Muhammad had come all the way from Boston for the meeting, but the commissioner was adamant. He canceled the meeting.

Years later, Giuliani's communications chief Cristyne Lategano said that Bratton had initially agreed to meet with Sharpton, only to be ordered not to do so by City Hall. "Here we are, seven days into the new administration, and the police commissioner is meeting with Al Sharpton," she recalled. "It made no sense whatsoever. It was a wake-up call that maybe Bratton wasn't the right choice." Bratton says he never agreed to meet Sharpton.

Bill Lynch, Dinkins's trusted aide, had always felt that "it was better to have Sharpton pissing in your tent than pissing on it" and accorded Sharpton a place at the table during racial disputes. But the new mayor felt that Sharpton represented the worst of New York's racial politics. The poor saw Sharpton as a man who could force the powerful to listen to their grievances, but Giuliani saw someone who intensified resentment between the races. The mayor and his advisers had decided from the outset how to deal with him: The mistake that Koch and Dinkins made, they decided, was to acknowledge him at all. Giuliani set out to ignore him. Any spotlight Sharpton would get, he'd have to get for himself—and he'd have to work doubly for it.

Sharpton was furious. "This is an insult and affront to our community," he huffed after Bratton's snub. Other black leaders attacked the administration's lack of "sensitivity." But the new mayor supported Bratton's move. "It seems to me that it's not wise to turn this city over to people who divide us," Giuliani said. The cops had been "the only victims" of the mosque incident, he insisted. "If we can't stand up for those police officers despite the color of our skin," he said, "this city's in more trouble than I think people believed it was." He was sending a message that City Hall was through with Sharpton's brand of politics, and no degree of pressure would force its hand.

Watching this play out from a distance, Rudy Washington, the new commissioner of business services, couldn't help but shake his head. A month earlier, after Election Day, he had been asked once again by Giuliani's chief confidant, Denny Young, to dine with Sharpton, this time at the Manhattan Ocean Club, a plush East Side restaurant. And once again, Sharpton seemed eager to keep the lines of communication open with Giuliani.

The reverend told Washington, as he had at their lunch in Queens during the campaign, that he was disgusted with the state of the city under Dinkins. Minority neighborhoods were filthy, crime-ridden, and neglected by city services. He was hoping Giuliani would address the problems. Once again, no offers were made or accepted, but both sides seemed eager to maintain a discreet relationship.*

It was yet another milestone in Sharpton's secret history of communications with the Giuliani camp. Their contacts went back to the '89 campaign, when Sharpton furnished Giuliani aides with intelligence picked up from the streets. His information was sometimes relayed by Arthur Bramwell, the African American leader of the Brooklyn Republican Party since 1993 and a lifelong friend of Sharpton's. Bramwell says he doesn't doubt that Sharpton was playing both sides of the fence in Giuliani's races against Dinkins. "Sharpton was anti-Dinkins, no question about that," Bramwell says. "He was anti-Dinkins, period. That goes back years. He wasn't anxious to do anything for Dinkins." Sharpton denies he helped Giuliani in either race.

But now, in the days following the snub at One Police Plaza, the reverend was working in overdrive against the new mayor. "Under what arrogance does the Giuliani administration choose who can talk to them?" he demanded, speaking at an NAACP breakfast. "We're not going back to being disrespected and disregarded!" The crowd jumped to its feet and applauded. Within days, Giuliani's invitation to speak at a Harlem church was withdrawn. A Harlem minister called him a "fascist." A huge audience at a Martin Luther King Jr. tribute in Brooklyn showered him with jeers. When the mayor returned to City Hall, hundreds of demonstrators were there to greet him. Giuliani's fragile relationship with the black community was crumbling. Black leaders—most of them Democrats—had turned their backs on him from the moment he defeated Dinkins, he complained. Now, as black politicians in City Hall tried to discuss the mosque incident with him, he was refusing to meet with them.

It was a surreal moment. Under Dinkins, quiet diplomacy would have kicked in. But the new mayor, surrounded by white prosecutors, had no one around him who could bridge the divide. He wasn't in a mood for diplo-

---

*Sharpton denies criticizing Dinkins at the meeting, but several other participants confirm that he did so. Sharpton contends that the primary motive of the meeting was Washington's desire for Sharpton to keep up the pressure on Giuliani to hire more blacks in his administration. One participant agrees with Sharpton's contention; others dispute it.

macy anyway—that would just undermine the cops, he felt, and he was determined to demonstrate that the days of moral ambiguity at City Hall were over. The message went out: It was a police matter, nothing more, nothing less. And he was sending a message about Sharpton, too: "We have spent way more time on Reverend Sharpton than it's really worth," Giuliani told reporters. Sharpton wasn't just declined an audience with the police commissioner—the door to city government was slammed shut in his face. No matter how loud Sharpton hollered, no one was coming around the corner to apologize to him this time. For the next several years, the mayor refused even to utter his name.

There was nothing conciliatory about Giuliani's tone. Black officials, he told reporters, were "going to have to learn how to discipline themselves in the way in which they speak." He wanted New Yorkers to know that their new mayor couldn't be intimidated. The message was getting through, but in the process the mayor antagonized every black leader in town.

New York's mayors had historically dealt with racial crises by working feverishly to soothe passions. Lindsay walked the streets of Harlem. Dinkins employed diplomacy ("Al, call for peace!"). To do otherwise, the conventional wisdom held, would ignite the racial tinderbox. Rudy Giuliani's absolutist approach struck many as irresponsible and potentially dangerous. He'd urged his cops to storm a black religious institution, disparaged an activist whose ability to stir up anger in the black community had humbled mayors and governors for years, and refused to talk to a slew of black politicians he considered political enemies.

Giuliani believed that his predecessors had gotten themselves and the city into trouble by blurring the distinction between right and wrong. His strategy was to stake out a principle, send a consistent message, and refuse to compromise. He was well matched to the task: He had a powerful will, which armored him against pressure and allowed him to pursue his goals single-mindedly. He didn't equivocate. He spoke his mind, seemingly without fear of consequence. He was confrontational, dismissive, impatient.

In the mosque episode, his first crisis, Giuliani's strategy worked. The city's attention soon turned to other things, Harlem didn't explode in violence, and municipal government returned to normal. Sharpton was diminished, to the relief of a public that had grown weary of his game.

The lasting effect of the incident was more subtle: Giuliani had won just 5 percent of the black vote, necessitating some sort of bridge-building. But the mayor, feeling burned by the black leadership, was finished dealing with them. It was just two weeks into his mayoralty.

The mosque crisis was an unexpected skirmish. The war Giuliani wanted to wage was with the government he'd inherited.

New York's economy was in dire straits: Mirroring the national economy's anemic condition, it had endured thirty-eight months of recession. Hundreds of thousands of jobs had evaporated as corporations fled the city, but the size of city government had tripled during the 1980s alone—from $10 billion to $30 billion a year. A million people were on welfare.

The city budget deficit was floating somewhere between $2 and $3 *billion*, with higher deficits projected for the years ahead. This wasn't unusual: similar crises hit Dinkins every year of his mayoralty. Each year he'd cut some services, raise some taxes, sell off some assets, beg the unions to cooperate, and pray for better times. A succession of regimes had raised money to pay expenses by creating taxes and fees that other municipalities had never even heard of. Where other cities had only property taxes, New York had an income tax, a sales tax, *and* a property tax. The number of people who could pay the rising taxes was shrinking, while the number of people supported by the city was growing.

Blending the tenets of Reaganomics with his own innate pragmatism, Giuliani believed that if he could shrink the size of government and reduce the taxes that fueled it, the private economy would bloom again. Instead of cutting here and there, he wanted to shrink, sell off, or just eliminate whole areas of city government.

Changing the beast would be a monumental task. New York was a Democratic city steeped in the tradition of the New Deal. Its citizens took pride in providing more compassionately for the poor than any other city in America. Where Chicago and Boston had one municipal hospital, New York had eleven. Its welfare benefits were among the most generous in the nation. On any given day, city government was barraged by an army of inter-

ests. Black and Latino politicians wanted social services. The outer boroughs wanted their fair share. Unions wanted pay hikes. Corporations
demanded tax breaks. Lobbyists for a thousand community groups looking
for city funds greeted council members, commissioners, and mayoral aides
as they walked through the doors of City Hall each morning, while activists
demanding AIDS funds and homeless services demonstrated outside. Most
had legitimate, even urgent, needs for more aid. All had some degree of
political clout.

The budget gap gave Giuliani a powerful weapon. The city was in a crisis.
It couldn't afford to increase spending. It had to cut back to survive. In truth,
he was intent on keeping the government starved for money.

The mayor admired Ronald Reagan, he told his aides, for changing the
debate in Washington from how to spend money to how to shrink the size of
government. Reagan pulled it off, he concluded, by enacting tax cuts so
large they bled the federal government dry of funds, forcing leaders to find
ways to cut expenses. By the time Giuliani hired his two budget experts,
Finance Commissioner Marc Shaw and Budget Director Abe Lackman, he
had decided to do the same thing in New York. A city hooked on spending
would be forced by perpetual deficits to shrink the size of government. If the
deficits already before him weren't enough, tax cuts would ensure that New
York would spend the next few years talking about how to reduce the size of
its bureaucracy, not how to increase it. The advocate who wanted an extra
bus to transport kids to an after-school program would have to understand:
there was no more money in the bank.

Giuliani studied the $32 billion budget like a doctoral student. Lackman
and Shaw were his teachers. The two budget guys had known one another
for years—both had worked in the State Senate for the Republicans. Now
they were educating a prosecutor in the art and science of sculpting a government. The sessions began at City Hall in the mornings and continued
through the evening hours up at Gracie Mansion. Budget meetings would
sometimes include a dozen aides or so, but even those sessions turned into
colloquies between the mayor and his two experts. Other mayors had been
flummoxed by the avalanche of calculations and categories and relied upon
aides to translate the budget to them. Giuliani actually began to grasp it.

On February 2, he walked to the mayor's podium in City Hall's Blue Room and presented his preliminary plan. "Not only do we have limited resources," he told an audience of reporters, "but we have the city on the course of disaster." He described a government spending beyond its means, smothering the city's economy in the process. His proposed solution was dramatic: He wanted a reduction of 15,000 employees from the city payroll and another 2,500 from the Board of Education. He wanted $1 billion in spending cuts from city agencies. He wanted to sell off city hospitals, merge the housing and transit police into the New York Police Department, and consolidate the Emergency Medical Service into the Fire Department. He wanted the unions to cough up $300 million in productivity givebacks. He wanted to fingerprint welfare recipients to eliminate fraud. He proposed $55 million in immediate tax cuts and $750 million within four years. He was the first mayor in two decades to propose that the city spend less money in the following year than it had the year before.

Lackman sat behind him, but Giuliani was the star of the show. He had charts on top of charts to illustrate his points and lectured his audience like a teacher. "I didn't create that gap," he said, thumping on a chart, "or that one, or that one, or that one. I inherited this chart."

Later that day he delivered a televised address. Sitting beside an American flag, his face heavily pancaked, the mayor told the citizens of New York that they faced perhaps the biggest budget deficit in city history. "Without decisive action now," he said, "that gap will grow to $3.4 billion by 1998, which would be a calamity for the people of New York City. I don't intend to let this happen."

The reaction was instantaneous. The underclass depended on city services more than any other group, and its representatives saw this as a bullet heading directly at them. "This document jumps on poor people," a black councilman, Enoch Williams, said. Stanley Hill, the African American leader of the city's biggest union, District Council 37, echoed Williams. "Mayor Giuliani was elected by 53,000 [sic] votes," he told New York 1. "He's got to represent all the people in this city." Liberals fumed that the mayor was turning his back on the weakest members of society. The protests, with their undercurrent of racial resentment, grew as the days followed.

The city's transit police chief, Michael O'Connor, was outraged at the mayor's plan to merge his troops into the NYPD. There were obvious reasons why it would be more efficient to combine three bureaucracies into one, but the departments had successfully protected their turfs for years, in part by scaring the public. "What I'm fearful of," O'Connor told New York 1, "is we won't be able to serve the riding public as well as we have in the last three years."

The City Council's twenty-two-member Black and Hispanic Caucus released a list of "nonnegotiable" demands for the mayor, mainly rollbacks of his plans to cut health care and education. The mayor's proposals, Councilwoman Una Clarke told a reporter, would create not "a leaner city, but a meaner city."

A few blocks away, at 30 Worth Street, all hell was breaking loose in the boardroom of the Health and Hospitals Corporation. Giuliani had pronounced municipal hospitals obsolete: Vast numbers of beds were lying empty every day as patients took their business to plusher private hospitals, which were happy to accept their government Medicaid payments. He wanted to sell off the city's venerable old institutions, places like Bellevue in Manhattan, where generations of young internists had earned their battle scars treating men with gunshot wounds, and the fortresslike Kings County Hospital, where the poor of Brooklyn had their babies and mourned their dying. As a kind of get-to-know-you present to HHC, the mayor cut off the city's subsidy of $350 million, forcing hundreds of layoffs and throwing the corporation into a tailspin. Its sterile board room suddenly came alive with regular interruptions from community activists waving placards reading "JOBS NOT JAILS" and chanting slogans. "We're not going to sit down here and let this board preside over the sale of hospitals and take money away from poor people," an activist named Sidique Wai lectured the board.

As opponents of Giuliani's plans announced themselves loudly, usually on the front steps of City Hall, his proposals were having their effect inside the bureaucracies. On a single day in March, HHC chief Dr. Bruce Siegel, trying to be heard over the catcalls of protestors, announced plans to lop 2,200 people off the payroll and cut the central board by half; in Brooklyn, Schools Chancellor Ramon Cortines grudgingly unveiled a plan to cut

2,000 jobs from the Board of Education payroll. At City Hall, a small army
of AIDS activists stood by the barricades at the perimeter of the building
heckling Deputy Mayor Fran Reiter because the administration was considering doing away with the Division of AIDS Services, whose workers
helped clients obtain benefits. *"People are dying! We don't want barricades!"*

Thousands of protestors, union members, politicians, and lobbyists were
fighting one man, who stood alone each day at a podium inside City Hall's
Blue Room, a solitary figure facing a sea of skeptical reporters. He was an
army of one, firing shells, launching missiles, and engaging in hand-to-hand
combat with the enemy. Each day brought a new assault on the people he
branded as the protectors of the status quo. Faced with defiance from the
HHC board, he threatened to do away with it altogether. "It was constituted
by the city government," he said. "It could be reconstituted." He refused to
grovel before the chief of the independent Municipal Assistance Corporation, who held the purse strings on $200 million Giuliani wanted. "It's our
money," he told reporters. "It's not his. It isn't his role . . . to be suggesting
the budget priorities or political priorities of the city."

It was a jaw-dropping spectacle for reporters used to Dinkins's preternatu-
ral, sometimes maddening, caution. Giuliani seemed the anti-Dinkins,
speaking his mind without a hint of diplomacy. A friend one day became a
target the next: City Council Speaker Peter Vallone's criticism of his jails
policies was "irresponsible" and based on "misinformation." The mayor was
often condescending: When former Police Commissioner Ray Kelly—
whom he'd almost reappointed—defended his stewardship of the community policing program, Giuliani said, "It sounds to me like he's really kind of
lost control now." When Mark Green tried to climb aboard the privatization
bandwagon, suggesting that the police have patrol cars repaired in private
shops, Giuliani scoffed, "Green's suggestion is the most idiotic thing I ever
heard of." In fact, the NYPD had been testing out the very idea Green proposed. But the mayor was spotting enemies all around him.

Much of the civic leadership was appalled. "It's not the way a responsible
public official talks," sniffed *New York Newsday*. But Giuliani was setting the
terms of the dialogue, throwing his critics on the defensive. In a not-so-
subtle way, he was intimidating them.

Privately, internal debate was raging over which services should stay and which should go. The social services commissioner, Marva Hammons, had dropped a bomb in the laps of the administration when she proposed to meet her budget-cutting goal by eliminating the Division of AIDS Services. The uproar it incited nearly paralyzed government: AIDS activists held a sit-in in the corridors of City Hall and had to be dragged out of the building one by one. Two dozen protestors were arrested.

The pressure made Giuliani more defiant, but Fran Reiter was worried. The sole Liberal in the upper administration, she was afraid some AIDS patients would fall through the cracks without the caseworkers at the division. Lackman, the budget director, was fighting to do away with the office entirely. The arguments raged during 8 A.M. staff meetings, budget conferences, and late-night bull sessions through the week leading up to Giuliani's final budget presentation in April. Reiter was at Gracie Mansion for a dinner party as the deadline approached. She managed to pull the mayor aside. "Can I talk to you when dinner's over?"

"Sure, absolutely," he said. "People generally clear out about eleven o'clock. We'll go inside, we'll sit down and talk about whatever you want."

Their conversation took place closer to eleven-thirty, over a glass of wine in the living room. "You're getting close to making a decision on all of this budget stuff," she said. "I'm going to take one last shot at this issue. And that's it, because I'm running out of steam here."

"Go ahead," he said.

She made one last pitch to save DAS. She said it was flawed but still necessary, even for people with AIDS who were living longer from the advent of new drugs. They still needed help navigating the bureaucracy, she argued. Giuliani listened, asked questions, and challenged her. Thirty minutes later, she'd won her case. "You're right," he said, picking up the phone. It was well past midnight. He was calling Lackman at home. "I've made a decision on DAS," he said. "Take it off the table."

It was a triumphant moment for the deputy mayor. Giuliani might be an unmovable object in public. Behind closed doors, she felt, he was a supremely thoughtful man.

Virtually all the Dinkins holdovers found the new mayor more intellectually curious than his predecessor, more interested in policy, and far more decisive. "He had an amazing amount of patience," a former commissioner recalls of his agency's budget presentations. "Those meetings would last three hours. We had long, convoluted discussions on whether it made sense to hire more staff to offset overtime and whether overtime was cheaper than straight time—really nuts-and-bolts operational stuff. And he was unbelievably engaged during those things, asking really good questions the way any sort of good administrator would." The few times the commissioner tried to do the same under Dinkins, Deputy Mayor Norman Steisel would roll his eyes as if to say, "You're killing me here." "He'd call me afterward and say, 'Hey, what the fuck were you doing?' " the commissioner recalls.

But Giuliani could also be demanding to the point of abusiveness. Aides and commissioners often recoiled in embarrassment over his treatment of his closest advisers. Denny Young, the quietest, most reflexively loyal of all his aides, came in for especially harsh treatment from the boss: As other aides looked on, Giuliani would scream at him for failing to carry out a task he'd been handed. Even Powers, Giuliani's closest friend, a man others viewed as the only person who could speak to him as an equal, suffered public tirades. The same commissioner who admired Giuliani's mind remembers him going "ballistic" at Powers at a Gracie Mansion staff meeting. "I turned to [a mayoral aide] and I said, 'That's his best friend? Wow!' "

Another Giuliani aide who had worked for the prior administration recalls a dozen acts of kindness and encouragement from Giuliani and says Dinkins exploded more frequently at his advisers. But the memories of Giuliani's outbursts remained vivid for their sheer, devastating rationality. "A lot of people, when they start yelling, they start getting a little wacky," the ex-aide says. "He doesn't, which makes it more intimidating."

As the budget protests grew to a cacophony, Peter Vallone was watching the mayor quietly. The day Giuliani presented his preliminary budget plan, the speaker of the City Council praised the mayor's "excellent presentation." His only disappointment, Vallone said, was that the mayor hadn't included his own pet tax cut—one for co-op owners.

It was a telling response from the Democratic leader, for Vallone had tremendous power over Giuliani's fate. The speaker was a soft-spoken man, a devout Catholic who'd lived his entire life in a four-block area of Queens. His amiable personality belied a ruthless management style, however. He controlled the City Council like an old-fashioned ward heeler, rewarding loyal members with bonuses and committee posts and punishing disloyal ones with banishment. He could pass or bury any piece of legislation Giuliani came up with, or override a mayoral veto with 10 votes to spare.

But Vallone and his burly chief of staff, Kevin McCabe, had already found much in common with the new mayor and his number two, Peter Powers. Vallone was a Democrat—nearly every council member was—but a conservative one. He had little problem with the mayor's push to rein in government. He and McCabe were also taken with Giuliani's competence. Watching his budget presentation, McCabe kept thinking that this man wasn't just briefed and prepped and going through the motions. He was actually driving the train.

Giuliani and Powers took pains to romance McCabe and his boss, holding meetings every Friday with them and keeping the lines of communication open even in the worst of times. They made a convivial group, these four guys from the boroughs, all of them Catholic school graduates: Giuliani, McCabe, and Powers had all attended Bishop Loughlin High School while Vallone had graduated from its Manhattan rival, Power Memorial.

If they were on the same cultural wavelength, they were also on the same ideological one: Vallone's political base was a conservative section of Queens that had voted overwhelmingly for Giuliani. Much to the chagrin of the more liberal members of his party, Vallone's agenda was similar to the mayor's: lower taxes, more police protection, less entitlement spending for the poor.

Giuliani barely knew the names of the other fifty council members in his first years in office. "They just didn't fit the definition of somebody that was needed," recalls McCabe. It wasn't that he didn't try—a bit. The mayor held the annual Gracie Mansion reception for all the members and their wives in 1994, but the tradition died soon afterward. "I think he was having a hard time making believe he really wanted to be there for that long with these people," McCabe says. The mayor even showed up at the council's annual beach outing—in a suit. He didn't stay for long.

He did, however, show tremendous deference to Vallone and McCabe. In the span of three years, McCabe suffered the loss of two brothers and two nephews, and Giuliani showed up at the McDonald-Leahy Funeral Parlor in Queens to pay his respects at three of the four wakes. At the wake of his brother Terry, McCabe remembers, Giuliani brought his top lieutenants. "It was him, Powers, Mastro, Denny Young—he brought everybody with him," McCabe recalls. Giuliani even sent condolence notes to McCabe's mother. "It was just a very decent thing for him to do," McCabe says. "It made my family feel a lot better."

The mayor was giving the city an extraordinary display of power politics. While he negotiated quietly with the council speaker, he played hardball with virtually everyone else. He arm-twisted the Municipal Assistance Corporation into handing over the $200 million, then used it to offer severance to 15,000 workers he wanted off the payroll. The unions screamed that he'd devastate city services, but Giuliani pledged that he'd lay the workers off if he couldn't buy them out. The unions capitulated. The HHC board, bullied and threatened by City Hall, agreed to make budget cuts, as did the Board of Ed. In the end, the overwhelmingly liberal City Council swallowed his plan virtually whole. It even approved his proposal to fingerprint welfare clients, a move that struck terror in the hearts of civil libertarians. With Vallone leaning on them, even the members of the Black and Hispanic Caucus rolled over and voted for the budget. The mayor had met none of their nonnegotiable demands.

Mark Green was sitting in his office at the Municipal Building when he heard some disturbing news: a man in a car had sidled up to a van full of young rabbinical students on the Brooklyn Bridge, pulled out two 9mm semiautomatic guns, and opened fire, wounding four young men. It turned out that Green had been driving on the bridge at about the same time. He called his security detail, got into his car, and headed for St. Vincent's Hospital to visit the wounded students.

As he was driving north along Sixth Avenue en route to the hospital, he got a call from Randy Mastro, Giuliani's chief of staff. "The mayor's very upset you're going to the hospital," he told Green. "He doesn't want you to go."

"Why not?"

"If you go, it will turn into a media circus."

"Randy, I'm not Madonna," Green told him. "I'm just going as a public official very upset with what's been reported. Trust me, if the public advocate goes, it really will not lead to a media frenzy."

Mastro repeated himself. "The mayor doesn't want you to go."

"Well, I don't work for you," Green said. "And I'm going."

The new administration had gotten off to a quick start. Its leader was decisive and competent, his aides smart and efficient. But the number of people mistreated by Giuliani and his apparatchiks was growing. The mayor would seize an issue, escalate the stakes to a crisis point, and fight the opposition until it cried uncle. Then he would move on to the next battle, leaving behind a trail of embittered politicians whom he'd belittled, insulted, or humiliated.

It wasn't pretty to watch, but this one-man wrecking crew was systematically shattering an edifice that had been maintained by a vast Democratic consensus for decades. Giuliani cared less that he was going to run out of friends than that everyone knew he was boss. His new regime was obsessed with establishing his primacy and was willing to put the muscle on anyone who threatened it. Green had gotten the message. Their next target was William Bratton.

4

The Big Sweep

Late in the afternoon on a breezy April day in 1994, Police Commissioner William Bratton and a large entourage of his lieutenants marched into the fifth floor conference room of the New York Civil Liberties Union in midtown Manhattan. Already gathered around a long table were a dozen of the city's best-known civil rights leaders and advocates for the homeless, people who were routinely quoted in the papers slamming city officials for inaction or insensitivity. They were eager to meet him.

The event was the brainchild of Norman Siegel, executive director of the NYCLU and perhaps the best-known civil rights advocate of them all. He had proposed the summit meeting to Bratton because the advocacy community was worried about the new mayor and his police commissioner: The two were heralding a new style of aggressive policing and were vowing to take the city back block by block. The word on the street was that the cops were getting nasty.

Poker-faced as usual, Bratton stood in front of the room and, using his dry, almost clinical language, gave a brief description of his plans. He also extended an olive branch to his audience: We may not always agree, he said, but we can agree to disagree.

Mary Brosnahan rose to speak. She was the director of the Coalition for the Homeless, a diminutive woman who glowed with passion for her cause, a kind of Florence Nightingale for the homeless. She was already angry about the new commissioner's comments about the city's squeegee men: "They should get off the booze, get off drugs, and get off their asses," Bratton told reporters soon after his arrival in New York. "If they're committing other crimes, we'll be more than happy to lock 'em up, and then they don't have to worry about washing windows—they can do it in Sing Sing." The tabloid press loved his new-sheriff-in-town shtick, but the protectors of the poor weren't impressed.

Brosnahan said that her staff had been getting complaints about the cops from homeless people ever since Bratton came to town. They were being singled out and given summonses by the police purely on the basis of their appearance, she charged. And she placed the blame on him.

"We have a waiting room filled with people that have been terrorized by the police," she said. "These people don't need to be terrorized—they need help!

"The message that is coming very clearly from you and the mayor to the police officer on the beat is that homeless people are fair game. *The fish rots from the head down.*"

Bratton peered at her with disdain. He didn't like her or her philosophy. When he ran the city's transit police a few years back, a hundred homeless people were dying every year in the subways. They were bitten by rats, stricken with frostbite, killed by speeding trains. People like Mary Brosnahan, he felt, fought his efforts to get the homeless off the subways for political reasons. He suspected they wanted to keep these subway dwellers in the face of the public to force politicians to devote more money to the cause. That was criminal, he thought.

"Subways are not for sleeping. Subways are not for living," he responded. "We're going to flush the homeless people off the street in the same successful manner in which we flushed them out of the subway system."

The new police commissioner was putting the advocates on notice that the streets of New York were in for a sweep.

Siegel watched the goodwill in the room evaporate. There were arguments over Bratton's plan to go after truants. The commissioner saw it as a way to keep teenagers out of trouble. The activists saw it as a way of harassing young black kids. There was no meeting of the minds whatsoever. At least we're talking, Siegel thought to himself. We should keep the dialogue going. But even that was optimistic. It was the last meeting the two sides would have.

At fifty, Siegel was as idealistic as a first-year law student, a gentle man with curly hair, hangdog eyes, and a soothing voice, kind of a Jewish Boy Scout. These were qualities that made him a natural protector of the underdog, and he had honed them, to the annoyance of almost everyone in New York at one time or another, as head of the NYCLU. Many New Yorkers hated him for opposing Ed Koch's efforts to fight the homeless situation: Siegel had beaten back Koch's attempt to remove a mentally disturbed homeless woman from the streets and have her institutionalized. Much of the public couldn't understand why he was protecting a person's right to sleep on a heating grate, but he'd received support from many of his neighbors on the Upper West Side, who appreciated his defense of individual liberties.

Even as liberalism was falling into disfavor around the country, the Upper West Side remained proud of its heritage as an intellectual center of the left. Norman Mailer had lived there, as had Isaac Bashevis Singer, who strolled down the canyon of grand prewar apartment buildings each morning to get his vegetarian chopped liver at the Famous Dairy Restaurant on West 72nd Street. The great political wars on the Upper West Side had not been fought between Democrats and Republicans but between Democrats and Democrats: JFK vs. Stevenson; RFK vs. McCarthy; Humphrey vs. McGovern. Independence, Missouri, may have given the world Harry Truman, but the Upper West Side gave it Ruth Messinger.

Lately, though, Siegel was beginning to feel like an outcast in his own neighborhood. Liberal guilt was practically invented on the Upper West Side, but his neighbors' sympathy for the less fortunate was clearly running out. The streets were a disaster zone. Homeless people were strewn across blankets on sidewalks while panhandlers worked the corners. Deranged men, half-naked or reeking of urine, screamed at passersby, lost souls in search of an elusive peace. Early on in the crisis, a resident's interaction with a homeless person would produce a momentary bout of sympathy or guilt, but those days were long gone. Now most people just accepted them as human street furniture.

Siegel still saw the homeless as human beings, people like anyone else who needed help. He tried to be sensitive to the man who periodically ranted to himself on his street: Siegel would talk to him, give him some money once in while, even as his neighbors took detours to avoid him. People were loath to walk down Broadway and brave its gauntlet of misery. Outside the 72nd Street subway station, where LBJ and RFK once spoke to large crowds on flatbed trucks, people frowned as panhandlers took shifts working the entrance. These Upper West Siders were Democrats, Siegel knew, but a lot of them had voted, quietly, for Rudy Giuliani. They were prepared to let the mayor do the dirty work while they closed their eyes.

The civil rights lawyer and the new mayor had begun their careers together at NYU Law School, class of 1968. Siegel was a campus activist; Giuliani was a bookworm. One organized Law Students Against the War in Vietnam and the Law Students' Civil Rights Research Council; the other stayed in the library. Years later, when Siegel assumed the NYCLU post, he watched his old classmate on the evening news all but pronounce people guilty when they'd only been indicted. He was ruthless, Siegel decided, and everything since then had only confirmed it. When the Giuliani campaign commercial first aired showing the candidate playing catch with his son, Andrew, Siegel felt Giuliani's throwing style was awkward and rigid, like Nixon's. When the news showed Giuliani dancing the Lindy with old Italian women at senior citizen centers, he seemed relaxed and comfortable, while in black neighborhoods he looked tight and uneasy.

Since the election, the new mayor and his police commissioner had given Siegel and his fellow advocates a hundred new reasons to worry. Giuliani and Bratton had set in motion one of the largest-scale sweeps of urban criminality in American history. The mayor promised during the campaign to free police to go after street-level drug dealers, and Bratton had issued the orders. In one fell swoop, the police department abandoned years of self-restraint, adopted through decades of corruption and brutality scandals, and fanned out with a vengeance.

The "Broken Windows" theory was now departmental policy. Petty drug dealers were busted, even if all they carried were nickel bags and loose joints. A yuppie smoking pot in Washington Square Park could find himself incarcerated in a city jail for a night. People caught urinating in the street, jumping a subway turnstile, playing loud music, or drinking beer on a stoop were ticketed, interrogated, and checked for outstanding warrants and parole violations. Guns were confiscated and traced. And the squeegee men—all seventy-five of them, it turned out—were soon history. Summonses for so-called quality-of-life infractions jumped from 175,000 to 500,000 that year; the number of misdemeanor arrests exploded from 90,000 to 220,000; and 15,000 additional prisoners made the bus trip to the city's massive jail complex on Rikers Island in 1994.

The timing could not have been better for the administration. The public was ready for dramatic action. Dinkins's Safe Streets, Safe City plan had pumped up the size of the police force by nearly 8,000 officers. President Clinton's crime bill would soon pour hundreds of millions of dollars in additional funds into the effort. The crack epidemic, meanwhile, had peaked: the cross fire from semiautomatic gun battles that had splattered the blood of so many children across the city's housing projects had started to quiet down.

The homeless became another target of the NYPD crackdown. Bratton formed a thirty-five-member squad to roust them from their makeshift beds, cardboard boxes, and shantytowns and offer them a place in a shelter. If they refused, they'd be moved along or in certain cases arrested. As for the panhandlers, the Supreme Court had ruled that anti-loitering laws were unconstitutional, but the police attacked the problem from every other conceivable angle. If beggars were approaching people in their cars, they were cited for impeding the flow of traffic—a violation of Penal Law Section 240.20 (5). If they made physical contact with passersby, followed people, or even made menacing gestures, they could be charged with harassment, Section 240.26 (1).

In short order the homeless who'd changed the character of New York City seemed to vanish, and the landscape changed dramatically. It was an eerie development. The average number of homeless single adults in city shelters actually went *down*. Where did they go?

Clearly many went to jail, while others were simply moved along by police day after day. Rikers Island became just another shelter for some, another city institution with hot meals. But thousands more started to receive the housing that advocates like Brosnahan had cried out for. Just as Dinkins's police expansion bloomed under Giuliani, so did his expansion of special housing for the homeless. An agreement he'd signed with Governor Cuomo had created 7,500 units of supportive housing for single adults. Thousands of additional residences were created for people with AIDS, many of them homeless. And that was on top of Ed Koch's mammoth housing construction program of the late 1980s.

At the same time, the nation was experiencing an unparalleled expansion of housing for poor single adults. Under Clinton, the new leaders of the Department of Housing and Urban Development in Washington made homelessness their number one priority and doubled funds for the problem. New York City's allocation in one year alone was $100 million. The federal aid Dinkins had long hoped for had finally come through—in time to benefit Giuliani.

Yet the advocates were besieged. Mary Brosnahan witnessed an increasing tide of misery at her office downtown, whose waiting room became a crowded way station for homeless people in desperate need of help. The numbers showing up at soup kitchens swelled. At the NYCLU, Siegel was hearing increasing reports of young black and Latino men being jostled by cops. Five teenagers—three blacks and two Latinos—were hanging out in broad daylight in front of a building one of them lived in on 85th Street and Amsterdam Avenue when a cop told them to get off the street. When the kids told him one of them lived in the building, the officer snapped back, "Don't give me any fucking lip. When I come back in fifteen minutes and you're here, you are all going in." Sure enough, when the cop returned, he arrested them all. Siegel took up their case and got the charges dropped. He couldn't convince any of their families to sue, however: all feared retaliation from the local cops. In their neighborhood, as in dozens of other minority communities, anger over police harassment was beginning to grow.

But with the public starting to take notice of the changing atmosphere in the city, Siegel's warnings about the excesses of Giuliani's tactics fell on deaf ears. The journalists who interviewed the attorney became increasingly skeptical of his complaints. It took all he had to convince the City Council to reject an administration bill to strengthen anti-panhandling laws. "Remember your roots," he told council members; "remember how people would come here with pushcarts. Your grandparents would be out on the Lower East Side of Manhattan: we all begged. Are we going to forget our roots?"

A year later, the council passed the bill. To Siegel, the new regime was criminalizing poverty. It all had racial overtones. But Norman Siegel was fighting a losing battle. He was on the wrong side of history.

It was smoky as usual. The thicket of yuppies and social climbers clogged the bar at Elaine's, making it hard for Deputy Police Commissioner Jack Maple to weave his portly frame back to his usual table in the dining room. With his homburg, bow tie, and spectator shoes, he was as outrageous as any character in the place, a nineteenth-century dandy in a 1990s hot spot. It was a role he seemed to relish. Spotting his friends beneath a dark mural of bearded satyrs playing the violin, Maple flipped his hat over the bust of George Plimpton, which looked out skeptically upon the clique like an archangel guarding the sacred traditions of the place.

He needn't have worried. Maple, his boss Bill Bratton, and the department's youthful press secretary, John Miller, clearly had a reverence for Elaine's. Weren't they a latter-day Rat Pack, after all, startling the establishment by day at One Police Plaza and catching bad guys by night on the city's mean streets? They were hard-living urban cowboys, eager to brag about their conquests into the morning hours at the most venerable celebrity hangout in Manhattan. Back at City Hall, their swinging behavior was driving the boss crazy. But that only made it more fun.

Bratton and his crew must have felt like the toasts of the town. Their crime-fighting exploits were covered on the front pages while their social exploits were making the gossip columns. In a few short weeks, the commissioner's innovations and get-tough attitude toward crime had made him a star. Three months into the new administration, crime was already falling by double digits.

In his clubby little squad of mavericks, the commissioner played the adult. He was the only married man in the bunch: his wife, Cheryl, would often cook dinner for the bachelors. Miller was the fair-haired kid, a star crime reporter for WNBC-TV who'd given up a huge salary to play cops and robbers. He had blond curly hair, penetrating eyes, TV-star good looks. With his pinstriped suits and white pocket handkerchiefs, he'd always seemed a little too well dressed to be a reporter. He seemed more in his element at Elaine's than in Little Italy, where he'd made his reputation stalking John Gotti outside the Ravenite Social Club. When he jumped to the other side to work for Bratton, he joked ostentatiously about the salary cut he'd taken. "Anybody got a dime?" he asked reporters at a City Hall event. Like Bratton, he was cocky.

Maple, Bratton's chief anticrime strategist, was the genius of the bunch, the guy with a computer in his head. He could spit out crime statistics and deployment figures like a baseball fan ticking off batting averages. He knew that in 1993 there had been 1,946 murders, 86,000 robberies, 99,000 burglaries, 112,000 car thefts. Back at One Police Plaza, they were calling him "Rain Man."

It was a heady time for the crew. They had taken a sclerotic old bureaucracy and shaken it up, even changed the culture somewhat. A department that for the most part kept business hours was now running full throttle nights and weekends, same as the bad guys. Precinct commanders who used to see crime statistics every three months were now getting them daily and were expected to shift their resources to address new crime trends.

Ground zero of the crackdown was the new Computer Comparison Statistics room at One Police Plaza—Compstat—where computers were spitting out daily crime statistics and police deployment was being adjusted with military precision. Precinct chiefs were grilled by police brass as a large computer screen flashed local crime figures. "Captain," Maple would ask, "what are we going to do about the shootings in those housing projects? How are we doing with the buy-and-busts? Are we debriefing the prisoners?" The management of the department had been brought to a new level of sophistication.

As this evening at Elaine's progressed and one drink led to another, the conversation drifted into dark humor. The jokes were about the mayor and his aides: how grim they were, how mean they could be. The war stories Bratton's crew exchanged weren't so much about criminals but about deputy mayors and press secretaries, and who at the table had been chewed out by one of them this time. Giuliani and Bratton were the hottest crime-fighting team since Batman and Robin. But the boys at Elaine's tonight knew that behind the scenes, the relationship was falling apart.

At City Hall, Giuliani was rapidly asserting his dominance over city government. The mayor's moves had an operatic quality to them. The tension would mount around his office, aides would start scurrying around the corridors faster, and at the chosen moment he would unleash a bomb-shell that seemed to stop time. His flair for the dramatic gesture was illustrated when a thousand Legal Aid lawyers went on strike, set up pickets outside City Hall, and stranded tens of thousands of indigent defendants without representation.

Spurning backdoor diplomacy, Giuliani raised the stakes and canceled the city's contract with the group. Then he announced he was ready to replace every lawyer on the staff if they didn't return to work the next morning. "There are many lawyers in this city that are looking for work, and maybe they can have options that they didn't have," the mayor told the press. Humiliated, the lawyers folded and signed a new contract that evening.

Another Giuliani Moment came in the closing days of his yearlong fight to merge the city's three police departments. None of the mayor's predecessors had been able to overcome union and bureaucratic resistance to the idea. But Giuliani was expert at finding leverage and exercising it, no matter how angry it made the chosen opposition. The autonomous Metropolitan Transportation Authority controlled the transit police, but City Hall paid the bill. Giuliani decided to withdraw the city's entire $320 million contribution to the MTA and threatened to use the money to rehire the cops on the NYPD payroll. It was an extraordinarily hostile act, but the mayor didn't care. The MTA board capitulated and relinquished control of the transit force. The Transit and Housing Authority police departments merged with the NYPD.

An unmistakable air of machismo filled the air around the mayor's office. Weakness was out at City Hall. Giuliani was new to municipal government, but he seemed to have no self-doubt. There was an adrenaline rush around him. He walked quickly, purposefully, always surrounded by a large retinue of aides and detectives. His morning staff meetings were suffused with an air of conquest. "He would swagger in with his cup of coffee and tell his war stories about whatever had gone on," a commissioner recalls. "Everybody would cheer him on, like 'Oh, you're so tough and so powerful and strong.'"

Cops were the heroes of choice in the Age of Giuliani. Every month brought a press conference at City Hall featuring the mayor and police officers who'd performed acts of heroism. "I thought to myself, 'Arlene, remember your academy training, take your time, take a deep breath, think what you're going to do,'" recalled Officer Arlene Beckles, a Police Academy instructor who foiled a robbery attempt at a beauty parlor where she was having her hair done. Before a packed news conference, the mayor had Bratton promote her to detective on the spot. He also promised to officiate at her wedding. Another press event featured five officers who had refused to accept a bag filled with $254,000 in cash as a bribe. The mayor, four of whose uncles were cops, idolized the men in that profession and rhapsodized about the department they worked for. "When this police department is motivated to act, there is nothing quite like it in law enforcement," he said. At yet another press conference he recalled consoling the grief-stricken family of a murdered police officer. His voice shrank to a whisper as he described his inability to sleep after he'd returned to Gracie Mansion. He'd stayed up for hours, he recalled, asking himself and Donna what more he could have done for them.

On January 7, 1995, Giuliani and Bratton appeared at an elaborate press event at City Hall to mark their accomplishments in the war on crime. Standing in front of detailed charts, they trumpeted extraordinary news: Crime in New York City had fallen in every major category in 1994. Murders alone plunged 19 percent, the largest drop in recorded history. A whole generation of scholarship holding that police had little to do with the rise and fall of crime was being discredited on the streets of New York.

Critics claimed that Giuliani and Bratton had simply come to power at a lucky moment. In cities across America, crime had been a rising fever through the 1980s. Now the fever had broken: Murder was down 21 percent in Los Angeles and 13 percent in Boston. The crack epidemic, which had spawned warfare in ghettos all over the United States, was ending after a decade of carnage. The mayor and his police commissioner seemed to be taking credit for a nationwide trend.

The numbers, though, showed that New York was not just "riding a wave and claiming to be the entire ocean," as Al Sharpton would put it. Halfway through 1995, crime was down by 1 percent across the country but by 16 percent in New York. Bratton pointed out correctly that of the 67,000 fewer crimes committed across America, 41,000 were in New York City. The city was driving the national trend, not following it.

A battle for the credit was shaping up in New York. The public was viewing Bratton as the hero of the city's crime plunge, and Giuliani was growing resentful. Giuliani had campaigned on a promise to arrest low-level drug dealers and other petty criminals; he had loudly proselytized for the "Broken Windows" theory throughout the campaign; he had hired Bratton because he agreed with his philosophy of policing. Bratton and his crew clearly had taken the concepts to a higher level of sophistication and effectiveness than anyone had done in the past. But Giuliani wanted the world to know that it was he who'd started the ball rolling. As Mark Green learned on inauguration day, the mayor didn't like sharing the spotlight.

On the face of it, the mayor and the commissioner seemed cut from the same cloth. Both were raised in working-class Catholic families. Both were cultural conservatives who disdained the radical activism of the sixties. Both spent their careers in law enforcement. But temperamentally they were a mismatch. Where Giuliani had once considered becoming a priest, Bratton was a Sunday school dropout. Where the mayor lived and breathed the work ethic, Bratton often got by on his charm. Where Giuliani was almost ascetic in his pursuits, Bratton loved glamour. Where Giuliani's men were stern and serious, Bratton's gang was right out of the frat house.

Their troubles began at the end of Bratton's first week on the job. On Sunday, January 16, his image graced the front page of the *Daily News*. An "exclusive" banner ran across a huge picture of him staring ahead and looking visionary. The headline read "TOP COP BRATTON—I'LL END THE FEAR." Inside, the new commissioner talked about his tumultuous first week on the job and about the plans he had for the city. "My number one priority is fear reduction," he told the paper. He had nothing but praise for Giuliani. "He lets me run the department," he said. "Very frequently, in interviews with a chief, I hear 'Whatever you want, commissioner,' but that's not what I want. I'm looking to turn around that mentality of waiting to hear from on high."

It didn't take long. According to Bratton, his phone rang shortly after the *Daily News* hit the stands. He and Maple were summoned to Peter Powers's office at City Hall. When they arrived, the deputy mayor was in a bad mood. "We need to be aware of these stories," Powers said. "The mayor is very concerned. We will control how these stories go out. The mayor has an agenda, and it's very important that everybody stay on-message and that the message come from the mayor."

"I've known Rudy since we were kids, okay? I'm his best friend, and I couldn't get away with this. If I was doing this stuff, he'd fire me." If it kept up, he said, they'd find another police commissioner.

That was all. After a week on the job, Bratton had been threatened with termination. His offense: good publicity.

The mayor's distrust of Bratton continued to grow. Hours after John Timoney was promoted at City Hall to first deputy police commissioner, he was called up to Gracie Mansion. In a basement conference room, Peter Powers chewed Timoney out for failing to thank the mayor while the cameras were rolling. Bratton looked on in amazement.

Bratton and his aides came to think of that conference room as a torture chamber. "We used to joke that they'd throw the windows open so that it'd be ice cold in there and then, when they'd attach the electrodes, they'd throw cold water on you so that when they throw the electricity on it'd hurt even worse," Bratton recalls. "You had to basically engage in dark humor because they were in many respects a sadistic group of people." Maple says he always imagined that Giuliani, who didn't participate in the torture sessions, was secretly watching them through the eyes in the portraits on the conference room walls.

At the dawn of the administration, Police Spokesman John Miller had worked as a team with Giuliani Press Secretary Cristyne Lategano. The two ran marathons together, joshed with each other at press conferences, even played piggyback around the press office. They soon developed more than a professional relationship, sometimes openly smooching at restaurants and bars—notably Hogs and Heifers, a raunchy biker bar tucked away inside the meat-packing district in downtown Manhattan.

But increasingly the mayor came to view Bratton as a showboat and his press office as a renegade operation, feeding reporters flattering stories about the commissioner instead of the mayor. Lategano's relationship cooled with Miller, and she started to make vitriolic phone calls berating him for cutting the mayor out of news stories. Bratton's crew started referring to Lategano as the "Dragon Lady."

The conflicts continued. Bratton says the mayor chewed out Miller for failing to include Giuliani in a press conference announcing the arrest of two suspects in the robbery at Vera Wang's wedding boutique. "You know, I have the distinct impression that someone over there is putting someone else's agenda ahead of mine," Giuliani said, referring to police headquarters.

On Wednesday, February 8, 1995, the boom fell. Convinced he was being excluded from the limelight, Giuliani ordered a full housecleaning of the police department's public relations office, and a tearful Miller resigned in protest two days later. It was a humiliating public rebuke for the police commissioner, and speculation mounted that he too would quit. But he didn't. Chastened, Bratton withdrew into the seclusion of his office at One Police Plaza and quietly smoldered.

5

The Control Machine

Lou Carbonetti hadn't seen Rudy Giuliani in twenty-five years. The two had never been very close, but their fathers, Louie Carbonetti and Harold Giuliani, were best friends in the late 1950s, two plainspoken Italian men who loved baseball. Harold frequently traveled up from Brooklyn to visit the Carbonettis on 108th Street in East Harlem, and sometimes he'd slip Lou a dollar as a present, which made the child extremely happy. Sometimes Harold would come by with Rudy, his only son, and the two friends would take their kids to the Yankees game.

Decades later, in 1986, Lou started reading about Rudy's exploits as a U.S. attorney and about his interest in entering politics. He called the prosecutor, had a short chat about old times, and arranged to come down to his office to reconnect. As a gesture, Lou framed an old 8 × 10 photo he'd found, showing their fathers standing together at Louie's uptown Democratic club.

At their small reunion at the U.S. Attorney's Office, Lou presented his old friend with the photograph. Giuliani was touched. He had pictures of his dad, but none like this: Harold, a bar owner, rarely dressed up, but he was wearing a dress shirt and tie here. Thanking Lou warmly, Giuliani slipped the photo out of the $69 frame and set it aside. "Lou, I can't take the frame," he said, handing it back to his childhood friend. Gee, Carbonetti thought, the stories about him are true. This is one stand-up guy.

As he set out to capture the mayoralty in 1989, Rudy Giuliani wasn't interested in being viewed as another politician. He'd prosecuted the municipal scandals and seen the filthy underside of the business. He'd been disgusted by how Donald Manes and Stanley Friedman, two reigning Democratic bosses, had been handed whole areas of city government as political rewards, then used those fiefdoms as dumping grounds for cronies, hacks, and crooks. Things would be different under him, Giuliani vowed. Patronage was a "municipal plague," and he called for a "dramatic break" from the practice. "From the day that I started exploring running for mayor," he told the *New York Times* in 1989, "I have made it clear to every political leader almost from the first discussion we have had that there will be no jobs or patronage—only decisions made on merit."

But somewhere down the line, most likely as he was making the transition from prosecutor to politician in the lean years between his '89 loss and his '93 rematch, Giuliani had a change of heart. By the time he charged up the steps of City Hall in 1994, the new mayor was determined not just to replace the top officials of government with political allies but to replace employees at *all* levels of government. The first Republican mayor in a generation wanted his own people to staff the city government, be they sympathizers or cronies of sympathizers. Far from being loath to hand jobs to friendly politicians, he was intent on doing so.

The man he chose to carry out this mission was Lou Carbonetti's son.

Sweet-faced and heavyset, Tony Carbonetti had worked at only one job in his short career prior to joining the Giuliani campaign in '93—managing a bar in Boston. To Giuliani, though, he had the single greatest qualification for entrance into his constellation: total loyalty. He was a Carbonetti, after all, a member of the family. He was eager to learn, still impressionable, and a quick study, with a good amount of common sense. After working tirelessly on the campaign, he was rewarded with a job in the chief of staff's office working for Randy Mastro. Carbonetti was given the title of appointments director and placed in charge of handling patronage for City Hall. Not bad for a twenty-three-year-old without a college degree.

From the outset of the new administration, Ray Harding had been upset with what he felt was the slow pace of housecleaning. Commissioners had been hired during the transition, but deputy and assistant commissioners hadn't been replaced, leaving hundreds of Dinkins appointees in agencies throughout city government, theoretically able to undermine the agenda of the new administration. "Don't let the new commissioners become too reliant on the Dinkins people," Harding warned Giuliani. "Take the hit for firing people early and all at once instead of dragging it on for months." But transitions are short, the Giuliani crew was exhausted after the November victory, and the incoming team was wary of lopping off experienced bureaucrats. In the top tier of the administration, only one man, Corporation Counsel Paul Crotty, the chief lawyer, had ever served in city government before. The outsiders needed a few insiders.

Carbonetti went to work. Fielding thousands of résumés, he gave priority to Liberal Party acolytes—including both of Ray Harding's sons, Robert and Russell—followed by people recommended by Republican allies like Guy Molinari in Staten Island and State Senator Guy Velella, the Bronx Republican chairman. Some of Giuliani's relatives got jobs, like Catherine Giuliani, a cousin, who was named a Queens community coordinator at a $44,000 salary, and Christopher Halligan, a son of a Giuliani cousin, who also got a community coordinator's job, with a $40,000 salary. Raymond Casey, the husband of one of Giuliani's cousins, was named special counsel to the mayor's commissioner of labor, making $75,000, and his son Jeffrey Casey was named special assistant to Ninfa Segarra, a $35,000 job.

Tony's father, Lou Carbonetti, wasn't forgotten: he was named director of the mayor's Community Assistance Unit, with a starting salary of $77,000. He had to resign under pressure a year later, after being promoted to commissioner, amid headlines claiming that he'd failed to report back debts on his business and possessed two different driver's licenses with two different names.

The mayor argued to reporters that it was necessary to staff city government with people who agreed with the policies of the new administration. "Of course we are hiring supporters," he said. "Who else would we appoint?"

What he didn't tell the public was that a young commissioner had refused

to hire a candidate sent by City Hall because three of the references furnished by the prospective employee had used the word *scum* to describe
him. Or that a City Hall referral had demanded a deputy commissioner's
job in his interview because his father had contributed to the Giuliani campaign. Or that a Housing Authority worker who received his position
because of his ties to the Jewish community had been arrested on the job for
exposing himself to two women. Upon his arrest, he had Central Booking
call Bruce Teitelbaum in the chief of staff's office to bail him out, since Teitelbaum had gotten him the job in the first place. A panicked Teitelbaum
refused.

One agency administrator who was forced to swallow dozens of patronage
hires estimates that 60 percent of them were qualified while 20 percent had
no experience for the jobs they applied for. The last 20 percent, he says,
"were dirtbags."

Government might not be hiring the best and the brightest, figured one
of Giuliani's commissioners, but the mayor didn't care. "These guys came
in with sort of this disdain for government," he recalls. "Their approach to
hiring was 'What the hell difference does it make? We're going to run everything from City Hall. We can have a chimp as a commissioner.' They
thought that they were going to be involved in everything and they were
going to make the decisions. And that's what they did."

The Health and Hospitals Corporation became a favorite dumping
ground for City Hall's patronage hires. The organization, which runs the
city's eleven public hospitals, is quasi-independent, with its own governing
board and a separate payroll. It could swallow up new hires beyond the
range of scrutiny that city agencies received. "There's a person's résumé
coming over the fax," Carbonetti would tell hospital executives. "Have him
hired by Friday. Salary's got to be around fifty thousand."

Some were qualified, and some were not. "The cockier ones would come
and say, 'I worked hard in the campaign and this is owed to me—here I
am,'" a former hospitals official says. "A lot would tell me, 'I feel sorry for
you. It must be hard.' I'd say, 'It is.'"

Mastro would often step in when agency officials resisted swallowing Carbonetti's hires. When the public saw the bearded, cherubic former assistant

U.S. attorney, Mastro was usually on television arguing the party line for Giuliani's policies. Roaming the corridors of City Hall, he was always ready with a gracious smile and a bear hug for a disgruntled councilman or an eager lobbyist. But behind the scenes he often played the role of enforcer for the boss. "I don't want an explanation, I want you to do it!" he'd say. "I told you the salary had to be a hundred thousand." One high-level corporation official came to dread Mastro's calls. "He would talk to me like I was scum," the official recalls.

The timing could not have been more inappropriate. Giuliani was cutting hundreds of millions of dollars from the hospital system, attacking it for being a bloated "jobs program" instead of a health care provider. Giuliani's cuts forced the layoff of hundreds of hospital workers. Meanwhile, the mayor's men were on the phone forcing patronage hires down the throats of terrified hospital executives. "There was a Gestapo mentality about these guys that was scary," says the hospitals official. "There was the sense that you could lose your job if you don't cooperate. These were people who'd cut your head off."

City Hall wasn't just replacing executives. Carbonetti was routinely forcing agencies to take mid- and low-level hires, down to the men who dug up the streets. When the Department of Environmental Protection tried to hire twenty-five street laborers, the hires were intercepted by Carbonetti. "You can have five," he told a DEP official. "I'll take the other twenty."

"These are unglamorous jobs," a City Hall official conceded, "but I can't tell you how many calls we'd get from politicians telling us they needed these jobs."

The patronage operation existed on two planes. It was a vehicle for payback, a way to bolster the political power of Giuliani as he eyed a reelection battle down the road. But it was also part of a larger effort at message control that obsessed the mayor even more. Giuliani was a Republican mayor in a Democratic town, and he believed the knives were out for him from every direction. A ditchdigger could leak an embarrassing story about Giuliani's government just as easily as a deputy commissioner. From the mayor's perspective, the more loyalists out there, the better.

The message control machine extended far beyond the patronage folks in the chief of staff's office. They were merely staffing the troops. The Press

Office was keeping them in line. Cristyne Lategano was expected to come over from the '93 campaign to City Hall as the junior member of the two-headed press team headed by campaign communications chief Richard Bryers. But when Bryers decided not to join the administration, the twenty-eight-year-old Lategano was on her own.

The new press secretary proved a ferocious loyalist, willing and able to terrorize the spokespeople who worked at the city's agencies. The polite relationship that had traditionally existed between the City Hall Press Office and its dozens of satellites was thrown out the window under her reign.

Lategano ordered press secretaries throughout city government to run even the smallest public statements by City Hall for approval. At the Department of Environmental Protection, which oversaw the city's water supply, press officers routinely supplied a *New York Times* clerk with the city's reservoir level each day, which would run in agate type on the paper's weather page. According to a DEP source, when City Hall got wind of this, the order came down to the agency: The reservoir numbers had to be run by Lategano's office every day before being released to the newspaper. When no one was around to give the agency its okay, the paper of record would have to print "NA," for not available. Lategano denies any knowledge of this.

On a larger front, Lategano had helped dislodge John Miller as chief spokesman at the police department once she and the mayor concluded that he was serving Commissioner William Bratton's agenda and not the mayor's. But Giuliani wasn't satisfied. As he prepared to release his second budget in 1995, he decided that Ray Harding had been right—there hadn't been enough of a sweep of personnel. Giuliani sent down the order to swing the ax far and wide and rid government of all officials who did not believe in his agenda.

The mayor explained to reporters that his new budget was "truly an attempt to reengineer the way in which city government operates." Government officials were going to have to get with the program or get out. "Sometimes the manager that's there is capable of doing it," he said. "Sometimes the manager that's there is so boxed in to the old way it was done, or has personal relationships with the people that are there, that that person is incapable of doing that."

In one bloody week, dozens of mid-level managers were fired throughout city government. The mayor's office also fired four department spokespeople on the grounds that they were not supporting Giuliani's agenda. These were career public relations officials, people who'd served a long line of mayors of different political stripes: the evidence that they were blocking Giuliani's program was specious.

Mastro handled much of the fallout. The chief of staff felt he was in a no-win situation: the mayor was calling for heads, while commissioners were besieging him with desperate requests to stave off executions of valued aides. To some commissioners, Mastro played the good guy, voiding orders that would have cost people their livelihoods. To others, he was a hatchet man.

Former personnel commissioner Lilliam Barrios-Paoli recalls that Mastro was willing to listen to reason when she resisted hiring candidates sent down by his office. "We'd argue back and forth until we'd reach some accommodation," she says. "Clearly, he had things he needed to do. I never found him to be the ogre or the unreasonable person others might have found him to be."

The mayor succeeded in creating a climate of fear throughout municipal government, which may have been his goal all along. Commissioners, scared of retribution from City Hall, stopped speaking to the press. Reporters who reached out to them were rebuffed and directed to the City Hall Press Office. Lategano took a page from David Garth's campaign strategy: editors were called when she deemed a story unfair. Jerry Nachman, the news director at WCBS-TV, learned that City Hall operatives weren't content complaining to him about his station's coverage—they were talking to his boss, Budd Carey, the general manager. After a while, he says now, "they were no longer dealing with Budd—it was with Budd's new boss, the president of the owned television stations division."

At New York 1, hopes for an improved relationship with the new administration faded. Giuliani refused to appear on the set of *Inside City Hall*, the nightly political show. The bunker mentality at City Hall was a carryover from the '93 race, when Giuliani believed the press was treating his campaign against a black mayor with suspicion. The adversarial relationship didn't abate after the 1993 campaign. It grew.

I t was late at night at Gracie Mansion in July 1994 and the mayor was angry. Sitting in the study on the mansion's main floor, eating his dinner on a coffee table, he pored over the press coverage of what reporters were calling Rentgate. *Newsday* had disclosed that more than a dozen members of the Giuliani campaign, most of them now on the City Hall payroll, had received thousands of dollars worth of free rent from landlord William Koeppel, a top fund-raiser for the Giuliani campaign. The revelations triggered accusations that Giuliani had accepted illegal campaign contributions from Koeppel and that the officials had violated disclosure rules.

The mayor had been unable to spin his way out of this quagmire by insisting that such rent breaks were common practice. Realtors like Nancy Packes, president of the Madison Avenue powerhouse Feathered Nest, were popping up in the media disputing his assertion. "It's an unwarranted consideration, no matter how you want to slice it," opined Packes in *Newsday*. She was shooting him down in the *Times* and on WABC-TV as well.

The telephone rang at Gracie Mansion. An old associate from the U.S. Attorney's Office was calling the mayor to remind him that Nancy Packes was once married to Edmund Rosner, a lawyer Giuliani helped prosecute for attempting to bribe a police officer in 1972 and again for drug trafficking in 1987. The real estate expert had a conflict of interest! Packes had split with Rosner more than a decade earlier, but Giuliani had found a way to discredit her.

He had an aide fetch him a copy of the book *Prince of the City*, which detailed the prosecution of Rosner. He flipped excitedly through its pages. There it was. "Every era has a public enemy number one among lawyers," an assistant U.S. attorney says in the book, "and Rosner is ours."

Giuliani sent his press aides to work. The administration had its lists of friendly reporters and unfriendly reporters, and calls went out to some of the former. So feverishly did they go about finding a journalist willing to print the Rosner revelation that the story ended up running in two different columnists' pieces on the same day, July 26.

"But who is Nancy Packes?" asked Hilton Kramer of the *New York Post* in his weekly column critiquing the *New York Times*. "When she was Mrs. Edmund Rosner, she was the wife of an attorney who was successfully prosecuted by a U.S. Justice Dept. team that included Rudy Giuliani."

"Packes was married to Edmund Rosner," reported columnist Jim Sleeper in the *Daily News*, "a mob lawyer convicted of bribery in 1972 by a team of prosecutors including young Rudy Giuliani."

The facts about Packes were true. She was a bit player in Rentgate, not someone who necessarily deserved to have her association with a criminal she'd divorced ten years earlier splashed across the city's news pages. But she had messed with Rudy Giuliani.

The message that you either fell into line with the boss or risked disaster seemed to get through to everyone in municipal government—with the exception of Marilyn Gelber.

The newly named commissioner of the Department of Environmental Protection had come to the job by way of the Brooklyn borough president's office, where she'd served crusty old Howard Golden for seven years as his executive assistant. Like Golden she was a Democrat, but the career city planner considered herself more of a policy wonk, removed from his world of deal-making and back-slapping. Short and bespectacled, with salt-and-pepper hair, she arrived in the Giuliani administration hoping to pursue the environmental causes she'd worked on in Brooklyn, like recycling and clean water protection. Giuliani—reformer, nemesis of hacks—seemed like the perfect boss.

Gelber had marveled at the mayor's use of power in his first months on the job. She watched in awe when he unveiled his first budget without a printed speech—without even *notes*—and handled questions more deftly than Dinkins or Koch had ever done. He seemed to realize that understanding the budget was key to understanding his power, she thought. What she didn't understand was that the new mayor was also exercising his power in less high-minded ways.

Something in Gelber's personality made it impossible for her to stomach even a hint of politics intruding upon her job. It was an odd trait for a woman who had spent years working for Golden. Dour as a mortician, incapable of smiling, Golden seemed a throwback to the kind of political boss who made his deals at weddings and funerals. But Gelber knew him as a man smart enough to hire talented people and ethical enough to keep politics away from the work of his staff. She expected the same from Giuliani.

In October of 1995, Deputy Mayor Peter Powers informed Gelber that he had an applicant he wanted hired for the job of deputy commissioner overseeing the Bureau of Air, Noise and Hazardous Materials. It was the division of DEP that dealt with chemical spills and other crises, a highly technical area. Gelber's staff was already well along in its search for candidates, but Gelber agreed to throw his name into the mix.

Tom Michaels was a Brooklyn man who had spent much of his career on the public payroll. He'd worked at city hospitals, a community board, and the state housing department. At the time he submitted his résumé to the new administration at City Hall, he was running an outfit that acted as a traffic cop for public works utilities, letting one know when another was doing work on the same street corner. He was only vaguely qualified for the job he was seeking, and in fact had applied for the far less specialized position of deputy commissioner for administration.

Half of Michaels's cover letter focused on his devotion to Giuliani and his work in the '89 and '93 campaigns. Just to hammer home the point, Michaels attached two form letters from Giuliani and his staff thanking him for his help in the campaign; an invitation to a Giuliani for New York Finance Committee meeting; a get-out-the-vote letter Michaels had written to Giuliani supporters; a press release on Friends of Giuliani letterhead mentioning his political club's endorsement of the candidate; and, finally, a list of references beginning with the Honorable Rudy Giuliani, Mayor, City of New York.

Brought into DEP's general counsel's office, Michaels seemed to treat his job interview as a formality, which irritated his questioners. "He wasn't even excited about the fucking job," recalls one of the three. "At least you'd get excited about it, you know—'Yeah, I care about the environment, I love clean air.' Something, anything!"

Gelber had him marked as a political hack and resisted his hiring for months, despite repeated calls from Powers inquiring about the delay. She finally relented, she says, after City Hall held some other appointments hostage.

But Gelber was stubborn. Instead of making the best of the situation, she proceeded to treat Michaels with outright hostility. His first day on the job, he says, he approached the commissioner and asked what he should do first. "Her response was 'You should start looking for another job.' " At a staff meeting a few days later she refused to introduce him. When he ventured to speak, she cut him off. "You will speak only when you're spoken to!" she said, according to Michaels, as others looked on in shock.

The situation deteriorated. An aide to Gelber eyed Michaels's secretary sending out a mailing for a political club he'd helped found, the Fiorello LaGuardia Good Government Committee. Gelber chewed him out, then called Powers to tell him about it. On April 9, 1996, she dashed off a furious memo to Powers. "I want to alert you that, this afternoon, I dismissed Thomas Michaels from his position as Deputy Commissioner of the Department's Bureau of Air, Noise and Hazardous Materials.

"Mr. Michaels has shown himself to be insubordinate and without the capacity to show good judgment. . . . He has added no value to the operations of the Bureau and created additional work burdens for me and senior Department managers trying to cover his inadequacies. . . . He has shown no leadership abilities and he has not demonstrated even an elemental grasp of his Bureau's responsibilities after four months on the job."

The City Hall crew was amazed at Gelber's arrogance. She had come out of Howie Golden's office—was hired as a *gift* to Howie Golden—but was making an issue of a patronage hire "as if she'd gotten her own job through the *New York Times*," in one City Hall aide's words.

Powers was enraged. Aside from the petulance she was displaying over Michaels, he felt Gelber wasn't doing a very good job as commissioner. In 1993, before she assumed her post, DEP had taken over the water billing system from the city's Finance Department. Citizens had been complaining about their bills ever since. At every town meeting the mayor attended, citizens harangued him about inaccurate water bills.

Powers says he kept getting assurances from Gelber that things were being remedied. She in turn blamed the water billing problems on City Hall's refusal to permit her to hire an additional thirty customer complaint representatives. They were holding up the hires, she felt, to award them to administration cronies.

In response to the billing complaints, DEP launched its Night Out program, in which agency employees equipped with laptops were sent into communities to sit down with citizens and review their billing records. Several local elected officials wrote to the agency to take advantage of the program.

Then City Hall stepped in. An assistant to Powers named Seth Kaye contacted Gelber's chief of staff, Ben Esner, with an order: Powers wanted copies of any letters DEP received requesting a Night Out. City Hall, not Gelber or her staff, would decide which officials would get DEP's help.

The sole criteria would be politics.

Officials out of favor with the administration were not to be granted their requests. Instead, Giuliani functionaries would find friendly politicians and offer them the chance to sponsor the events. "Why give your political enemies a pat on the back when you can easily serve the same neighborhood with someone we like?" an administration member who was involved in that process says. "You didn't want to do it with an unfriendly councilman, so you did it with an assemblyman instead."

Gelber was embarrassed. Officials she'd known for years were calling her with service requests, and she was powerless to help them. East Flatbush Councilman Lloyd Henry, a soft-spoken Episcopalian minister, requested that DEP workers come to his district to answer constituent complaints, but the administration refused to grant permission. A few weeks later, City Hall got Congressman Ed Towns to sponsor the event instead—outside of Henry's district.

"Here I was, blindly going about responding based on my judgment of whether this was a useful appearance to do," Gelber recalls, "and I was just being told, 'No, no, no—you don't make those decisions. Where it involves an elected official, we're going to make those decisions for you.'"

The policy tied Gelber's constituent service operation up in knots. Esner was constantly on the phone with Powers's office trying to extract permission to perform basic services for customers. "There was the regular day-to-day service delivery stuff, which was like 'Clean the catch basin,' Esner recalls. "They never said, 'Don't go clean the catch basin,' but they'd say, 'Clean the catch basin, but don't write back to councilperson so-and-so to let them know. Or if you do write back, make sure that we see the letter before it goes'—that kind of thing."

It was a practice reminiscent of Tammany Hall, the old New York Democratic political machine that used government to reward friends and punish enemies. Giuliani's administration was systematically enforcing practices that he once dismissed as the very thing that was wrong with city government.

DEP was hardly alone in chafing under his control. Police Commissioner Bratton was enraged that the mayor's aides kept overturning his decisions to send NYPD officials to community meetings called by administration critics like Public Advocate Mark Green and Manhattan Borough President Ruth Messinger. "Anybody who was on whatever enemies list they must have had—everything had to be cleared through them as to could you go to this meeting or give this information out," Bratton recalls. "It was that type of political control that I took great offense at. And it got worse and worse."

A few years later Councilman Henry was the subject of yet another strong-arm tactic by the administration. The administration's welfare commissioner, Jason Turner, stormed out of a City Council hearing after suffering verbal abuse from Henry's fellow Brooklyn councilman, Stephen DiBrienza. Henry moved to issue a subpoena to force Turner to return to finish his testimony. That prompted Jake Menges, the mayor's liaison to the council, to walk over to Henry and mete out his punishment. "You've just lost your fucking Beacon School," Menges told Henry, referring to a program that kept public schools open in the evenings for community use. Unfortunately for Menges, the incident was caught on tape by New York 1 political reporter Melissa Russo. Compounding his situation, Menges, unaware that she had the evidence, lied to Russo when she asked him whether he'd made the comment.

When Giuliani heard about the problem, he called Menges into his upstairs office. "Did you say it?" the mayor asked the young aide. "Yes," Menges said. He apologized and offered his resignation. Then the two of them viewed the video of Menges's exchange.

"It looks like you were defending Jason," the mayor said, referring to his welfare commissioner.

Menges informed the mayor that he'd heard rumors that City Council Speaker Peter Vallone was considering banning Menges from the City Council chamber. "I'll tell him to drop dead," Giuliani said.

Giuliani was loyal and forgiving with his aides and far less generous with outsiders. Menges kept his job: Randy Mastro issued an apology and revoked Menges's threat to Henry.

On May 8, a small gossip item appeared in the *Daily News*. "It looks like some city commissioners can take a stand for independence and not feel the wrath of City Hall," it stated. "Environmental Protection Commissioner Marilyn Gelber just fired Deputy Commissioner Tom Michaels, who was pushed for the job by powerful First Deputy Mayor Peter Powers." It speculated that Powers was mellowing because he was thinking of leaving the administration.

This was not a good thing for Marilyn Gelber.

Randy Mastro called her that morning. "We don't know what's going on here," he told her. "But reinstate him. Reinstate Tom Michaels. He's not fired." The item—which Gelber swears she did not plant—effectively ended her relationship with Powers, City Hall's second most powerful man.

Four days later the *News* caused her an even larger headache. "GETTIN' SOAKED," the headline read. "CUSTOMERS SAY THEY'RE DROWNING IN ERRORS ON WATER BILLS." It was a massive investigation into the water bill mess, featuring, among other examples, a Queens homeowner who received a bill from the city for $27,000. "My kids do like to shower a lot," she said, "but this is ridiculous." The story touched a nerve with homeowners, who deluged the paper with hundreds of additional horror stories.

Embarrassed, Giuliani instructed Powers to appoint a team to resolve the mess. Powers in turn appointed an operations aide, Lawrence Schatt, to take over DEP's water billing operation, a public rebuke to the commissioner. By now the deputy mayor had lost all trust in Gelber.

But Gelber wasn't finished antagonizing City Hall. Early in the morning on June 17, a steam pipe ruptured on the Upper East Side. As supervisor of DEP's hazardous materials unit, this was Tom Michaels's responsibility. Following what he interpreted as procedure, he headed toward his office in Queens, awaiting word from the site as to whether asbestos was involved. He was alerted that there was a positive test for asbestos just as he approached headquarters. He swerved around and drove off to Manhattan.

By the time he arrived, Commissioner Gelber was on the scene along with a phalanx of city officials and a large contingent of television cameras. Michaels says he confirmed that the situation was under control, then walked to get a cup of take-out coffee with a professor from Hunter College who was studying the agency's air monitoring program. Gelber, watching him like a hawk, dashed off a memo later that day to Powers. "I write to express my continued concern about the lack of leadership displayed by Deputy Commissioner Tom Michaels," she wrote. "Although notified of the emergency at 7:11 A.M., Mr. Michaels failed to arrive at the site until three hours later and then disappeared to have breakfast for another hour."

The pipe rupture cleanup job went on through the night. The next morning, Gelber came back to the site and was enraged to find that Michaels was nowhere to be seen. When he did arrive, she exploded at him. *"How dare you come to an emergency late!"* she yelled in front of a group of city officials. *"You're fired—get out of here!"*

And then she sent off another memo to the deputy mayor. "For your information, effective immediately, I am removing Deputy Commissioner Tom Michaels."

About a week later, Gelber was at City Hall for a meeting. She had helped ink a deal between the Giuliani administration and some upstate counties that averted the need for the city to build an $8 billion filtration plant—a big win for the city that Powers felt she had almost botched. After the meeting, he asked her to stay behind.

"I want you out," he said. "And I want you out by tomorrow."

And that was it for Marilyn Gelber. A woman who had come into the Giuliani administration largely as a patronage hire self-destructed over another patronage hire. Gelber learned the hard way that in the Giuliani regime, there was no fighting City Hall.

6

The Mayor and His Little Victim

J ake Menges was one of the true believers of the Giuliani regime. He was blond and mop-topped, a kid like Tony Carbonetti who joined the campaign fresh out of school and rose to a high position at an early age. Having survived the "Beacon School" controversy, he'd risen to become the administration's director of intergovernmental affairs—a big job for someone under thirty.

But now, as he sat on the edge of a hospital bed in the pediatric ward of Lenox Hill Hospital, he was just another nervous parent. A few hours earlier, doctors had removed a cyst from the throat of his four-year-old son, Gardner, who was lying near him wounded and scared, with tubes sprouting from his mouth and layers of bandages covering his throat. Father and son were in need of a little reassurance when a knock came at the door: the mayor of New York City stepped in. "Jake, I'm sorry to intrude," he said. "I just wanted to come by and bring Gardner this hat." Rudy Giuliani was carrying a New York Police Department cap.

For the next half-hour, as a grateful father looked on, Giuliani and young Gardner tossed hockey cards around the bed like old friends, occasionally stopping to check out the basketball game on the tube. "Do you know who that is?" Mr. Menges whispered to his son. "Yeah, Dad," Gardner responded, "it's the mayor."

It was an act of kindness that Menges would never forget. "He's an extremely loyal friend," he says of Giuliani. "There's a very warm and caring side about him."

Such acts of kindness toward his staff were common. On the night before Giuliani delivered his budget presentation in February 1995, his chief advance man, Rick Friedberg, learned that his father had died. Giuliani showed up at Friedberg's apartment after he found out and sat with Friedberg's grieving mother until 4 A.M. "The guy could've just paid his respects," Friedberg says. "He didn't have to sit there and hold the hand of a seventy-five-year-old lady." The next day Giuliani delivered the eulogy at her husband's funeral.

For those who worked closely with him, the mayor's image was an unending source of frustration. Rudy Giuliani on a personal basis could be warm, wise, and open-minded. The man the public saw, on the other hand, was often ruthless and seemingly eager to destroy anyone who got in his way. That vast dichotomy between his private and public lives would never be so apparent as when he decided to hound the chancellor of the New York City school system out of his job.

Ramon Cortines was a gentle, soft-spoken man of sixty-two, a lifetime educator who was awaiting confirmation as an assistant secretary for education in Washington when New York's Board of Education offered him its top job. He was small and balding, with wire-rimmed glasses, the picture of an earnest teacher. In his quietly righteous way, Cortines felt he was on a mission of his own, which was to redeem urban education from its ignoble state. "Attempting to make urban school districts work challenges me," he told a *Times* reporter. "People say New York can't be done. Well, I'm not willing to give up on our big cities." The Californian had no experience in New York City and little preparation for the ordeal he was about to suffer when he landed at JFK International Airport on September 1, 1993.

New Yorkers had come to regard the disastrous state of the public schools as a fact of life in the city, like the cold winters and the high crime rate. For parents, the public schools were the end of the line, the choice when there were no other choices. Members of the upper middle class had long since abandoned the school system in favor of private schools, while much of the middle class had turned to Catholic schools or fled the city altogether for the suburbs. That left more than a million kids, 80 percent of them black and Hispanic, crowded into the haunted old fortresses that had served in many cases since the days of Teddy Roosevelt. Fewer than half the students in those buildings could read at grade level.

Political warfare had left the governance of the public schools tied up in knots. John Lindsay's vision for school decentralization had spawned a network of corrupt and inept neighborhood boards with vast powers over the schools in their domain. Labor contracts made it next to impossible to fire incompetent principals and teachers. School custodians ruled their buildings like corrupt fiefdoms. There was no consensus about how to repair the system, just an eternal war between conservatives and liberals, upstaters and downstaters, over whether lack of money or bad management was responsible for its decline. Ideological wars had paralyzed the seven-member Board of Education. A yearlong feud over a multicultural curriculum advocating tolerance of gays and lesbians had led to the ouster of the previous chancellor, Joseph Fernandez.

Giuliani, like his tutors at the Manhattan Institute, held the Democratic establishment in contempt for the increasing dysfunction. In his eyes, the ruling party was too dependent on the unions to question their hegemony and too accustomed to the status quo to challenge the bureaucracy. True enough, Dinkins and company had laid the blame for the sorry state of the schools on the Republican-dominated State Senate, which repeatedly thwarted efforts to fund urban schools as generously as suburban ones. Giuliani, on the other hand, believed that if kids weren't being educated, money wasn't the problem. The system needed radical surgery.

In early February 1994, soon after he took office, Giuliani took his first stab at bringing Cortines into the fold. He invited the chancellor up to Gracie Mansion, where the mayor proceeded to make his case. Thousands of heads—2,500 by Giuliani's estimate—needed to roll at the Board of Ed. The bureaucracy was out of control, eating up huge amounts of money that should have been going to the classrooms.

The mayor was giving marching orders to a man who did not work for him and had a vastly different approach. Giuliani was impatient for results, a human bulldozer; Cortines was neat, methodical, patient. The mayor wanted a full-scale war on the bureaucracy; Cortines wanted to improve the quality of education in the classrooms. As Giuliani ticked off his ideas, the chancellor sat and listened politely. Then he thanked the mayor and left. The mayor thought they'd struck a deal.

John Beckman feared he was in over his head. As a deputy press secretary under Dinkins, he was a statistics and analysis guy, the one who'd write the thirty-five-page press releases that accompanied the mayor's management reports. Now, as chief spokesman for the schools chancellor, he was playing for higher stakes. Government flacks were often grizzled journeymen hardened by years of political warfare. Beckman, by comparison, was thirty-two, a graduate of Philips Exeter Academy and Dartmouth, an idealist who believed in the leaders he worked for. He was enchanted by Cortines, by his dedication to education and his refusal to let politicians manipulate the city's children. He admired the chancellor's gentlemanly style—how at staff meetings he wouldn't sit down until the women in the room took their seats. He admired the way Cortines arrived at work each day at 6 A.M., answered his own phone calls until his secretaries arrived hours later, and worked until 8 at night. He considered his new boss a man of integrity.

On March 31, 1994, the chancellor responded to Giuliani's call for wholesale layoffs at the Board of Ed with a plan to cut 678 positions and 513 unfilled jobs from its payroll. City Hall was decidedly underwhelmed. "Maybe this day I'm particularly frustrated," Giuliani said on a radio talk show. "I've asked the chancellor to find 2,500 positions in a school system bloated with administrators." Giuliani felt Cortines had gone back on his agreement to cut those positions from the payroll. "He says one thing to me and another to the press," the mayor complained to his aides.

Beckman, called by reporters for a response, gave a dismissive one. "The mayor's reaction has been born of a misunderstanding, as angry reactions often are," he told a New York Times reporter. The same story quoted the chancellor's budget director as well, who didn't even grant Giuliani the benefit of a misunderstanding. "We've said from the beginning that you can't make a 2,500-person cut," said Leonard Hellenbrand. "That's not doable unless one believes that there are hundreds and hundreds of people just twiddling their thumbs, and that's not the case."

Perhaps in another time and place, people would have looked at this as normal parrying between city institutions, the yapping and yelping of bureaucrats. In the eyes of the Giuliani camp, this was full-scale defiance. Giuliani was furious. "Look," he told reporters outside police headquarters, "I've lived in this city a lot longer than he has," referring to Cortines. "Don't tell me that there are only six or seven hundred useless bureaucrats at 110 Livingston Street. . . . Part of the problem could be that coming from out of town maybe he doesn't realize that he's been captured by the school bureaucracy." That accusation—"captured by the bureaucracy"—would grow into a refrain.

Cortines was taken aback by the mayor's fury, but the worst was yet to come. At about 9:30 that night, he was driving back from a community meeting to Board of Ed headquarters with Beckman when the car phone rang. It was City Hall. Beckman studied Cortines's face as he spoke: "If this is going to be a constructive conversation, great. I don't want to come to a session where you're just going to beat me up." The chancellor nodded a few times and hung up. He was being summoned to Gracie Mansion.

Several hours later, Beckman was fast asleep in his Lower East Side apartment when the telephone rang. A reporter was calling for a response to a late-night City Hall press release announcing that Cortines had agreed to cut 2,500 staffers from the Board of Education payroll. Beckman knew nothing about it. Sitting up in his bed, he called Cortines but got his answering machine. Then he reached out to Cristyne Lategano. It was 2:30 in the morning.

The mayor's press secretary called back and confirmed the story. "You're telling me you put this out at twelve o'clock at night?" Beckman said. "These are really crappy tactics." Lategano insisted that Cortines had signed off on the statement. The conversation went downhill from there.

When he arrived at work at 8 A.M., Beckman walked straight into Cortines's office. The chancellor was at his desk as usual, looking as though nothing were wrong. Calmly, he explained to Beckman that Giuliani and his aides had brought him down to the conference room at Gracie

Mansion—the "torture chamber" used to browbeat Bill Bratton's wayward lieutenants. This time, Giuliani himself sat in on the grilling. He put it bluntly to Cortines: lop off 2,500 heads—including Beckman's and Hellenbrand's—or City Hall would appoint a "monitor" to investigate the board. It was Giuliani's version of Double Secret Probation—there was no such thing. But the threat sounded ominous enough. Giuliani gave him twelve hours to comply.

It was a classic prosecutor's gambit: Bring a reluctant suspect into a small room and tell him to come clean or else. The chancellor was cornered. He capitulated on the 2,500 layoffs, provided they were spread out over fifteen months. But he wouldn't fire Beckman and Hellenbrand. And he made a threat of his own: I know how to run a school system, he said, and if you try to appoint somebody to watch me, I'll resign.

Beckman tried to make sense of this bizarre confrontation. The situation was so far over the top that it was almost comic. The mayor had personally worked Cortines over in the dead of night, then humiliated him with a public rebuke. Now Cortines was threatening to quit after just a few months on the job. Deputy Mayor Peter Powers was calling every five minutes seeking an answer from Cortines about whether he'd fired two of his closest aides by the noon deadline.

None of the soft-spoken educator's advisers were equipped for this: His budget man was a former math teacher. The chief of staff was a former English teacher and guidance counselor. Beckman, a mid-level flack and policy wonk under Dinkins, was the closest thing to a political player that Cortines had on staff, and that wasn't saying much.

Nervously, Beckman offered to bow out. "I'm a pretty decent press secretary, but pretty decent press secretaries in this town are a dime a dozen," he said. "So I here and now offer you my resignation. It's much easier to find a good press person than it is to find a decent chancellor."

Cortines wouldn't consider it. "You really don't understand," he said. "If I'd said yes to this, I'd never be able to say no to anything they asked for." Instead he instructed his spokesman to draft a press release announcing the chancellor's resignation. A few hours later, when Giuliani made good on his threat and announced that Herman Badillo—Giuliani's unsuccessful running mate in '93—was being appointed as Special Schools Monitor, Cortines instructed Beckman to release the statement.

Beckman moved ahead on his boss's orders. He dialed Michael Goodwin, editorial page writer at the *Daily News*. "Listen, I'm sending you a press release announcing Ray's intention to resign," Beckman told him. "I wanted you to hear it from me first." Goodwin laughed. "Well, that's a funny joke," Goodwin replied. "I'm not kidding," Beckman said. He read Goodwin some of the lines of the press release. Goodwin cut him off. He started shouting to a colleague. *"Art! Art! Come here!"*

Carol Gresser read about the late-night encounter in the morning paper as she got dressed in her Queens home. The president of the Board of Education was a high school PTA president and an after-school volunteer when she was appointed to the board by the borough president in 1990. With her beauty parlor hairdo and fashionable outfits, Gresser had never lost the image of Queens housewife and political novice, but she was learning fast. A Giuliani ally, she had started to sour on him at his first State of the City speech. She'd been flattered to be offered a seat in the dignitary's section, but after listening to him rail against the evils of the Board of Ed, she walked away feeling suckered.

At the same time, her admiration for Cortines was growing. She had fallen for him at his first interview back in 1993, when he dazzled search committee members with his articulate vision for the school system, and she had been a fan of his ever since. At Board of Ed headquarters, Cortines often eschewed formality by dropping into her office to chat. The two dined together, sometimes with her family. He received invitations to her home, which was usually off-limits to politicians.

Alarmed by newspaper accounts of the Gracie Mansion showdown, Gresser got on the phone with Cortines. "I'm not staying," he told her.

"Ray, you can't do that," she said. "I mean, the children need you."

He was resolute. "I have my integrity, and I'm going to do what I think is right," he said. It was a nightmare. After just eight months on the job, another chancellor was halfway out the door. Gresser frantically called people who might be able to talk sense to either Giuliani or Cortines. Michael Petrides, the Staten Island board member and an adviser to the mayor, agreed to speak to him but called back saying Giuliani wouldn't budge. She tried Ed Koch: there was nothing he could do.

Her last hope was the governor.

Mario Cuomo didn't have a role in this local spat, but he agreed to try to help. He'd been governor for twelve years and was facing a widespread perception that he'd run out of gas. Cuomo had nevertheless announced his plans to run for a fourth term and was willing to play hero in a desperate moment. He was still a powerful moral force in the state, a brilliant, intimidating man with a fiery intellect and a smoldering temper. People tended to listen when he spoke.

The problem was that he couldn't get Cortines on the phone. The governor tried to reach the chancellor for hours, but Cortines wasn't interested in talking to him. Flummoxed, Cuomo left a pleading message on Cortines's home answering machine. "Chancellor Cortines, this is Mario Cuomo. You have to return my phone call. I'm the governor."

Charmed, Cortines replied. Within a day, Cuomo had negotiated a truce: Beckman and Hellenbrand's jobs were saved, but Badillo's appointment as schools monitor stood. All 2,500 jobs would be eliminated. Cortines would stay on. The deal was sealed in the living room of Gracie Mansion. Giuliani poured drinks to celebrate the pact; then he and Cortines emerged into a room jammed with reporters and dutifully shook hands for the cameras as Carol Gresser looked on in relief. It was a picture the Board of Ed president would later place on her wall, a memento of a rare smile being shared between the tormentor and his victim.

A few months later the wooden doors of the grand old mansion swung open for Ed Koch. The former mayor was celebrating his seventieth birthday at a dinner party thrown for him by Rudy Giuliani. Since the '93 race, Giuliani had paid homage to Koch, sought his counsel, appointed his former aides, held him up as a role model. Koch in turn had defended him in the press and praised him in his newspaper columns. "You think I was tough?" the former mayor quipped to an audience one night. "*This* guy is tough!"

But Koch was growing weary of the new mayor as he neared the end of his first year in office. Famously belligerent himself, he was finding Giuliani increasingly abrasive. *"Don't interrupt me!"* Giuliani had bristled on the phone with him one day, and the reprimand still burned in Koch's memory.

The birthday boy made his way through the small crowd, taking a kiss on the cheek and a slap on the back here and there. The staff at the mansion was happy to see their old boss back again and welcomed him warmly. He looked a little softer and a little balder than he had in the 1980s, and he seemed a bit quieter since he'd settled into the role of elder statesman, but he could still be the life of the party when he was in the right mood.

Giuliani had insisted on taking care of all details of the party, down to the guest list, an act of generosity that didn't sit well with Koch. How would Giuliani know who he wanted for this milestone and who he didn't? The former mayor peered around the room: there were friends from past wars, like Diane Coffey, his former chief of staff, and advisers he'd passed on to Giuliani, like David Garth, his old strategist, and Henry Stern, the former and present parks commissioner. There was Dan Wolf, founder of the *Village Voice* and a political confidant. Allen Schwartz, Koch's first corporation counsel, now a federal judge, was there as well.

Koch looked for his old friend David Margolis. The two had been friends since the 1960s; Margolis had been the man who saved Koch's life by performing the Heimlich maneuver on him at a Chinese restaurant in 1981. Koch had appointed Margolis's wife, Barbara, as his protocol chief. He was nowhere to be found. Making his way through the crowd, Koch spotted the strangely familiar face of a partner at his law firm, Jonathan Margolis, a real estate lawyer thirty-one years his junior, a man he barely knew. When Margolis walked over to shake his hand, he broached the obvious. "I don't understand why I'm here," he told the former mayor.

Koch knew. Giuliani had invited the wrong Margolis. It was an innocent mistake made in the course of a good deed. But to Koch it was an irritating reminder that Giuliani listened to no one but himself, regardless of the consequences. Jonathan Margolis and his wife sat at the dining table, a little embarrassed to be surrounded by Koch's closest friends.

Some months later, Koch would have another, more disturbing interaction with Giuliani when Koch's brother Harold died. It was a hard passing for Koch to take, for Harold had been his big brother and role model. When Giuliani found out about it, he told Koch he wanted to speak at Harold's funeral. It wasn't something Koch wanted, but one doesn't say no to the mayor of New York. Members of the mayor's staff also insisted that Giuliani speak first, which did not go over well with the Koch family. And so, before a large crowd of mourners at the Riverside Memorial Chapel on Manhattan's Upper West Side, the mayor eulogized a man who was not a friend of his and proceeded to get his facts wrong. When he talked about Harold's wife, Gail, and her son, Andrew, members of the audience rolled their eyes. Andrew was not Gail's son—he was born to Harold's first wife. Koch felt that Giuliani once again trampled on people's feelings because of his arrogance.

The former mayor was coming to resent Giuliani for another reason. Koch had struck up a friendship with Ray Cortines and had started giving him advice about how to deal with the man at City Hall. And what he was hearing about the mayor's behavior was troubling him.

As a way of protecting the schools from political interference, state law made the chancellor answerable only to the Board of Ed, whose members were chosen by the mayor and the presidents of New York's five boroughs. Giuliani had no patience for a system that prevented him from getting his way: voters would hold him accountable for the schools, he argued, so why shouldn't he have the power to run them? He also didn't appreciate that the occupant of the office was exercising his independence.

The Board of Education was famously resistant to change. Its bookkeeping was almost impenetrable, making it impossible for outsiders to know how many employees worked there and what they did for a living. The whole operation seemed to exist in a fog, which had frustrated a long line of New York City mayors, who were obliged to fund it but who had no power to control it.

Seeking to circumvent his lack of authority over the system, as he had with the appointment of the "monitor," Giuliani commissioned a study of its management structure. He also had Herman Badillo commission an audit to find out how the schools were spending tax dollars. Both studies found massive waste at the board. Convinced the system was throwing away millions on useless administrators, the mayor—still coping with a severe fiscal crisis—swung an ax at the chancellor's budget requests. "I am not afraid to kick the living hell out" of the system, he told an audience.

For his part, Cortines went about his business with a kind of monkish asceticism that was a marvel to behold considering the circumstances. Determined to stay focused on his agenda, he left it to Beckman to handle the daily parrying with the mayor, while he launched efforts to trim special education, raise educational standards, experiment with year-round schooling, and buy more textbooks. He assumed control over a half-dozen failing schools. Educators and parents applauded his innovations.

The chancellor seemed blind to the mayor's sensitivities. He dismissed Giuliani's studies as biased and inaccurate. He hired David Dinkins's former economic development chief as his chief of operations, which infuriated City Hall. He complained publicly that the mayor's budget cuts would force teacher layoffs and bigger class sizes. The mayor didn't take the charges lightly.

In December of 1994 a frustrated Giuliani publicly called for the chancellor's ouster. "If I had my druthers, I would say we should find someone who wants to make changes rather than someone who has to be forced into them," he said, urging the Board of Ed not to extend Cortines's expiring contract.

At about that time, Howard Koeppel, one of Giuliani's closest friends, ran into Cortines having dinner at an Upper East Side restaurant. The two struck up a conversation about the chancellor's troubles.

"Perhaps you could talk to your friend and tell him to give me more respect. I'd appreciate it," the chancellor told him, according to Koeppel.

"I like you," Koeppel told him, "but you two just don't agree on the same things."

"People sometimes don't agree on the same things," Cortines reportedly said, "but you don't have to have words. Just disagree and then go on and try to work it out. It seems like I can't work anything out with him."

"When he makes up his mind, he's set in his ways," Koeppel replied. "I understand what you're saying, but I don't think it's just you. That's the way the mayor is."

"Well I'm sensitive, and I don't like to be treated that way."

Koeppel says he promised to mention something to Giuliani. He got his opportunity a few days later when the two were in the mayor's basement office at City Hall.

Koeppel says he told the mayor about his conversation. The chancellor was taking all the criticism personally. "Maybe there's another way of handling it," Koeppel told the mayor. "If he has to leave, he has to leave. But maybe you don't have to beat up on him, you know?"

"I've tried to talk to him," Giuliani said, according to Koeppel. "The guy is impossible. He's fighting me tooth and nail—I can't seem to get him to agree on anything." His aggressive campaign against Cortines, he said, was his only choice. Koeppel realized it was a lost cause.

The public watched in amazement as Giuliani intensified his attacks on Cortines. "New York's mayors have always played by unwritten rules that demanded they get along with leading players in government," *Times* columnist Joyce Purnick wrote. "That code of political conduct does not seem to govern Mr. Giuliani. New York has not seen a mayor like him in recent memory, if ever."

It wasn't clear why Giuliani thought so poorly of Cortines. He was disparaging him as if he were a jaded bureaucrat, incapable of innovation. In fact, Cortines was an energetic reformer who was launching new initiatives to improve the quality of the schools. His major sin seemed to be that he didn't share Giuliani's fervor to destroy the bureaucracy. The mayor was waging a holy war against him because of a difference in ideology

City Hall's effort to have the Board of Ed fire the schools chief was a losing battle. Business leaders, educators, the teachers union, and even allies of Giuliani's rushed to Cortines's defense. Within the administration, Giuliani was being pressured to lay off. "We were scared," says a former high-level aide. "His poll numbers went in the toilet over the Cortines thing. There was no question he was doing damage to himself and his public image. But he kept his own counsel on this. He felt it was the right thing to do."

With the city rushing to Cortines's defense, the Board of Education defied the mayor and gave the chancellor another two-year contract. But it seemed more a victory for Gresser, who coordinated the effort to keep

Cortines, than for the chancellor himself. Privately, Cortines was smoldering. "I am trying very hard to please this man, and it doesn't seem that I am
able to," he told Gresser. "We are caught in a situation that's almost like, kiss
the ring and we'll give you another buck, but if you complain, you may not
get the kind of money you need," he told a legislative committee in a rare fit
of pique. The schools, he said, shouldn't "have to go across the river and
genuflect" to City Hall.

Try as he might to ignore the mayor, it was clear that Cortines was being
affected by Giuliani's assaults on him. In May, 10,000 teachers, parents, students, and union members marched across the Brooklyn Bridge to protest
budget cuts to the schools. They were all there—Carol Gresser, teachers
union chief Sandra Feldman, and a phalanx of politicians. All except the
schools chancellor, who told Gresser he would march and then changed his
mind because he didn't want to antagonize the mayor. "Ray was scared to
come march with us," Gresser recalls. "The mayor let it be known that he
would be very angry if Ray marched, and Ray didn't march." She was angry
with Cortines for letting Giuliani intimidate him.

The mayor didn't show much gratitude. Having learned that violent incidents in the schools were on the rise, he embarked on a new crusade—to put
3,000 school safety officers under the control of the Police Department.
Gresser and Cortines balked, citing the grim specter of police officers
patrolling school halls. That sparked yet another round of public battering
from City Hall. "I think most parents and most teachers would feel far safer if
this were in the hands of the NYPD rather than in the hands of the school
board and the chancellor, who has not shown a great capacity at management
in general and certainly not in the area of law enforcement," Giuliani snarled.

It was war by sound bite, the only weapon at Giuliani's disposal. He had
little power over the chancellor, but he had his podium in the Blue Room
from which to fire his missiles.

Cortines, just back from a trip to the West Coast, was incensed. Reading
scores in the public schools were starting to rise, but City Hall was attacking
him. "He's made it very clear that no matter what I do or say, unless I acqui-
esce to all of his wishes, that I am not a good manager and I am not showing
leadership," he said. "If the Board of Education doesn't think I'm doing a
good job they should get rid of me. I don't work for the mayor."

"He shouldn't be so sensitive about it," Giuliani snapped back in response. Cortines, he said, was being "precious" about the criticism.

It was a hard fight to watch. Giuliani's aggression toward Cortines made for a painful psychodrama, in which the mayor played the role of school bully, Cortines the class sissy, and Carol Gresser the overly protective mother. The next day at City Hall, addressing the chancellor's complaints about his attacks, Giuliani let loose. "The chancellor should stop it," he said. "He should grow up, and what he should do is understand that he has got to embrace change and stop whining about it, and stop playing little victim. He is *not* a victim. He is the person running that system. He is not running it effectively if he's had a 25 to 30 percent increase in crime on his watch."

On one hand, Giuliani was right. Crime in the schools was running rampant, the poorly trained school safety officers were botching the job, and the leadership was acting defensively. Without the power to order up changes, Giuliani's only weapon was the force of his argument. He was using a sledgehammer to break through the shell protecting Cortines and the board.

On the other hand, Giuliani's words were cruel and vaguely homophobic.

The back-and-forth continued until Cortines walked into Carol Gresser's office a little more than a week later and handed her a note. After a friendly chat, he left her to read it. The note thanked her for the support he'd received from the board and expressed gratitude for being allowed to serve the people of New York. "No Regrets!" it was signed. "Ray Cortines." He was gone.

The mayor had tormented the man until he bent to his will. Giuliani, for one, was satisfied. "I know that they've called me a bully," he said the day Cortines resigned. "I know that they called me all kinds of names. You want my reaction to it? I won't quit."

How could the same man who nurtured Jake Menges's sick child at his hospital bed be capable of degrading a decent man? Giuliani always maintained it was never personal for him. "This has always been about issues for me," he told Purnick in December 1994. "I never got angry at Ray Cortines. I don't dislike him. It plays out that way because of the public impression of the two of us—me being very strong and tough, him being easygoing and nice and friendly."

"I'm very tough but not difficult to get along with," he said. "And I'm very reasonable."

It was always about something much larger than personalities to him. Giuliani had a mission—in this case, to reform the schools—and in his calculations, the mission was more important than the people who stood in the way of it. Ramon Cortines was expendable. Saving New York was not.

But it was difficult to persuade New Yorkers that his sadistic behavior was carried out for a good cause. The more personal Giuliani's attacks grew, the more the mission seemed to take a backseat to his own sense of competition, which dictated that all battles had to be won regardless of the costs. By the end, the mayor, who was such a controlling man, seemed out of control.

The Cortines saga raised a novel issue: Can voters appreciate an effective leader if they find him offensive? A poll taken long after the Cortines episode showed that more than half the public believed Giuliani didn't have a likable personality, but over 60 percent felt he was doing a good job. The mayor claimed that it was more important to be respected than liked. But his treatment of Cortines raised the issue to a higher level. Many New Yorkers started wondering whether Rudy Giuliani had a heart.

7

Rudy and Mario

Al D'Amato was furious. Here it was, an opportunity for Rudy Giuliani and him to patch things up and show the world they were friends, and the mayor had gone and pulled another stunt. The senator arrived at City Hall with the governor and the state comptroller for a press conference urging voters to pass a referendum calling for a multimillion-dollar investment in environmental protection. There should have been good feelings all around, but instead the senator was outraged. He and the comptroller, Carl McCall, were brought upstairs to wait in an out-of-the-way meeting room. The governor, on the other hand, had been ushered into the mayor's wing downstairs.

"What is this?" D'Amato said. "We're up here, they're down there—if this is the way he wants to treat me. . . ."

McCall, a Democrat, hadn't expected red-carpet treatment from a Republican mayor—especially *this* Republican mayor—but D'Amato, the state's reigning Republican, saw this as a deliberate slight from his longtime nemesis, Giuliani. "Do you believe this, Carl? Do you believe they're treating us like this?"

The senator got on the phone to his Washington office shortly before his old press secretary, Zenia Mucha, who arrived with the governor, walked in.

"I gotta go," D'Amato told the person on the other end and hung up. He turned to Mucha. *"Who the fuck do they think they are?"* He was screaming. At first D'Amato wanted Mucha to go downstairs and communicate his sentiments to the mayor. Thinking again, he decided he wouldn't stand for the indignity a minute longer. He grabbed the state comptroller's lapel. "Come on, Carl," D'Amato said. "We're not putting up with this shit!"

He proceeded to lead the comptroller, who stood a head taller than D'Amato, out of the room and down the hallway, where they were intercepted by a crowd filing in for the start of the press conference. A confrontation was averted, though just barely.

The senator's outburst at City Hall took place long after the 1994 governor's race had faded into history. But Rudy Giuliani's decision to insert himself into that contest left D'Amato—and a legion of Republicans across America—bitter for years. It would be hard, in fact, for *anyone* who witnessed the mayor's behavior in that tumultuous period not to see him differently. Giuliani's decision to throw a tight election into total chaos, a result of some grand concoction of principle and arrogance, became one of his career's defining moments and would haunt him for years to come.

Against the better judgment of his advisers, Mario Cuomo decided in 1994 to make a run for a historic fourth term as governor of New York State. With the bags under his eyes grown long and his famous oratory beginning to grate on New Yorkers after twelve years, he was hugely vulnerable to a challenge. The state was in a recession, his popularity was down, and he seemed not only defensive about his leadership but angry that people would question it. He was, after all, the man who'd inspired millions to oppose Ronald Reagan's economic program with a soaring keynote speech at the 1984 Democratic Convention in San Francisco. He was an author, an intellectual, a towering figure in a profession filled with mediocrities. He'd become accustomed to his singular role in American public life, and had grown increasingly imperious despite the deteriorating conditions of his state.

He took pains to cultivate the city's new mayor, perhaps hoping to dampen Giuliani's support for whoever the Republican candidate for governor turned out to be. Cuomo hired as chief campaign strategist David Garth, the irascible architect of Giuliani's '93 victory, and closely aligned himself with Liberal Party chief Ray Harding, Giuliani's top political adviser. With City Hall drowning in red ink, the governor came to the mayor's rescue whenever he could, altering the state budget to take hundreds of millions in expenses off the city's hands. Cuomo was counting on massive support from city voters in November, so he was cultivating Giuliani's city as well as its mayor.

The chemistry between the governor and the mayor was fascinating to behold. At their public events together, Giuliani seemed genuinely nervous in Cuomo's company. Here was an older Italian politician who was brilliant, famous, and powerful, a role model for a neophyte mayor who had grown up venerating Italian men. Giuliani seemed eager to impress him. His Italian-American press secretary, Cristyne Lategano, saw Cuomo as a hero.

As the public romance between the two men flowered, Al D'Amato was methodically positioning himself to play kingmaker in the Republican Party. With no heavyweight candidates emerging to challenge Cuomo, the senator waged a successful arm-twisting effort within the state GOP to anoint an obscure state senator named George Pataki as its nominee. It was an odd choice: Pataki came from the Westchester suburb of Peekskill, which he had served as mayor and then as state senator without attracting much notice in the political world. But he neatly fit the description that D'Amato's political adviser Arthur Finkelstein had cast for the ideal Republican candidate: he was from upstate, was pro-choice, pro-death penalty, and had voted against Mario Cuomo's last budget. He was also genial and handsome in a Jimmy Stewart kind of way, a lanky, somewhat shy man with a crooked smile and a nice word to say about everyone. But he was ambitious enough to place himself in D'Amato and Finkelstein's hands and serve as a vessel for their strategies.

In May, D'Amato cajoled, threatened, and browbeat the state party into handing Pataki its endorsement. New Yorkers knew nothing about the candidate, and Finkelstein did little to change that: polls showed that the key to victory was to make the election a referendum on Cuomo, whose popularity was hovering at a dismal 36 percent. Pataki's position papers ran just a few pages in large type and were bereft of specifics. His speeches were short and vague. He promised to sign a death penalty bill and to cut taxes 25 percent, hoping to capitalize on the nationwide tax-cut fever that New Jersey's new governor, Christie Whitman, had sparked the previous year. Day after day, week after week, with an almost robotic discipline, Pataki leveled the same attack on Cuomo's leadership, using the same language. "Mario Cuomo says that he can't cut spending, he can't cut taxes," he told crowds. *"Mario, let me tell you something. You're right, you can't—but I can!"* What he lacked in eloquence, he made up for in repetition.

Giuliani already owed a debt of gratitude to Cuomo for commissioning the report on the Crown Heights riots that helped sink Dinkins's mayoralty. As their alliance bloomed, the mayor was in no rush to endorse an opponent. In July, Giuliani started talking to the candidates for governor, including Republican Richard Rosenbaum and Independent Tom Golisano, but never seemed to have time to meet with Pataki. On one occasion Pataki came to City Hall to have a sit-down with the mayor, only to be kept waiting on a bench inside the building as Giuliani attended to a police incident. Neglected, the candidate and his aides finally gave up and left.

Giuliani seemed to enjoy torturing Pataki. On a radio program, the mayor took aim at the stealth strategy that was at the heart of the candidate's campaign. "George Pataki doesn't take positions that tell me what he's going to do as governor of New York," Giuliani complained. He added, "The candidate has elected to have a campaign strategy that is to be nonspecific. Essentially, the strategy is to kind of take up all of the vote that would be there, people who might be uncomfortable with Mario Cuomo having four more years."

Then he turned his focus on Cuomo. "Some people disagree with things that he's done, as I do in some cases. But in other areas, Mario Cuomo has been very, very good to the City of New York, and he has the interests of the city at heart."

These were words of heresy in the eyes of D'Amato and the state Republicans, who were left to guess why the mayor wasn't helping out at this critical moment: perhaps he was tormenting D'Amato as payback for the senator's support of Ron Lauder in 1989. D'Amato and Giuliani had struck something of an uneasy peace after that election: Giuliani didn't oppose D'Amato's reelection in 1992, and D'Amato stayed out of the '93 mayor's race. But feelings of resentment still ran deep in both men.

There were other theories. If he supported Pataki, Giuliani would be just another Republican falling into line behind Al D'Amato, whom he detested. But if he helped Mario Cuomo pull an upset victory, Giuliani would take D'Amato's place as kingmaker.

Pataki and his aides tried to extract some intelligence from the Giuliani camp about the mayor's intentions. The Republican candidate was ahead in the polls, and his tax-cut plan was going over well with the public, but he suffered from the perception that he was little more than Al D'Amato's ventriloquist dummy. The expectations were so low for the Yale graduate that they sometimes worked to his advantage. "Even when he stumbles a bit over an answer or makes an occasional awkward move," reported Charisse Jones of the *Times*, voters "say he is more handsome than they thought, warmer than they thought, smarter than they thought." But the candidate was clearly in need of the kind of validation that the mayor of New York could give him.

On October 23, a rainy Sunday night, Pataki finally received some information out of the mayor's camp. A mutual friend told him that Giuliani had huddled with his advisers that evening at Gracie Mansion to discuss the governor's race. The friend said that Giuliani couldn't guarantee he'd endorse Pataki, but he wouldn't endorse Cuomo. He didn't want to hurt Pataki.

The next day at about noon, Pataki's burly campaign manager, Rob Ryan, made contact with Giuliani's press secretary, Cristyne Lategano. The two of them had worked together in ex–State Senator James Wallwork's losing bid for governor of New Jersey, and both had fled to New York at about the same time. Ryan, working the connection, got Lategano on the phone. She gave him a similar answer, he remembers. "Look, I can't say we'll endorse Pataki," she allegedly told him, "but we'll do nothing to hurt you." Ryan was encouraged.

At the Gracie Mansion meeting, Giuliani had listened for hours to advisers who were deeply split on the issue. Republicans like Deputy Mayor Peter Powers, Labor Commissioner Randy Levine, and Budget Director Abe Lackman were advising the mayor to fall into line with Pataki. A neutral stance would be read as a rebuke to his party's candidate, they said; endorsing Cuomo would be high treason — "insanity" in Levine's words.

Harding had brought Giuliani a word of advice from Cuomo: Stay neutral — or, as the governor put it, "aggressively neutral." Describe the qualities New Yorkers need in a governor — and make it clear that only Cuomo had them. Cuomo had done the same thing himself in the 1989 Democratic mayoral primary when he telegraphed his support for David Dinkins over Ed Koch by stating that New Yorkers needed a mayor who could bring the races together.

Giuliani finally arrived at a decision. He instructed Harding to inform the governor of it the next day at precisely the moment Giuliani walked into the City Hall Blue Room to announce it.

The next day Lategano notified newsrooms across the city that a mayoral budget speech was being canceled and would be replaced by a late-afternoon announcement about the governor's race. So much drama had built around Giuliani's endorsement decision that every television station in town rushed camera crews down to City Hall; most ran heavy cables out the Blue Room window, which snaked across the steps of City Hall to satellite trucks preparing to beam the announcement live.

As Giuliani walked toward the Blue Room and the capacity crowd assembled there hushed, television stations around the dial cut into their programming. WABC-TV interrupted *Oprah* to air the bulletin from City Hall.

Harding, seated at his desk in midtown Manhattan, called Cuomo's secretary, Mary Tragale, and asked to speak with the governor. She said Harding had just missed him — he'd gone into an elevator and headed off for a midtown event. A few minutes later, Cuomo returned Harding's call from his car as he traveled up the West Side Highway. Harding informed Cuomo about the mayor's decision. "If you turn on your radio, you'll hear him doing it," the Liberal Party chief said.

The governor tuned in.

At the same moment, Peter Powers placed a call from his City Hall office to Guy Molinari in Staten Island, who'd been working hard to elect Pataki. Powers broke the news to him.

"He's crazy!" the borough president yelled. "I can't believe this!"

At Cuomo campaign headquarters on Third Avenue, the telephone rang and someone shouted that Giuliani was making an announcement on television. A dozen staffers rushed into a corner office and gathered around the tube.

Inside the Pataki camp on Lexington Avenue, fifty volunteers and staffers were at work when the mayor came on the tube. They abandoned their desks to huddle around the television.

What they saw was a man sweating profusely. Giuliani, who rarely perspired and never read from prepared texts, was at a podium nervously reciting the speech he was reading through big thick glasses. A thousand camera flashes lit up his face.

"The election this year presents a fundamental dilemma causing many of us probably to do the same thing, agonizing over a decision we have to make, the choice we have to make for governor," Giuliani began.

"I'm proud to be a Republican. I've already endorsed the Republican candidates for attorney general, comptroller, and the United States Senate. But the next governor of New York must do more than just advance a few ideas and assist a political party.

"From my point of view as the mayor of New York City, the question that I have to ask is, 'Who has the best chance in the next four years of successfully fighting for our interests? Who understands them, and who will make the best case for it?' Our future, our destiny is not a matter of chance. It's a matter of choice.

"My choice is Mario Cuomo."

In the privacy of his car, the governor absorbed the news and smiled. His car had already arrived at his midtown stop, but he sat in the front seat with his driver, glued to the radio.

The mayor wasn't done.

"I've come to the conclusion that it is George Pataki who best personifies the status quo of New York politics—a candidate taking as few positions as possible, all of them as general as possible, taking no risk and being guided, scripted, and directed by others."

At Cuomo headquarters, Joel Benenson, the bearded campaign spokesman, was watching with astonishment. "I can't fucking believe it," he muttered. In his wildest fantasy scenario, the mayor would endorse Cuomo solemnly, call it the toughest decision of his life, and cast it as a choice between two qualified candidates. Instead Giuliani was tearing into Pataki as an empty suit, a puppet of Al D'Amato's, an enemy of the people of New York City. Benenson and the people around him started to laugh, giddily, at each insult the mayor hurled at his fellow Republican.

"Senator Pataki has almost uniformly voted against the interests of the city and often the metropolitan region. . . . Mario Cuomo is his own man. I prefer dealing with someone who is his own man."

"The sense that I've gotten from George Pataki is that it is very much a campaign out of a political consultant's playbook. There are clichés, there are slogans, there's the right sound bite, there's the right position. You become specific only for as long as you have to, and then you become general again."

Giuliani had made a calculated decision that if he was going to endorse Cuomo, he wanted to help ensure that he'd win. "If we're going to do it," Peter Powers had said, "we might as well go all the way."

At Pataki headquarters the clutch of workers watched the disaster unfold in silence—"as if someone had hit us over the head with a mallet," one recalls.

That was just the beginning for them. In the days following the endorsement, the floor fell out from under the Republican's campaign for governor. By Wednesday the campaign's internal polls showed that Pataki had gone from leading Cuomo by 7 points to trailing him by 13 points. Aides were shell-shocked. Kieran Mahoney, Finkelstein's hard-nosed young deputy, brought out a bottle of scotch and took a few swigs when he got the news. "FREEFALL" read the front page of the *Daily News* a few days later.

It is for times such as these that political strategists are paid so handsomely, and Arthur Finkelstein went into action. On Thursday morning the paunchy middle-aged consultant, who worked so far behind the scenes that he could walk past reporters unnoticed, arrived at Pataki headquarters. Wearing his tie draped around his neck like a scarf, he took off his shoes, poured a cup of coffee, and told Ryan to get out a tape recorder. "We're gonna do an ad," he said.

He'd read newspaper stories that Giuliani was counting on $150 million in state aid from Cuomo, and he'd dreamed up a mischievous commercial called "The Deal." He started dictating a script charging that Cuomo had bought Giuliani's endorsement with taxpayer money. Eating a pastrami sandwich from Sarge's Deli that he'd ordered with extra fat, Finkelstein and the small group hammered out the wording in a few hours. The campaign's ad man, Tony Marsh, turned the commercial around the next day. Finkelstein ordered it beamed by satellite to television stations across upstate New York, which started airing it on the six o'clock news Friday night.

Pataki, meanwhile, started echoing the charge at his public events. "What's the price of a deal, Mario?" he asked at a Queens rally. "Let me tell you the answer: nine billion dollars. Four hundred million dollars. One hundred and fifty million dollars. It's going to cost us fourteen hundred dollars for every household in Kew Gardens and all across this state." The numbers were based on recent Cuomo initiatives that benefited the city and the suburbs. The charge was speculation at best, but that was beside the point. The Pataki team was exploiting the legendary hostility between the glamorous city and the neighboring upstate communities it overshadowed.

Giuliani, meanwhile, was luxuriating in the uproar he'd ignited. The national media was in love with the endorsement story, as were all the hundreds of thousands of liberal Democrats in his city. For the first time since his heyday as a crusading U.S. attorney, he was embraced by the city's Democratic establishment and the media. New Yorkers who felt skittish about the Republican suddenly felt he was one of them.

The mayor brought the top members of the Cuomo campaign to Gracie Mansion and gave them a pep talk. "I want to do anything in my power to make sure the governor wins," he told them. His aides proceeded to meet continuously with Cuomo's aides. Giuliani's people were pushing for joint appearances, road trips, commercials. They wanted the mayor to join the president when he came to stump for Cuomo. It was classic Giuliani overkill: he was hijacking the Cuomo campaign. The governor's brain trust, left breathless by the sudden flush of good news, didn't resist.

Several days later Giuliani ventured outside the city limits with Cuomo and saw how the rest of the state was feeling about his endorsement. He and the man he endorsed journeyed to a rally in front of Babylon Town Hall in Long Island, where four hundred people awaited. Not everyone had come to cheer. Republicans came bearing signs reading "RUDY THE RAT" and "BENEDICT RUDY." The jeers and heckles were so loud that Giuliani, standing by Cuomo, could barely be heard introducing the governor. *"You're a whore, Giuliani!"* yelled a man from the audience, eliciting a round of catcalls back and forth between the Cuomo and Pataki supporters in the crowd. As the mayor attempted to ignore him, the heckler loudly persisted. *"You're a whore."*

Cuomo, a far more nimble politician than his friend the mayor, stepped to the microphone and pointed to the heckler. "Excuse me—wait, wait, wait. What was that? I didn't hear you. What did you say?"

The protestor, who owned a local nightclub, stiffened.

"What did you say?"

"I said Giuliani's a whore," he responded, a bit more meekly.

"Can I tell you something?" Cuomo said. "The way you use the word, you look to me like a guy who's very familiar with the species."

The punch line sent the Democrats in the crowd into a frenzy. As Giuliani watched blankly, the old master all but took a bow.

Yet the pair's troubles were only beginning.

Several advisers successfully pushed for the mayor to fly upstate on Cuomo's behalf that weekend to bolster the liberal governor's weak standing in the conservative region. Some Cuomo aides worried that the mayor might spark a backlash by unleashing deep-seated anti–New York City sentiment. But the momentum from Giuliani's endorsement was the best thing the Cuomo camp had going for it. Until the endorsement, says Garth, "Mario was going nowhere."

A few Cuomo advisers say they resisted the idea but were outvoted. "Garth and Harding insisted on it, and when we tried to stop it, they got belligerent about it and said we couldn't do this to the mayor," recalls longtime

Cuomo aide Sandy Frucher. Garth and Harding say they don't remember arguing for the trip. At least Giuliani was willing to hit the campaign trail, Garth says. "You couldn't get Mario out of the Governor's Mansion," the strategist recalls. "He wouldn't go anywhere. At least Rudy Giuliani was ambulatory."

Cuomo says it was Giuliani himself who pushed for the upstate trip. "Rudy was the one who wanted to do it mostly," he recalls. "I just felt, this is wrong."

On Saturday morning, wearing a dark navy suit and a crisp white shirt, Giuliani headed for the hinterlands. Cuomo's aides had limited Giuliani's stops to airports, fearing that downtown rallies could provoke ugly confrontations between Pataki and Cuomo supporters. But that one attempt at stage-managing wasn't nearly enough: the Pataki camp had organized protests at all Giuliani's stops.

The mayor was in too ravenous a mood to notice that disaster was looming. Intoxicated by his desire to win at all costs, he shed all restraint and ripped into Pataki and D'Amato as if they were common criminals. "Al D'Amato was instrumental in raising ten million dollars for George Pataki, four hundred thousand of it illegally," the mayor told reporters. "Go ask Al, were there any deals—or did Al just do this because he's for good government in the state of New York? Ask them how many jobs—is it four or five thousand jobs Al's been promised?"

As the day progressed, the mayor encountered more protests. Fistfights broke out near his plane on the airstrip in northern Syracuse. In Rochester dozens chanted "Traitor!" inches away from Giuliani as nervous aides escorted him to his airport press conference. In Oriskany near Utica, more than fifty protestors chanting "Let's make a deal!" drowned out Giuliani's event. On one occasion the mayor and his entourage were trapped inside his plane waiting for police to clear angry protestors away from it. Inside the small aircraft, gallows humor started to seep in. "Time to get my head banged in," Giuliani said. The trip had turned into a fiasco. The Pataki strategy had turned the Giuliani endorsement into a symbol of the unholy alliance between Cuomo and the hated city, and now its mayor had come upstate to rub it in everyone's face.

The surreal quality of the weekend continued when the mayor returned to City Hall the next day. With his friends now his enemies and his enemies now his friends, Giuliani had a brainstorm: He had an intermediary reach out to Public Advocate Mark Green and ask him if he was interested in appearing at a joint press conference to denounce D'Amato. Much of Green's political career had been pegged on dethroning the senator: He ran—very unsuccessfully—against D'Amato as the Democratic Senate candidate in 1986; he also filed a complaint against him with the Senate Ethics Committee, which resulted in an embarrassing reprimand of D'Amato. The public advocate accepted Giuliani's offer.

For the first time since the '93 election, Green was invited into Giuliani's office, and the two foes talked like old friends, cracking jokes at D'Amato's expense. Then they walked out of City Hall together and ambled down the steps of the building to a group of mystified reporters, where for twenty minutes the two political adversaries took turns bashing George Pataki as a puppet of an ethically challenged Al D'Amato. "If the D'Amato-Pataki crew ever get control, ethics will be trashed," Giuliani said. Wow, Green thought, that's strong stuff.

There was an operatic dimension to the events, in which Pataki seemed like a wounded puppy on the sidelines while Giuliani battled D'Amato in the Last Great War. Beating Al D'Amato for primacy of New York State Republican politics became Giuliani's last great prosecution, the final piece of business he'd left unfinished when he moved from the courthouse to City Hall. D'Amato seemed to grasp the personal nature of the fight even as he publicly denied its existence. "This is not a contest between me and Giuliani," the senator told a reporter. "That may come someday."

But Mario Cuomo was paying a price for Giuliani's zeal: The election became more and more about Rudy Giuliani and less and less about the governor. And thanks to Finkelstein's commercials hammering home "The Deal," Giuliani was quickly becoming a liability.

With Pataki's charges of a Cuomo-Giuliani conspiracy sinking in with the public, the Republican's numbers started to creep up once again. Each day Cuomo's lead shrank a bit more. On the Sunday before Election Day, the Pataki camp took its last poll. The state senator was only 2 points down. Giuliani had made his endorsement a week too early.

On Election Day, the Cuomo camp received reports that voters were turning out in droves upstate. An astronomical 70 percent of voters there went to the polls compared with fewer than 50 percent in New York City. Giuliani's upstate trip had apparently fired up the *anti*-Cuomo vote there. At the same time, voters there and across America were flocking to the polls to vent their anger at President Clinton for his failed effort at health care reform and to support Republican Newt Gingrich's Contract with America. It was all working against Mario Cuomo.

That night at the Sheraton Hotel the governor was in a suite with his family watching the returns on television when his son Andrew got a phone call. The elder Cuomo knew it was all over from watching the expression on his son's face. He gathered his family in a huddle. "We're going to hear some bad news," the governor said in a small voice. And then he went to see Rudy Giuliani, who was staked out in Ray Harding's suite at the same hotel, watching the returns as if it were his own election on the line. Cuomo, who had never called to thank the mayor for his endorsement, told Giuliani the bad news and expressed his gratitude. And then, in a spirit of generosity, he told a plain untruth.

"I lost this without your help," Cuomo said.

Rudy Giuliani's high-flying adventure had come crashing down in flames. His supreme confidence in his own instincts had caused him to march triumphantly into the mouth of disaster. George Pataki, the new governor, would not even take his phone calls for three weeks and harbored anger that would plague their relationship for years. Leaders of the national GOP, who had considered Giuliani a rising star, were disgusted with his actions. Only the residents of New York City, who were used to feeling the disdain of outsiders, appreciated what Giuliani had done.

As a result of his miscalculation, the mayor would have to humble himself repeatedly to regain the favor of his fellow Republicans. As D'Amato demonstrated with his outburst at City Hall four years later, some people would never trust him again.

8

The Press Gal

It was a strange request to get from the chief of staff, and in truth it wasn't so much a request as an order. Standing around Randy Mastro's small office, half a dozen aides to Mayor Giuliani were being told they had to go to a birthday party.

The honoree was Cristyne Lategano, the communications director, and the last-minute order was triggered by a ruling from Giuliani himself. Several days earlier, two young assistants from the mayor's Press Office, Lenny Alcivar and Kim Serafin, had taken it upon themselves to plan a thirtieth birthday celebration for their boss, and they asked Michael Lewittes, a gossip columnist for the *Daily News*, to invite some of Lategano's friends. Lategano and Lewittes had dated for three or four months and spent many happy nights table-hopping at Elaine's with Bill Bratton's crew, when that was still acceptable behavior for a City Hall employee. Lategano and Lewittes were just friends now, but Giuliani didn't care. He ordered the guest list torn up. Alcivar was instructed to disinvite Lewittes, and he reluctantly did so, explaining that the mayor didn't want the press participating in a staff event. With just hours until it was scheduled to begin, Giuliani had the party reconstituted to include only Lategano's coworkers at City Hall. He wanted it kept within the family.

It fell upon Mastro to corral a group together, but that was easier said than done. Behind the wall of solidarity that separated the administration from the outside world, Cristyne Lategano was widely disliked by members of the mayor's staff. Standing around Mastro's desk, his assistants were groaning at the prospect of having to pal it up with her. By now the chief of staff was used to getting complaints about Lategano's growing influence at City Hall. "If you want to take her on, you take her on," he'd reply, knowing a losing battle when he saw one. Today was no different. "I'd encourage you to be supportive of her," he told his charges.

On the car ride uptown to the restaurant, Therese McManus, the gruff mother hen of the group and the director of special events and community services, sang an ode to Cristyne, *"Happy Birthday, You Fucking Asshole,"* as Tony Carbonetti, the appointments director, chuckled. Hating Cristyne was one of the bonds that kept the crew together. McManus pulled over at a Korean deli to buy Lategano some flowers and a few lottery tickets. "I'll say it's from all of us," she said.

When they arrived at Jim McMullen's on the Upper East Side, Lategano was there, a wisp of a girl with long brown hair and a shy smile. Also sitting at the table was the mayor of New York City. Lategano sat there beaming, protected by the glow of her number-one fan. For two hours, her colleagues wore tight smiles and exchanged knowing looks as the most talked-about woman in city government bathed in the affection of the boss.

It was a measure of the incendiary effect that Lategano had inside City Hall that even her birthday party became controversial. People were amazed that a woman so young had become the second most powerful person in city government—and remained standing as everyone who'd competed with her for the mayor's ear fell away one by one, including his best friend and, to a large degree, his wife.

Lategano was Rudy Giuliani's alter ego. No one had more influence with him or exercised it as brazenly—or as irresponsibly at times. In the running dialogue the two maintained from morning to midnight, she fed his distrust of outsiders, of blacks, of reporters, of his own employees. She disparaged commissioners and aides as disloyal, with secret motives and hidden agendas. She spread malicious gossip. A person who joined Giuliani's campaign barely able to write a press release ended up shaping his mayoralty more than any other single adviser.

When her time at City Hall was over six years later and the two had finally parted, Lategano sat with a reporter in a half-empty Italian restaurant in SoHo and argued unconvincingly that all the talk about her was much ado about nothing.

"You're only as powerful as people allow you to be, or as much as they think you are," she said. "But I was really just the director of communications. I was the press gal, that's all."

Like any small-town girl starting out on her march to fame and fortune, Cristyne Lategano entered her hero's life by writing him a fan letter. A Brooklyn native who, like Giuliani, had spent her teenage years growing up on Long Island, she was working in 1989 as a staffer to Congresswoman Helen Bentley in Washington—her first job out of college. Having followed Giuliani's career for years, she expressed to him how proud his exploits as a crusading prosecutor had made her feel to be an Italian-American. Flattered, the mayoral candidate passed her letter along to his chief scheduler, Therese McManus, who called Lategano down for a job interview.

The experience ended in frustration. As Lategano was arriving at campaign headquarters, Giuliani's mother fell ill, and he canceled the interview to rush to the hospital. Soon after Lategano returned to Washington, McManus called and hired her over the phone. But that would end in disappointment as well: She lost the job on her first day, when campaign manager Russ Schriefer met her and decided she wasn't right for the position.

Lategano got a job the next year working for ex-Giants receiver Phil McConkey, who had decided almost on an impulse to enter the race for the New Jersey congressional seat vacated by Jim Courter. Operating on a shoestring budget, he hired three kids, all in their early twenties, to serve as campaign manager, press secretary, and fund-raising chief. Their pay was a few hundred dollars a week, a free bedroom in his country house, and all the McDonald's food they could eat.

U.S. Attorney Rudy Giuliani, February 21, 1985. (Anthony Pescatore, New York *Daily News*)

Mayoral candidate Giuliani at the June 13, 1993, Puerto Rican Day Parade with running mate Herman Badillo. (Misha Erwitt, New York *Daily News*)

Giuliani kisses wife Donna Hanover Giuliani after declaring victory over David Dinkins in the 1993 mayoral election, November 3, 1993. (Linda Cataffo, New York *Daily News*)

Giuliani delivers his inaugural address at City Hall as his son, Andrew, steals the show, January 2, 1994. (Frances M. Roberts)

Three top Giuliani aides *(left to right)*, Peter Powers, Denny Young, and Randy Mastro, at a mayoral press conference in City Hall's Blue Room, January 29, 1994. (Frances M. Roberts)

Schools Chancellor Ramon Cortines during a New York *Daily News* editorial meeting, May 5, 1994. (Evy Mages, New York *Daily News*)

Giuliani and Governor-elect George Pataki exit their first post–Election Day meeting at 38 East 37th Street on November 29, 1994. Pataki, smarting from Giuliani's endorsement of Mario Cuomo, refused to speak to Giuliani for three weeks after the election. (Bill Turnbull, New York *Daily News*)

William Bratton shares a light moment with Giuliani as the police commissioner announces his resignation at City Hall on March 26, 1996. Bratton aide Jack Maple is on the right. (Frances M. Roberts)

Cristyne Lategano leads Giuliani toward Queens Borough Hall on August 27, 1997, to accept the endorsements of several Democrats in the '97 race for mayor. (Misha Erwitt, New York *Daily News*)

Giuliani thanks Ray Harding on election night, November 4, 1997. (Frances M. Roberts)

Liberal Party boss and Giuliani confidant Ray Harding outside a party meeting at the Intercontinental Hotel, April 18, 1998. (Frances M. Roberts)

Cristyne Lategano *(far right)* makes her own recording of a mayoral interview at the Dominican Independence Day Parade while Governor George Pataki looks on, August 16, 1998. (Frances M. Roberts)

Al Sharpton addresses the Wall Street rally protesting the killing of Amadou Diallo, March 3, 1999. (Frances M. Roberts)

Former Mayor David Dinkins *(with raincoat, second from left)* marches with Al Sharpton and Congressman Charles Rangel at a Diallo protest at One Police Plaza, March 15, 1999. The three were arrested at the demonstration. (Richard B. Levine)

Hillary Clinton announces her candidacy for the United States Senate at SUNY Purchase on February 6, 2000. (Andrew Savulich, New York *Daily News*)

An emotional Donna Hanover, speaking hours after Giuliani publicly announced their separation, accuses her husband of maintaining relationships outside their marriage, May 10, 2000. (Jennifer Altman, New York *Daily News*)

DAILY ◉ NEWS

504   www.nydailynews.com   **NEW YORK'S HOMETOWN NEWSPAPER**   Saturday, May 13, 2000

WALKIN' MY BABY BACK HOME

Rudy and Judi take E. Side stroll after dinner at Italian restaurant

SEE STORIES ON PAGES 2 & 5

TODD MAISEL DAILY NEWS

Giuliani and "good friend" Judith Nathan captured on the front page of the New York *Daily News* taking a long stroll after dinner on May 13, 2000. Two days earlier he announced that he was separating from his wife, Donna Hanover. (Todd Maisel, New York *Daily News*)

Judith Nathan with her pet on May 14, 2000. (Yola Monakhov, New York *Daily News*)

Lategano was hired for the fund-raising job, but before long she was virtually running the operation, working harder and clocking longer hours than
her two male colleagues—and engendering their jealousy as a result.
McConkey marveled at her determination to win what was by all measures
an uphill battle. "She was very protective of me and would do anything in
her power to make me look good with the press," he recalls. The candidate
ended up in second place, losing to Dick Zimmer by only 2,700 votes, and
gave Lategano much of the credit. "She would throw herself in front of a
truck to protect her boss," he says. "If she believes in what the person's
doing, she'll do anything."

A few years later, when she was winding up a stint as President Bush's
New Jersey campaign spokeswoman—another losing battle—Lategano
wrote to Giuliani again. Her father, Joseph, a banker, was appalled that she
was offering herself once again to a group that had treated her so shabbily,
but she sent in her résumé shortly before Memorial Day weekend in 1993—
just as Richard Bryers was searching for a low-profile substitute for the campaign's quick-witted but undisciplined press secretary Ken Frydman. Bryers
hired Lategano shortly after interviewing her at Bloom's Coffee Shop on
Lexington Avenue.

Lategano hadn't been on the campaign trail for very long when she suffered yet another humiliation. It was early September, and after walking for
miles under the hot sun glad-handing his way through Manhattan's Labor
Day Parade, candidate Rudy Giuliani announced he was hungry. The press
secretary took off with Giuliani and Herman Badillo, his running mate, for
a nearby Burger Heaven. As the three of them sat down to order, Therese
McManus entered the restaurant in a huff, accompanied by Giuliani's
advance man, Todd Ciaravino. "What are you guys doing?" she demanded.
Lategano was just the press secretary—she should have cleared the lunch
break with the mother hen, who was bigger, older, and had a lot more standing with Giuliani. The two candidates were needed back at the parade,
McManus informed the three. Bashfully, the two candidates got up to leave
the restaurant. Lategano offered to wait for the food and get it wrapped.

But McManus wasn't done with her. "Don't you *ever* do that again!" she
screamed at the new girl, pointing her finger. The dressing-down began

inside the restaurant and continued all the way back to the parade. McManus was renowned for her explosive temper, and the press secretary was getting the full force of it as strangers looked on. For Lategano, it was terrifying: The trauma of the tongue-lashing would remain with her for years. Sheepishly, she approached Giuliani and apologized for the mistake, hoping perhaps for some comfort. "Don't worry about it," the candidate said. "It was my idea to go to the restaurant.

"And don't let anyone push you around," he added.

He would protect her from that moment on.

Lategano was a rank beginner in many ways: Her press releases needed massaging, and she had little knowledge of the city for someone who'd spent years growing up in Brooklyn. David Garth, the campaign strategist, looked upon her as Bryers's assistant. "She was the one who, when Richie didn't want to answer the phone, she'd do it," he says.

But in other important ways she fit in well.

In his U.S. attorney days Giuliani had been a good guy in the eyes of New York City's reporters. It wasn't just that he was accessible; he was also fighting the same battles they were, looking for wrongdoing in high levels of government. As a result, the prosecutor formed bonds with many of the city's journalists. It was thus perplexing to watch him turn on the press when the '93 mayoral campaign commenced. Garth had warned him that the New York media would have little sympathy for his battle to unseat the city's first black mayor, and Giuliani moved decisively to seize the offensive.

Lategano had little trouble adopting the campaign's antagonistic posture. As a Bush spokeswoman, she'd already honed a talent for attacking the news organizations that covered the campaign. Responding to a *Time* poll showing Bush lagging in the bellwether suburb of Middlesex County, New Jersey, Lategano denounced the magazine. "The magazine is biased against George Bush, like the rest of the press, who have done one hell of a job on him. *Print the truth.*" Sure enough, soon after starting with the Giuliani campaign, she was spitting out curt one-sentence answers to reporters' questions and justifying the withholding of Giuliani's daily schedule from New York 1 as a way of punishing the station for what she called its biased coverage.

When Giuliani won the mayoralty and the strategy was carried over to City Hall, the high command decided to keep the team of Bryers and Lategano intact. As Bryers pondered whether to accept the communications director's job, Lategano, at twenty-eight, became the youngest mayoral press secretary in New York City history. Insiders were surprised that someone of her age and modest experience had landed a job that had been held by Pulitzer Prize–winning journalists and public relations veterans, but she was loyal and groomed in the art of attack, which made her a natural choice for Giuliani. Besides, Bryers would be supervising her.

While the middle-aged men who were settling into the senior jobs in the new administration were getting good reviews for their handling of the budget and the Harlem mosque crisis, Lategano's press operation started off as a picture of chaos. Press releases had misspellings. Calls went unanswered or were handled by clueless underlings. Lategano, harried and short-tempered, frequently screamed at her young charges, some of whom were just out of college.

Yet she was clearly on the same wavelength as the mayor. Standing alone at a lectern in front of a room full of reporters and cameramen each day, Giuliani seemed determined not to end up a sitting duck in a room full of hunters. He was always in full battle mode, accusing his questioners of sloppy work, biased reporting, unclear thinking. His tone was often condescending: he laughed off questions as silly or ridiculous and lectured his audience about the facts he felt they'd mangled. Cristyne Lategano stood to his left, keeping a watchful eye on the crowd, shouting "Next question!" at strategic moments, and "Thank you!" when things got too hot for her principal.

The loyalty and protectiveness that Phil McConkey appreciated in his young aide were now focused on Giuliani. The mayor became the center of her universe. Previous press secretaries assigned deputies to accompany the chief on routine public outings, but she popped up at most events herself. Each day the mayor and Lategano, surrounded by a cloud of plainclothes cops, would breeze out of City Hall, fly down the steps, and disappear into the white Chevrolet Suburban idling there. While most New Yorkers were settling into bed at night, she would set out on a hunt through Manhattan for newsstands selling the early editions of the next day's papers. She lived

on the Upper East Side, but she would often travel to the docks outside the
New York Post building way downtown on South Street, where deliverymen
filthy from newsprint would flip her a fresh copy of the next day's paper.
Sometimes she'd take a midnight trip over to the *New York Times* building
in Times Square, where the delivery guys insisted on collecting change
from her for a copy of the early edition.

If the phone didn't ring in the middle of the night with the news of a cop
who'd been shot or some other calamity requiring the mayor's attention,
she'd rise at 5 A.M., take a jog around the neighborhood, and head to Gracie
Mansion to start the day with Giuliani. Sometimes he'd swing by her place
and pick her up. As the white van barreled down the empty avenues of Manhattan, she'd give him the news, prepare him for his day, and initiate live
interviews with radio stations eager for a piece of the mayor. And the two
would talk about how the world perceived Rudy Giuliani, and how he could
stay ahead of his adversaries.

It was a routine that started to catch the attention of the men at City Hall
and particularly of Peter Powers. Although he was one of four deputy mayors, Powers was the undisputed second-in-command in the new administration, with unparalleled access to Giuliani earned from thirty years as his best
friend and confidant dating back to their days at Bishop Loughlin. Powers
was the man who saved the '89 campaign from disaster and helped steer the
'93 effort to victory. They were family. Giuliani trusted Powers for his loyalty
but also for his judgment: Beyond the warm smile and a genial, small-town
courtliness, Powers possessed a lawyer's mind and a judge's wisdom. He was
the yin to Giuliani's yang, a soothing influence who could calm his hot-
tempered friend with a tap on the knee or a knowing glance. With his balding pate and ruddy features, he reminded David Garth of Karl Malden in
On the Waterfront, the priest who tried to talk sense into people hell-bent on
violence.

Settling into the prestigious center office in the mayor's suite, Powers was
plainly bothered by Lategano's deepening relationship with Giuliani. As the
number-two man in the building, he wanted everyone to report to him. The
lowly twenty-eight-year-old press secretary, by virtue of her extraordinary
access to Giuliani, had managed to skirt the chain of command.

He also watched as Lategano's fierce devotion to the mayor got her into trouble. Her disorganized press operation was making the lives of the reporters down the hall in Room 9 a nightmare, and her dealings with them were often hostile. The days when reporters could sit around and schmooze with the mayor's press secretary were clearly over. In the view of this mayor and his spokeswoman, reporters for the city's daily newspapers had consumed far more energy than they were worth. Giuliani could get his message out better in an unfiltered five-minute interview with a starstruck television anchorman than he could by arguing his case to a skeptical government reporter.

Lategano also had credibility problems. Seeking to blunt the effect of embarrassing revelations about the financial troubles of the new Youth Services commissioner, John Brandon, she called up City Hall reporters late one night with news that the Department of Investigation was looking into financial irregularities committed by *David Dinkins's* Youth Services commissioner, Richard Murphy. In the light of day, it was obvious that the administration had cooked up the Murphy story as a diversion, untroubled by the damage being done to an innocent man's reputation. DOI eventually cleared Murphy of the charges. But Lategano was rapidly losing the respect of the reporters who covered the administration.

Watching all this from his office on Park Avenue, David Garth, like Powers, was also growing unhappy with the new press secretary. The blunt-spoken media strategist had no official role in the administration but felt a degree of ownership in it. He'd elected Giuliani, after all; the suits downtown had to listen to him. Stomping up and down the hallways of his media consulting firm, the portraits of John Lindsay and Ed Koch and all the other politicians he'd elected peering down at him, the white-haired bulldog growled about Lategano's incompetence. Staffers at City Hall were grumbling about her treatment of them, and reporters were angry that she was regularly calling their bosses to complain about their work. It was one thing when Garth yelled bloody murder at the reporters who covered his candidates: he had standing in this town, and a campaign is warfare. It was quite another for this little shrub at City Hall to piss off the entire New York City press corps in one fell swoop.

"She didn't know the role of a press secretary," Garth says. "She was going to out-Garth Garth. When I do a campaign, I do a campaign to win. When you're mayor and dealing with the press, that's the beginning of a longtime relationship. It's the difference between a one-night stand and a love affair."

The strategist had assumed that Bryers would join the administration, but as it turned out, Bryers wanted no part of it. So Lategano was running the show when she was just supposed to be someone's deputy. Quietly, Garth, Powers, and Ray Harding set about interviewing candidates for communications chief. Someone needed to supervise Cristyne Lategano.

A stopgap measure of sorts soon arrived in the form of Jacquelyn Barnathan, a young news producer at the local Fox station. City Hall had approved Lategano's request to hire a first deputy press secretary to help strengthen her fledgling operation, and the two women had grown friendly. Garth knew her father, Jules Barnathan, an executive at ABC News, from the old days, and considered her a sharp woman. Powers signed off on her too.

Barnathan knew she was walking into the lion's den: at her interview, Garth warned her that Lategano was incapable of running her office and needed assistance from someone with a better understanding of the media. Barnathan and Garth agreed to stay in touch as she learned her way around the press office.

With Powers acting as Barnathan's guardian angel down at City Hall, she and Lategano began working side by side. The friendship didn't thrive.

Privately, Lategano felt Barnathan was a spy for Garth. "I knew that she was giving him information, and that didn't bother me," Lategano says. "I didn't have anything to hide. If she wanted to be press secretary—which everybody told me that she was trying to do—let her try out for the job."

Clearly threatened by the presence of her new chief aide, Lategano complained to Giuliani that Barnathan was inept, lazy, unable to deal with the press, and—worst—disloyal, because she came from the New York media. "She's in bed with the press," she told the mayor and his aides. "You can't trust her."

Barnathan was certainly not the heavyweight that Garth had hoped for: while an accomplished producer, she was a beginner as a flack. Yet

Lategano went out of her way to freeze her out. When Giuliani informed his inner circle, on October 23, 1994, that he was going to shelve his budget speech and endorse Mario Cuomo instead, Barnathan was kept out of the loop, and she ended up getting yelled at by reporters for denying rumors of the impending endorsement.

Though Garth helped hire her and Powers tried to protect her, Barnathan was at the mercy of Lategano, whose ability to make her life miserable was ultimately too great. She canceled Barnathan's Christmas vacation, telling her she didn't deserve it. She held up a promised $2,000 bonus. Eventually she had Barnathan banished from City Hall altogether and sent to work at another building. The first deputy press secretary lasted eight months.

Lategano later claimed it was all Barnathan's fault. "I . . . knew that Jackie wasn't going to last too long, because she liked to go home at five-thirty," she said. "She liked to take her weekends and liked to take her vacations. And I like Jackie very much, but she couldn't keep up with the mayor."

As the outside world marveled at Giuliani's confrontations with racial activists and union leaders, talk about Cristyne Lategano started to consume the conversations of the deputy mayors, commissioners, and assorted aides and hangers-on who traveled the corridors of the mayor's suite each day. For a neophyte press secretary, she seemed to have a lot of influence with the boss.

Aides to the mayor watched with concern as Lategano played to Giuliani's natural suspicion of people outside his small circle of trusted aides. Lategano would tell the mayor whether certain people were good or loyal, keenly aware that the most important value to the mayor was loyalty. His preoccupation with loyalty became her preoccupation. "I expect you to lie down in front of a running train for the mayor," she was overheard telling someone. "If you work for the mayor, you've got to agree to take a bullet for him."

"Bratton has his own agenda," she told Giuliani about his police commissioner. She argued that Marilyn Gelber, his environmental protection commissioner, was serving the agenda of Brooklyn Borough President Howard

Golden, her old boss. The mayor seemed to get angrier the more Lategano
wound him up.

Often she was right about people—Lategano was more perceptive than
many of the older male aides around her. Often she seemed bent on confirming Giuliani's worst instincts. But her efforts would have gone nowhere
if Giuliani hadn't been receptive to them. Lategano was really just displaying what she had learned from the boss himself. When Giuliani was hit with
a controversy, he'd gather his aides and run through a drill: "What do we
have on this person? What's their problem? Who are they and how do we
discredit them? What's the ammunition?" Lategano was Giuliani's protégée: She was displaying all she'd learned.

Thumbing through the *Daily News* in 1997 one morning before an 8 A.M.
staff meeting, Giuliani noticed a story about a pilot program that the city's
Department of Transportation was considering that would allow drivers to
prepay parking fees. "And now, from the great minds that brought you alter-
nate-side parking: A high-tech gizmo smart enough to take your money as
soon as you pull into a parking space," wrote reporter David Lewis. Agency
officials were looking at the gizmos as possible replacements for parking
meters, he reported.

"What's this?" Giuliani said to Lategano, pointing to the story.

"Chris Lynn must have leaked it," she said, referring to the city's colorful
and outspoken transportation commissioner. "He's off on his own agenda."

"There is no pilot program," the mayor announced. "Done."

Later that day Lynn was informed by City Hall that his entire press staff
was fired.

As it turned out, Lewis learned about the program from reading about it
in legal notices. But the mayor was furious. Five DOT employees were let
go—only to be offered their jobs back when the mayor's press office was
inconvenienced by phone calls redirected from the shuttered DOT press
office. Lynn says Lategano told him she knew nothing about the firings. As
for the pilot program, it was never heard about again.

Powers would wax philosophical as others complained about Lategano.
"Don't preoccupy yourself with trying to get even with her," he counseled a
staffer, "because eventually she'll get what's coming to her." But at other

moments he allowed that he was aggravated as well. "She's giving him bad advice," he fumed to a colleague. "She's driving the rest of us away."

There was something profound taking place as Powers and Lategano waged their quiet power struggle. They seemed to be fighting a war over Giuliani's soul. Where Powers would advise caution, she'd advise aggression. When Guy Molinari attacked Giuliani for deserting his party and endorsing Cuomo, Lategano encouraged the mayor to go for the jugular. She worked him into rages over his old mentor's criticism. "That psychopath!" Giuliani exclaimed. But Powers held him back. "Think of the long run, the big picture," he counseled his friend. The borough president would come back to the fold, he predicted accurately.

Inevitably, as gossip proliferated about Giuliani's late-night dinners with his young press secretary, speculation began to grow that Giuliani and Lategano were having an affair. No one could prove it, but *New York* magazine deftly handled the rumors with a cover story entitled "The Woman Behind the Mayor," which featured a shot of Lategano looking over Giuliani's shoulder. The article stated there was no evidence of a romantic relationship. But the day the story came out, Dominic Carter of New York 1 News put a microphone to Giuliani at a crowded Long Island news conference and asked him point-blank if he was having an affair with Lategano.

"If you had any decency you wouldn't ask that question," the mayor replied icily. "But your profession has sunk to such a low level of decency that you feel compelled to ask that question."

Then he answered it. "No, I'm not," Giuliani said, "but it's really outrageous that you ask it."

Shaken, Giuliani's wife, Donna, retreated from public life. The city's first lady, a member of Giuliani's inner circle in the '89 and '93 campaigns, a woman he'd called "my lover" in his inauguration speech, stopped showing up at events with her husband, and eventually dropped "Giuliani" from her name altogether, claiming it was better for her acting and television career.

Husband and wife began a long estrangement that erased her image from public view for years to come. While the Giuliani family continued to live at Gracie Mansion, Hanover no longer took part in his meetings and she rarely appeared with her husband at social events. When Hanover won raves for her movie debut in *The People vs. Larry Flynt* in 1997, the mayor skipped the premiere. Hanover maintained that this was all designed to allow her to establish a separate professional identity. But the truth was much sadder, as the public would come to learn later.

Lategano was suddenly exposed as the most reviled woman in city government ("Why Does Everyone Hate This Woman?" read *New York's* inside headline). Decades earlier, she seemed to have anticipated that she would be misunderstood by a cruel world. Her high school yearbook motto was borrowed from Antoine de Saint-Exupéry's *The Little Prince*: "It is only with the heart that one can see rightly; what is essential is invisible to the eye."

The ordeal brought Giuliani and his press secretary closer together. Unable to staunch the attacks, he tried dearly to help her withstand them. "You've got to let it roll off your back," he told her. "You can't take it too seriously. As difficult as today is going to feel, you'll look back on this and you'll grow from it and you'll learn from it."

The press secretary was understandably shell-shocked. "During the darkest days," she recalled years later, "I would listen to him and just think he was speaking a foreign language."

Whether or not they were romantically involved, the mayor and the press secretary were functioning as a team from morning until midnight. If she didn't travel to Gracie Mansion in the morning, he'd drive to her apartment building and pick her up in his van. They would eat lunch at his desk at City Hall, sometimes waving in a deputy mayor or some other staffer to come and join them. She socialized with him at night, dragging him once to a dive in the meat-packing district called Hogs and Heifers, where women danced on the bars and pulled their bras through their sleeves (something she had, in fact, done on another occasion). Giuliani was a man under enormous pressure, having launched a succession of titanic battles with members of the city's permanent government. It seemed to give him comfort to have a sidekick who was focused like a laser on his image and constantly on guard against enemies, real or imagined.

Meanwhile, Garth was interviewing a stream of candidates for the communications director's position, though his recommendations to City Hall went unheeded. Convinced Lategano was bad-mouthing the applicants to the mayor, he kept pushing to find a boss for the renegade press secretary. And then she found out what he was doing.

A source close to Lategano claims she was laughed at by the mayor and a room full of his aides when she told them she thought Garth was supporting her for the communications director's job. Feeling humiliated and double-crossed, Lategano went into her office and called up the media maven. "I can't believe you stabbed me in the back this way!" she yelled,

"Who do you think you are, talking to me this way?" Garth shot back.

"You're someone I don't respect!" she said. A few seconds later she slammed the phone down. Teary-eyed and shaking with rage, Lategano waited a few moments, then decided to call him back and apologize for losing her temper. He didn't take the call.

Not long after that, on March 31, 1995, Giuliani called a press conference to discuss Lategano's future. Some in the press corps assumed she'd be leaving the administration, but they underestimated his loyalty to her. The mayor handed her a $25,000 raise, bringing her salary to $102,000, and gave her the communications director's job. She gained control over the press office, speechwriting, research, and public scheduling.

Standing beside her in the Blue Room, the mayor dismissed assertions that her operation had halted the flow of information to the press and cut some reporters off completely from access to administration officials. "I think they have done a remarkable job in conveying the message of an administration that, whether you've noticed it or not, has made more change in this city in sixteen months than I think has ever been the case before, with the possible exception of the first sixteen months of Fiorello LaGuardia," Giuliani said.

In fact, the press operation under Lategano was now running smoothly and efficiently. Many of the amateurs had been replaced by people with more experience. While reporters fumed about lack of information from the administration, Lategano was quietly helping the mayor's image by choreographing elaborately staged press conferences and booking him on a never-ending string of nonthreatening television interviews. The harried look of her early days was gone. She seemed more poised, as if she'd grown up.

The new communications director looked sheepish as she took the podium. "I'm a little nervous," she said, "because I usually don't talk to you guys, and I try not to, as you know."

That day, without so much as a conversation with the mayor, David Garth ceased communication with the administration he had helped bring to power.

The rumors of an affair served to obscure the extraordinary imprint that Lategano was having on Giuliani's mayoralty. She may have seemed shy in public, but in private her voice was becoming increasingly important.

Her new scheduling duties gave her vast control over the mayor's activities. Determined to protect him from hostile audiences, she weeded out invitations from organizations representing African Americans, fearing his appearance would produce video on the evening news of Giuliani being booed once again by blacks. Her protective instinct flowered at the scheduling meetings in Giuliani's office. When the mayor was invited to speak at the J&R Jazz Festival, an annual event at City Hall Park that drew thousands, Lategano opposed it, according to an aide who participated in the meeting. The audience at a jazz festival, she argued, would be largely black. Lategano denies she urged the mayor to skip the event.

Another aide to the mayor recalls Lategano convincing Giuliani not to attend a rally for the New York Housing Authority's Inner City Games, which promised to draw thousands of minority kids and their parents. Lategano's argument was the same: "He'll get booed," she said, according to the aide. The decision was a shock to Ninfa Segarra, the mayor's Puerto Rican deputy mayor. "These are *kids*," she argued, to no avail.*

Publicly, the mayor and his aides were denying that he was avoiding mixing with black New Yorkers. But privately, a slew of high-level officials, including Deputy Mayors Fran Reiter and Segarra and Chief of Staff Randy

*Segarra says she can't remember what was said in the conversations about the games.

Mastro, were frustrated by Giuliani's aversion to facing black audiences—and by Lategano's constant feeding of that instinct. Giuliani had defeated the city's first black mayor, and a number of David Dinkins's political supporters were making it hard for Giuliani to mend fences with the black community. The media, meanwhile, were quick to point out every heckle that greeted Giuliani's appearances in minority neighborhoods. Fearing the obstacles before him, Giuliani avoided them altogether instead of confronting them—with Lategano's encouragement. The consequences of his continuing estrangement from the black community would prove disastrous.

Commissioners throughout city government had grown terrified of Lategano and would file into her office requesting permission to launch programs and hold public events. Once, riding in the van with the mayor, Lategano was besieged with phone calls from commissioners seeking her blessings. Giuliani seemed oblivious to the climate of fear she had created. "Tell them to stop bothering you," he told her. Lategano shrugged.

Aides to the mayor were infuriated by the role she was playing. "Nine people would agree on something in a meeting: six experts, two political guys, and Rudy Giuliani," recalls one high-level aide. "Ten minutes later, he'd call and say he'd changed his mind. You'd go back to his office and say, 'What happened?' And she'd be sitting there with him."

Lategano's influence disturbed many people but perhaps none as much as Powers. While honest and widely respected, he was hampered by insecurity about his relationship with the mayor, which had the effect of driving the two friends apart. Clearly the most powerful deputy in the administration, he insisted that he be given the title of first deputy mayor. "I must be first among equals," he told the mayor. Giuliani confided his frustration to other aides. "Peter's driving me crazy insisting he must be first deputy mayor," he said.

Powers eventually got his promotion. But his fears about his standing in the scheme of things didn't abate. When Deputy Mayor for Economic Development John Dyson left the administration in April 1996, Powers lobbied intensely for Richard Schwartz, Giuliani's young policy adviser, to get the job. Instead the mayor gave it to Fran Reiter, who had been deputy mayor for planning and community relations. Denied the opportunity to control another deputy mayor, Powers was angered.

The shift in power from Giuliani's boyhood friend to his young press aide was dramatic. In the first year of his administration, the mayor would reflexively buzz his secretary in a crisis and shout, "Get Peter in here!" Now, increasingly, he was calling for Cristyne. The press secretary was taking the place of a man who was twice her age, wiser, and decades closer to Giuliani.

Frustrated at his inability to keep the mayor and Lategano apart, and burned out from the internal politics, Powers announced his resignation in August of 1996. Interviewed several years later, he denied that Lategano was the cause of his departure. "I actually stayed longer than I planned," he said, adding that financial considerations played a role. As for his relationship with Giuliani: "All I'll say is, we were as close the day I left as on the day I arrived."

Asked to describe his feelings about Lategano, he declined. "I don't care to comment on my feelings," he said. "If I did, I would hire some guy, sit on a couch, and talk about my feelings."

With Powers gone, Lategano was rid of her only real rival for influence with the mayor. Randy Mastro was promoted to deputy mayor for operations, and soon forged a nonaggression pact with the communications chief. No longer competing for the role of chief confidant, she seemed liberated. In the clubby atmosphere of the mayor's office, where almost everyone was a male attorney, the boldest—and most brazen—voice belonged to the young communications director. Her ideas were sometimes extreme.

By the start of 1996, Ed Koch had finally had it with Giuliani. Already upset with his rough treatment of Ramon Cortines, Koch exploded in anger when Giuliani refused to reappoint two Brooklyn judges recommended by a judicial screening system designed by the former mayor. Giuliani maintained that he was trying to install better-qualified candidates, but one of the two new judges he appointed had flunked out of law school twice and never earned a law degree; the other, an assistant district attorney with ties to Brooklyn's Orthodox Jewish community, had tried just seven cases in six years. "I have only contempt for Mayor Giuliani's decision, his hypocrisy, his judgment," Koch fumed.

The break between the two was big news, and Giuliani was confronted with two unappealing choices: fire back at a hugely popular elder statesman he still respected—or suffer Koch's withering criticism. Gathered in his office with Lategano and a group of aides, the mayor and his brain trust tossed around ways to respond.

Lategano had a suggestion. "Weren't there rumors of Ed Koch having an affair with Herb Rickman?"

The room fell silent. "When he was mayor, wasn't Rickman living at Gracie Mansion the whole time?" she continued. "Can't we get something out like he was fooling around with Herb Rickman?"

It was an old chestnut in political circles, never proved, that Koch was romantically tied to his former special assistant Rickman.

"Everyone looked at her like she was crazy," recalls one senior aide to the mayor. "It was 'Let's attack Koch's character.' That was her MO."

Lategano denies she made the comments. "I can tell you for sure, every single time that I've been in the presence of the mayor, no conversation regarding Ed Koch's personal life ever came up—because I don't think Rudy Giuliani would have tolerated it." She also said she'd never heard of Rickman at the time of the alleged conversations.

But a second senior aide to the mayor heard Lategano make that suggestion "more than once" in other meetings and conversations at City Hall. "She doesn't understand that some things are off-limits," the official says. "She doesn't understand that in politics, you're never someone's enemy forever." Giuliani, the aide says, "would just ignore it and wait for the subject to go away."

By all accounts, the mayor seemed used to Lategano's excesses, waving off her more extreme suggestions as silly or just ignoring them. It was the kind of environment in which colleagues could speak freely, and people said outrageous things sometimes. The question is what it said about him that he was comfortable with advisers who harbored such malicious thoughts.

A legion of those who ended up on Giuliani's bad side blame Lategano at least in part for their troubles. "She did everybody in," says William Bratton. "Powers, Miller, Dave Garth. Everybody. She did them all in. She has a tremendous way of getting between people close to the mayor."

As for the communications director, she says she can't understand why so many people who worked with her want to hurt her.

"People I'm sure were very angry or insecure about my position with the mayor," she says. "It happens all the time in not only government but in newsrooms, any kind of work environment or teaching environment—people don't like the teacher's pet. They don't—right? So you taunt them, you tell rumors about them, you lie about them.

"And I always just thought: 'I can get through all of this because I'm just going to do my job.' And the more the lies came out and the more the taunting, I just wanted to work harder and do it better. So in a sense, they were just challenging me to do even more work.

"And obviously that's what I did."

9

Ragin' Rudy

In October 1995, almost two hundred heads of state descended on New York for a mammoth celebration of the United Nations's fiftieth anniversary. The streets were clogged with limousines, and a traffic gridlock alert was declared for all of Manhattan as Russian President Boris Yeltsin and Chinese President Jiang Zemin arrived, with Fidel Castro, Jacques Chirac, and Yitzhak Rabin close behind.

The timing couldn't have been better. Peace had been breaking out in the most violent corners of the world as the fallout continued from the collapse of the Soviet Union. Just a few weeks earlier, Israel's Rabin and Palestinian Liberation Organization leader Yasir Arafat had signed an accord in the White House East Room transferring part of the West Bank from Israeli to Arab hands. It was the latest of many developments signaling an era of extraordinary harmony.

The UN anniversary was an event of international importance, larger than any one nation or political figure. But by the end of the week, one man had single-handedly managed to disrupt its message of world harmony and make himself the center of attention. He wasn't even a president or prime minister. The only citizens he ruled over lived in the five boroughs of New York.

As the host city for the UN event, New York was well prepared for the moment. The police had spent months designing special security precautions, while other arms of government staged elaborate ceremonies to honor the guests. One of the highlights was a concert at Avery Fisher Hall at Lincoln Center. The New York Philharmonic was scheduled to perform Beethoven's Ninth Symphony before an invitation-only crowd of presidents, premiers, and other dignitaries.

Rudy Giuliani arrived early to prepare his welcoming remarks, and his aides were buzzing up and down the theater's sweeping staircases. Bruce Teitelbaum, the curly-haired deputy chief of staff, was watching the guests arrive from an upstairs railing. The aide, harried, rumpled, and perpetually glued to his cell phone, was Giuliani's link to the Jewish community, particularly the Orthodox Jews who were a vital part of the mayor's political base. Peering down upon the grand lobby, a knitted yarmulke pinned to his thinning hair, Teitelbaum noticed the crowd start to buzz. Someone had swept in surrounded by dozens of people, like a rock star, and begun making his way upstairs. Teitelbaum watched the figure approach him until he realized it was Yasir Arafat, dressed in his customary kaffiyeh and military uniform. The PLO leader and a handful of his aides walked to a small room that led to a private box seat near the stage and closed the door behind them.

Teitelbaum was stunned. Just a few days earlier, Giuliani had instructed him to keep Arafat off the guest list, along with six other heads of state whom the mayor deemed terrorists. The aide rushed downstairs and found Randy Mastro, who had brought his parents to the event. The chief of staff insisted on seeing Arafat with his own eyes before going to the mayor. Once he spied Arafat settled into his box seat, Mastro and his deputy headed to a small room backstage, where Giuliani was sitting with Gillian Sorensen, the UN undersecretary general in charge of the three-day celebration.

"Mister Mayor," Mastro said, "Yasir Arafat is here."

"He wasn't invited," Giuliani said sternly. "Throw him out."

Sorensen was horrified. "You can't do that!" she said. "Chairman Arafat is part of the UN commemoration. He's here as an official observer with the approval of the United States. He has tickets for the concert."

Giuliani barely acknowledged her. "Throw him out," he repeated.

Sorensen protested again, a note of panic entering her voice. Giuliani waved her away. "Gillian, I don't want to hear it," he said. The concert was about to start. People had already taken their seats.

Given their orders, Teitelbaum and Mastro bounded toward Arafat's box accompanied by a member of the mayor's security detail. Teitelbaum knocked on the door until one of the chairman's aides came out. Teitelbaum and Mastro handed him their business cards, which the aide proceeded to hand to the PLO chairman. Charmed that the mayor of New York had sent two emissaries to greet him, Arafat came to the door and extended his hand. Teitelbaum declined to shake it.

Mastro spoke in a soft voice. "I've been asked to speak to you by the mayor," he said to Arafat. "This is a mayoral event by invitation only and you were not invited. And while the concert is about to start and you're already here in these seats, the mayor would prefer that you leave since you weren't an invited guest."

Arafat apparently didn't understand what he was being told, because he smiled and nodded in response. But another aide to Arafat understood Mastro well. "Do you know who you're talking to?" he yelled, grabbing Mastro's arm.

"Of course I know who I'm talking to," Mastro replied. "We would like you to leave. You were not invited, and Mr. Arafat was not invited, and we would like you to leave."

"This is terrible!" the aide yelled. "This is terrible that you should make this request!" He waved a letter of invitation at them.*

Mastro's voice remained low. "I can't force you to leave," he said. "No one is going to attempt to physically remove you. But you've come to an event to which you were not invited, an event sponsored by the mayor, and the mayor would prefer that you leave."†

---

*Giuliani claimed the Lincoln Center event was run by the city. UN officials, however, assert that it was a joint event and that they distributed many of the tickets out of the UN building, including, perhaps, the ones used by Yasir Arafat and his aides. The Giuliani administration's ticket distribution operation, meanwhile, was engulfed in chaos: The tickets were lost for a day, and when they were recovered, the city's UN liaison office was thrown into an uproar when hundred of aides from various missions showed up on the day of the event demanding them.

†Pressed for his version of the conversation a few days later, Arafat added one detail. When Mastro made his request, Arafat said he looked at Mastro and said, "Go to hell."

Mastro and Teitelbaum left to report back to the mayor, who was satisfied with what he heard. "Look," Giuliani said. "We've asked him to leave; there's really not much else we can do." The lights were down. The orchestra had started to play. Giuliani sank into his seat, having successfully sparked a diplomatic incident.

Twenty minutes later, the PLO chairman and his entourage got up and left Lincoln Center.

After the concert, Mastro took his family out for dessert, and Teitelbaum went home to sleep. When he awoke the next morning, Teitelbaum's copy of the *New York Post* had the Arafat story on its front page. "RUDY BOOTS ARAFAT—PLO Chief Embarrassed at Lincoln Center." The paper gleefully recounted the chairman's travails inside.

Not everyone interpreted the event so favorably for the mayor. Clinton administration officials were appalled: Arafat had a history of terrorism, but he had wagered his future on negotiating a peace settlement with Israel, representing the best hope for Mideast peace in decades. "We don't think this is right," said State Department spokesman Nicholas Burns. "He's the leader of the Palestinian people, and he is negotiating peace with Israel. He should be given the respect and dignity and hospitality in the United States that the leader of the Palestinian people deserves."

Besieged with questions about the incident later that day, Giuliani was defiant, pointing to the 1985 killing of Leon Klinghoffer aboard the *Achille Lauro* cruise ship and other murderous acts attributed to the PLO. "When we're having a party and a celebration, I would rather not have someone who has been implicated in the murders of Americans there, if I have the discretion not to have him there," he said.

As for the Mideast peace process, the mayor claimed he had *helped* it. "Maybe it'll make it more realistic," he told reporters at City Hall. Giuliani seemed to be operating far out of his depth.

Ed Koch, one of the most prominent Jews in the city, was disgusted and joined David Dinkins for an unprecedented joint press conference. "Mayor Giuliani has behavioral problems dealing with other people," Koch told reporters. Giuliani responded by sending staffers to research comments Koch had made about Arafat in the past. Sure enough, the former mayor had once called Arafat a "murderer."

"In the words of Ed Koch, what I did was ask a murderer—that's the way he described Yasir Arafat—to leave an event that was private," Giuliani said.

The back-and-forth between the former allies intensified: Giuliani said Koch "turned around on an issue of conscience for himself just in order to get a little publicity." Koch said Giuliani was "demonstrating those very qualities that he exhibited as a prosecutor . . . a viciousness and mean-spiritedness that no great mayor can have."

Critics asked whether Giuliani was simply pandering to Jewish voters. Indeed, thousands of letters poured into City Hall from Jews praising Giuliani's tough stand with Arafat. Some were concentration camp victims who called the mayor a hero.

Pandering or not, Giuliani was clearly enjoying the international furor he'd kicked up. As the days progressed, his rhetoric became more defiant. On October 26, he appeared before an audience of fund-raisers for the United Jewish Appeal and brought up his actions at Lincoln Center three days earlier. "When I write my memoirs," he said, "these are some of the things I will be proudest of."

He went even further in a conversation with an aide. "My only regret," he told him, "was that I didn't throw Arafat out myself."

At City Hall in the mid-1990s, such improbable battles were commonplace, and the stakes were always cinematically high. The mayor was a junkie for action, always in search of a fight that would astonish the citizenry. His ability—or was it a need?—to spot a potential battle was always on display. Some of his wars were for fundamental change in the city; others weren't as important. But they helped establish his reputation across America as a fighter.

For the people who worked under him, Giuliani's intensity could be variously inspiring or alarming. He needed only four hours of sleep a night, a trait he inherited from his mother. His staff grew used to late-night meetings at Gracie Mansion and to even later phone calls at home from the boss. The mayor seemed intent on running the city by himself, dashing off to fires, police shootings, water main breaks, and other calamities that struck New York more or less daily. When a paralyzing snowfall blanketed the city, he monitored the cleanup himself and shoveled snow for photographers. His critics said the mayor couldn't stand to be left out of a picture, and his

resentment of William Bratton's press coverage proved them right. But there
was more to his style than mere vanity: He needed to be in control, barking
orders like a general.

He could be frightening: A young aide had to duck when the mayor
started throwing telephones inside the van, furious that a staff error had kept
him from rushing to the hospital bedside of an ailing former mayor, Abe
Beame.

But that intensity also drove him to take on seemingly insurmountable
problems.

R udy Washington was surrounded. Four hundred angry fish handlers were
inching toward him, burly old guys with faces red from the early morning wind, some of them taunting him with shouts of "nigger." Several were
brandishing the fish hooks they used to smash the windows of truck drivers
who refused to pay extortion money. A few dozen cops were on hand, badly
outnumbered. Day One of the city's drive to take the Fulton Fish Market
out of the hands of the Mafia wasn't going well.

The mayor's commissioner of business services, a wiry man with a straggly
beard, reached for his cell phone to call Randy Mastro at his Greenwich Village apartment. It was 4 A.M. "Someone's gonna die tonight!" Washington
told the deputy mayor. Mastro, who'd been up all night directing the effort
by phone, tried to reassure him. The cops were sending in reinforcements,
he said. "Don't do anything, Rudy! I'm going to call the mayor." Washington hung up and waited for fate to run its course, closing his eyes and pressing his arms close to his bullet-proof vest. Perhaps God intervened, because
the crowd became distracted by a noise in the background and moved to
other targets. The moment passed.

A few hours later, Washington and Mastro, weary from a night without
sleep, marched up the steps of City Hall, walked through the grand rotunda,
and bounded up the staircase to the daily 8 A.M. staff meeting. The mayor
was sitting at a large round table, surrounded by aides. Before the gathered
audience, the two reported that the Mob, which had already burned a building to the ground in defiance of the mayor, had brought the market to a

complete halt overnight. Giuliani didn't pause. "If people don't go back to work tonight, I'll shut down the market altogether and no one will be able to do work there," he said. "Then we'll reconstitute the whole operation." Later that day he made the same threat in front of a room full of reporters.

Giuliani's vision for cleaning up the city included wresting mainstays of city life back from the Mob. Most of the city's chief executives had preferred to leave criminal matters to prosecutors. But Rudy Giuliani *was* a prosecutor.

The Mafia was fixing prices, limiting competition, and extorting protection money, driving consumer costs up by hundreds of millions of dollars a year—"a Mob tax," Giuliani called it. At the fish market, trucks arrived each morning from up and down the Eastern Seaboard, packed with two million pounds of the day's catch. Only the "unloaders" were allowed to take the fish off the trucks and bring them to the wholesale shops that lined the downtown market area, where buyers from restaurants and grocery stores shopped. In reality, they were a price-fixing cartel that extracted kickbacks from truckers in return for serving them. The Genovese crime family was reputedly running the show.

With Mastro placed in charge of cleaning up the operation, Giuliani basically regulated the cartel out of business. All companies were required to apply for licenses, and anyone who failed a background check was disqualified. The city disqualified dozens of unloaders and found a company to replace them.

The old guard tried mightily to intimidate the new workers—the warehouse was set ablaze, and groups of marauding fish handlers tried to scare truckers away from the market. But after a few scary nights, hundreds of police officers secured the area. The Mob was soon chased out of Fulton Street.

Giuliani extended the battle to the commercial garbage hauling industry. Prosecutors believed the companies that hauled trash away from Manhattan's restaurants and office buildings were controlled by the Genovese and Gambino crime families. Four carting associations ran the industry, using violence to intimidate potential competitors and setting prices artificially high. In 1995 all four groups and seventeen people were indicted on charges ranging from attempted murder to arson. The case gave Giuliani a chance to step in.

Acting in rare concert with Public Advocate Mark Green, the mayor prevailed upon the City Council to create the Trade Waste Commission to conduct background checks, carry out fingerprinting, and issue licenses. Those members who couldn't pass the scrutiny of the commission were bounced. New companies were invited into the once-insular industry, and competition bloomed for the first time in memory.

The results were striking. The Metropolitan Museum of Art's trash bill declined by 40 percent. The managers of a building in the Wall Street area reported that its annual trash bill fell from $1.2 million to $150,000. Another bastion of the Mafia was cleansed by the former prosecutor at City Hall.

The annual Feast of San Gennaro was a Little Italy ritual dating back to the mid-1920s, when residents organized to pay tribute to the patron saint of Naples. New Yorkers had long since lost interest in squeezing past hordes of tourists for the privilege of breathing in the smoke of grilling sausage and frying dough, but the eleven-day event drew a million people a year from the tri-state area, making it the city's largest street festival. Giuliani had boycotted the feast for twenty years, convinced that the Mafia had taken over this New York institution. In 1995 a round of indictments gave him a chance to sweep it free.

A federal grand jury charged two vendors with lying on behalf of a reputed Genovese soldier named Thomas Cestaro, who allegedly oversaw the operation of the festival from a Mulberry Street social club. Organizers claimed the festival was clean, but with people with names like Tony "Waterguns" Pisapia running the show, it didn't take a stretch of the imagination to envision what was taking place.

True to his nature, Giuliani began the campaign with an ultimatum. "There will not be a San Gennaro Festival unless an independent monitor oversees the financial transactions regarding the festival," he had Cristyne Lategano tell the press. City Hall was withholding the feast's permit.

Giuliani's expertise at finding the levers of power in a battle was on display again. Where prosecutors could attack only individuals, the city had the ability to shutter the operation entirely. Italian-Americans were his most passionate supporters, but Giuliani was intent on auditing the books of the

Society of San Gennaro and was willing to end the party if he didn't get his way. The society agreed to the monitor.

The following January, former prosecutor John Sabetta released his findings: The nonprofit society was a fraud, a Mob-connected operation that raised $360,000 but donated just over $11,000 to charity. Its president had been paid a $30,000 salary to run the two-week festival and given an $83,000 interest-free loan. Its previous chief was a reputed associate of the Genovese family.

Giuliani denied the group a permit for the first time in sixty-eight years and dispatched Randy Mastro to reconstitute the operation. A new group was found to run the show; City Hall prevailed upon the Roman Catholic Archdiocese to oversee the finances. The full force of city government was thrown into the effort: electricians and other city workers flooded Mulberry Street and worked feverishly to bring the electrical system up to code.

On the first night of the new Feast of San Gennaro, September 12, 1996, Giuliani took his first trip to the event in two decades. The mob-buster was back, determined to eradicate the scourge of the Mafia and salvage the good name of the city's Italian-Americans. "It's going to be a feast that actually delivers money to charity," he declared, strolling down the narrow streets with a clutch of reporters and plainclothes detectives. As he walked by the old storefront headquarters of the society, the people sitting outside its doors just scowled at him.

As for the feast, the new organization in charge of the festival ponied up $150,000 to charity in its first year.

Thanks to major efforts from prosecutors, Giuliani managed to wipe the Mafia from areas it had dominated for so long that people barely even complained anymore. No one criticized his in-your-face style this time. "The bully boys of the market have had their way for too long, at everyone else's expense," the *New York Times* editorialized. The mayor's actions, it said, were "bold." The *Daily News* gushed even more. "The customer winning. Now that is reinventing government."

On a hot summer night in July 1996, a TWA flight carrying 230 people sailed off a runway at Kennedy Airport and flew out over the Atlantic

Ocean en route to Paris. Twelve minutes later, it exploded into a fireball, raining down bits and pieces upon the waters off Long Island before plunging into the ocean. Dozens of bodies bobbed up in the waters near the crash. All passengers were feared dead.

More than a hundred panicked relatives rushed to the airport to get information about their loved ones. Rudy Giuliani rushed there as well.

The scene was chaotic. Ambulances, police, and emergency vehicles converged, followed by a swarm of television news vans, reporters, and photographers from up and down the East Coast. The relatives were directed to a nearby Ramada Inn and settled in for a tense vigil in a hotel ballroom. The networks were reporting that the plane had simply disappeared off the radar screen; there was no warning from the pilots on Flight 800 that something was wrong. Suspicion mounted that a bomb had gone off on the plane.

As the hours passed, the mood inside the Ramada Inn became increasingly desperate. The mayor was there, comforting people and keeping vigil for an attorney friend named Kirk Rhein who was scheduled to be on the flight. Yet TWA would not confirm which of their friends and relatives had actually boarded the plane that evening. They beseeched TWA employees for the passenger list, but none was provided. Giuliani grew angry at the lack of response from the airline, which had sent grief counselors to the hotel but no managers with hard information.

The mayor finally got hold of an airline manifest. It was not a definitive source, as it didn't take into account those passengers who'd been bumped from other flights or who used other people's tickets. But it was better than nothing. Giuliani took it upon himself to go from person to person to break the news to them that their husbands, wives, and friends were dead. He stayed with them through the night.

By daybreak, he was livid. "Let me tell you about TWA," he told reporters. "The upper management of TWA has abandoned the families. If they were city employees, they'd be fired."

He stayed at the hotel throughout the day, criticizing TWA mercilessly at every juncture. Company spokesmen and the president of TWA himself, Jeffrey Erickson, argued haplessly that the company needed to check flight data from dozens of connecting flights before it could confirm that passengers had indeed gotten on board Flight 800. It would have been cruel to tell someone a relative had died when he or she had not, he said. But the process took more than eighteen hours, leaving the mayor with a huge target. Forever incapable of doing anything halfway, Giuliani went on a rampage, tearing apart the reputation of one of the world's best-known corporations. He appeared on *Good Morning America* and blasted the company before the entire nation. He did the same on *CBS This Morning, Larry King Live,* and *The Charlie Rose Show.* He spoke to CNN, MSNBC, the local broadcast television stations, and New York 1. He even held his weekly radio broadcast from the hotel the following day, attacking TWA for "incompetently handling" the notifications—and then lying about it.

If it seemed that he was serving his own interest as well as that of the relatives, it was hard to reproach him for it. He had a keen instinct for knowing a vulnerable target when he saw one. And his willingness to personally direct the city's disaster response and help the families for hours, even days, gave him credibility—as a TWA spokesman found out.

"It's very easy to criticize when you're outside the process of actually having to compile the information," the spokesman told an interviewer for CBS.

"I *wasn't* outside the process," the mayor of New York City shot back at him. "I've been here since eleven o'clock at night . . . and the gentleman from TWA decided to go home last night to get some sleep. I've sat here with families, and I also lost someone on that plane who was a friend of mine. So don't you tell me that I'm outside the process!"

Giuliani knew the world didn't care if he was making life miserable for the people at TWA. The message sinking in with people was that he was a hands-on leader who wasn't afraid to fight.

The wars against the Mob, against Arafat, against TWA were sideshows compared with the main drama of Giuliani's first term: the fight to reshape city government.

When he took office in 1994, the local economy was still in the grip of a recession that the rest of the country was shaking off, and tax revenues were plummeting. Expenses were outrunning income by $2.3 billion. After implementing a battery of spending cuts and worker buyouts, the mayor learned that revenues had fallen short by an additional $1 billion. For all his budget-cutting, Giuliani's reward entering 1995 was a new gap of over $3 billion.

It was the kind of demoralizing cycle that had plagued Dinkins each year of his mayoralty. But, unlike Dinkins, Giuliani welcomed the crisis as a chance to scale back the size of city government. The city, he said in a televised speech in February 1995, was in need of "reality therapy."

"I see this crisis as a historic opportunity," he said, looking blankly into the camera with his hands folded. "It is a chance to do what was politically unthinkable just a few years ago."

Many of his ideas were innovative, if controversial. He announced plans to consolidate a host of city agencies, merge the Emergency Medical Service into the Fire Department, and combine the three police departments into the NYPD. He pushed for concessions from the city's municipal unions, demanding that their members pay health insurance deductibles like everyone else. He proposed selling off most of the city's public hospitals, calling them an anachronism in an age in which even the finest hospitals were happy to treat anyone receiving Medicaid.

Other proposals were more far-fetched. He announced plans to sell off the city's water supply to raise more than $2 billion in cash. He proposed eliminating all the fire alarm boxes across the city to cut down on false alarms.

The mayor went about the crusades in his usual tactful way. He branded the criticism of his labor deals from a nonpartisan budget watchdog group "outrageous," "off the wall," and "crazy." His negotiations with the unions had failed to obtain productivity or health insurance givebacks, but his critics were being "political" for pointing that out.

When State Comptroller Carl McCall, a Democrat, issued a report questioning the mayor's fiscal policies, Giuliani lashed out at him in the same way. "From the day that he took over the job of comptroller, he's acted in a partisan, political way," Giuliani said. "Clearly, he has some kind of political agenda." Then the mayor proposed eliminating the comptroller's New York City watchdog office altogether, claiming that New York already had enough oversight.

City Comptroller Alan Hevesi expressed alarm at putting the water supply in private hands. The mayor responded, "I don't know that Mister Hevesi yet understands this transaction." When the comptroller ultimately sued to block the deal, Deputy Mayor Peter Powers charged Hevesi with "playing politics with the children of this city," because the proceeds were partially earmarked for school repairs. A mild-mannered man, Hevesi was insulted. "The people of this city are getting tired of the administration labeling as political anyone who disagrees with them," he told a reporter. "They have done this fifteen or sixteen times and it's getting boring."

In a matter of months, Giuliani had angered and alienated some of the most powerful officials in the state, people with whom he might have been expected to develop working relationships. He was a Republican in a city of Democrats. Everyone was suspected of acting politically. Cristyne Lategano wasn't the only suspicious one in the mayor's wing.

Unable to schmooze, much less build consensus for his programs, the mayor ended up losing several key battles. Vallone took him to court over the plan to sell off city hospitals and won. Hevesi won his lawsuit to bar Giuliani from selling the city's water supply. The City Council beat back the mayor's proposal to eliminate the fire alarm boxes.

He was more successful taking on the welfare system.

For generations, New Yorkers prided themselves on being protectors of the poor. John Lindsay, alarmed by the riots sweeping America's inner cities, launched ambitious campaigns in the sixties to sign people up for welfare, advertising the availability of benefits and relaxing the city's eligibility screening procedures. The welfare rolls doubled—from 538,000 in 1965 to 1,165,000 in 1971. New York City's welfare population grew larger than the total populations of fifteen states. The federal government's welfare program, Aid to Families with Dependent Children, wasn't enough: The state established its *own* welfare program—this one for healthy, childless adults— and the city was its financial partner in the endeavor, called Home Relief. The largely white ruling class watched passively as a huge, increasingly dysfunctional culture divorced from the working class mushroomed in the city's poor neighborhoods. Illegitimacy in the inner city skyrocketed: In 1970, 445,000 of the 600,000 children on welfare were living in homes without fathers. But to question the wisdom of the welfare culture was to risk being tagged a racist.

Giuliani had said little about changing the welfare system in his 1993 campaign, but as 1995 dawned, he zeroed in on it. Almost 250,000 New Yorkers, most of them single men, were receiving Home Relief payments of $325 a month, at a cost of $1.9 billion a year. "Somebody come in and justify that program to me," Giuliani told his staff, "because otherwise I'm getting rid of it." The state legislature stood in the way of eliminating Home Relief, but it did not prevent the mayor from making it harder for people to get benefits. At the mayor's behest, Senior Adviser Richard Schwartz oversaw the design of a tough new eligibility verification system. All new applicants were to be interviewed twice about their identities, living situation, medical histories, and income. Welfare workers were to visit their homes and interview neighbors and landlords about their living arrangements and outside income. Their names were to be run through computers to ensure they weren't receiving benefits in other states. Their fingerprints were to be scanned. Then, presuming their applications survived the screening procedure, they were to be put to work cleaning up city parks or painting city property in exchange for their checks.

The system produced results more dramatic than Giuliani had envisioned. In its first three months, welfare bureaucrats rejected almost 60 percent of new applicants for Home Relief. The mayor took pains to describe his motives as nonideological (though the changes would ultimately become an integral part of his ideology). The new rules, he said, were implemented to rid the system of cheaters who were giving honest clients a bad name. "Home Relief in New York City was a very user-friendly system," Giuliani told the press, standing side by side with Governor Pataki in a triumphant City Hall press conference. "It was a system saying, 'Please come and take the money.'" A few months later he turned the screening procedure on existing recipients and predicted that 100,000 people would be dropped from Home Relief by the end of the year.

Advocates for antipoverty groups complained that the mayor had stacked the system against the most desperate New Yorkers. "They've made it so complex to apply that it's sort of like setting up a New York City marathon," complained Liz Krueger, a well-known advocate for the poor. "Now they're making everyone run this marathon, and some people are far less able to do so than others."

But that was just the beginning. When Giuliani unveiled his preliminary plan to plug the $3 billion budget gap in February 1995, he asked the state to cut $1.2 billion in welfare and Medicaid spending, which would have saved the city a comparable amount in matching funds. Giuliani became the first mayor in memory to lobby the state for *less* aid.

The uproar was instantaneous. *New York Newsday*, the outpost for the liberal opposition, howled in outrage. "It's war on the welfare poor," *Newsday*'s City Hall bureau chief Michael Powell wrote. He pointed out that the city was handing tax breaks worth $339 million to seven of the city's "richest" companies even as it was saving $200 million from welfare cuts. It was a simple zero-sum game in the eyes of the critics: the rich against the poor, with the mayor on the side of the wealthy.

Manhattan Borough President Ruth Messinger, a liberal warrior from the Upper West Side, echoed Powell's point. "All entitlements—not just for the poor—must be on the table," she said. Protestors popped up on the steps of City Hall every day to rail against Giuliani's insensitivity to the poor. Fernando Ferrer, Messinger's counterpart in the Bronx, warned that the proposals "endanger the social fabric of the city."

Responding to the rhetoric of compassion became a huge challenge for the mayor. Privately, he viewed the protests and denunciations "sort of non-emotionally and almost analytically," says a former aide.

"His view was, 'I'm here to make change. They're the problem,' " the aide recalls. He looked upon the people denouncing him outside his office as part of the city's permanent government, playing their part just as the realtors and the lobbyists played theirs. In his view, these social service advocates and liberal politicians were married to a rotting system for financial or ideological reasons and were protecting their interests by filling the airwaves with sympathetic depictions of welfare recipients going hungry.

He fought back in a predictably combative fashion. The critics outside were "apostles of dependency." The advocates were "special interests." His liberal critics were defenders "of the old way of thinking." Giuliani once again had no coalition behind him and no well of constituent support—polls showed that his popularity was a meager 46 percent. All he had was the force of his will.

At the end of the '95 budget cycle, Governor Pataki relented to the Democrats who controlled the State Assembly and threw in the towel on his proposed welfare cuts, sticking Giuliani with yet another budget hole to fill.

But the mayor's drive to change what he called the culture of dependency in the city was succeeding. He talked Stanley Hill, the amiable leader of the city's biggest municipal union, into accepting the workfare program, assuring the labor chief that his members wouldn't be displaced by welfare clients earning a fraction of their salaries. The City Council didn't stand in his way.

Giuliani had history on his side. He came to power at a time when welfare was being reexamined across America and Bill Clinton, intent upon steering the Democrats on a moderate course, was pledging to "end welfare as we know it." A handful of localities were already tinkering with the welfare system.

By the time President Clinton signed the welfare reform bill in 1996, New York City had the biggest workfare program in the country. In a matter of two years, Giuliani managed to shave almost 250,000 people off the rolls, with more to come. The program was criticized as inhumane, and when a fifty-year-old woman working for her benefits collapsed and died in Coney Island and a fifty-seven-year-old man with high blood pressure suffered a heart attack after he was required to scrub sanitation trucks, the criticisms seemed valid.

But Giuliani's program was destroying a wretched status quo, and the defenders of the welfare system seemed to be working off an outdated script, one that called for the defense of even the most unsuccessful government programs.

For all of his commando tactics and antisocial behavior—perhaps because of it—Giuliani looked like the reformer, while the Democrats seemed the enemies of change.

Things were going well for Police Commissioner Bill Bratton as 1996 began. *Time* magazine made him the cover boy of its January 15 issue, which heralded the drop in crime across America. Standing in a trench coat near a squad car under the Brooklyn Bridge, his collar turned up like Bogart's, the commissioner was the picture of cool. Inside, a story about the "slim, well-tended man who wears his reading glasses slung low on an impressive nose" paid glowing tribute to him as a kind of Patton-like figure. The story quoted him addressing his commanders: "You proved that police can change public behavior. For that you should be proud. Now get your feet off the desk. It's 1996."

Having lain low since the Press Office fiasco and the departure of his spokesman John Miller, Bratton was creeping back into the limelight. Celebrating his second anniversary at the NYPD, he told the *Daily News* that the department was on track to cut crime by half in many categories by the end of the decade. "We've won the World Series," he boasted. Despite the past tumult between City Hall and One Police Plaza, he said, he was in no rush to walk away from his job. "I'm at the top of my game, so why would I leave?" he asked.

It was a reasonable question. Bratton was Rudy Giuliani's ace, the man who handed him the accomplishment for which the mayor would always be remembered, the historic plunge in crime. But that wasn't the way Giuliani was seeing it. His prediction about Bratton in '93—"*He's going to be such a prima donna that he won't remember who's the commissioner and who's the mayor*"—was being proved correct.

Every day brought news to exacerbate the mayor's apprehensions. The commissioner scheduled a parade to honor the NYPD—on his birthday. He signed a six-figure deal to write a book about his crime-fighting successes.

Cristyne Lategano saw him as a man with his own agenda. Cognizant that Giuliani had doubts about Bratton's loyalty, she stoked the mayor's resentments. "He's trying to upstage you," she'd tell Giuliani about his commissioner. The mayor would grow increasingly agitated the more Lategano talked. "Denny, get Bratton on the phone!" he'd bark.

The antipathy surfaced publicly in March, when Giuliani rejected some personnel moves that Bratton was planning for the NYPD. The story leaked in the *Times* the next day, fueling a new round of questions about Bratton's relationship with the mayor. Both insisted publicly that their partnership was fine, yet Bratton's comments to the press seethed with understatement.

"I don't profess that the two of us skip down the lane hand in hand," the commissioner told the paper.

Events began to snowball. Bratton's term expired in February, and Giuliani refused to reappoint him until City Hall lawyers scrutinized the propriety of his book deal. Then the *Daily News* reported that Bratton and his wife had "winged aboard" a private jet belonging to Wall Street takeover king Henry Kravis and spent an all-expense-paid weekend "in high style" at the tycoon's villa in the Dominican Republic. Giuliani's lawyers launched a review of all the commissioner's travels. In the corridors of City Hall, mayoral aides quietly assisted reporters in their hunt for new Bratton peccadilloes.

Bratton saw the writing on the wall. "These were prosecutors," he recalled. "They were familiar with creating damage through investigation. I had seen them do it at the U.S. Attorney's Office, I had seen them hound Schools Chancellor Ramon Cortines out of office." The feud reached the front pages.

On the morning of March 26, the commissioner took a walk from One Police Plaza to City Hall, where he was mobbed by an army of reporters and cameramen on hand to record the fall of Batman and Robin. "On a day like this, all is well with the world," the commissioner said, smiling, before he hustled up the steps to see the mayor. A few minutes later, it was over.

The two held a friendly press conference at which each congratulated the other for a job well done. But the world saw Rudy Giuliani's worst side this day. The mayor had facilitated the departure of the most successful police commissioner in city history because he was getting too much good publicity. He had grown incensed with his limelight-loving appointee until he was no longer willing to share the limelight anymore. Then he resorted to torment, as he had with Cortines, to get his way.

Giuliani gave Bratton's job to Fire Commissioner Howard Safir, a decent man with a blue-chip record at the Drug Enforcement Administration and the U.S. Marshall's Service. Because he was an old friend of Giuliani's and loyal beyond reproach, Safir was tagged as a puppet from the outset and doomed to suffer years of ridicule. But the mayor was satisfied. He staged a swearing-in ceremony for Safir on the steps of City Hall so grand that it rivaled mayoral inaugurations. There were bagpipes, marching bands, and hundreds of smiling loyalists. Designed to herald a new era for the police department, it seemed more like a state-sponsored glorification ceremony thrown by some communist dictator, a phony spectacle intended to prop up a bureaucrat. Safir dutifully played out his part under the smiling approval of his boss, the mayor. It was hard not to be a little embarrassed for both of them.

The Bratton episode was Giuliani's most disastrous battle to date. As in the Cortines war, the mayor got his way, only to horrify the public in the process. The world learned that he had a monstrous ego, a personality flaw that was not only self-destructive but was hurting the city as well.

Yet Giuliani was a package: the drive, or inner turmoil, that caused him to pick fights with both the Mafia and his own police commissioner was directed by a compass in his own head, and there was no way to get him to focus only on the bad guys. He was a marvel to behold when fighting for underdogs like the relatives of the passengers killed on Flight 800. But the mayor sometimes focused his rage on people just because he found them personally threatening, like Bratton, or offensive, like Yasir Arafat, or because they stood in the way of his ambitions, like Cortines. Whatever rage Giuliani was born with or had learned as a boy growing up in Harold and Helen Giuliani's home in Flatbush was a gift and a curse. The city was stuck with both.

10

"Happy King Day!" Giuliani
and the Black Community

The streets of Brooklyn were still thick with slush from a week-old snow-storm when the Reverend Al Sharpton and a crowd of followers moved toward the foot of the Brooklyn Bridge. Bundled up in dark coats and long scarves, they were preparing to commence an annual ritual, the traffic-halting march across the bridge to honor the Reverend Martin Luther King Jr.'s birthday.

On this cold January morning in 1996, however, they were greeted by a battalion of New York City police officers, stationed to prevent the reverend and his group from taking over the bridge's roadway. The orders had come from One Police Plaza that Sharpton would no longer be allowed to para-lyze traffic.

The new year had not been treating the reverend well. A public that was forever taking his measure had seen him at his worst, caught on videotape exhorting a Harlem audience to boycott a "white interloper" who operated a store on 125th Street. Three months after the speech, a street activist walked into the store with a gun, told all the blacks to leave, sprayed the remaining employees with gunfire, doused the store with paint thinner, turned the .38-caliber pistol on himself, and pulled the trigger. Eight people died in the inferno that followed.

The debacle was another nail in the coffin that Rudy Giuliani was building for Sharpton's career as a civil rights leader, a confirmation that he was the same old race-baiter in a three-piece suit. The mayor was rubbing his contempt in Sharpton's face this morning.

Faced with the prospect of mass arrests, the minister had another idea. As cops in riot helmets looked on, he waved his minions away from the bridge and turned them around, soldiering them through the streets of downtown Brooklyn without telling them where they were being led. As befuddled officers and reporters ran alongside, Sharpton brought his cavalry to the Brooklyn Academy of Music, where the mayor of New York was scheduled to speak. Wearing a three-piece suit under his dark wool coat and silk scarf, his long mane of hair shimmering in the sunshine, Sharpton stormed into the grand old building and walked down the center aisle with a few dozen people in tow, chanting, "*You say get back, we say fight back!*" The audience of perhaps a thousand middle-class black residents, most of them decked out in their Sunday best for the Brooklyn borough president's annual salute to King, had come to hear the day's keynote speaker, Rudy Crew, the African American schools chancellor. Some clapped as Sharpton and his renegade crew threw the proceedings into chaos. The invading army lined up with their backs to the stage, a short distance away from Giuliani, who was standing in the wings awaiting his turn to speak. "You let us say something and we'll leave you—or you want us to sit in?" Sharpton asked the flustered emcee, who capitulated to the threat and gave him the microphone to scattered applause.

"We hope you listen to the right Rudy—Rudy Crew!" Sharpton told the crowd in his husky voice, standing at a podium with a giant photo of Martin Luther King Jr. hanging behind him. "When Rudy Wallace Giuliani comes on—no, he's not about Dr. King; he's about the ones that tried to stop him from marching!"

Some audience members stood up and cheered with their arms raised in solidarity as Sharpton compared the mayor to the southern segregationist. "Happy King Day to the young people!" Sharpton said by way of farewell. As audience members applauded, he went on his way, barreling back up the aisle toward the exit.

Minutes later, Giuliani was introduced—to a hail of boos and catcalls. "I don't think you perpetuate the spirit of Dr. King by making anyone feel unwelcome," he said sternly, wagging his index finger at the crowd. But the heckling continued. He stood alone at the podium, angrily fending off a hail of derision. The day belonged not to the leader of the city but to his nemesis.

For a while, Giuliani seemed well on his way to retiring Sharpton from his singular role as New York's preeminent orchestrator of racial protests. The mayor's strategy of ignoring him and his various demands had worked well, forcing Sharpton to seek attention in other places. But by the time that raucous day in Brooklyn rolled around, Giuliani had bungled his relationship with the black community so badly that he effectively invited Sharpton back into the limelight.

On the day after his 1993 triumph over David Dinkins, Giuliani looked like a politician who understood the power of symbols. Working on just a few hours of sleep following his victory party, the white prosecutor traveled to Harlem, evoking John Lindsay's famous walk through the neighborhood in the 1960s. As a swarm of reporters and cameramen recorded the historic moment, Giuliani entered the Salem United Methodist Church and held an impromptu community meeting in the church basement, assuaging the fears and anger of black residents who'd just lost their grip on City Hall.

"Whatever stereotypes you have, please don't believe for a minute that I want to put together a government of all one group," he told them. "I am very mindful of the fact that I won only 51 percent of the vote. I need to spend time with you. I need to get an understanding of the problems you have here." Then he traveled downtown to City Hall for an extraordinary joint press conference with Dinkins, calling on the city to come together.

It was impressive, but it would be his last gesture of reconciliation to the black community for a long time. The new mayor, it turned out, was far more interested in destroying the symbols of appeasement by which City Hall had kept the races mollified over the years.

Two weeks into his mayoralty, he eliminated the city's eight ethnic liaison offices—small bureaucracies that catered separately to blacks, Latinos, Jews, gays, Asians, and even European-Americans. Giuliani felt they served to balkanize the city instead of unite it. Two weeks after that, he gutted a Dinkins affirmative action program for minority and women contractors. None of his four deputy mayors was black, a fact he seemed almost proud of because it showed that merit supplanted tokenism in his administration. One of them, John Dyson, sparked not one but two racial controversies by using bizarre and insensitive language. The first was the "two white guys" memo he wrote during the transition; the other was his equally bizarre statement to a newspaper reporter, during a dispute over the hiring of a black city subcontractor, that the comptroller "ought to know the difference between a bid and a watermelon." Giuliani dismissed demands for Dyson's resignation, saying the deputy mayor had admitted he'd made a mistake.

To the mayor, it was a more honest way of governing, a color-blind, apolitical approach that treated every situation on its merits, as if there were no special sensitivities at stake.

"I'm coming from a very simple place," he said on a black radio station soon after the January 9, 1994, Harlem mosque incident. "It's called the law. Everybody has to follow it. Everybody will be dealt with in precisely the same way if they don't, and I'm going to work hard for every single person in this city, irrespective of race, religion, ethnic background."

The problem was, there *were* special sensitivities at play in the city he was running. Black leaders were holding every development at City Hall up to the light and looking for evidence of insensitivity or racism. The enormous job of serving the vast black underclass was fraught with gigantic racial minefields, particularly for a white man who had just upended the city's first black mayor. Black New Yorkers depended more heavily upon municipal services than any other group. Black children filled the public schools; black students filled the City University system; black patients filled the wards of the municipal hospitals; black prisoners filled the jails. Giuliani's budget cuts and welfare reform plans hit the city's black residents hardest.

Moreover, Giuliani's crackdown on crime had police officers acting increasingly aggressive on the streets of the city's black neighborhoods. Young black men were being jostled by cops, asked for identification, ques-

tioned about their intentions, patted down for weapons. The police department—never a friendly organization in the eyes of minorities—descended
upon Harlem and Bedford-Stuyvesant like an occupying force under Giuliani, and its officers were treating residents like suspicious characters.

These were legitimate concerns, but the mayor was not hearing them. He
had few trusted black advisers. Few blacks had campaigned for him, and
those who did learned that they did so at their own risk: Rudy Washington,
an entrepreneur and president of a local Rotary Club, was slapped in the
face by a woman on a Queens street when he campaigned for Giuliani
against Dinkins in 1989; he also received a steady stream of death threats.
The Reverend John Brandon, who hosted Giuliani in the basement of his
Harlem church the day after the election, lost his job because his congregation was so infuriated over his alliance with the Republican mayor.

Those minority group members who landed jobs with the administration
found it next to impossible to gain entrance into Giuliani's inner circle. The
fraternity of white prosecutors around him always felt free to drop into the
chief's office to gossip and strategize, whereas deputy mayors Ninfa Segarra
and Rudy Washington (who became Giuliani's first black deputy mayor in
1996) felt uncomfortable seeing the boss without a meeting. Segarra was
widely perceived as the least influential of Giuliani's deputy mayors. Washington fared somewhat better, though he never shook the derisive view of
the black Democratic establishment that he was chosen, as one elected
Democrat says, "almost because he had no relationship with the African
American community."

Black leaders shunned the new mayor almost from the start of his tenure.
The new mayor felt that Harlem's politicians were offering him cooperation
in private conversations, then bowing to Democratic Party pressure and criticizing him in public. Angered by the Harlem mosque incident and still bitter about Dinkins's loss, religious leaders and Democratic politicians were
getting Giuliani disinvited from speaking engagements and church appearances and leaning on others to do the same. Sharpton had managed to get
the Baptist Ministers Conference of Greater New York to ban him from
dozens of churches. The day Giuliani was confronted by Sharpton at the
Brooklyn Academy of Music, organizers of the annual King Day celebration

at Harlem's Convent Avenue Baptist Church had barred the mayor from attending and instead welcomed Dinkins, its minister claiming, "He's still our mayor."

It was the kind of situation that would test the diplomatic abilities of even the most nimble of politicians, and Giuliani wasn't a diplomat. He felt spurned by the black community, and Cristyne Lategano, worried about the disastrous news stories that appeared every time a black audience heckled him, reinforced his instinct to avoid those situations altogether.

The mayor was increasingly resentful. Because of his policies, crime was plummeting in minority communities. Old ladies could walk the streets of Harlem with their grocery bags without fearing they'd be mugged. Drug dealers weren't selling crack on the corner anymore. Gunfire wasn't lighting up the night at the city's housing projects. By 1997, murders had fallen to a thirty-year low. The mayor would recite the crime statistics daily, pointing out that the city was starting to flower again, opening the way for new jobs for the unemployed. It was a compelling argument, one that the black Democratic leadership stubbornly refused to acknowledge.

Yet Giuliani was his own worst enemy. Even as his aides pondered how to repair his deteriorating relationship with the black community, he was systematically alienating some of the most important black politicians in town.

Of all New York's black leaders, State Comptroller Carl McCall had perhaps the best potential to establish a working relationship with Giuliani. Tall and handsome, with a blue chip résumé — Dartmouth College graduate, an ordained minister, state senator, New York City Board of Education president, vice president of Citibank — he was a moderate man by ideology and temperament, more comfortable in a boardroom than on a protest line. He was the kind of corporate citizen that Giuliani usually felt comfortable doing business with. But McCall was close to the Harlem Democratic leadership, which included Dinkins and Congressman Charles Rangel. McCall had worked hard for Dinkins in the '93 race and had even taken some knocks back then for bending over backward to praise Dinkins's handling of the city's crumbling finances. The new mayor's camp viewed him with suspicion.

Soon after Giuliani's triumph in November '93, McCall invited the mayor-elect to his Manhattan office to brief him on the city's fiscal situation.

It was a cordial meeting: McCall and his staff went over the numbers, detailing the budget gaps Giuliani would be facing, and then the two politicians retired to McCall's office, where the comptroller offered the new mayor his cooperation. They shook hands and said good-bye.

But it was not long before Giuliani decided the comptroller had it in for him. As Giuliani labored to close massive budget deficits, McCall's office issued reports warning that the mayor's revenue estimates were too optimistic. The comptroller also urged the State Financial Control Board to meet more frequently to monitor the city's finances under Giuliani. McCall characterized his actions as part of his institutional responsibilities. But the mayor was furious, and he let the world know it in November 1994, when he endorsed a fellow Republican, Herbert London, for the comptroller's job. Under McCall, Giuliani said, the comptroller's office had become "the partisan political operation of the Democratic Party of New York City."

"We need a comptroller who is going to return the office to being an apolitical office," Giuliani said.

The die was cast. The mayor had decided the Democrat was "political" and thus an enemy. McCall won his race, but the relationship was doomed. After a brief meeting at City Hall following McCall's reelection, Giuliani did not meet with him again for five years. When the comptroller sent auditors in to conduct a routine assessment of city services in 1997, Giuliani had them thrown out and banished from municipal property, charging that McCall was trying to embarrass him before the '97 election. It took a judge's order to reinstate them.

At worst, McCall was guilty of intensifying his oversight over a mayor from another political party. But Giuliani's reaction was the political equivalent of nuclear war. He set out to tarnish McCall's reputation, then froze him out and treated him as a nonperson. He was vilifying New York State's highest-ranking African American leader.

"I could never figure out where it came from," McCall says of Giuliani's animosity. "I think that I could have been helpful to him, not only just as the chief fiscal officer of the state, but as someone from the black community who was certainly willing to meet and talk with him."

Instead, the mayor's antagonistic behavior convinced McCall that he had little interest in the black community. "Maybe Giuliani didn't want to have those kinds of relationships," the comptroller says with a trace of anger. "He wanted to cater to other people and wanted to show other people that he was ignoring this community. This community hadn't done anything for him politically, so therefore 'I'll ignore them.' "

In fairness, Giuliani was on the attack against a lot of Democratic politicians, black and white alike, using the same amount of vitriol. In his inner sanctum, where he and Lategano sized up who could be trusted and who could not, who was a friend and who was an enemy, the city's black establishment was placed on the same side of the page as the fiscal monitors, the New York Civil Liberties Union, Upper West Side liberals, and advocates for the homeless. They were all part of the same firmament that had brought the city to a state of collapse in the name of justice and compassion. Now that a reformer was declaring the game over, they were protecting their turf. These were enemies that had to be neutralized.

The mayor's own history with blacks was limited. He was born in Flatbush, a white working-class section of Brooklyn, and moved at the age of six to the largely white suburb of Garden City, Long Island. He studied at St. Anne's, a parochial school, then began commuting to Brooklyn to attend Bishop Loughlin Memorial High School in 1957. Bishop Loughlin was an overwhelmingly white all-boys school, where conformity was expected, crew cuts were the norm, and the boys and girls danced together at sock hops. The black kids were a few blocks away in the rough neighborhood, Fort Greene, hanging out in gangs on stoops, alongside men drinking from bottles in brown paper bags. Loughlin students would pass them quickly as they walked to the subway station, where the G train would whisk them away to Queens Plaza, the Long Island Railroad, and the suburbs.

The future mayor chose as his college a largely white, all-male Catholic school, Manhattan College, whose tranquil New York City campus was an oasis from the upheavals of the civil rights movement. Giuliani finally plunged into the center of urban rebellion in 1965, when he entered NYU Law School, right off Washington Square Park in Greenwich Village. His political sympathies were with the blacks protesting for civil rights down south. But his worldview was largely shaped in white ethnic neighborhoods and Catholic schools.

A former campaign aide recalls watching Giuliani at a party on Long Island in 1992, clad in shorts, with legs like "big, heavy white tree trunks."

"He looked for all the world like the stereotype of the Italian middle-class unassimilated suburban homeowner, grilling the sausages," the aide remembers. The image remained with him as he got to know Giuliani. "He had never traveled and had never been exposed to people other than himself," the former aide recalls. "He had a very parochial, narrow experience."

He first displayed a willingness to buck the sentiments of the black community in the early 1980s when, as an associate attorney general in the Reagan Justice Department, he oversaw the administration's hugely controversial Haitian refugee detention program. With Florida overwhelmed by a flood of refugees who'd fled the regime of Jean-Claude "Baby Doc" Duvalier, the U.S. government set up vast detention centers as officials decided what to do with them. To the horror of America's black leadership, thousands of other refugees were turned back at sea by the Coast Guard, while Giuliani argued that they were economic and not political refugees.

As mayor, Giuliani bristled whenever he was challenged on the topic of his relationship with minorities. Asked by the Washington Post to answer criticism that he was ignoring minority residents, he replied by citing the dramatic drop in crime in minority neighborhoods. "They are alive, how about we start with that?" he said. "You can't help people more directly than to save lives."

It was an answer that spoke volumes about his estrangement from the city's black community. Its members and leaders had never supported him, and he didn't need them to win in the future. It wasn't clear that Giuliani even cared all that much that he'd dodged one of the great challenges of his mayoralty, which was to bring the black community in under his wing after toppling the city's first black mayor. They were alive—thanks to him.

In the summer of 1996, the phone rang at the ramshackle headquarters of Al Sharpton's National Action Network in Harlem. Queens Assemblyman

Gregory Meeks was the young firebrand heading up the Council of Black Elected Democrats, a statewide group representing dozens of black politicians. Like Sharpton, he was an outsider who forced his way into power without the initial support of the black establishment. Sharpton was one of Meeks's few early supporters.

The assemblyman was calling to ask the reverend's help with an ambitious plan: He wanted to unite the black community around an opponent to Giuliani in the upcoming 1997 mayor's race. Meeks was organizing a summit meeting of the city's black leadership. He would bring the politicians; he asked Sharpton to bring the ministers.

Sharpton, who had been laboring in a kind of exile from municipal politics since the Harlem mosque episode, had been growing in stature nonetheless. In 1994 he challenged Pat Moynihan for the Democratic nomination for U.S. Senate, a losing battle strategically selected to show off the minister's ability to draw black votes. Sure enough, he drew a respectable 178,000 votes. Now he was aiming his sights back at City Hall, looking for revenge against a mayor who refused even to say his name. Sharpton agreed to help plan the summit.

The meeting took place on a sleepy summer morning at the Sugar Hill Disco & Restaurant in Bedford-Stuyvesant, a Caribbean and soul food mecca and a hangout for local politicians. In a private room, groups of elected black leaders from around the city mixed with some of New York's leading black ministers. Every pocket of the black power structure was represented: the Harlem clubhouse and its rival in Brooklyn; Manhattan state legislators and Brooklyn congressmen; the state comptroller and city councilmen; Baptist ministers and Pentecostal ministers. The atmosphere was electric: Hatred of Rudy Giuliani had united a dozen quarreling factions. Clergymen and councilmen alike compared slights and insults from City Hall over the years. Giuliani had refused to meet with most of the people in the room and had attacked a good number of them. "No one felt they were being represented by Giuliani," Meeks recalls. "If there was one thing we needed to do, it was get rid of this mayor."

The group concurred that the best hope for taking down Giuliani lay with Carl McCall. But the comptroller was there to tell the group to forget it. He was the latest major politician to decline to run, a sign that Democratic political advisers believed Giuliani's war to clean up the city had rendered him unbeatable in '97. With no obvious second choice, the group agreed to set up a screening process. Letters would be sent out to candidates inviting them to speak to the group. A candidate selection panel was formed. They were on their way.

It didn't take long after the meeting ended for all that cohesion to unravel. The Brooklyn Democratic organization was courting City Comptroller Alan Hevesi, who was flirting with a run. The Manhattan Democrats were uniting behind Borough President Ruth Messinger. The black politicians in those boroughs were being pressured to follow the lead of their county organizations, and the newspapers were reporting defections daily. Reading the reports, the ministers who'd joined in the effort were infuriated that the politicians were deserting the group.

Al Sharpton, who'd brought the ministers to the Sugar Hill, got on the phone with Greg Meeks. "What's going on?" Sharpton asked.

"Man, I don't know," Meeks replied. "Everybody made their commitment, and nobody's keeping it."

"Here we go again," Sharpton said. "Y'all are cutting your deals and leaving the community out."

The unified effort was falling apart, which angered Sharpton but also intrigued him. He was thinking about his own ambitions.

About six months later, on the same January morning on which Bill Clinton was sworn in for a second term as president of the United States, saying "the divide of race has been America's constant curse," the Reverend Wyatt Tee Walker, a former aide to Martin Luther King Jr., stood before a crowd of hundreds packed into the National Action Network in Harlem on King's birthday. "We're going to make history here today," he said.

"I bring you the next mayor, the Reverend Al Sharpton!"

The crowd jumped to its feet. A band in front of the auditorium struck up a beat. Sharpton walked to the podium amid a loud and jubilant cheer. "No justice . . ." He beckoned. "No *peace!*" the audience responded. "No justice . . . *No peace!*" The call and response grew louder. "No justice . . . *No peace! No justice . . . No peace!*"

"What do we want?" he asked. *"Justice!"* "When do we want it?" *"Now!"* He had the look of an experienced driver steering a car with one hand. He could do this in his sleep.

But he was just getting started. "If Martin Luther King were alive today, what would he do? Martin Luther King Jr. would not be at some nice ceremony where conservatives use the holiday they were against to give speeches.

"Last year we tried to march across the Brooklyn Bridge—we learned that from Martin Luther King Jr. We were stopped by the present mayor." The audience responded rhythmically. *"Teach!"* they yelled.

The auditorium was the shape of a long rectangle, with Sharpton in front, a long bank of television cameramen in back, and rows of cheering supporters in between. Framed pictures of Sharpton adorned every wall, along with photos of Jesse Jackson and James Brown, his two mentors. The room, which he called the House of Justice, was his monument.

Sharpton's volume was rising as he turned his sights on the mayor.

"His numbers are as bad as Ed Koch's were in the black community, and there has been no Howard Beach or Bensonhurst under his watch," he said. "It is *him* that is the polarizer!"

The crowd applauded. Clenched fists pumped the air. *"Oh yeah,"* people said. *"Teach!"*

"The quality of life may be better for Giuliani, but it's not better for a majority of the people who live in New York.

"Giuliani told the city for three years we were wrong about police mistrust. Now he acknowledges it because he knows now that our voices are being heard. He ignored the problem of education. Now he acknowledges it.

"He talks about, well, crime is down. Yes, we know it's down, because we helped bring it down. It was civic groups and community groups like us that went and closed crack houses.

"He wants to be a kinder and gentler Giuliani. I agree, but we need a relaxed Giuliani in retirement."

As the crowd hollered with delight, he turned back to the subject of Dr. King. "Why would someone think that after twenty years, the end of the century, that we would throw in the towel and give up our fight?

"I am a continuation of the dream!"

The crowd jumped to its feet. *"RUN, AL, RUN!"*

The reverend took a breath.

"I've decided, on this day, in this place, that I will seek the office of mayor of the City of New York."

The House of Justice erupted. Sweat was pouring down Sharpton's face. "I know we can win," he thundered. "Because Martin Luther King won. Because today, from Johannesburg to Harlem, they are singing 'We Shall Overcome.'

"I can fly!" Sharpton yelled. "I can fly!"

On cue, amid pandemonium, the band to his right struck up the anthem from the movie *Space Jam*, "I Believe I Can Fly." Sharpton, caught up in the rapture of the moment, started singing. *"I believe I can fly. I believe I can touch the sky."*

A gospel chorus led by his wife, Katherine, joined in, clapping and singing, and then so did the audience. As he sang, Sharpton held his arms aloft and flapped them like wings, prompting the politicians behind him to do the same; before long the roomful of people were waving their arms. *"I believe I can fly . . . I believe I can touch the sky."* Sharpton had gone from activist to politician to preacher to entertainer, and now, as he belted out this childlike song, waving his arms like a bird, he seemed a child himself, reveling in fantasy.

About an hour later, Rudy Giuliani, Police Commissioner Howard Safir, and a small crowd of plainclothes detectives walked into Harlem's Convent Avenue Baptist Church. For the first time in four years, the Baptist Ministers Conference of Greater New York had reversed course and invited Giuliani to address its King Day observance. It was a promising sign to the mayor on a day that had already held out some promise: the audience at the Brooklyn Academy of Music had treated him respectfully that morning, a marked improvement over the drama of the previous year.

The mayor and Safir, looking visibly uncomfortable as they made their way to the front of the ninety-eight-year-old Gothic Revival church, were seated off to one side of the pulpit. David Dinkins sat in the seat of honor in the middle of the stage, next to the Reverend Dr. Shellie Sampson Jr.

Giuliani was introduced to a hail of boos. He walked to the pulpit.

"Praise God," the mayor began, standing before several hundred well-dressed parishioners. *"Praise God,"* the audience responded.

In a hushed voice, he launched into a speech that tried to draw connections between his world and the world he was visiting this afternoon. He spoke of Martin Luther King Jr.'s message. "What is the lesson that he taught us that comes from this book"—he held up a Bible—"and that comes from all of our great religious traditions?" he asked the crowd. "It is that we are all children of the same God—all of us." The audience cheered, momentarily drowning out a band of hecklers in the audience.

Giuliani continued, but the hecklers, many of them acolytes of Sharpton's, persisted in yelling at him from all corners of the church. They shouted, "Murderer," and "What about Lemrick Nelson?"—the young man convicted in the Crown Heights case. Giuliani grew flustered as the booing grew louder. "We should just try to get to the end," he said, finishing his brief talk a few unhappy minutes later. He sat back down with Safir. Both men looked grim.

A short while afterward, the mayor exited in defeat and Sharpton arrived from the National Action Network—to a hero's welcome.

Sharpton was reaping the benefits of Giuliani's racial problems, but he was no bystander. He was doing everything in his power to keep Giuliani alienated from the black community, whether by getting him banned from events or by having him booed at those events he did attend. That was always the thing about the reverend: he was never as innocent as he claimed. He would manipulate events to his advantage, then step in as the hero. His first cause was always himself.

Yet with no dialogue taking place between the mayor and the mainstream black elected leaders down at City Hall, Sharpton had the stage to himself, and he used it brilliantly. He was turning out to be the only man in town clever enough to outmaneuver Rudy Giuliani.

11

The Gang Cracks Up

It was a beautiful day in Southampton. The breeze was soft and almost chilly, a welcome relief from the dank humidity back in the city. It was 6 P.M.—social time—and a stream of millionaires and socialites were pulling up to the estate of Broadway theater mogul Jimmy Nederlander and flowing into his house for the opportunity to lavish campaign contributions upon Rudy Giuliani.

The mayor was in a relaxed mood as he worked the crowd. So many celebrities had signed on to the host committee it was hard to keep them straight: there were Bill Blass, Marvin Hamlisch, Susan Lucci, Dina Merrill, Patricia Duff, and Ron Perelman. Giuliani circled around the expansive living room, shaking a hand or taking a compliment, and wandered back to the tent rising above the Nederlanders's vast lawn. There were as many Democrats as Republicans, maybe more, a sign that even New York's liberals were grateful to have their neighborhoods safer and the homeless off their streets. The wealthy had come to show their appreciation.

Howard Koeppel was one of them. A jaunty middle-aged man with silver hair and a Florida tan, he was the mayor's Good Time Charlie, a happy-go-lucky millionaire who often tooled around Manhattan with Giuliani in the mayor's van, grabbing a pizza at Patsy's or racing up to Gracie Mansion for a late-night snack. Koeppel was an unlikely sidekick—an openly gay car dealer from Queens with an Asian lover twenty-three years his junior. While he loved politicians, he didn't know much more about politics than the customers who walked through the doors of Koeppel Volkswagen or Koeppel Mazda each morning. But Giuliani loved him for his sense of humor and his obvious devotion to him, and Koeppel adored Giuliani back, becoming not just his number-one fan but one of his biggest fund-raisers.

As the party started to wind down, Koeppel had an idea. He'd driven a refurbished 1935 Ford Coupe to the party, knowing that the mayor was a car buff, and he approached Giuliani with a kind of conspiratorial look.

"How'd you like to have some fun?" he asked.

"What do you want to do?" the mayor said.

"When was the last time you drove a car?"

"I don't know, I can't remember—why?"

"Do you have your license with you?"

"Yeah, I always have my license—want to see it?"

Giuliani pulled it from his wallet and showed it to Koeppel.

"Okay," the friend said. "How would you like to drive my car? I'll let you drive it all the way back to the city."

Koeppel described the vehicle: on the outside it was an old classic, fire-engine red; on the inside it was refurbished with pink velvet seats, a new motor, automatic transmission, power windows, air conditioning, and a stereo system—"a Jewish hot rod," Koeppel called it.

The mayor was intrigued. "I'll tell you what," he said. "You get in your car and I'll get in my car and we'll meet down the road so we won't have a scene in front of the house. I'll explain to Intel what I'm going to do."

A few blocks away from the party, Giuliani exited his van with a plain-clothes detective from Police Intelligence and got behind the wheel of the dream car, with Howard Koeppel sitting next to him and Koeppel's lover, Mark Hsiao, sitting in back with the detective.

Giuliani slipped one of Hsiao's opera tapes into the stereo system, turned up the volume, and took off. The windows came rolling down as a stream of arias blasted from the speakers, with the mayor shouting above the wind and the music, explaining the plots of the different operas to Koeppel. The mayor was liberated, bathing in the moment like a teenager behind the wheel for the first time. People were staring as he raced the shiny red antique down the Long Island Expressway, his passengers bouncing up and down on sixty-two-year-old coil springs. An unmarked New York City police car was struggling to keep up with them.

About seventy miles later, they arrived at the foot of the Triborough Bridge and slowed down to pay the toll. Koeppel reached into his pocket to find three dollars, but Giuliani waved him off and pulled a five-dollar bill from his pocket.

The toll booth clerk was staring at the car when the hand stretched toward her with the bill. She took the money, looked at the car again, and did a double take at the sight of the mayor of New York sitting behind the steering wheel. Searching for words, she smiled nervously. "Mayor, I can't take your money," she said.

"Everybody pays!" he snapped back.

"Yes, sir," she responded, fumbling for his change. Giuliani took his two dollars and his receipt, put his foot to the pedal, and drove off to Manhattan.

The mayor must have felt like the master of all he surveyed as he crossed the expanse from Queens to Manhattan and took in the glorious view of the city skyline. The city was rising back to life under his mayoralty. Just as Robert Moses, an emperor of another age, had used his sheer will to build the bridge on which Giuliani was traveling, Giuliani had willed his vision of the city upon the people and their government. As he drove through the streets of Manhattan on this summer night in 1995, the armies of vagrants, peddlers, and drug dealers that had predominated on the sidewalks during the Koch and Dinkins years were gone, vanquished by Giuliani's newly emboldened police force. The small parks that Moses had created during the Great Depression with an army of unemployed WPA workers were cleaner than they'd been in years, swept and scrubbed by Giuliani's own army of public workers, the workfare brigade.

Turning north on First Avenue, Giuliani could see people walking their dogs and dining in restaurants, middle- and upper-middle-class New Yorkers who had stuck it out as less hardy souls fled for the suburbs in the stampede that began under Lindsay. There was less desperation in the air, even confidence that the deterioration had stopped. People were encouraged by the signs of life the city had begun to show: a 40 percent drop in the murder rate in two years, a 35 percent drop in car thefts. People had stopped exchanging war stories about their muggings. The very word, a staple of daily conversation in the seventies and eighties, was falling into disuse. Even race relations had improved since the defeat of the first black mayor: there hadn't been a significant racial conflagration since the Harlem mosque incident.

A mile or so south, the corpse of Times Square was beginning to show some life as well. Bulldozers were wiping away peep show houses and porno theaters; construction cranes harkened the creation of new hotels, theaters, and megastores. Hope was returning to the city, and with it the confidence of New York's corporate chiefs, entrepreneurs, and developers. As the 1997 election year dawned, the city's economy had finally started to participate in the nationwide boom. Budget deficits were shrinking, and the unemployment rate, still hovering at 9 percent, was starting to fall.

As Giuliani drove uptown toward Gracie Mansion, he knew that his police were out in force uptown in Harlem and in the ghettos of the Bronx, patting down young black men for guns, throwing them up against the walls of buildings if they talked back or seemed suspicious. It was the underside of the crime fight that he never talked about. The removal of weapons was one of the reasons for the miraculous drop in crime. Black leaders resented the seemingly racist policies that made the young of their communities prime suspects, but the cops were being urged to go where the guns were. When the leaders complained, Giuliani always had a ready answer: crime was plunging in black neighborhoods more than anywhere else. The cops were saving their communities from the ravages of crime.

Rudy Giuliani was not handsome, like Lindsay, or funny, like Koch. He couldn't even qualify as irascible, like his hero LaGuardia. He was a bit grim, and not all that sympathetic. But he was growing on New Yorkers because he was competent, hardworking, and as feisty as a cabdriver. David Letterman invited him to repair a pothole on his show one night: Giuliani gladly cooperated, happy to be portrayed as the mayor who ran the town single-handedly. To millions of New Yorkers, Giuliani was more than just an effective, if abrasive, leader. He had come to embody their personal security, and those politicians seeking to oust him were suddenly being considered potential threats to that.

The essential dynamic of this election year—that the people of this city were safer than they had been in decades—gave the mayor supreme confidence about his chances in November.

Wake up, sleepyheads!" Actor Nathan Lane, the master of ceremonies at Ruth Messinger's first major fund-raiser, was barely exaggerating. Some five hundred people who'd paid $1,000 each to come to the Grand Ballroom of the Sheraton Hotel were eating dinner in something approaching silence.

The Manhattan borough president had waited years for her shot at the mayoralty. She had earned her fame as an Upper West Side firebrand, neighborhood activist, battler of real estate interests, and zealous City Council member. In the old days she had lived in an Upper West Side collective, sleeping on a mattress on the floor, boycotting broccoli in solidarity with migrant workers. She'd protested the Vietnam War and fought for the civil rights of blacks, women, gays, and lesbians. With her frizzy black hair and floral skirts, she was the quintessence of the Upper West Side liberal politician. Her candidacy for mayor was the logical next step in her long public career.

But at this moment in February 1997, there were signs that the old rules were changing for the town's Democrats. A Republican at City Hall had helped reverse the city's decline by discarding the policies of the left, and he was winning the grudging admiration of New York's famously progressive electorate. In Washington, Bill Clinton was salvaging his party's fortunes by parting with liberal orthodoxy and fighting the opposition for the political center. Now Ruth Messinger, the proudest liberal in town, had moderated *her* politics, soft-pedaling her big government, antidevelopment message and stressing her bona fides as a mother and a wife, someone who could bring people together. Even her physical appearance had changed: A serious policy wonk famous for her disdain of fashion, she'd styled her hair, purchased a rack of power suits, and donned a pearl necklace.

Messinger's speech on this night was about *values*, a word Clinton had appropriated from the right to communicate his concern for middle-class interests. "The truth is, values do matter," she told the crowd. "And the most important value we need coming from City Hall is the value of community—to get New Yorkers to start pulling together and stop pulling apart." The city, she said, needed "partnership, not partisanship," "collaboration, not confrontation," "consensus-building, not confrontation."

The muddled message only intensified the undercurrent of doubt rolling through the audience. Rudy Giuliani was throwing people off the welfare rolls, arresting homeless people, threatening civil liberties. Didn't this signal a call to arms? Wasn't it the responsibility of the Party of Compassion to fight back? Or was it political suicide to argue with success?

The mayor's poll numbers were not prohibitively high, but a legion of politicians had decided not to risk the race against him. Friends had warned Messinger that this was a losing battle, that the mayor would be hard to beat, and that people would be too scared of retribution from City Hall to donate money to her. She kept telling them that someone had to stand up against this guy.

Others weren't as brave. Geraldine Ferraro, Mark Green, Alan Hevesi— even William Bratton, his former police commissioner—had toyed with running, only to back off. David Dinkins, furious that the opposition was rolling over for his nemesis, flirted with running himself, fueling visions of a disaster of unimaginable proportions for his party. Eventually Dinkins ceased his threats and endorsed Messinger. Fernando Ferrer, the Bronx borough president, launched a run for the job that went nowhere, and pulled out four months later, weakly claiming that he was withdrawing to spare the Democrats a harmful primary fight.

That left three people: Ruth Messinger, Councilman Sal Albanese, a gadfly with little hope of winning, and Al Sharpton. The field, said Ed Koch, offered "a miserable choice." A bellwether of the city's middle class, he said he'd have no alternative but to vote for Giuliani, a man he likened to a scorpion.

Given the advantages of a growing economy, a safer city, and a confused opposition, Giuliani's journey to reelection in 1997 seemed assured. But things started going wrong.

Increasingly, in the course of this pivotal year, the mayor was playing referee between warring members of his once-united team. The inner circle of the '93 race consisted of David Garth, Peter Powers, Ray Harding, and Rudy

Giuliani, with Donna Hanover Giuliani, Harding loyalist Fran Reiter, and some others playing important roles. Now the old gang was starting to crack up.*

Garth was astonished by the success of Giuliani's first term, and he was tempted to reprise his act as master strategist. "I thought Rudy Giuliani had the best four years I'd ever seen or read about," he says. "He had a knockout campaign just sitting waiting for him. The record was impeccable."

But while the strategist and the mayor he'd elected had never argued, the two were separated by a vast divide. Garth's contempt for Cristyne Lategano was deep and public. "I didn't want to work with her," Garth recalls. "I thought she fed his worst instincts, always telling him 'Don't take that shit.' She called to meet with me, but I wouldn't meet with her. I wanted nothing to do with her."

And Giuliani was wary of Garth. It wasn't just his disdainful treatment of Giuliani's closest adviser. It was his monumental temper, the resignation threats, the brooding refusals to answer the phone. Garth was a genius, perhaps the best political mind in the state, but his volcanic personality was a turnoff, even to his admirers, and his hard-to-get act through 1996 compounded City Hall's wariness. Harding and others were trying to broker a reunion between the mayor and the strategist, but the efforts were going nowhere.

Powers, a rock of stability throughout Giuliani's political career, was expected to reprise his successful role as campaign manager in '97. But he had been making a gradual transition back to the private sector since leaving City Hall, and the prospect of jumping back into the fray wasn't appealing. In early 1997 Powers announced that he had decided not to run the Giuliani campaign after all. The decision threw the nascent reelection effort into disarray with the election year already under way, and it put Powers on a collision course with the woman Giuliani chose as his replacement—Fran Reiter.

The two were charter members of the Giuliani team, deputy mayors who'd worked tirelessly for the candidate in '93 and believed in the causes

---

*Carl Grillo, the widely respected head of the '93 field operation, died in December 1996. Robert Wagner Jr., a close adviser to Giuliani, died shortly before Giuliani took office.

he represented. But their relationship unraveled soon after they took up res-
idence at City Hall. Powers, the soft-spoken voice of moderation in the
administration, was a marked contrast to his outspoken, often abrasive peer.
A native of Manhattan's East Village, Reiter smoked like a chimney and
loved a good, loud argument. He was Catholic, a loyal Republican; she was
Jewish and a Liberal.

Their resentments flowered in the spring of 1996 when Powers lost his
campaign to convince Giuliani to promote Senior Adviser Richard Schwartz
to the deputy mayor's job vacated by John Dyson. When the mayor gave the
job to Reiter (she had been deputy mayor for community affairs), she and
Powers descended into a cold war. Each felt the other held a grudge. "Fran
indicated a coolness after she got it," Powers recalls. "I sensed it was like a
political campaign—you're either with me or against me." By the time Powers left the administration, the two deputy mayors weren't on speaking terms.

Tensions only got worse when the mayor handed Reiter the reins of the
reelection operation in March of '97 and Powers assumed the largely ceremonial job of campaign chairman. Reiter was horrified by the operation she
inherited. Powers had arranged a "totally inadequate" office for the campaign, she says. "He had rented a relatively small space that you could never
run a campaign out of. He had hired only one person, and the phones
weren't in, the computers weren't in—nothing was done."

"For three months," Reiter says, "Peter had done absolutely nothing. I
inherited, three to four months into the election year, a nonexistent campaign organization. And Peter then disappeared."

Powers says he was in constant contact with the mayor and was trying to
"stay out of her hair" to let people know she was in charge. As for the office,
he says he was just saving money in the run-up to the campaign. "This is a
fiction in Fran's mind that she would walk into a campaign that was totally
done," Powers says. "There was plenty of time to do that. It would've been
money that needn't have been spent."

Acknowledging the animosity, Powers asked Reiter to sit down with him
for a détente in the spring of 1997. The two went out for dinner at Fresco, an
opulent midtown Italian restaurant that played host to a daily power scene
for the city's political elite. There the former and current campaign man-

agers set out to clear the air. But before long, the conversation devolved into bad family therapy.

Powers complained that Reiter had snubbed him by not inviting him to her going-away party at Gracie Mansion. "We have to work together," he told her, "and sending a message to me by not inviting me to a party is not an adult way to deal with this." Reiter told him he had nerve: she had hosted him at her country house, an invitation she'd never before extended to a professional colleague, and he not only failed to thank her, but neglected to invite her to his birthday party.

Then the Schwartz matter came up. "How can I ever forgive you for that?" she said. "I thought you were my friend." Powers maintained he was just doing his job. "I owe my loyalty to the mayor, not to you," he said. "I always give him my best advice." By the time dessert menus were handed to them, things had gotten ugly. *"You tried to fuck me on becoming deputy mayor for economic development!"*

Ray Harding had managed to keep a safe distance from the turmoil precisely because he was physically removed from it all. As grand pooh-bah of the Liberal Party, he rarely needed to set foot into City Hall. When Rudy Giuliani needed his considerable sagacity, he would reach him by phone or join him after hours for a late-night strategy session over dinner or at Gracie Mansion.

But Reiter was Harding's protégée, and his lobbying for her over Schwartz had put a strain on his friendship with Powers. Harding had also gotten himself into a huge conflict-of-interest mess. Cashing in on his access to City Hall, he accepted a position at the law firm of Herman Badillo, Giuliani's unsuccessful '93 running mate for comptroller. Harding left his dusty old Liberal Party office behind for gleaming new digs on the seventeenth floor of a Third Avenue office tower, and the newly renamed firm of Fischbein Badillo Wagner Harding plunged into the influence-peddling game. In the years following his arrival in April 1994, its lobbying practice swelled from three clients to sixty, as a swarm of companies seeking help from the Giuliani administration came its way. It all drew relatively little notice until the *New York Times* ran a front-page story about the arrangement in February 1997. Reporter Clifford Levy noted that Harding lobbied, among others, Peter Powers.

Harding maintained that he tried to avoid meeting with officials with whom he had relationships, preferring to meet with their staffs instead. He also argued that, as a lawyer with years of experience dealing with local government, he was entitled to earn a living lobbying City Hall. Giuliani was forced to defend Harding as follow-up stories detailed the work Fischbein Badillo was doing for its clients. One client, represented by Badillo, was a construction company facing the loss of its city contract after a building's roof collapsed, injuring five workers.

The law firm, suffering withering scrutiny from the press, eventually suspended its lobbying business, though it continued to perform similar "legal work" for companies seeking business from the Giuliani administration. The mayor was cornered into proposing an all-out ban on lobbying of city government—which he later discarded as impractical. Harding was an indispensable ally of Giuliani's, but he was now a liability as well, a living emblem of cronyism in a reform administration.

As for Donna Hanover Giuliani, she had long since become a nonentity in the mayor's professional life. A woman who was used to playing a Hillary Clinton–like role in Giuliani's political career, she retreated from public view about the time that *New York* magazine published its cover story about Lategano's growing role in the administration. No longer a political adviser to Giuliani, Donna was barely serving as First Lady anymore, limiting her appearances to an occasional charity event as she went about her film and television news careers. The rumors about Lategano and Giuliani persisted, erupting in episodic waves of feverish gossip that traveled through the phone lines connecting the city's reporters with government aides and one another.

Internally, the rumors were sparking concern among the mayor's advisers. It was the middle of an election year, the worst possible moment for a sex scandal. Giuliani's aides tried to bring up the subject with the mayor.

The task of getting Giuliani to focus on the "Cristyne problem," as it was known in the mayor's wing, fell at one point to the newest member of the mayor's inner circle, Adam Goodman. A media maven from Baltimore, he was David Garth's replacement. Boyish, sweet, and nonthreatening, he was widely liked among the mayor's high command. Sitting in Giuliani's upstairs office at City Hall with a group of aides one afternoon, Goodman took a stab at it.

"The stories—they're out there, about you and Cristyne," he said to the mayor. "Really, we should talk about it."

Giuliani held up his hand and cut Goodman off. "Let's not talk about that," he said.

Goodman persisted. "You have to deal with it," he said, in as gentle a voice as he could muster. "We should talk about how you respond to it. You can't ignore it."

Giuliani said that his relationship with Lategano was nobody's business. That's what he would tell the press. And that was the end of it.

Goodman dropped the subject. It was the way those conversations always went: The mayor flatly refused to discuss the issue with his aides.

The rumors finally exploded into the open on August 4. *Vanity Fair* published a story by writer Jennet Conant entitled "The Ghost and Mr. Giuliani," which slammed the New York media for covering up the story of Giuliani's crumbling marriage and his affair with Lategano. "Even members of the mayor's own staff are questioning the objectivity and independence of the local media, which seems content to sit on the marriage story until it's broken elsewhere," Conant charged. Her proof that Giuliani was sleeping with Lategano came from unnamed former aides who agreed that the two had become "intimate" during a series of overnight and weekend campaign trips to Georgia, Michigan, and Massachusetts.

Two deputy mayors, Randy Levine and Randy Mastro, had worked behind the scenes for months to get the story killed by pressuring executives at Condé Nast, the magazine's parent company. Having failed, the administration went into damage-control mode. Aides produced documents proving that Lategano did not even go on the Michigan trip and that the Massachusetts foray was actually a day trip. But the tabloid press, which for months had been trying fruitlessly to confirm the rumors, seized on the *Vanity Fair* story to release their pent-up frustration. "CITY HALL SOAP," the *Daily News* front page roared. "Mag says Rudy was 'intimate' with top female aide; City Hall blasts allegation as 'pure fiction.'" Even the Giuliani-friendly *Post* couldn't resist. "RUDY MARRIAGE FUROR," its front page screamed. "Aides rip mag over report that Hizzoner, Donna may split."

The saga remained on the front pages most of the week. "ALL IN THE

FAMILY," the *Daily News* shouted the next day. "Donna Hanover says Giulianis will endure as Rudy, Cristyne deny affair."

Lategano, thrust into the center of this growing feeding frenzy, denied that she and the mayor were having an affair. After a New York 1 News reporter announced that editors he'd interviewed at the *News* and the *Post* conceded they had no idea whether the *Vanity Fair* story was true, Lategano pulled the reporter aside at a mayoral press conference the following day. "Thank you," she said sadly.

Giuliani reacted predictably. "I have said all I'm going to say about it, and if you want to in that way delve into people's personal lives and embarrass yourself and show that you have no decency, continue to do it," he said to a reporter at an outdoor press conference a few days after the story broke. "It's like a broken record. It's like a sad, perverse broken record."

Donna, meanwhile, proved intriguingly elusive throughout the furor. The magazine had failed to prove its case that her husband and Lategano were "intimate," but it was clearly onto something in its portrait of a troubled marriage. The city's First Lady issued no statement of support for her husband; there would be no joint photo opportunity to prove their marriage was intact. After wading past mobs of reporters with barely a comment for days on end, she finally consented to brief newspaper interviews in which she refused to say whether she loved her husband or even whether he was a good mayor. "I've said what I mean when I said we're a family, and we're going to stay together," she told the *Daily News*. "My children and I will continue to live at Gracie Mansion with Rudy as a family, after the election, if he wins." And then yet another member of the original Giuliani campaign brain trust went into seclusion. It would not be her last word on the matter.

Two weeks later, Al Sharpton stood at his pulpit in the House of Justice auditorium, peering out upon a half-filled room. Only the die-hards had come out on this lazy August morning to hear the reverend explain why his mayoral campaign had yet to catch fire. Delivered with the fervor of a preacher's sermon, his message was more like the spin of a failing candidate. "I know how to pace a campaign," he told the crowd. "If you peak too early, people will forget by the time you need them to remember. We're getting ready to pump it up now!" The small audience clapped supportively.

Business was slow in the racial outrage industry. Cops continued to harass black kids on the streets of Harlem, and a handful of young blacks and Latinos had died in police incidents since Giuliani took over. But nothing had yet stirred the community to anger on the scale of a Bensonhurst or a Howard Beach. The mayor was scoring a 40 percent approval rating in the *black* community. The essential truth of '97—that life on the streets was calmer, safer, saner—was just as relevant to the poor of Bed-Stuy as to the prosperous of Brooklyn Heights. All three Democratic mayoral candidates were being ridiculed as losers in pursuit of a lost cause.

"They say the polls are against you," Sharpton continued. "The odds were always against me. I wouldn't know how to act if they were going my way." His fans gave him an encouraging cheer. But a tone of desperation punctuated the reverend's speech this summer morning.

Unbeknown to Sharpton, however, an incident that had taken place six hours earlier in the bathroom of a Brooklyn police station house was about to put him back in business.

It was no mere case of police brutality. It was an act of savagery, "a tale straight from the police dungeon," as *Daily News* columnist Mike McAlary would call it. In the early hours of Saturday, August 9, a police officer named Justin Volpe had helped break up a fight outside Club Rendezvous, a Flatbush nightclub popular with Haitian immigrants, and was punched in the head and knocked to the ground in the process. Infuriated, he grabbed a thirty-year-old immigrant named Abner Louima—the wrong man—and arrested him for assault and disorderly conduct. Volpe and some fellow officers placed Louima in a squad car and drove him to a deserted street, where they took turns pummeling him.

When they brought Louima to the 70th Precinct station house to be booked, Volpe was still in a rage. As other cops looked on, he took Louima, who had been strip-searched, into a nearby bathroom, his pants draped around to his ankles. *"Why did you curse at me on the street? Why did you punch me?"* Volpe asked Louima, throwing him against a bathroom wall. Then Volpe punched him in the chest and threw him to the ground.

With Louima facedown on the bathroom floor, Volpe grabbed a piece of wood he'd broken off from a broom handle. He demanded an apology. *"Do you have anything to say?"* Louima mumbled something back. Furious, Volpe took the stick and jammed it up Louima's rectum, sodomizing his captive with his primitive weapon. As a final insult, the cop took the stick and shoved it into Louima's mouth. *"Look what happened!"* Volpe screamed at his victim. *"Look what you made me do!"* He threw the stick down, picked Louima up, and dragged him out of the bathroom, confiding to a fellow cop, "I just broke a man down." Left bleeding in his cell for over an hour, Louima was finally taken by ambulance to Coney Island Hospital, where he was treated for a puncture to the small intestine and injuries to his bladder, outfitted with a colostomy bag, and then handcuffed to a hospital bed.

On Monday morning, Harold Nicolas, Louima's cousin, called almost every television station in the city to alert them to the case. The only person who took him seriously was a young assignment editor named Sean Sullivan working the lobster shift at New York 1 News, who took down the information about Louima's ordeal and passed it along to police reporter Aram Roston.

That night, Mike McAlary received an anonymous tip about the case on his voice mail at the *Daily News*, probably from a cop. On Tuesday, Roston and McAlary separately interviewed Louima at his bedside in the Intensive Care Unit of Coney Island Hospital. Later that evening, Police Commissioner Howard Safir called Giuliani to tell him about the case as the mayor was watching his son's Little League game. Not long afterward, New York 1 broke the Louima story. Sharpton says he spoke throughout the day with McAlary about the case. "I'm going front page in the morning," the columnist allegedly told the reverend that night. "You should get involved with this one. This is not Tawana Brawley."

The Louima story was horrifying, and news of it blew through the city like a hurricane. With anger mounting over the NYPD's harassment of minorities, and brutality complaints climbing at the Civilian Complaint Review Board, police misconduct was becoming the Achilles' heel of Giuliani's mayoralty. His advisers feared the case could prove devastating to his reelection effort. The mayor's first reaction was deft. Breaking with his practice of granting the benefit of the doubt to cops, he condemned the alleged incident as "reprehensible" and paid a highly unusual visit to Louima at his hospital bed, accompanied by Police Commissioner Howard Safir.

Watching the developments from his perch at Fischbein Badillo, Ray Harding was worried. Safir said his department was investigating "management failures" at the precinct, but that wouldn't be enough to staunch the political hemorrhaging that could ensue. What about Volpe's co-conspirators? What about the cops who saw Louima being marched into the bathroom naked, or who heard his screams coming from the bathroom? Why didn't anyone at the precinct house report this to the department? What about the commanders who allowed this to take place?

Sitting at his desk with his sleeves rolled up and his tie undone, Harding dialed up Denny Young at City Hall. The mayor's soft-spoken counsel was Giuliani's liaison with the NYPD. He was also the man who usually ferried the most urgent and confidential information to the mayor.

"This is outrageous," Harding told Young. "The mayor has to get ahead of the curve on this."

Young, as nonthreatening a figure as Giuliani had in his inner circle, listened attentively.

"If you talk to Rudy," Harding continued, one long syllable at a time, "I have no doubt that he'll recognize that what the police department is doing doesn't rise to the level of what this situation is all about."

Young promised to convey the message to Giuliani. Safir had to move decisively.

Whether in response to Harding's advice or to the increasing fury of the public's reaction, Safir ratcheted up his response. At a news conference televised live, he and the mayor announced a full-scale shake-up of the 70th Precinct. The precinct commander was removed from his post, and his second-in-command was transferred; a desk sergeant was suspended; ten officers were placed on desk duty. "They are responsible for the activities in that precinct," Safir said. Giuliani pledged to fire any police officer who refused to come forth with information about the guilty officers.

Their words came as Louima, speaking to TV reporters from his hospital bed, confirmed a reported quote from Volpe as he was assaulting him. "He said, 'Stupid nigger . . . know how to respect cops,' " Louima recalled. He said Volpe then told him, "This is Giuliani time. It is not Dinkins time."

It was an extraordinary line, a searing metaphor that seemed to make Giuliani as culpable for the atrocity as Volpe. As it turned out, it was also a lie. Five months later, Louima admitted that he'd made up the quote. For the duration of the mayor's race, however, Giuliani was implicated in the incident by the victim himself.

The Louima tragedy was the greatest threat to Giuliani's mayoralty since he'd taken office. He went into full battle mode. After shaking up the precinct, he formulated another damage-control measure, forming a commission on police-community relations. With great fanfare he named some of his biggest critics to the panel. For a few days, the surreal became the norm at City Hall: Giuliani swung the doors of the mayor's office open to the people he most reviled. The man at the center of the Control Machine even ceded the spotlight of a mayoral news conference to commission member Norman Siegel of the New York Civil Liberties Union. As the mayor stood by, Siegel proceeded to trash Giuliani's record on police brutality. "If this task force is about public relations and it's meaningless, the Civil Liberties Union will quit," Siegel said, standing a foot from the mayor. But it was worth the pain to Giuliani, because Siegel had agreed to become part of the solution instead of a critic.

While the mayor did his best to protect himself from the Louima fallout, he had little to fear from the political opposition. Ruth Messinger's campaign strategist, Jim Andrews, wanted to keep his candidate as far away from the Louima story as possible. On the face of it, the incident seemed like a golden opportunity. But Andrews felt that to be seen as soft on crime or anti-cop in Rudy Giuliani's New York, where people were cherishing their newly found safety, would be disastrous, especially for a candidate who'd been fighting the perception that she was an old-fashioned liberal. So despite the storm over Louima's torture, Messinger traveled to the Upper East Side and held a press conference about domestic violence. Predictably, only her response to a reporter's question about Louima made it to the evening news: "I see this case right now as a single, isolated, horrible, terrifying story," she said. Two days later, appearing on CNN's *Inside Politics*, Messinger went further and completely endorsed Giuliani's response to the crisis. "I think what the mayor has done in the last few days is right on target," she said.

But the seductive powers of the "Giuliani time" quotation ultimately proved too great for Messinger. Eleven days after the Louima story became public, the borough president rose to the podium at the Evangelical Crusade Church in East Flatbush on a Sunday afternoon and let loose.

"Giuliani time is a time when it's out of fashion to care about the poor and homeless," she said. "Unemployment is at depression levels in some boroughs and neighborhoods. It's Giuliani time. Some ninety thousand children will be forced to go to school in closets and stairwells and locker rooms and bathrooms. It's Giuliani time. And what did they chant when they beat and brutalized Abner Louima? 'It's Giuliani time.' Why did they chant his name? Why? Because Giuliani time is a time of cold shoulders and hard hearts."

It was the most spirited speech of Messinger's oddly subdued campaign, an arrow piercing to the heart of Giuliani's policies. But it was suicidal. Journalists pointed out the bizarre inconsistency of her responses to the tragedy. Messinger says she came to feel more strongly about the matter after meeting with Louima and members of the Haitian community. Yet Giuliani criticized her remarks as representing "pandering of the worst kind, almost at the verge of really severe irresponsibility." Even Sharpton piled on, agreeing with Giuliani that she was pandering. "When the case first happened, Messinger had nothing to say about the case for two or three days," he said. "Now that she sees this is a sustained issue, she's trying to act as if she never supported the mayor in the first place." Messinger's campaign, already devoid of a coherent message, became an object of derision.

Sharpton, finessing the politics of the Louima case far more capably than his mainstream competitor, spoke at marches and demonstrations held in the wake of the assault and seemed reinvigorated by the passions it incited. When Primary Day finally rolled around, he handed a devastating humiliation to Messinger, winning a surprising 32 percent of the vote and depriving her of the votes needed to avoid a runoff election. Eight days later the Board of Elections reversed itself after a recount and announced that Messinger had actually scraped by the runoff threshold by 658 votes. Sharpton agreed to endorse

Messinger—after one of his aides reportedly tried and failed to shake the Messinger campaign down for a six-figure contribution to his National Action Network.* Messinger had her nomination, but the episode only contributed to the air of comedy surrounding the Democrats as the fall election began.

Giuliani had worked long and hard to arm himself for the '97 battle. He was on his way toward raising $10 million (compared with Messinger's $3.75 million) by schmoozing the realtors, developers, lobbyists, bankers, and corporate executives who made up New York's permanent government. As a piece of his reformer's mantle frayed, he chatted up men named Trump, Rockefeller, Rudin, Speyer—an endless stream of fat cats and the people who worked for them, all of whom required access to City Hall. The mayor insisted they got no favorable treatment from his administration, even as his minions quietly squeezed businessmen doing business with the city.

The mayor was willing to go to extremes to win this race, even if it meant forging an alliance with Al D'Amato, the man he held in greater contempt than just about anyone. Two years after Giuliani waged war on the senator and his hand-picked candidate for governor, he appeared with the senator before hundreds of Republicans at a D'Amato fund-raiser. The mayor hugged D'Amato and held his hand as D'Amato chanted, "Rudy! Rudy! Rudy!" George Pataki, who loathed the mayor, played his part by introducing him as "the great mayor, Rudy Giuliani." All the members of D'Amato's gang—State Republican Party Chair Bill Powers, Conservative Party Chair Mike Long, even Trent Lott, majority leader of the United States Senate—smiled as Giuliani and the senator sealed this devil's pact. "Since Al D'Amato has been in the Senate," Giuliani announced, "New York has not had a stronger advocate fighting for the city." Members of the crowd shook their heads and made cynical jokes to one another.

The mayor also took a new interest in schoolchildren in '97. His pollster, Frank Luntz, had determined that education was the mayor's biggest problem.

---

*The assertion is made by the Messinger campaign's chief researcher, Evan Mandery, in his book *The Campaign*. Messinger denies knowledge of the call, as does Sharpton.

Having slashed Ray Cortines's budget requests by billions of dollars before hounding him out of town, Giuliani was clearly vulnerable on the issue. With Messinger making the schools the centerpiece of her campaign, Giuliani made maximum use of his alliance with the new chancellor, Rudy Crew.

In his State of the City speech in January, Giuliani bestowed an embarrassment of riches upon Crew. There was Project Read, a $125 million program aimed at increasing literacy in schools and housing projects across the city. Then he announced that he was restoring $75 million in funding for arts education. The mayor's campaign to destroy the bureaucracy of the school system took a backseat for the campaign season.

Giuliani developed an intense new interest in visiting schools and reading to young children. Over and over again he trooped to public schools around the city, with the press corps in tow, opened up children's books, and read aloud to his new friends. *"Everyone got on a school bus. They rode and rode. At last they stopped at a white house."* The photo ops inside school classrooms became so routine that the mayor commissioned a book to be written especially for the events. Entitled *What Will You Be?* its main characters were the mayor and his dog, Goalie.

Crew couldn't cooperate enough. He joined Giuliani on a handful of sojourns to city classrooms and read aloud with him side by side, a popular African American schools chief bestowing his blessings on a mayor up for reelection. Crew's office, meanwhile, was barring Messinger from entering school buildings, claiming that political events were not permitted inside public schools. The Democratic candidate was forced to hold her press conferences on the streets outside, while the mayor was granted the run of any school he wanted.

Giuliani had defused the Louima crisis by making unorthodox gestures across wide boundaries, and he was reaching out for campaign support in the same fashion. The previous October, Howard Koeppel and a small group of gay men with connections to City Hall convinced Giuliani to accept an invitation to the annual fund-raising dinner for the Empire State Pride Agenda, the state's most influential gay lobbying group. It would be by far the largest group of gays and lesbians the mayor had ever addressed.

The group itself had been seriously split over whether to extend the invitation: a board member resigned in protest at a special meeting on the issue, and the group's cochair, Jeff Soref, was warned by activists that his apartment building would be picketed.

The gay community was a reliable constituency for the Democratic Party and had been a critical component of David Dinkins's Gorgeous Mosaic. But the rules in New York City were changing. The 1,100 well-dressed men and women in the Grand Ballroom of the hotel on this night were affluent, successful, and appreciative of the city's rebound. Like a lot of other New Yorkers, they had qualms about handing the city over to Messinger. While the activist wing of the gay movement loathed Giuliani, the yuppies were open to persuasion.

For a Republican, Giuliani was progressive on gay issues. He favored hate crimes legislation and supported domestic partnership benefits for gay and lesbian couples, though he opposed gay marriage. Koeppel was touched when the mayor told him that if he ever changed his mind on the marriage issue, he'd perform the wedding ceremony for Howard and Mark first—at Gracie Mansion.

Going into the fund-raiser, Giuliani was apprehensive. Several advisers had tried to talk him out of attending, fearing he'd be heckled. Sitting in a private room at the Grand Hyatt, he seemed nervous. "You know, Howard, I'm tired of getting booed, and I'm not looking forward to this," he said, his knee bobbing up and down as he spoke. Koeppel put his hand on the jittery knee. "Could we stop the motor for a minute?" Koeppel said. "I could just imagine the press if you didn't go. Everybody is expecting you. You're not just the speaker, you're the mayor of these people. These people are your constituents."

"I'm just tired of getting booed," Giuliani said. "If I get up there and they start booing me, I'm going to leave."

Giuliani did not like venturing into unfriendly territory. Koeppel held his breath as the mayor made his entrance.

The audience seemed almost stunned when Giuliani walked in, as if he were a figure from another world. Yet the very fact of his arrival caused a sudden eruption of gratitude. The audience jumped up and roared with approval, bathing the mayor in a sustained standing ovation. Giuliani stood at the podium in a state of shock—"like a deer caught in the headlights," Soref recalls. He had come prepared for a hostile reaction and had written his speech accordingly. And he delivered it, a broad call for people to respect the viewpoints of those who disagree. Ethan Geto, a public relations executive and gay activist, had written Giuliani a list of talking points highlighting his accomplishments on gay issues, but the mayor largely ignored it.

Ten minutes into his delivery, he was heckled by three audience members, who challenged him on AIDS education and gay marriage. "I wouldn't hiss you, I wouldn't boo you if I disagreed with you," Giuliani responded. Then he continued, ticking off his administration's accomplishments combating crime. While the crowd was on his side and the hecklers were vastly outnumbered, Giuliani's supporters felt he missed an opportunity by taking such a defensive posture.

When it came time for the Pride Agenda to make an endorsement in the mayor's race in '97, the group was once again torn. Ruth Messinger had a spotless record on gay issues. She had played the game of identity politics for years, backing everything from gay marriage to gay adoption; she had boycotted the St. Patrick's Day Parade after organizers banned a gay Irish group from marching, and supported a public school curriculum teaching tolerance of gays and lesbians. She expected the community's support in return. Giuliani, on the other hand, wasn't nearly as close to the community, whose leaders were mostly Democrats. He had taunted Ray Cortines with vaguely homophobic epithets and run him out of town. He had defended a supporter, the Reverend Ruben Diaz, on religious grounds when Diaz loudly warned that the Gay Games, an Olympics-style event, would spread AIDS. He marched in the St. Patrick's Day Parade and opposed the multicultural curriculum. He supported a handful of gay rights but opposed others.

In the end the group voted to stay neutral in the mayor's race. Giuliani was the favorite to win, and the group wanted to build bridges to moderate Republicans. Besides, the economy was coming back, crime was down, and many gays and lesbians felt he'd done a good job as mayor.

"He was an incumbent, and he was willing to meet with us and explore some issues," says a board member. As for Messinger, "Everyone was dissatisfied by the kind of campaign she was running." It was an embarrassing rebuke to the Democrat, and it undermined her ability to raise cash and support in the community. Messinger had unquestionably been an old and loyal friend to gays and lesbians. But the rules had changed.

The friendly greeting at the Pride Agenda dinner was a harbinger of things to come. On September 11, the day after the Democratic primary, Giuliani walked out of City Hall and down the tree-lined path to the fountain at the other end of City Hall Park. The Democratic borough president of Queens, Claire Shulman, walked by his side, arm in arm with Charlie Hughes, the African American leader of the school cafeteria workers' union. The mayor took the podium in front of dozens of local Democrats who were deserting Messinger. There was Priscilla Wooten, a black councilwoman from Brooklyn; Nettie Mayersohn, a white Catholic assemblywoman from Queens; Nathan Leventhal, the Jewish president of Lincoln Center and a deputy mayor under Koch. A cloth sign towering above them read "Democrats for Giuliani."

The mayor's handlers distributed copies of his new campaign commercial, starring Shulman, a well-known Democratic politician. "Great things are happening," she said, describing falling crime and growing employment. "Even the Mets are doing a little better since he became mayor."

The dominoes were just beginning to fall. The next day Giuliani stood outside the front doors of City Hall with Stanley Hill, the executive director of the largest union of city workers, the 120,000-member District Council 37. A middle-aged African American with weary eyes and a bush of gray hair, Hill cited the five-year contract signed in 1996, which froze salaries for two years, and praised Giuliani for honoring its no-layoff pledge. And then Hill did what no man in his job had ever done and endorsed a Republican for mayor of New York City. "This mayor gave us a no-layoff pledge, and he has kept that pledge," Hill said, shaking Giuliani's hand in gratitude. And then he walked down the steps, looked into the camera of a Giuliani campaign film crew, and made a commercial for the mayor's campaign.

Two weeks later, Giuliani brought two black Democratic congressmen to the City Hall rotunda. There, before the New York City press corps, he accepted the endorsements of the Reverend Floyd Flake, one of the best-known and most respected politicians in New York, and Edolphus Towns, a relatively obscure Brooklyn congressman. "It would be unfortunate if New York City returned to the era of drive-by shootings, children unable to play in playgrounds because of rampant crime, and young men and women involved in illegal drug dealing found dead in alleys," Flake said. Later he told reporters he sided with the mayor because Giuliani was likely to win.

The fruits of a lot of behind-the-scenes romancing were blossoming. Deputy Mayor Randy Mastro had been building relationships with a handful of black Democrats around the city who were not in the Dinkins-Rangel orbit, meeting them at diners or calling to say hello while other black leaders were denouncing Giuliani on television. Deputy Mayor Randy Levine, Giuliani's smooth-talking chief labor negotiator, had done the same with the union leaders. But it was the probability of Giuliani's reelection and the knowledge that he rewarded his friends and punished his enemies that were leading so many erstwhile critics to his door. The Democratic firmament was cracking under the weight of Giuliani's steamroller.

The mayor's strategy was to attack Messinger relentlessly as a member of the far left and capitalize on people's fears of returning the city to the pre-Giuliani era. Messinger was struggling daily to convince voters she was a moderate. She even turned on the labor movement, calling for unions to make productivity concessions and for government to privatize some services. But Giuliani wasn't going to let her get away with it. He was on a crusade to discredit New York–style liberalism altogether and intent on gluing Messinger to an old and failed ideology.

Speaking to the press, the mayor portrayed his Democratic opponent as an ideological twin of Al Sharpton's. "They're identical," he said. "It depends on the order in which you place their names: Sharpton-Messinger, Messinger-Sharpton. This is essentially the same set of viewpoints, and the question is, do you want to take this city and put it in their hands?"

His campaign commercials went further. Giuliani researchers uncovered two pieces of evidence that Messinger, her protestations notwithstanding, was a member of the lunatic left. One was a *New York Times* clipping about a party thrown at her Upper West Side brownstone in 1979 in honor of an inmate convicted in the killing of a guard in the Attica prison uprising. The article said that the party, for inmate John Hill, was held to celebrate Governor Hugh Carey's commutation of Hill's sentence. It all evoked images of "radical chic" parties in the sixties, at which affluent white New York liberals lavished money upon leftist groups like the Black Panthers. Messinger said she couldn't remember the party, while two lawyers who attended it said that Messinger lent her apartment for the affair but was not present.

The other reputed smoking gun was a 1995 letter that Messinger sent to the City Planning Commission opposing Giuliani's zoning plan to curtail the number of sex shops in New York. The letter pointed out that sex shops had "invigorated" the quality of life in gay neighborhoods like the West Village and were "an important part of our city's economic and tourism-industry base." In the letter she extolled her own less restrictive plan to limit sex shops.

"Messinger: Sex businesses give New York character," ran the words of a Giuliani commercial, distorting the Democrat's view. Giuliani made a speech about it: "You think it lends character to the city," he said. "I think it destroys the character of the city."* In one fell swoop he was warning of a rollback of his quality-of-life campaign and denigrating Messinger as a liberal extremist.

Messinger also tried her hand at attack ads but floundered. One commercial criticized Giuliani for education cutbacks that had forced teachers to hold classes in school bathrooms. The video was a staged shot of child actors huddled together around bathroom urinals. Rudy Crew, coming to Giuliani's aid yet again, flew into a fury over the ad, denouncing it as grossly misleading. In truth, some classes were being held in bathrooms in New York's public schools, but Messinger found herself suddenly fighting Crew, one of the most popular public figures in the city. The media played up the controversy over the exaggerations in the staged ad, overlooking its basic

*Giuliani based the "lends character" comment charge on a television anchorwoman's summary of a story about Messinger's letter. Neither the borough president nor the reporter used that phrase.

truth. Messinger's campaign team came off yet again as The Gang That Couldn't Shoot Straight.

The Giuliani camp was turning out quality work. The research into Messinger's past had paid off. The wave of endorsements for the mayor was undermining Democratic Party unity. Adam Goodman's attack ads were effective, as were his positive commericals romantizing the rebirth of city neighborhoods under Giuliani's reign. Cristyne Lategano was calling the shots from City Hall, reviewing Goodman's scripts before they got passed on to the mayor. The communications chief, always mindful of the boss's image, urged Goodman to cast the mayor in a Reagan-esque light. "I want 'Morning in America,'" she told him. "Think 'Morning in Bay Ridge.' " The adman, well aware of who wielded the power in Giuliani's orbit, always made sure to keep Lategano happy.

It was especially impressive that Team Giuliani was producing such good work considering that its members were fighting a civil war.

Fran Reiter, running things uptown at Giuliani campaign HQ, was grow-ing increasingly resentful at the lack of cooperation she was getting from the boys downtown at City Hall. The happy crew of the '93 race had all gone on to cushy City Hall jobs, and few were returning on their off-hours to help her. Reiter was training a new team, largely made up of inexperienced kids and volunteers. Peter Powers, she claims, was MIA, while Deputy Mayor Rudy Washington was useless. "Talk about absent without leave during the campaign!" she says of Washington. "Nothing we asked him to do he did. Nothing."

He wasn't the only one, she asserts. "Randy Levine played golf every week-end for the campaign," Reiter recalls. Deputy Mayor Ninfa Segarra? "That's like, don't bother," she says. The only one to help, Reiter says, was Randy Mastro. He was a busy man: Aside from supervising government operations, he was fighting a quiet though bitter war against Levine. Both were protégés of Giuliani, former prosecutors who competed for his affections. Both spent considerable energy thwarting the other's rise to the job of first deputy mayor.

But one thing seemed to unify the folks downtown: utter contempt for

Fran Reiter. Her bombastic personality was alienating her from much of Giuliani's inner circle. With the exception of Ray Harding, her mentor, only Mastro and Cristyne Lategano had a kind word to say about her.

It was an incumbent's campaign this time around, not an insurgent's; everyone but Reiter had assumed that the reelection campaign would be run out of City Hall. Moreover, Reiter was on television nearly every night, seemingly concerned with her own image as much as Giuliani's.

The tension between Reiter and the others finally erupted into the open at a fall meeting of the high command, held at campaign HQ. Predictably, the fight was between Reiter and Peter Powers.

With Giuliani presiding, Powers voiced concern that Reiter had not put together an effective field operation, a worry that others in the high command had whispered about. Giuliani supporters needed to be convinced to go to the polls on Election Day, bused to polling places if necessary. "What's our plan if voter turnout is low?" Powers asked her across the table. Reiter gave him her assurance that she had a detailed strategy.

"What's the plan?" he persisted. The two went back and forth a few rounds, until Reiter exploded. *"I'm running the goddamn campaign, and I've got a plan!"* she shouted.

"Excuse me for asking," Powers shot back. "I'm sorry, I don't think you have a plan."

Giuliani had to break it up. "Let's step back," the mayor said. "The question is whether we have a plan." He turned to Deputy Chief of Staff Tony Carbonetti and asked him to join Reiter's operation in the last three weeks of the campaign and help her with the field operation. Carbonetti was a protégé of Carl Grillo's, the widely respected field coordinator in '93 who had died in 1996. He was a natural replacement for Grillo, but Giuliani had been reluctant to lose him to the campaign. Now there was no choice.

Things deteriorated in the days that followed. Reiter refused to give Carbonetti office space at campaign headquarters. He, Rudy Washington, and others would have to find room to work in another office, she told them. "These guys march in, and I've got this young crew who've busted their butts sitting there looking at these people that they have never seen for six

months march in and try to tell them that they were doing a lousy job,"
Reiter recalls. "I was furious."

The dispute made its way back to Giuliani, who was livid. He got Reiter
on the phone and ordered her to find space for his lieutenants. "I'm sending
them back there," he said. "And you better fucking throw people out of their
offices to make room for them if you have to!"

The mayor slammed down the phone and shook his head. "Do you fucking believe this?" he asked an aide. "She just doesn't listen." Then he called
Ray Harding to complain about it.

The pressure on the campaign to pump up the vote didn't exist just
because Giuliani wanted to guarantee a win. He and his advisers wanted a
big win. Term limits dictated that his second term would be his last. Some
of his aides harbored national aspirations for the mayor; some thought he
could run for president in 2000 on the strength of his record in New York.
But he'd have to win reelection by a landslide to impress the party bosses in
Washington.

Rudy Washington fretted about the vote-pulling operation and thought
Reiter was bungling the campaign. He expressed his fears to the mayor and
received a jolting response. "Put together a plan to take over the campaign,"
Giuliani told Washington.

The deputy mayor took the instructions to heart. Focusing on the field
operation, he held meetings with commissioners and others familiar with
different areas of the city and mapped out a thirty-page memo detailing
which districts needed vote-pulling help along with the names of people
who could work those areas.

A few days later, Randy Levine called Washington and told him the
mayor wanted him to present his plan that evening on the front porch at
Gracie Mansion. Fran Reiter would be there.

It was a Friday night. Except for Ray Harding, the entire high command was
in attendance, chatting and sipping wine. Washington showed up with a large
box, from which he distributed copies of his plan. Apparently only the mayor,
Levine, and Washington knew what was about to unfold. "Rudy, you have
some ideas for the campaign?" Giuliani said to Washington. It was his cue.

"This is a plan to pull out the vote," Washington announced.

Reiter was blindsided. "What is this?" she asked, infuriated.

"Calm down, Fran," Giuliani said. "Let Rudy talk."

As smirks bloomed across the porch, Washington made his presentation. Randy Mastro was trying to contain Reiter, who was fuming in her seat. When Washington finished, Giuliani thought for a moment. "That's interesting," the mayor said. The words hung in the air.

"I'll take my leave now," Washington said. And then he left.

Washington wasn't given control over the campaign, and Reiter wasn't booted from it. But Giuliani had deliberately sent her a message that he wanted the field operation bolstered, and he'd taken her down a peg in the process.

Reiter remained defiant. "We were about to win a huge victory—there was no question," she says. "There was no way that Peter, Randy, and Rudy Washington were going to try now at the eleventh hour to wrest control of this so that they could all be heroes on election night."

The bottom line, she says, is that she won and they lost. "They tried their coup, it didn't work, and they sort of disappeared," Reiter says. "Mostly they failed because they are grossly incompetent. You can quote me on that."

The mayor did win a big victory over Ruth Messinger on election night, beating her by 16 points amid the lowest turnout in decades, even winning the Upper West Side. He barely won Manhattan, and he lost the Bronx. But he won 20 percent of the black vote, 43 percent of the Latino vote, and perhaps as many gay votes, which was impressive for a Republican. The left was vanquished.

The turmoil within his campaign was a problem but not a fatal one. In the end the two people who mattered most in the Giuliani administration— Rudy Giuliani and Cristyne Lategano—called the shots. Ray Harding, Fran Reiter, Adam Goodman, the two Randys—they were a constellation hovering around the mayor. He focused on one or the other as he needed them, sometimes playing one off against another if he felt it in his interest. Much of the feuding was stoked by him.

The most surprising thing to emerge on Election Day was a comment that Giuliani made in his victory speech at the New York Hilton's Grand Ballroom. Bathed in applause and the warmth of a hundred politicians, advisers, and union leaders surrounding him—everyone but his wife—the mayor lowered his voice and apologized to New Yorkers who felt left out during his first four years.

"We have to do a better job to include all of you," he said to the packed ballroom. "We have to reach out to all of you. If we haven't, I apologize. I'm sorry. It's my personal commitment we will try endlessly and tirelessly."

They were the words that Giuliani had refused to utter in four years at City Hall, the kind of words that can heal old wounds. They were words he routinely spurned because they indicated weakness, and it took an emotional high point like his reelection to make him comfortable enough to say them out loud. New Yorkers had to wonder whether they'd ever hear them again.

12

Demon

The most disastrous year and a half of Rudy Giuliani's mayoralty began with a vision. When he stepped in front of City Hall on the first day of 1998 to take the oath of office for his second term, Cristyne Lategano wanted the public to see more than just a mayor. Thanks to term limits, this was the start of his last term at City Hall. The communications chief wanted America to think of him as a president.

Lategano ordered up a special backdrop for the occasion: an American flag so huge that it reached virtually from one end of City Hall to the other. Giuliani's other aides were appalled: "If you put a flag that size behind Rudy it'll make him look like Patton," one adviser complained. But it was a losing battle. "Don't argue," another aide told him. "She's convinced him to do it."

Sure enough, when Giuliani stepped forward and raised his right hand on January 1, a frigid Thursday morning, his background was a blanket of stars and stripes.

It wasn't just the mayor's communications chief who had big plans for him. An outbreak of presidential fever had overtaken the Giuliani camp. Invitations to hit the presidential trail were pouring in from Republican state chairmen around the country since his landslide victory over Ruth

Messinger, and he was preparing to hit the road to gauge interest in a presidential run. In California, a Field poll of Republican voters ranked New York's mayor ahead of John McCain, William Bennett, Lamar Alexander, and Pat Buchanan. "Someday I will see him sworn in as president," his mother, Helen, vowed on inauguration morning. Outside of the festivities, a vendor hawked "Rudy for President" buttons.

It was a heady time at City Hall. A Quinnipiac College poll would soon confirm that Giuliani was outrageously popular in New York City, with a 74 percent approval rating. Even a majority of black New Yorkers were happy with him: 57 percent liked the way he was handling his job. He and his aides had been celebrating since election night. He guest-hosted *Saturday Night Live* — and appeared in drag (as he'd famously done the year before at the annual Inner Circle Dinner). On New Year's Eve, he invited aides and supporters to a 12:30 A.M. private screening of *The Godfather*, his favorite movie.

When he rose to deliver his inaugural speech, he struck a tone of triumph.

"Four years ago, when I stood here and said New York City is the capital of the world, there was doubt. There was fear. There was a feeling that New York City's best days were behind us.

"I didn't accept that. Many of you didn't accept it either. And over the last few years, in an exercise of human will and determination, you and I together have changed the direction of the city more than in any four-year period in history."

The frostbite temperatures were causing anguish in the audience, but Giuliani again gave his speech without a coat, as if to belie any hint of weakness.

In one respect the mayor could have benefited from a closer race in '97. Messinger had frequently complained, without effect, that the incumbent had put forth no agenda for a second term. As Giuliani delivered his speech it became apparent that she was right. His boldest idea was to spend $64 million to hire more cops. "The NYPD will reach 40,000 officers and be at its greatest strength in its history," he pledged.

As the beginning weeks of his second term unfolded, it was clear he had perhaps one or two big battles on his mind. In his State of the City speech, he proposed a radical reform of the City University system, calling for an end to its decades-long policy of admitting anyone who applied. The once-prestigious university was a "disaster," he said.

The mayor assured the hundreds gathered inside the City Council chamber that he had plenty of energy left as he began his second administration. "If you think that I've run out of enthusiasm for the job because I'm a lame duck, watch out!" he said. "This is my chance to do all of the things that I was too timid and restrained to do in the first administration." The line got a big laugh.

But in truth, Giuliani was casting about for new ideas. His election night promise to reach out to alienated constituencies may or may not have been sincere, but it produced no new programs, initiatives, or rhetoric. The minority community was chafing under repressive police tactics, but Giuliani and his police commissioner, Howard Safir, chose to ratchet *up* the pressure, nearly tripling the size of the NYPD's Street Crime Unit, whose members spent their nights in high-crime neighborhoods frisking young men for guns. These days they were seizing almost half the illegal guns confiscated by the entire department.

Those two decisions—to further militarize the streets of minority communities while eschewing efforts to improve relations with the people who lived there—drew few headlines. But they would prove calamitous.

As he searched for a new cause to champion at the start of his second term, Giuliani came upon an article in the Manhattan Institute publication *City Journal*. It proposed that he launch a second phase in his quality-of-life campaign, based around the concept of restoring civility to New York. The author was Jonathan Foreman, a young Englishman who had been revolted by the anarchy he'd witnessed on the streets of India during a recent stay. Freshly committed to the cause of civic order, Foreman proposed that New York City impose strict law enforcement on reckless motorists, irresponsible taxi drivers, dangerous bikers, and owners of screeching car alarms. "As much as graffiti or squeegee men, they send the message that no one is in charge," he wrote of the annoying alarms. He named his essay "Toward a More Civil City."

Soon after its publication, Foreman received a surprise call from the mayor's office inviting him to a speech Giuliani was set to deliver at Lincoln Center on Ash Wednesday. Its title was "Creating a More Civil City."

Giuliani had evidently been to church that morning and showed up with a giant cross smeared on his expansive forehead. He walked to the podium and looked out upon 150 invited friends and supporters.

"If we don't act in a civil manner here, we can't thrive as individuals or as the capital of the world," he said.

"Just like everyone contributes to the chaos, everyone can contribute to the order and safety that we bring about. When we further the quality of life and advance the city of New York as a more civilized city, we reinforce the notion that all of our actions affect each other."

The police, he said, would forthwith begin a crackdown on speeding drivers, litterbugs, reckless taxi drivers, and dangerous bicycle riders. Furthermore, in accordance with Foreman's recommendations, he announced that his administration would discipline city employees who acted discourteously to members of the public. Conversely, members of the *public* would be expected to treat city employees with civility. He also adopted Foreman's call for the public schools to start teaching civil behavior to their students.

Many of the proposals were sound. There wasn't a New Yorker alive who hadn't been awakened in the middle of the night by the jarring blare of a car alarm. And no one could deny that New Yorkers, as a rule, drove like maniacs. But the mayor's emphasis on civility as the overarching theme of his proposals triggered a wave of derision. With his crucifix boldly stamped above his eyes, Giuliani could have been Saint Augustine describing the City of God to a town of pagans. Why would a man so practiced in the art of the insult choose to lecture New Yorkers about the value of civility?

The press was merciless. "BE POLITE OR ELSE, GIULIANI WARNS IN ANNOUNCING CIVILITY CAMPAIGN," read the *New York Times* front page. Few could resist mocking a civility campaign led by a man who once appeared on the David Letterman show to promote the slogan "New York City: We Can Kick Your City's Ass."

The months that followed were dominated by one bizarre battle after another as Giuliani sought to implement his vision of a more civil society. Having conquered murder, robbery, and even car thefts, he worked his way down the food chain of maladies—until he arrived at jaywalking.

New Yorkers considered it an inalienable right to traverse the city's road-ways at whim and took pride in the disorderly spirit of the city's streets. This was Manhattan, not Cincinnati. But Giuliani felt citizens were endangering their safety and that of others by crossing streets in defiance of traffic lights. "In most cities, this is not a big issue," he said. "In most cities, there is a bet-ter understanding of respect of the rights of other people." Amid a loud and almost unanimous chorus of ridicule, Giuliani ordered police to hand out jaywalking tickets to bewildered citizens.

To some it seemed that the mayor was trying to squash the city's anarchic spirit. But that was just the beginning. He released new proposals to curtail reckless behavior by the city's taxi drivers, triggering a wave of resistance. On May 13, 1998, almost all the city's cabdrivers staged a one-day strike, a remarkable feat for a nonunionized industry. The streets of Manhattan fell eerily silent. It was if someone had dropped a neutron bomb on the city.

Giuliani was primed for the fight. "If they would like to stay home forever, they can stay home forever as far as I'm concerned," he said at a City Hall press conference. "The city will function very well without them." In the days that followed, he raised the stakes, warning the drivers to abandon a plan to demonstrate against the proposed rules by driving en masse into the city. "If they disobey an order of the police, they'll be arrested," he announced. "If they want to proceed to close down the city of New York, we'll take their medallions away from them. If they think I'm kidding, give us a try." Most of the drivers backed down. But polls showed that the public increasingly sympathized with the cabbies because the man at City Hall seemed to be bullying this group of largely low-paid immigrants. Giuliani had accomplished the impossible: he had turned a class of workers famous around the world for their rudeness into sympathetic figures.

Giuliani also took aim at the city's food vendors and street artists, who glutted some of the busiest areas of midtown selling their wares. He met sim-ilar resistance: some eight hundred vendors abandoned their hot dog stands and coffee carts for a day to stage a demonstration near City Hall, provoking a wave of anger among citizens who depended upon them for their morning and noontime meals.

The mayor seemed to be looking for fights in all the wrong places, and the response from the public was quizzical. Were rude taxi drivers and pro-

liferating hot dog vendors the biggest problems facing the city? He was battling the very things that made New York the maddeningly chaotic town it
was. And that may have been the idea. From the standpoint of a politician
traveling around the country seeking support for a presidential run, this was
an effective way for Giuliani to distance himself from the things other Americans hated about New York.

A cloud of megalomania began to waft over Giuliani's second term. Soon
after his reelection, *New York* magazine launched an advertising campaign
ribbing Giuliani's ego. Bus ads boasted that the magazine was "Possibly the
Only Good Thing in New York Rudy Hasn't Taken Credit For." Giuliani didn't
laugh it off. Instead he pressured the Metropolitan Transportation Authority
to rip the ads down. The matter ended up in court, with an inevitable First
Amendment victory for the magazine and the equally inevitable wave of
sympathetic press for it.

Administration lawyers were constantly fending off lawsuits charging Giuliani with exercising dictatorial control. His continuing refusal to release
information to the media triggered a battle with the *Daily News*, which won
a court order forcing him to hand over memos of internal inquiries into
malfeasance at city agencies. After he unilaterally banned press conferences
from the steps of City Hall, citing security threats, a judge forced him to
rescind the rule. He yanked a multimillion-dollar contract from an AIDS
advocacy group that criticized his administration—until a judge ordered it
restored.

His growing arrogance reached a peak on March 26, when his twenty-
eight-member Task Force on Police-Community Relations, formed in the
heat of the Abner Louima crisis, released its findings. Its members—clergymen, journalists, political opponents—had worked for seven months to
weave together ideas for easing tensions between the police force and the
minority community. After $15 million and hundreds of hours spent in
meetings, they had produced 150 pages of recommendations.

Giuliani laughed them off. At his daily press briefing, he noted that the
panel's members recommended changing the title of the police department's deputy commissioner of community affairs to deputy commissioner
for community relations.

"I think that's Recommendation 9B," the mayor said sarcastically. "So that's a good change. We can change it from affairs to relations."

Otherwise, he said, he'd already enacted some of their proposals and opposed some others. "And some of the things," he said, "are unrealistic and make very little sense."

With those few comments, the mayor insulted not only his allies on the panel, but everyone who believed that the commission had not been just a public relations ploy to get the mayor off the hook from a racial crisis in the middle of a reelection campaign. He seemed to be laughing in their faces, telling them they'd been had.

Those disparaging comments would cost Giuliani dearly.

Amadou Diallo came home from work around midnight, as usual. It had been another long day selling videotapes and tube socks outside the C & B Convenience Store in lower Manhattan. It wasn't much of a business, just a little mouse hole on 14th Street, a bargain district where the poor and almost poor roamed about looking for cheap sneakers and paper towels. But the job helped pay the rent on Wheeler Avenue in the Bronx, where Ahmed, as his friends called him, lived with three roommates. Ahmed was twenty-two years old, a shy man with a slight stutter who had come to America in search of excitement. Before he left his mother in Guinea, he promised her that he would remain faithful to the Muslim rituals he'd learned growing up in West Africa, and he kept his pledge. Five times each day, he walked back into the store's cramped little storeroom, kneeled down on a small carpet next to a dog food dish and a bowl of water, and prayed.

As he settled into his apartment this evening, Ahmed flicked on the television and said good night to a roommate, Momodou Kujabi. Then, for some reason, he left, perhaps to grab a meal.

About forty-five minutes later, Edward McMellon, Kenneth Boss, Richard Murphy, and Sean Carroll were cruising toward Diallo's building at 1157 Wheeler Avenue in an unmarked police car. They were four young police officers, all wearing bullet-proof vests underneath their street clothes.

It was the standard garb for members of the Street Crime Unit, the maverick squad whose motto was "We Own the Night."

Carroll, riding in the front passenger seat, spotted Diallo on the stoop of his building. "Back up," he told Boss, the driver. "I got something on the right."

Carroll thought it was strange that Diallo was peering up and down the street, then retreating into the building and emerging again. Maybe he was a burglar. Maybe he was a serial rapist they'd been hunting.

Carroll and McMellon got out of the car first. From the sidewalk outside the building, McMellon called out to the young man. The two cops claim that McMellon flashed his badge and said, "Sir, please, New York Police— we need a word with you," and then repeated the line.

Diallo, they say, turned away, prompting Carroll to call out to him. Then Diallo started to dig into his pocket, worrying McMellon. "Please show me your hands," the cop allegedly shouted.

But Amadou Diallo did not hear him or understand him. Instead, Carroll says, he pulled an object from his pocket that looked like a gun and pointed it at McMellon. It stopped the heart. "*Gun!*" Carroll yelled.

The cops opened fire, exploding a hail of bullets at their target. McMellon walked backward as he fired, and fell down the building's steps, firing at Ahmed even as his back hit the concrete. Thinking McMellon had been shot, Carroll kept firing, and Boss—standing behind the two cops with Murphy—opened fire as well. Murphy says that he too thought Diallo was firing a gun, and he started firing in response.

The slight man at the top of the stairs was being riddled by gunfire. Bullets were tearing through his heart, his lungs, his liver, his kidneys; they were spraying up and down his legs; they ripped through his spinal cord and his spleen. By the time the shooting stopped, the four cops had fired off forty-one shots, nineteen of which struck their target. With the gunfire ringing in his ears, Carroll ran up to Diallo—who was lying on the ground, still moving—and tried to take what he thought was a gun out of his hand. "*Where's the fucking gun?*" he shouted. "*Where's the fucking gun?*" Carroll discovered there was no gun. It was a wallet.

Horrified, the officer frantically lifted Diallo's shirt to resuscitate him but saw blood spurting from bullet wounds in his abdomen. "Oh my God!" the officer said, taking his victim's hand and rubbing his face. *"Please don't die. Keep breathing!"* Diallo was losing consciousness. *"Oh my God!"* Carroll repeated. *"Please don't die!"* One of the officers called for help. *"Give me a bus and a boss!"* he yelled into his police radio, meaning an ambulance and a supervisor.

The four officers were stunned. They'd just executed a man for taking a wallet out of his pocket.

About six hours later, the telephone rang at the home of Mohamed Jalloh, the president of the Guinean Association of America. Habib Bah, an association member, was calling to tell him that one of Bah's relatives, Amadou Diallo, had been shot and killed in the early hours of the morning. His body was at Jacobi Hospital in the Bronx.

Jalloh knew the drill. Guinea was a tiny country, and the Guinean community in New York was a close-knit group, one that looked after its own. Every time a Guinean immigrant died, Jalloh's job was to trudge to the hospital, claim the body, contact the family back in Africa, and make arrangements to have it shipped home for burial. He'd gone through this ritual thirty-nine times since 1990. Only thirteen of these people had died of natural causes; the rest were mostly drivers for private car services who'd been murdered by robbers.

A quiet, middle-aged man, Jalloh dutifully set about his morbid task, assuming that yet another working-class countryman had fallen victim to a thief. It was only when he arrived at the hospital and encountered a crowd of police officers that he learned that Amadou Diallo's killers worked for the NYPD.

Kyle Watters, the Guinean Association's attorney, was eating lunch at Asia de Cuba, a trendy Manhattan restaurant, when Jalloh reached him by cell phone with the news. The attorney, a garrulous man in his late thirties, was white but had spent so much time around Jalloh and the association's members that he barely noticed their heavy accents anymore. Watters asked his client about the dead man: Did he have a gun? A knife? Did he die in a struggle? Jalloh answered no each time. He was simply gunned down trying to get into his building. Watters headed up to Wheeler Avenue.

The phone rang at the National Action Network, the creaky second-story Harlem walk-up that served as Al Sharpton's headquarters. The voice on the other end belonged to another member of the Guinean community. Speaking in the clipped accent of a West African immigrant, he told Sharpton about a countryman who'd been shot nineteen times by police up in the Bronx. Sharpton said he'd look into it.

The reverend was used to fielding calls from people with tall stories. Sometimes the callers were crackpots or hysterics or people with too much time on their hands. But sometimes they were sobbing relatives reporting that the cops had just killed a son or a brother or a friend. On this morning, word of Diallo's death was filtering in from a handful of outraged Guinean immigrants acting independently of their leader. Sharpton ran through the usual drill. Was the incident drug-related? Did the dead person have a weapon? Was this an injustice or the unhappy result of a drug deal? He only had time for civil rights cases—he was an activist, not a Legal Aid attorney. They assured him that this was an outrage beyond imagination, a police assassination of an unarmed man who'd been trying to enter his own building.

By day's end, Sharpton was convinced enough to call a press conference for the following morning.

At about the same time, Jalloh was convening an emergency meeting of the Guinean Association in the basement of Harlem's Sokoboly Restaurant, the unofficial community headquarters for the city's Guineans. The topic was Diallo's death, and whether to allow Sharpton to enter the case. Many were adamantly opposed, fearing that the minister would exploit Diallo's death and inflame people's passions for his own purposes. Jalloh was one of them. He worried that Sharpton would turn the killing into a crusade against Mayor Giuliani. The Guineans were a peaceful people, respectful of authority, Jalloh argued. It was only right to deal with the leader of the city. Jalloh was also wary of antagonizing the mayor. Giuliani had a reputation for vindictiveness, and some of Jalloh's members had immigration problems that could be unearthed at the mayor's whim.

Others argued in favor of Sharpton. With the activist would come the city's media, and that would ensure that the NYPD couldn't sweep the case under the rug. The cops had already given them reason to harbor that fear. After the shooting, police officers brought Diallo's roommates to the station house and questioned them about the case for hours without telling them Diallo had been killed. Other cops had searched Diallo's apartment after the shooting, claiming they were looking for his ID. The community suspected that they were really looking for evidence with which to smear Diallo. Jalloh was outvoted: Sharpton would be welcomed.

The turnout at the next day's press conference was impressive. Reporters and cameramen filled the street outside the Sokoboly. Sharpton stood before a tree of microphones alongside Jalloh. "There is no way that I can even imagine," Sharpton bellowed in preacher's cadence, "that one can justify shooting at a human being forty-one times." He called for a federal investigation—and for a rally outside Diallo's home the next day. Meanwhile, Watters tracked down Diallo's father, who was traveling on business in Vietnam. In that phone conversation, Saikou Diallo retained Watters to represent the family. The lawyer passed the father's name and number along to City Hall: Mayor Giuliani wanted to call him to express his sympathy.

It was snowing on Sunday, February 7, a bad omen for a demonstration, but when Sharpton's car turned the corner onto Wheeler Avenue, he knew the Diallo case was something special. There were over a thousand people on the narrow street in front of Diallo's building, so many that they almost filled the entire block. Diallo's black-and-white image was blown up on a big poster that one of his neighbors had hung outside her window. Another had hung a sign reading simply "WHY?" An African immigrant sitting near the site of the killing held her baby in one arm and a sign on which she had scrawled "Giuliani Stop New York People Death," or NYPD.

Sharpton, dressed in a brown camel hair coat and a silk paisley scarf, took a bullhorn and walked to the entrance of Diallo's building. With his back to the brick wall, inches away from a door still pockmarked with bullet holes, he shouted some chants of "*No justice!*" and the crowd responded "*No peace!*" There was a large turnout by the media. "We want to know what happened!" the reverend told the crowd. "But we already know that four policemen fired forty-one bullets at an unarmed man. There was no fight. There was no criminal. There's no justification for the slaughter of this young man!" As hundreds cheered, an African immigrant woman waved a sign reading "OH GOD! COPS KEEP KILLING 'R' BABIES." They held the entire police department culpable.

The emotions raging this day had been building in the broader black community for several years. The daily frisks of young black men by police officers were degrading and offensive and had turned the community against the very men and women who were protecting it. A string of young black and Latino men had died under questionable circumstances during Giuliani's reign. They included Anthony Baez—killed when a hot-tempered police officer threw him into an illegal choke hold after his foot-ball struck the cop's squad car—and sixteen-year-old Kevin Cedeño, shot and killed by a police officer who claimed the youth had lunged at him with his machete. It turned out Cedeño was shot in the back.

Giuliani only inflamed matters with his reflexive support of the cops. Still resentful of David Dinkins's vacillation in Crown Heights and his misplaced support of the family of a drug dealer in Washington Heights, Giuliani made it a practice to support cops until the facts proved them culpable. In Cedeño's case, he went a step further, releasing the boy's criminal record and criticizing his mother for allowing him out on the street late at night with a weapon.

Those cases had only drawn sporadic protest—usually orchestrated by Sharpton. Black New Yorkers, like whites, were happy with the peace that Giuliani had brought to the streets of their neighborhoods. But revulsion over police misconduct had been intensifying when Diallo was gunned down. Now, standing in front of this restive crowd, Sharpton felt an electric-ity in the air. He called for another demonstration on Tuesday, February 9.

The media seemed primed to treat the Diallo case as a watershed inci-dent. On the day after his killing, the New York Times ran the news as its lead story, accompanied by two sidebar pieces. The tabloids all placed the Diallo shooting on page one. New York 1 gave Sharpton and his cause so much air time that administration officials tagged it the "All Sharpton, All the Time" channel.

The nation's attention at the moment was riveted elsewhere. In Washington, Republican prosecutors were making their closing statements on the floor of the U.S. Senate in the impeachment trial of President Clinton. At City Hall, Rudy Giuliani arguably had time to defuse the Diallo story before the public had a chance to fix on it.

From the moment he learned of the shooting, Giuliani adopted a two-pronged response, advising the public to withhold judgment about the case until Bronx District Attorney Robert Johnson could investigate the facts, but defending the police against assertions that misconduct was rampant. "This individual incident is one of great concern, and it's one that should be investigated very thoroughly," he told the press two days after Diallo's killing. "But it would be very unfair to jump from this incident to accuse an entire police department and to take away from them the credit they deserve for being just about the most restrained police department in the country."

The statistics he put forth bore him out. In 1998 the NYPD had shot and killed nineteen civilians, compared with forty-one in 1990, when the police force was smaller and David Dinkins was mayor. Other cities with far fewer police officers were shooting and killing far more suspects.

But his statistics couldn't dispel a gut feeling among the city's blacks that Diallo's killing was inevitable given the department's hyperaggressive activity on the streets. Citizens already angered at the police department's treatment of their youth reacted to the apparent murder of this young man with a sickened feeling of familiarity. The numbers showed that blacks in New York were not being gunned down by cops with anything approaching regularity. But the daily interactions black citizens had been having with the department since Giuliani took office made them feel like sitting ducks for the mayor's army.

On the weekend following the shooting, Ray Harding paid a rare visit to City Hall to give Giuliani his assessment of the political damage. Lowering his large frame into a chair in the mayor's upstairs office, the Liberal Party leader described the intensity of the reaction he'd been receiving, and he warned Giuliani that Sharpton had the potential to define the story as it unfolded. Get ahead of the curve, he advised the mayor.

Giuliani listened intently, as he always did with Harding, one of the town's canniest political strategists. He told Harding that he'd conveyed the city's regrets to Diallo's father in Vietnam and offered to pay for his trip to New York to collect his son's body. City Hall had also reached out to Jalloh, asking the Guinean Association leader to set up a meeting between his group and the mayor. The Guinean Association agreed to hold that meeting—but only when Diallo's parents were in New York to join it.

Harding didn't need to tell Giuliani how important it was to get to Diallo's parents before Sharpton could. If the mayor could earn their trust, they could help him discredit Sharpton's protests before they got off the ground.

The mayor was angry. Critics were using Diallo's death to paint his police as out of control, and he told Harding he wouldn't stand for it. People wanted to see him launch a full-blown shake-up or denounce the cops in the case, as he'd done after Abner Louima's torture. But that would be pandering, Giuliani said. It would be irresponsible to denounce the police before the facts of the case were in. He wouldn't do it.

Just try to stay ahead of the curve, Harding warned.

On Monday Giuliani ratcheted up the sympathy level. "I feel terrible about what happened," he told reporters in the Blue Room. "My heart goes out to them. No one wants to lose a child, and the idea of even talking to the father and talking to him about his losing his son in a foreign country is a terrible, terrible thing."

The words did not penetrate. More than a thousand protestors again turned out for Sharpton's lunchtime rally the next day in front of the State Supreme Court, a few blocks from City Hall. This time the focus of the anger shifted from the NYPD to the mayor. A sea of signs waving in the air read "IMPEACH GIULIANI." One man carried a poster of Giuliani with a Hitler mustache, and a succession of speakers condemned him. Sharpton, wearing a dark green raincoat over a white collared shirt and purple tie, charged that the cops had declared open season on blacks and Latinos. "If they can shoot anyone forty-one times," he told the crowd, "they can shoot everyone forty-one times. It may start with blacks and Latinos, but it can go everywhere." He did not mention that only nineteen people had been killed by cops during the past year or that the number was far lower than in any year of David Dinkins's mayoralty.

At about the same time, a plane carrying Diallo's mother from Africa was landing at John F. Kennedy Airport. Watters, the lawyer for the Guinean Association, was there to meet her, along with a van and driver provided by City Hall, and some police officers who'd come at Watters's request. She was whisked away immediately by the attorney before a group of Guinean immigrants who'd come to welcome her could even get close.

But Kadiatou Diallo soon emerged. She had the van drive her to 1157 Wheeler Avenue in the Bronx, so she could see the doorway where her Amadou had been gunned down. When she arrived at the building, the media captured a heartbreaking scene. Mrs. Diallo, a beautiful light-skinned African woman in her late thirties, walked to the bullet-splattered entranceway as a throng of reporters and spectators looked on, and collapsed in sobs. "*Amadou! Amadou!*" she yelled, as if calling for him. She fell limp as men around her tried to keep her standing. "*Wait! Wait!*" It was an excruciating moment. The cameras recorded every wail.

Watters booked her into the ritzy Stanhope Hotel on Fifth Avenue in Manhattan. He and Jalloh escorted her there and bade her goodnight at the end of her exhausting day.

After they left, Al Sharpton arrived.

The reverend showed up with a neighborhood character from Harlem named Delores "Queen Mother" Blakely, a warm but eccentric lady well known in her community.* After overcoming the hesitations of the police officers stationed outside the hotel, they went upstairs and entered the room of the grieving mother, fully expecting her to tell them that she wouldn't be needing Sharpton's help.

They were wrong. "I'm being held like a hostage," Mrs. Diallo told Sharpton. "Will you help me?"

She was confused by the swirl of events and overwhelmed by strangers offering conflicting advice. Jalloh was insisting he was in control, but dissident members of his group were telling her that he and Watters were collaborating with Giuliani. Amadou Diallo's parents were divorced and barely on

---

*Sharpton claims Mrs. Diallo sent for him. Mrs. Diallo says he and Blakely just showed up at her doorstep.

speaking terms: Mrs. Diallo wasn't impressed that Watters had been retained by her ex-husband. She felt Jalloh and the lawyer were ordering her around. "Kyle Watters was telling me, 'I'm your lawyer. I can pay for everything,' she recalls. "I didn't want to be bribed." She decided she wanted nothing to do with him or Jalloh.

Sharpton, on the other hand, seemed intent on getting justice for her son, and she took an immediate liking to him.

"The police killed my child, and then they took me off the plane and escorted me to hide from the people who wanted to sympathize with me at the airport," Mrs. Diallo told Sharpton. "I don't want anything from them. Will you help me get a reasonable hotel that I can afford?"

For the racial activist, it didn't get any better than this.

After the two talked for a while about her son, Sharpton and Mrs. Diallo agreed that he would make arrangements to move her out of the Stanhope the next morning and into the Rihga Royal Hotel, a less expensive hotel. Eventually, Mrs. Diallo agreed to allow Sharpton to pay for her accommodations.

Sharpton went home for the night, leaving Mother Blakely behind to sleep on Kadiatou Diallo's couch. Blakely was virulently anticop and told Mrs. Diallo that she was staying with her to ensure her safety. "The police are out to kill you," she told Mrs. Diallo. "I'm here to protect you." The newly arrived visitor from Guinea thought she was deliberately trying to scare her. But Blakely was caring and maternal and made for a comforting companion. She would not leave Mrs. Diallo's side for the rest of her stay in America, and she soon assumed the gatekeeper's position at her door, even screening Mrs. Diallo's phone calls. The anti-Giuliani forces had begun to form a tight ring around the frightened mother.

The next day Mr. Diallo arrived from Hong Kong. Sharpton went to Kennedy airport with Jalloh and Watters. Saikou Diallo was met, like his ex-wife, by NYPD detectives and a member of the mayor's office as well as by a member of the Guinean embassy. He turned to the police detectives and pointed at Sharpton. "I'm going with him," he told them. Jalloh was Rudy Giuliani's best hope in this crisis. But the Guinean Association president and the group's lawyer were rapidly losing influence.

Trying his best to stay ahead of the curve, the mayor met with a group called the United African Congress at City Hall. He also held a photo opportunity with the family of the legendary black athlete Jesse Owens. But events weren't going his way, and Giuliani's anger was beginning to show. As both Diallo parents prepared to hold a live televised press conference at Sharpton's Harlem headquarters, the mayor stood before the press in the Blue Room and lashed out at the opposition.

"I understand the game of politics that's played here, the game of racial politics," Giuliani told reporters. "We're not perfect and we have a long way to go, but we're a lot better off than we were five, six years ago by being fair and evenhanded with people and not rolling over for racial, religious, and ethnic exploitation."

Things were about to get worse for him. In the morning Giuliani showed up at the Rihga Royal Hotel after a City Hall aide informed him that Diallo's parents had agreed to meet with him. When the mayor arrived, Mrs. Diallo refused to see him. "I was isolated with that woman in the hotel room," she recalls, alluding to Blakely. "They came to get me and said the mayor's waiting for you. I said no way—I wasn't briefed about the meeting." Her ex-husband, a quiet and passive man, wanted to meet with Giuliani but complied with Kadiatou, who said she was afraid of walking into a trap and being coopted by the mayor.*

Giuliani, who hated to be embarrassed in public, waited for an hour in an upstairs room, only to be informed by Watters that the parents had decided not to talk to him. The mayor and his entourage left the hotel blaming Sharpton for squashing the event. Upstairs, the parents gave an interview to Dominic Carter of New York 1 News. They criticized the mayor. "The police are here to protect the people, not to kill the people," Mrs. Diallo said.

Amadou Diallo's memorial service came later in the afternoon. Thousands of mourners filled the vast Islamic Center on East 96th Street in Man-

---

*Mrs. Diallo says that, at the time, she was under a serious misimpression about the American legal system. She believed that she would have to go to court to fight the police, as if the criminal trial were the same as a civil case. Had she known that the district attorney had responsibility for pressing charges, she says, she might not have been so antagonistic toward the mayor.

hattan and spilled out its doors. A line of local politicians streamed in to pay their respects. Giuliani showed up with Police Commissioner Howard Safir and a large contingent of plainclothes bodyguards and slipped into the building through a side entrance toward the end of the service. After paying his respects to Saikou Diallo and waiting for the pine casket carrying Diallo's body to be taken away, Giuliani and his entourage turned around to leave. As they made their way outside to a waiting van, the mayor's guards had to shield him from a vast throng of angry mourners. The camera caught one of them yelling at the mayor with his pointing finger inches from Giuliani's face. Giuliani just stared straight ahead and kept walking. The image of the mayor pretending not to hear a man screaming in his ear was the rage of the eleven o'clock news.

Jalloh was distressed. He wanted justice, not a war with City Hall. He wanted to sit down with Giuliani and talk. But he was losing control of the situation. Rival members of the Guinean Association had brought in O. J. Simpson lawyer Johnnie Cochran to offer the Diallo parents legal advice, making Watters expendable. Sharpton had promised to pay their son's funeral expenses, which was the traditional role of the association. Mrs. Diallo no longer needed Jalloh for advice, legal representation, or financial support. And while her ex-husband, who was willing to deal with the mayor, continued to be represented by Watters, it was Kadiatou Diallo who was calling the shots. She had made her decision: the only person she needed was Al Sharpton.

At the same moment that Giuliani was making his way through the crush of mourners in Manhattan, an even larger drama was playing out in Washington on the floor of the U.S. Senate. Standing before a hushed chamber, William Rehnquist, chief justice of the Supreme Court, announced a verdict in the impeachment trial of the president of the United States: "It is therefore ordered and adjudged that the said William Jefferson Clinton be, and he hereby is, acquitted of the charges in the said articles."

As the president's fate was being decided on this windswept Friday afternoon and the eyes of the world were on the Senate chamber, the First Lady was neither glued to her television set nor standing at her husband's side.

Hillary Rodham Clinton was having lunch in the family dining room of the White House with an adviser, discussing her future. And her thoughts were not so much on the proceedings in Washington as on events in New York City.

The Monica Lewinsky scandal had been a torturous ordeal for everyone involved, but for no one more than the president's wife. Deceived by her husband and humiliated before the world, Mrs. Clinton had drifted between isolation and stoicism, defending the president in public while suffering in the privacy, such as it was, of her home.

But on this momentous occasion, the First Lady was examining a plan with the potential to rescue her from her desolation. New York's senior senator, Daniel Patrick Moynihan, had announced the previous November that he planned to retire, and she was tossing around the pros and cons of entering the race to fill his seat. The audacious proposition had first been floated by Harlem congressman Charlie Rangel back in the fall at a Chicago church. Intrigued, Mrs. Clinton grew more interested after New Jersey's Senator Robert Torricelli floated the idea in a conversation with NBC's Tim Russert before a taping of *Meet the Press* in early January. After Russert reported Torricelli's comments on the air, speculation started mounting.

The First Lady asked Harold Ickes, a former deputy chief of staff to the president and a veteran of New York politics, to sit down with her and think the issue through. The two weighed the politics of the notion for four hours. She asked Ickes to set up some meetings for her with New York politicians, labor leaders, political strategists—anyone who had advice that could help her make up her mind. The prospect of running had captured her imagination, but she wanted to examine the idea carefully.

Three weeks later, on March 3, Mrs. Clinton set out for New York City to gauge the level of interest in her candidacy. She traveled to the Plaza Hotel in Manhattan to speak at a luncheon hosted by a Democratic Party fundraising group called the Women's Leadership Forum. The trip came in the heat of the speculation about her political future, and the event became the hottest ticket in town.

So many politicians, reporters, and party activists showed up at the palatial ballroom that security officers had to lock dozens of reporters out of the overcrowded room. Television cameramen from all over the world filled banks of platforms in back as nine hundred Democratic activists, most of them women, buzzed around excitedly. When the First Lady arrived, accompanied by New York's junior senator, Charles Schumer, the room exploded in cheers. The First Lady seemed taken aback. "I haven't seen so much electricity and excitement in a room in a long time," Schumer remarked.

Mrs. Clinton was months away from declaring her intentions, and many of her friends were still doubtful that she would pursue a run. Why, after eight years of investigations, special prosecutors, sex scandals, and impeachment hearings, would she willingly throw herself back into the political cauldron?

When she took the podium, she offered an answer.

"We cannot drop out of the political process and leave the arena to those with very specific agendas," she said. "You can say all you want about the flaws of our political system, but when it comes right down to it, somebody is going to make the decisions." Pundits would speculate about her intentions for months to come. But she had handed the public an insight into her thinking.

The emotional response from her audience was a loving embrace for a woman who had weathered a public nightmare. But the enthusiasm was also fueled by the prospect that this Democratic icon was thinking of coming to town to take on Rudy Giuliani.

Since Moynihan's retirement announcement, the mayor's focus had been shifting from the presidential trail. He'd met enthusiastic crowds in his travels, but it was becoming increasingly clear that he and his staff weren't prepared to put together a viable presidential campaign. The vice presidency was still a target, but that was a crapshoot dependent upon the needs of the eventual Republican nominee. Moynihan's Senate seat, on the other hand, was sitting open in Giuliani's own backyard. Gradually, his political ambitions shifted back to New York.

Charles Barron was worried. Sitting on a bench across from Al Sharpton and a handful of black activists in a dimly lit police wagon, he wondered how much they were accomplishing. More than a thousand people had come to Wall Street on March 3 to protest Amadou Diallo's killing and vent their anger at the police department and Mayor Giuliani. When Sharpton and friends kneeled down to stop traffic on Broadway, dozens of cameras recorded their arrests. But as the wagon made its way to the precinct house for booking, Barron couldn't help but feel he'd been down this road before. The protests came and went, the news programs aired snippets of footage, and people soon forgot that the marches had ever happened. The Diallo case needed something more intense, he felt, something sustained.

Barron had been fighting for the civil rights of blacks when Al Sharpton was just a groupie traveling the country with James Brown. He was a Black Panther in the 1960s and head of the Harlem wing of the Black United Front in the 1970s. In the 1980s he led New York's Free South Africa movement, coordinating daily nonviolent protests outside the country's consulate. For years he'd distrusted Sharpton as a showboat and an opportunist, only to bond with him when they spent forty-five days together in a jail cell—a result of their protests in Howard Beach.

Now the two were under arrest once again. "We need to do something different," Barron said. "We need to sustain the pressure. We should keep this thing going, like we did with South Africa."

In the 1985 anti-apartheid movement, Barron's job had been to coordinate the arrest schedule for celebrities and politicians volunteering for the cause. Politicians flocked to the demonstrations, eager to be seen being handcuffed in the fight against a racist government. David Dinkins had been arrested. So had the Reverend Herbert Daughtry, a Pentecostal minister and black activist who was riding in the van this evening.

"Let's do it," Daughtry said. "Maybe at City Hall or Gracie Mansion."

"No, they'll say it's political," Sharpton said. He thought for a moment. "We can do it right at the symbol of what we're fighting—police brutality. Let's go to One Police Plaza."

Someone in the van wondered whether the organizers could keep a movement like this going for more than a few days. "I can guarantee you," said Barron. "People worried back then that the daily protests couldn't be sustained. Not only can we sustain it, we won't be able to contain it."

The Reverend Wyatt Tee Walker, once an aide to the Reverend Martin

Luther King Jr., listened to the conversation, his aging hands pinched by plastic handcuffs. A smile came to his face. "You know, you're a lucky guy," he told Sharpton.

"What do you mean?" Sharpton said.

"When we were trying to do the Voting Rights Act in the South, we searched the South and we had to find a Bull Connor. God gave you one. You're much luckier than we were."

Sharpton understood. Every revolution needs a villain. In this case, he was sitting at Fiorello LaGuardia's desk at City Hall.

Sharpton's civil disobedience campaign kicked off to a wobbly start the following Tuesday, March 9. A few dozen citizens responded to his calls for mass arrests to protest Diallo's killing, enabling him to spread them out at a pace of about five to ten per day. It was not hugely impressive, and other groups held far larger marches at City Hall and the Bronx courthouse, eclipsing his efforts.

But midway through the week, Congressman Charles Rangel called Sharpton and offered him a gift: He wanted to sign up to be arrested. An old-school rabble-rouser, Rangel was a baronial figure in Harlem, a fourteen-term legislator with a booming, sandpapery voice and a talent for bluster. David Dinkins was prone to calling him "my brother Charlie," and the close affiliation was not lost on the people who ruled City Hall. The mayor felt the Democratic congressman had sandbagged him early on in his mayoralty by privately promising to cooperate while publicly attacking him. For his part, the congressman had come to loathe Giuliani for his indifference to the black community.

"Rev, you're doing a good job," Rangel told Sharpton. "I think I'd like to come down either on Friday or Monday. Why shouldn't a member of Congress go and support you, so the mayor can't isolate you?"

It was no small favor for a mainstream Democrat to bestow some legitimacy on a street activist, and in that one phone call the congressman ensured that Sharpton's prestige in the black community would balloon. Rangel was angry from watching Giuliani belittle some Diallo protestors on New York 1. The congressman wanted to wipe the smile off the mayor's face.

On Saturday night, Sharpton got some even better news. He was at Madison Square Garden for the heavyweight championship fight between Lennox Lewis and Evander Holyfield, sitting at ringside with his wife and Kweisi Mfume, president of the NAACP. During a preliminary bout, Sharpton was approached by his lawyer, Michael Hardy, who was sitting twenty rows up and off to the side with Dinkins and Rangel. "Rev, Dave Dinkins said to tell you that he's going Monday and he's going to jail."

Sharpton was startled. He'd run into the former mayor in the men's room of an Italian restaurant the previous night, and Dinkins had talked about joining the protests. But there was no mention of going to jail.

"Dave Dinkins ain't going to jail," Sharpton corrected Hardy.

"I'm telling you. That's what he said."

Intrigued, Sharpton got out of his seat and strode up the aisle to hear it himself from the ex-mayor. The two joked about Sharpton's having gotten better seats to the match. "Michael told me you're ready to come and go to jail?" Sharpton asked.

"That's right, Al. I've thought about it and I'm willing to do it."

"Mr. Mayor, if I put this on the Daybook and it doesn't happen, you'll hurt us, you know," the reverend said, referring to the Associated Press daily calendar.

"Would I tell you something I'm not going to do?"

Sure enough, on Monday, March 15, David Dinkins, Charlie Rangel, and Al Sharpton, joined by Queens Congressman Gregory Meeks and two City Council members, sat down in front of the revolving doors outside One Police Plaza, as a clutch of cameramen and reporters encircled them. Reluctant to arrest an ex-mayor, police watched their act of defiance passively. Frustrated, the small group stood up, entered the building itself, stood in a circle, and linked arms. Defying a police lieutenant's request that they leave, the group was finally arrested and marched outside the building in handcuffs. The photograph was spread across the top half of the *New York Times* the next morning. Accompanying it was a story containing a derisive reaction from the mayor attacking both Dinkins and the press. "This is a great publicity stunt," Giuliani said. "Can't you figure it out? It's a publicity stunt, and you are, as usual, sucked into it."

The dam had burst. Hundreds of protestors jammed the plaza outside police headquarters the next day, and the next, while celebrities fought to make it onto Al Sharpton's appointment book to join the brigade against police brutality. Dinkins had always been adept at understanding the power of symbols, and he knew the public would be revolted by the image of New York's first black mayor being handcuffed by Rudy Giuliani's police force. After weathering six years of verbal abuse from the man who unseated him, Dinkins finally exacted his revenge.

For the next month, the city's attention was riveted on the events outside the windowless brick building housing the headquarters of the city's police force. Over 1,100 protestors were arrested for sitting down in front of the building's doors, including Susan Sarandon, Ossie Davis, Ruby Dee, Jesse Jackson, and a slew of politicians. Each day produced a satisfied smile on the face of some politician, labor leader, or activist being led away in handcuffs. The army of Rudy Giuliani's enemies was charging up the hill, led by the man Giuliani had vilified the most.

Sharpton had made a promise to the people of Kadiatou's Guinean village after attending Amadou's burial there. "One thing I promise is that I'll come back to this village one day to report we got these cops arrested," he told them. "I'm going to try to do whatever I can to get these creeps indicted." Unquestionably, the protests were geared to pressure the criminal justice system to come down hard on the four cops. But Sharpton happily conceded that he was also out to drive a nail into the coffin of Rudy Giuliani's political career.

He was joined by dozens of groups with similar motives. It seemed that all the people Giuliani had battled in the past had coalesced. Street artists, immigrant taxi drivers, AIDS activists, welfare recipients, City University students—all joined the demonstrations. Worried that previous marches against the mayor's policies had lacked visual punch, Robert Lederman, a street artist, spawned a genre of Giuliani-as-Hitler paintings, which became hot commodities at the protests.

Increasingly, Giuliani was being seen as a demon. His popularity plummeted 21 points the week of the Dinkins arrest, and his support among blacks virtually evaporated. Arts critic John Leonard, former editor of the *New York Times Book Review*, penned a diatribe against the mayor in the online magazine *Salon* that read like a kiss-off from the city's liberals. "The last five years in New York have been less about government than they've been about obedience training," Leonard wrote. "How mean is Rudy? So mean . . . he wouldn't spit in your ear if your brains were on fire."

New York magazine, the traditional voice of the city's upper middle class, featured a two-page cartoon of Giuliani as a battered and beaten Superman trying to fly as people threw tomatoes at him. "The Fall of Supermayor," it read.

Crises tend to snowball, and that is precisely what began to happen at City Hall. At the end of the tumultuous week that opened with Dinkins's arrest, Police Commissioner Safir, refusing to acknowledge that his police force was under siege, quietly skipped off to Hollywood to attend the Academy Awards, advising a City Council committee before he left that he wouldn't be able to attend a Monday morning hearing on the Diallo matter because of "a scheduling conflict." A camera caught him in a tuxedo shaking hands with an acquaintance, standing next to Helen Hunt. Every station in town slo-mo'd the image and broadcast it with punishing frequency.

It also began to seep in with the public that Giuliani had not met with most of the city's black leadership in years. Not with Rangel, nor with State Comptroller Carl McCall—the state's highest-ranking black official—nor with Manhattan Borough President Virginia Fields—the city's highest-ranking black official. They were partisan, Giuliani claimed, and not interested in solving problems. The estrangement was common knowledge at City Hall, but the news sounded bizarre in the current environment.

Giuliani and his aides viewed the developments with disgust. The demonstrations, they believed, were a "joke," in the words of one deputy mayor. Seeking to allay one another's anxieties, they spoke contemptuously about "arrests by appointment" at Sharpton's rallies, as when Jesse Jackson reportedly scheduled his arrest in time to make a flight out of town. Giuliani was appalled that a perception was taking hold that his police were gunning down African Americans left and right when in fact police killings were at their lowest point since 1990. The statistics showed that it was far more probable a black citizen would be killed by another black citizen than by a cop, but no one in the black community seemed to care.

Perception was outrunning reality, but the perception was fostered by Giuliani's policies. After nearly tripling the size of the Street Crime Unit in

1997, Safir doubled the number of citizens the cops stopped and frisked the next year, to 27,000—and that didn't include the frisks that cops never reported. The overwhelming number of those thrown against walls and frisked were black. Fewer than 5,000 of them were arrested, meaning that more than 20,000 innocent New Yorkers had been accosted by police in the past year. The mayor argued that the vast majority of criminal suspects were minorities. But were cops stopping people who fit the descriptions of alleged criminals—or who just shared the same skin color?

Giuliani and Safir repeatedly belittled the matter as a "courtesy" problem. The mayor told reporters that the demonstrations were getting "silly."

"I think they are over the top now," he said three days after the Dinkins arrest. "This is a piling-on time where everybody is hoping, 'Let me see if I can get on camera.' And, unfortunately, you keep obliging them." His comments added fuel to the public's anger.

The mayor's aides were split about how to handle the crisis. Ray Harding, Randy Levine, and Denny Young, fearing that the earth underneath them was trembling, were advising the mayor to be more contrite about Diallo's death, more understanding of the black community's anger. Cristyne Lategano and Tony Coles, the mayor's senior adviser, were the hard-liners: The crowds outside police headquarters were demanding the arrest of the four cops, which would have been illegal. They were calling Diallo's killing a murder when it may have been a tragic mistake. Don't give in to Sharpton, they argued to Giuliani. Don't undo all you've accomplished.

The mayor's one black deputy mayor, Rudy Washington, watched the Diallo crisis unfold with a sickened feeling. He believed from his own personal experiences that there was in fact a problem with the cops. But he was reluctant to tell the mayor. So he did the next best thing and helped convince Giuliani to meet privately with other blacks who might tell him the same thing.

Washington arranged a meeting between Giuliani and the Reverend Floyd Flake at the Fame Diner in Queens. The former Democratic congressman held an exalted role in Giuliani's life. Tall and thin, with a pastor's heart and a politician's mind, the minister was an iconoclast, so far removed from the Dinkins-Rangel orbit that he crossed party lines to endorse Giuliani in the '97 mayor's race. He was one of the mayor's few black allies.

Flake had watched with relief as Giuliani's police tactics put a halt to the rampant violence that was killing children in his district in the early 1990s. Members of his congregation were no longer being gunned down by gang members sporting Uzis. Sanity had returned to the streets of this middle-class black enclave during Giuliani's first term. But by the time the mayor and Rudy Washington sat down to breakfast with him, the police themselves had become a menace in his community. His parishioners were complaining that their teenagers were being routinely harassed by cops. Some black officers he knew were teaching black teenagers how to behave when stopped by cops—how to remain silent and what physical positions to assume when they were searched.

Flake stirred his oatmeal as Giuliani ran down the statistics for him. The use of force by his cops had plummeted since he'd taken over as mayor, he said. Sharpton was painting a distorted picture.

The minister listened patiently as the numbers came tumbling forth. And then he made his case. Behind those statistics were faces, he told Giuliani. The people complaining at his church that they were scared of the cops weren't Al Sharpton followers—they were black middle-class folks worried about the safety of their children.

Giuliani retreated to the numbers. Feeling the mayor didn't understand, Flake told him a story. About a year earlier, when he was still a congressman, Flake was driving his wife to his church at night and was waved down by a police officer standing at a divider. *"Nigger, didn't I tell you to stop that car?"* the officer yelled at him. After realizing that he'd flagged down a congressman, the officer let him go. Driving away, Flake kept wondering what would have happened if he *hadn't* been a congressman.

It brought back bad memories, Flake said. Growing up in Houston, he'd watched his father—a janitor—get stopped by cops whenever he drove a nice-looking car. Many African Americans recalled their own experiences when they heard about Diallo's killing.

The minister's case was eluding the former prosecutor sitting across from him. The numbers were the reality, the stories just anecdotes. Why should scars from past racism influence the city's crime-fighting policies? It was a sociological conundrum presented to a pragmatist. It wasn't computing.

The congressman studied Giuliani's face. Here was a man with almost no black allies besides himself. Calvin Butts, a Harlem minister, had made headlines by tagging the mayor a racist in an interview on New York 1 and Flake brought the matter up. "I won't join Calvin and call you a racist," Flake told the mayor, "because I just think you're mean to everybody."

Giuliani and his deputy mayor laughed nervously. "I think you're just mean," Flake repeated. "You've got a mean streak in you." The three of them laughed together now to break the tension. But they all realized Flake had meant every word.

Giuliani left the breakfast unpersuaded, and Flake left feeling contemptuous. He regretted endorsing the mayor. "Anyone who disagrees with him is considered almost as a personal enemy," the minister reflected later. "He treats everything as if it's a urinating contest, like he's got to win. That's not how you manage people in a city."

Giuliani was brought up in a white universe, Flake realized, but that didn't explain everything. "I felt that he was probably the nerd in the Charles Atlas comedy strip on the back of the comic book that got the sand kicked in his face all the time and finally got to a place of power and decided that he now had that authority to control those that would even dare to think about kicking sand in his face," Flake said later. "That's honestly how I feel."

Washington was frustrated. The mayor respected Flake, but he still didn't understand that the more he told blacks that their fears were unfounded, the angrier they got. The deputy mayor reached out to the other black Democrat who'd endorsed Giuliani in '97: Edolphus Towns, a Brooklyn congressman, was a far more obscure politician than Flake and was worried about being seen by his community as counseling the mayor in this crisis. At Towns's request, Washington sneaked him into City Hall, out of view of reporters and other politicians. He was brought into an entrance on the side of the building that led directly to the basement, then escorted into Cristyne Lategano's basement office and led up a circular stairwell into Giuliani's office.

The effort wasn't worth it. Their short chat produced more statistics and more exhortations to be sensitive to the community's anger. Giuliani wasn't moved.

On Monday, March 22, a week after Dinkins's arrest, Washington decided to speak up. The lone black man at the highest level of city government was watching a disaster unfold. Over a hundred people a day were being arrested at Police Plaza; Governor Pataki had felt the need to go on ABC's *This Week* and denounce Giuliani's handling of the affair; the press was savaging Commissioner Safir for jetting off to the Oscars. Giuliani had no credibility left on the issue of police misconduct, having scoffed at his own commission on police-community relations. Al Sharpton seemed well on his way to breaking Rudy Giuliani at last, and the mayor was increasingly isolated, unwilling to made the slightest public concession to the uproar.

The deputy mayor knocked on the mayor's door and asked to speak with him. Giuliani invited him inside. Before Washington could get beyond pleasantries, other aides began filtering in and plopping themselves down into chairs unannounced. There was Bruce Teitelbaum, the new head of Giuliani's campaign; Joe Lhota, the deputy mayor for operations; Deputy Mayor Randy Levine; and Senior Adviser Tony Coles. The boys club convened without so much as an invitation, leaving Washington feeling a little exposed. But he'd come to tell Giuliani something he needed to hear, and so he began to speak.

"I never told you this," Washington said to the mayor, "but a few years ago, I was going to see Howard Golden in Brooklyn and stopped off at a White Castle."

It was early in the morning, and Washington—then the city's commissioner for business services—was in his official city car; his taxpayer-funded chauffeur was behind the wheel. Washington was reading his *New York Times* as he waited for his driver to pull up to the fast food restaurant's drive-through window. As he ordered breakfast, Washington noticed that two police cars were sitting nearby. When his car pulled out of the White Castle lot, one of the cops motioned to his driver to pull over. An officer asked for the driver's license and registration. He turned to Washington and asked for his identification. "What are you doing with this car?"

"Did we do something wrong?"

"What are you doing with this car?"

"What's your problem?" Washington said. "Did we break the law?" He told the officer he was a city commissioner.

The cop didn't believe him at first. Eventually the officer threw the license and registration back into Washington's lap and departed. The commissioner felt the cops just saw him and his driver as two black guys.

Washington said there was another story he wanted to relate. On a Friday night in 1998, Washington came home from work, took his tie off, and drove off with his wife in their Voyager to go to dinner at a diner in Forest Hills, Queens. On the way home, a police car pulled him over. "Don't worry, baby," he told his wife. A young white police officer, perhaps twenty-five years old, asked for his license and registration.

Washington pulled out an ID from the Metropolitan Transportation Authority, on which he served as a board member. "Are you a board member of the MTA?" the officer asked him.

"Yeah."

The cop asked him to get out of the car. Washington opened the door and stood up, and the cop turned him around, pushed him against his car, and frisked him. "I'm taking you down to the station to check your ID," he said.

Horrified, Washington's wife, Deborah Cheney, started to cry. As the cops prepared to put him in their squad car, a superior officer, a lieutenant, pulled up and recognized Washington. "What are you doing? He's a deputy mayor!" He snatched the paperwork away from the cop and handed it back to Washington.

Washington had gone to Denny Young, the mayor's liaison to the NYPD, after the second incident. This is ridiculous, Washington told him. I've been stopped by police twice and humiliated, even once in my city car, because of my race.

Young was concerned. Not long afterward, he came back to Washington with a solution to his problem. He handed him a police identification badge with his name on it and urged Washington to keep it with him at all times. It should do the trick if cops pulled him over in the future, he said. The administration's own racial profiling problem was thus taken care of quietly.

There you have it, Washington told the mayor. You've got a problem with your police department, he said. You need to meet with black leaders, listen to them, and fix the problem.

The mayor looked at his aide. Washington was not among Giuliani's closest advisers, but he was unfailingly loyal and a member of the family. His story resonated. "Okay," Giuliani said. "I'll meet with them."

Meetings were set up with Virginia Fields and Carl McCall. Giuliani once again expressed regret over Diallo's death in the days that followed, and Safir announced he would revamp the Street Crime Unit. Giuliani also agreed to meet with small groups of black teenagers to hear about their experiences. It was a start, and it took place not a moment too soon. Three days after Rudy Washington's revelation, Floyd Flake showed up at One Police Plaza, sat down in front of its doors, and was arrested.

On Wednesday, March 31, the four officers who shot Amadou Diallo were indicted on charges of second-degree murder and reckless endangerment, which brought relief to both sides of the war. Giuliani was in the Bronx that afternoon, dedicating a street to fallen police officer Vincent Guidice. In a memorable performance, he threw aside his softened approach and called on New Yorkers to show more respect to the police, lashing out against "some of the worst in society." Giuliani never gave in.

Defiant on some days, contrite on others, Giuliani wasn't staunching the hemorrhage that was immobilizing his mayoralty. Safir, whose tin ear for public relations could be mind-boggling, addressed the problem by printing up tens of thousands of new wallet-sized Courtesy Cards for his officers, which listed the proper ways of speaking to citizens ("refer to teenagers as young lady or young man"). A new poll showed the mayor's popularity down by 30 points.

Frank Luntz was called in. The scruffy young pollster was a Republican prodigy, a key adviser to House Speaker Newt Gingrich in his heyday as leader of his party's revolution. No client had meant more to the pollster, though, than Giuliani, whom he looked upon as a heroic figure. Brought in by Garth to poll for Giuliani's '93 campaign, Luntz emerged as a key adviser to the mayor in '97, when Garth's shadow was no longer hovering over him.

Advisers had spent weeks trying to convince the mayor to allow Luntz to convene a focus group to help pinpoint his problems. Political strategists use such groups—consisting of ordinary citizens, prescreened to represent a desired constituency—to identify the public's deepest feelings about a politician. Giuliani believed from the start of Sharpton's protest movement that the crisis would eventually fade. But his aides were deeply worried. Worn down, the mayor finally agreed to the focus group, cautioning that he wasn't about to change his mind.

At 5 P.M. on Sunday, April 11, Giuliani and his high command descended on a focus group facility located in a midtown office building. Seated with his aides behind a large two-way mirror, he watched as an all-white group of New Yorkers sat around a table with a moderator, picking apart his response to the Diallo shooting. The mayor wasn't sensitive enough, they agreed; he wasn't apologetic enough. All the complaints he'd heard innumerable times from the editorial pages and the commentators and the liberal politicians and some of his own aides were pouring forth once again, this time from a group of average citizens talking among themselves.

It wasn't all bad. The group loved what Giuliani had done to clean up the city. But its members clearly felt that his police had made a mistake in the slaughter of the African immigrant. They wanted Giuliani to express compassion for Diallo and his family without reverting to his standard defense of the cops.

It must have been a humbling experience for the mighty leader of New York to listen for what seemed like an eternity as people once again criticized his handling of this wretched issue. What did they know about the situation? When it was finally over, and the mayor's crew convened to review the results, Giuliani was ready to explode. His target was Frank Luntz.

"This is a waste of time!" the mayor yelled. *"I've learned nothing from this. I am not going to turn against the police. I am not going to give in to the mob mentality!"*

Luntz was shaking, but no one stood up for him. Brought in to help turn the mayor around on the issue, the pollster was on his own.

Giuliani, who was red-faced, wasn't just angry at Luntz. He realized that it wasn't just the outside world calling for him to bend: it was many, if not most, of his own advisers. He was disgusted with their weakness.

"I'd rather not be mayor than do something unprincipled!"

In the age of Bill Clinton, who polled and focus-grouped every decision down to where to take his vacations, it was rare for a politician facing the abyss to reject the advice of his pollster. Giuliani was a remarkable man that way. In this case, though, the city could have used a little of Clinton's touch. It needed a leader with an ability to empathize, someone dexterous enough to tell every side a little of what it wanted to hear. Instead, it was led by an absolutist whose devotion to a principle had brought the city to a state of crisis. If David Dinkins had allowed havoc to flourish with his accommodationist policies, Giuliani was operating at the opposite extreme, fanning a community's anger by refusing even to believe its claim of injustice.

As the walls closed in further on Giuliani, his salvation ultimately came from Al Sharpton. Not knowing when to declare victory and move on, the reverend called for a monumental march over the Brooklyn Bridge on April 15. The media dutifully built up the drama. Protest organizers included Dinkins and three of his closest confidants—union organizer Dennis Rivera and longtime Dinkins advisers Bill Lynch and Ken Sunshine. All were simultaneously advising Hillary Clinton in her nascent campaign for the Senate.

Ignoring a basic rule of politics—don't build up expectations you can't meet—the organizers invited the media to witness the massive preparations for the march, which included the use of a vast phone bank operation. The hospital workers union paid for a television commercial promoting the event. Someone told reporters to expect 25,000 protestors.

When only 4,500 demonstrators showed up on the afternoon of April 15, the momentum in Sharpton's movement died.

Nonetheless, Giuliani's aura of invincibility was shattered. Many New Yorkers who had supported the mayor through two elections had come to see him in a different light. The hero who saved New York suddenly seemed a grim authoritarian tightening the reins of a racist state. Perhaps his great crime-fighting triumphs had been attained by repressing the civil rights of whole communities. One doubt begat another: perhaps the mayor had ejected 400,000 people from the welfare rolls not because they needed to break their cycle of dependency but simply because they were poor. Had Giuliani created a city just for the white and prosperous?

The mayor was practically inviting someone to step in and preach a return to compassion and generosity. As it happened, just such a heroine had been watching from the wings during his crisis, and was about to step out onto center stage.

13

The Reluctant Candidate

A soft dusk fell on the streets outside the Sheraton Hotel in Manhattan as a succession of television satellite trucks pulled up and settled in for the night, sending their masts shooting skyward. Upstairs, 1,700 guests filed into the Imperial Ballroom for the first major fund-raiser of Rudy's Giuliani's Senate campaign.

The room on this beautiful May evening in 1999 was filled with many of the people who had been present in the same space five years earlier, when the new mayor of New York City threw his first mayoral fund-raiser. They were always scheduled around his birthday: tonight the party celebrated Giuliani's fifty-fifth.

The usual crowd of lobbyists, developers, real estate interests, and Wall Street bond underwriters did their business, chattering around the maze of round, candlelit tables outfitted with bottles of cheap white wine. A large number of bearded Orthodox Jews milled about, having purchased tables at the behest of Giuliani aide Bruce Teitelbaum, his unofficial liaison to the Jewish community. The mayor himself walked in with a large entourage of aides, detectives, and the night's guest speaker, Florida's Governor Jeb Bush. After affixing a large button to his lapel reading "RudyYes.com"—his campaign web site—Giuliani headed for a long oval table in the middle of the room.

The crowd had settled in for a long night of speeches when a late-arriving member of the administration poked her head into the ballroom. Cristyne Lategano, once the most powerful woman in city government, looked a little forlorn as she made her way around the perimeter of the vast rectangular room, trying not to be noticed as the Boys Choir of Harlem belted out an inspirational hymn on stage. Wearing a blue shawl and black stockings, she was more casually dressed than most of the women in the room, giving her the vague look of an outsider. She finally reached the staff table, easily the worst spot in the house, and quietly slid into a chair.

Something was wrong. The rumors were that she was leaving city government, and when a reporter approached her to talk about it, she didn't deny it. "I'll be spending a lot of time away," she said.

The communications director seemed sad. "I already have the footprint on my back," she said. "I know you all want me to leave." She was referring to the city's press corps.

Lategano said she needed to attend to her sick mother down in South Carolina. But she and Rudy Giuliani were through as a team. After spending nearly every day together for five years, the two had quietly split up, for reasons only they knew. Now, watching from the lowly staff table as Giuliani mingled with the rich and powerful half a dozen tables away, she seemed as if she were already gone.

Later that evening, Lategano made a brief appearance at a party upstairs at the hotel, then accepted a ride home from mayoral adviser Herman Badillo and his wife, Gail. Sitting in the backseat, her long hair blowing over her brown eyes, Lategano was thinking about the future, pondering out loud about what she might do with her career. A chapter in her life had closed. Every word she spoke about Giuliani was phrased in the past tense.

Lategano always denied that she and the mayor had been lovers, but that was almost an extraneous detail by this point. The two had been inseparable, spending their mornings, afternoons, and evenings together. She'd watched over him, worried for him, protected him, and he had done the same for her. Their relationship was a marriage of some sort. A few months later, when she sat down and described what Giuliani had meant to her, Lategano grew wistful. "He was a role model," she said. "He was a father figure. He was the big brother that I never had. Definitely a family member. He was someone that I admired and respected. He was a hero to me."

Giuliani was starting the most high-profile endeavor of his life just as the person he'd relied upon most was leaving. Lategano was the one who'd kept him primed and focused. "She was like STP for Giuliani," an aide says, the person who could wind him up on an issue and keep his anger stoked. As she exited his life, he was left without his alter ego at a critical juncture. The nation was focusing in on Giuliani's titanic battle with Hillary Clinton for the U.S. Senate, and he clearly relished the attention. But behind the scenes he seemed curiously ambivalent.

His tight inner circle of advisers was his family, at least as much as his real family back at Gracie Mansion, yet most of the people he'd been closest to had either left or were on their way out. Peter Powers, his closest friend, was settled into his private law practice. Deputy Mayors Randy Levine and Randy Mastro, both former prosecutors who idolized the mayor, fought a long and bitter behind-the-scenes war over Mastro's unsuccessful campaign to land a first deputy mayor's title, and Mastro eventually left government in 1998. Levine would leave at the end of 1999 to become president of the New York Yankees.

Fran Reiter, part of the original Giuliani team, never returned to the administration after heading up the 1997 campaign, having alienated nearly everyone she'd worked with at City Hall. Giuliani rewarded her with the president and CEO's job at the Convention and Visitors Bureau, a well-paying though less powerful job, but she soon decided to pursue a run for mayor, an ambitious goal for a woman who'd never held elective office. He'd spoken to her about the idea before—even encouraged her. But Giuliani told his aides that when she last spoke with him, he'd shot her down. "Fran, how can you expect to win New Yorkers' support when you can't even get a single colleague who worked with you to support you?" he reportedly said. (Reiter denies he said that.) Lategano was given Reiter's job at the CVB.

Giuliani's inner circle was undergoing a wholesale changeover. Tony Carbonetti, the college dropout who manned his patronage operation, became Giuliani's chief of staff and would grow as close as a son to the mayor. Senior adviser Tony Coles was bumped up to deputy mayor and assumed the hard-liner's role vacated by Lategano. Joe Lhota, filling Mastro's job, was running day-to-day operations. And Ray Harding's son Robert, the budget director, landed a deputy mayor's post as well. Giuliani liked to keep things in the family.

Still adjusting to the new crew, the loss of Lategano, and the fallout from the Diallo crisis, the mayor had to adapt quickly to his new role as Senate candidate. Bruce Teitelbaum was dispatched to set up a campaign headquarters, recruit a staff, and build what would become a wildly successful fund-raising machine. There was no official start to the Giuliani-for-Senate effort: the mayor had disdained campaign kickoffs ever since the disastrous 1989 announcement on the day the Manuel Noriega story broke. The effort just evolved.

Heading into the summer of 1999, Giuliani was in a state of transition. Term limits prevented him from running for mayor again. But did this quintessential chief executive want to be a legislator, or had he just been seduced into running by all the attention? The question grew as he proceeded to send decidedly mixed signals about his interest in the job, while at the same time making some of the most self-destructive decisions of his mayoralty.

Hillary Mania was in full bloom when the First Lady of the United States—herself officially undecided about entering the Senate race—swept into the Grand Hyatt Hotel on April 29 for a State Democratic Committee fund-raiser.

It seemed as though every Democratic congressman, mayor, county executive, assemblyman, council member, and postmaster had turned out for the event. Mrs. Clinton was mobbed by politicians eager to say hello or share a photograph with her, as a vast contingent of reporters from media organizations across America watched behind a rope in the back of the room.

The very presence of this American icon seemed to fuel the Democrats with confidence. Locked out of City Hall for six years and the Governor's Mansion for five, they seemed giddy with the hope that someone had finally come to town to knock the block off Big Bad Rudy Giuliani.

There was a royal quality to her: When she fixed her glassy-eyed gaze on someone, bobbing her head in polite agreement, she didn't so much look at the person as evaluate him. While polite and friendly, she kept an unmistakable distance.

More than a dozen officials took turns paying homage to the First Lady and demonizing the mayor. None ripped into the Republican more enthusiastically than David Dinkins. "Too often good people are silent in the face of bad things occurring," he told the crowd. He proceeded to compare New Yorkers' silence in the face of Giuliani's malevolence to the public's failure to challenge apartheid in South Africa, slavery in America, and the return of the SS *St. Louis* with a boatload of German Jews to Nazi Germany in World War II.

But if the audience was expecting Joan of Arc, ready to do battle with the evil opposition, it was in for a surprise when Mrs. Clinton stepped to the podium. With red, white, and blue balloons floating in the background, she launched into a tedious litany of thank-yous, followed by a speech that seemed carefully designed not to offend.

Listening to schoolchildren at a public school that day, she said, she'd learned that kids wanted to be portrayed more positively in the media. She also learned that they wanted more adults in their lives, that their parents were working too hard, and that there weren't enough guidance counselors in their schools. Her boldest proposal was for smaller class sizes.

Turning solemn, Mrs. Clinton brought up the recent massacre at a public school in Littleton, Colorado. "We need a national conversation about, and a national campaign against, youth violence," she urged. "And we have to listen to them. Really *listen*."

It was a far cry from the militant tone struck by Dinkins. The Democrats' messiah was bland, programmed, and cautious. If there was a cause she was supposed to champion, she didn't seem to know it. A mythology had built up over the years about Hillary Clinton the liberal firebrand, muzzled from speaking her mind because of her official responsibilities. Unbound, however, she seemed kind of boring.

For the next several months Giuliani was able to sit back and watch his potential opponent plod and stumble through her transformation from First

Lady to candidate. For a Clinton, she was surprisingly lead-footed. Greeting the New York Yankees for a photo opportunity in the South Portico of the White House, the Chicago native donned the team's cap and announced herself a lifelong fan. It was an act of such transparent pandering that it reinforced her image as an out-of-towner, opportunistically claiming kinship with New Yorkers.

She took pains to establish her credibility with the locals, purchasing a house for herself and the president in suburban Chappaqua and setting off on a long trek through the state that she dubbed a "listening tour." She spoke with students at a community college in Valhalla, workers at a plant in Elmira, parents of schoolchildren at a church basement in Bedford-Stuyvesant. As weeks turned into months, the press contingent following her began to shrivel, a reaction to her aversion to controversy. Her game plan was to use the time to learn about the state and get her sea legs as a candidate. She could generate headlines later on.

At summer's end, her husband thwarted her hopes of making it through the season without generating news. He sparked just the kind of controversy Mrs. Clinton was hoping to avoid, highlighting her nearly impossible position as both candidate and president's wife. A chorus of human rights activists and Latino politicians, many from New York, had lobbied the administration on behalf of sixteen convicted terrorists from the FALN, a Puerto Rican nationalist group responsible for over a hundred bombings in the United States. None of the prisoners had been directly implicated in the bombings, yet most had received fifty-year sentences and had spent almost twenty years in jail. On August 12, 1999, Clinton offered them clemency. It was a move that presumably could help win his wife Latino votes.

An intense uproar followed. Police groups brought forth maimed and wounded officers, victims of FALN violence, to criticize the prisoners' release. Republican politicians cleverly linked the action to Hillary Clinton's need for Hispanic votes, charging that the president had done her a political favor. When it turned out that the prisoners' clemency petition had been opposed by the Federal Bureau of Investigation, the Bureau of Prisons, and two U.S. attorneys, the charge gained credence.

Trapped between the Puerto Ricans on one side and the law enforcement community on the other, Mrs. Clinton on September 4 called on her husband to withdraw the clemency offer. Her explanation was that the prisoners had taken too long to renounce further violence, a condition of their release. No one was fooled. Her Hispanic allies were outraged. Fairly or not, she looked like a pandering politician who'd gotten caught.

She looked even worse a few months later on a trip to the Middle East. Generations of New York politicians had made the pilgrimage to Israel to win Jewish support back home. Insisting she was traveling to Israel as the First Lady and not as a Senate candidate, Mrs. Clinton decided to balance her appearances in Jerusalem with an appearance in the Arab-occupied West Bank. In the interest of neutrality, she agreed to meet with the wives of the Israeli president and prime minister and then with the wife of Yasir Arafat. It was decision she would regret.

The First Lady traveled to Ramallah to dedicate a new $3.8 million maternal health care program financed by the United States. It was the kind of event she'd favored ever since the spectacular failure of her health care reform plan in 1994: it concerned children, and it seemed to be outside the realm of political controversy. But Suha Arafat was about to teach Mrs. Clinton that controversy in the Mideast is unavoidable.

Speaking at a lectern, as the First Lady of the United States sat behind her smiling politely, Mrs. Arafat launched into a tirade against the Israeli military.

"Our people have been subjected to the daily intensive use of poisonous gas by the Israeli forces, which has led to an increase in cancer cases among women and children," Mrs. Arafat said.

Mrs. Clinton remained silent. When the event ended, she gave Mrs. Arafat a hug and a kiss.

It took twelve hours for Mrs. Clinton to denounce the comments, a delay that allowed a furor to erupt that she couldn't contain. The Israeli government lashed out at Mrs. Arafat's comments, but that was nothing compared with the hostile reaction that greeted Mrs. Clinton's silence. Conservative Jewish leaders, Republicans, and the Clinton-hating *New York Post* denounced the First Lady for her complicity in a poisonous lie, even as she explained that her on-the-spot translation had been faulty. Her belated condemnation, her weak defense—and the fact that she'd gone to the West Bank at all in the midst of a Senate race—raised questions about her political skills and her campaign's competence.

So bumpy was the First Lady's entrance into New York politics that her campaign felt compelled to stage an event in late November to announce that she was not dropping out of the race. At a choreographed exchange at the United Federation of Teachers headquarters, union chief Randi Weingarten pretended to put the First Lady on the spot, asking her before a large audience whether she was in the race or not. "The answer is yes," Mrs. Clinton said, sparking an outpouring of thunderous applause. The First Lady was still honing her political skills, but she seemed fully committed to the campaign, whatever her shortcomings.

The harsh glare of scrutiny on the Democrat had allowed Giuliani to quietly put his house in order. Under intense pressure from national Republicans, Governor Pataki dropped a desperate effort to stop his nemesis from rising to statewide office and endorsed Giuliani in August. That forced a potential Republican primary rival, Congressman Rick Lazio, to withdraw from contention, leaving Giuliani unchallenged for his party's nomination.

The mayor stepped up his travels once again. Reveling in the attention of the national press, he took a swing through the Clintons' home state of Arkansas to poke fun at Mrs. Clinton as a carpetbagger. "I've never lived here. . . . I've never worked here. I've never gone to school here. It's the first time I've been here, but I think it would be cool to run for the Senate," he chortled to a Republican women's club.

"I'm just here listening," he said.

Then, in a demonstration of his pure chutzpah, Giuliani called New York and ordered the Arkansas flag raised over City Hall. That taught Arkansans everything they needed to know about New York's mayor.

Sunny Mindel always seemed a little overcaffeinated. The mayor's third press secretary was a short, frenetic woman with dark sunglasses, frosted blond hair, a big, toothy smile, and a loud, husky voice. Like her boss, she was a crisis junkie, though her harried style sometimes made Rudy Giuliani seem like a Buddha by comparison.

On the morning of September 15, 1999, Mindel had reason to be stressed. The administration was already in crisis mode, as the city prepared for the arrival of Hurricane Floyd, which had devastated much of the South with massive floods and dangerous forty-mile-an-hour winds. Giuliani was stationed at the city's new $13 million Emergency Operations Center at the World Trade Center, plotting out evacuations and school closings.

Amid the swirl of events, Mindel got a phone call from Douglas Feiden, a feature writer and former City Hall bureau chief of the *Daily News*. He was calling for the mayor's reaction to a British art exhibition heading for the Brooklyn Museum. It was entitled "Sensation."

The reporter described some of the works in the show. They included *The Holy Virgin Mary*, a depiction of a black Holy Mother featuring cutouts of pornographic photos and a big slab of elephant dung; *Self*, a sculpture featuring eight pints of the artist's blood, drained from his own veins; and *This Little Piggy Went to Market, This Little Piggy Stayed Home*, featuring the bodies of two pigs encased in formaldehyde.

Feiden pointed out that the Brooklyn Museum was partially funded by city tax dollars. What, he asked Mindel, did Giuliani think of "Sensation"?

Mindel told Feiden she'd get back to him. Tracking down the mayor, she filled him in on the details. "We're getting questions about this exhibit," she told him. Giuliani seemed too distracted by the storm preparations to pay much attention, but he sent her away with instructions to denounce the event. "Assuming the description of the exhibit is accurate," she told Feiden, "no money should be spent on it."

Feiden wasn't sure what she meant. Did she mean no city funds should be spent on it? Or that citizens shouldn't waste their money on it? "I'm going to have to leave the quote as it is," Mindel told him. She seemed to prefer to keep the response vague.

Over the next several days Mindel attempted, with limited success, to get the mayor to focus on the issue. "We're getting questions about this," she told him. "Reporters want to know if taxpayers should pay for this."

"No," Giuliani said. "I don't think so." And he resumed his business.

Her efforts continued. "It's a big issue," she told the mayor on another occasion. "The Catholic League will go after it. Cardinal O'Connor and the Catholics will go crazy over it."

Giuliani told Mindel to bring him more information.

In the eyes of two senior aides who watched her, the press secretary was eager to dive into the controversy. Even with Lategano out of the picture, there were people around the mayor who knew how to get him wound up. She brought Giuliani a clipping of Feiden's story in the *Daily News*. And she brought the issue up in an 8 A.M. staff meeting.

Then she got hold of the "Sensation" catalog and handed it to the mayor.

He flipped through the two-hundred-page book. One exhibit featured mannequins of naked children fornicating in a forest. Another featured a man tied up to a cross-shaped tree with his penis sliced off. Beside him was a headless, armless torso and its missing parts. There was a picture of an old man's naked corpse, entitled *Dead Dad*. Pages 96 and 97 featured a cow sliced into twelve pieces, each in its own glass case filled with formaldehyde. Marcus Harvey's infamous depiction of child-slayer Myra Hindley, created from what looked like tiny hand-prints of children, got its own page. And on page 133, Chris Ofili's *The Holy Virgin Mary* filled a page. She was depicted as an African woman with a large, wide nose, African garb, and big, wide lips. A circular stain appeared in the area around her left breast: that was the elephant dung. Cutouts of vaginas and anuses floated around her—a reflection of the sexual feelings the artist experienced when viewing paintings of her as a child.

The mayor's eyes squinted as he gazed at the photographs—a nervous tic. "This is fucking outrageous," he said. Then he took off his glasses and put the book facedown on his desk. "This is not art," he said. "I'm not going to fucking pay for this."

Mindel and others who were sitting around the mayor's desk knew what this meant. A Giuliani crusade was born.

Giuliani's commissioner of cultural affairs, an erudite patrician named Schuyler Chapin, was instructed to call the museum's director, Arnold Lehman, with an ultimatum: cancel the "Sensation" exhibition or the city would withdraw its $7 million annual contribution to the 173-year-old museum. It was typical Giuliani hardball, and it was soon accompanied by some flamethrowing rhetoric.

The exhibit, he told reporters, was "sick stuff."

"It offends me," he said. "The idea of, in the name of art, having a city-subsidized building have so-called works of art in which people are throwing elephant dung at a picture of the Virgin Mary is sick. If somebody wants to do that privately and pay for that privately, well, that's what the First Amendment is all about. The city shouldn't have to pay for sick stuff."

Chapin was infuriated by the order to cut off the museum and marched over to the mayor's office demanding answers. "No one would talk to me," he recalls. "They wanted to avoid me like the plague because they knew I wouldn't be happy about this." He finally cornered Deputy Mayor Joe Lhota at a staircase heading to the second floor.

"What is this?" Chapin demanded. "This is ridiculous!"

"We want a nuclear explosion," Lhota replied.

"Well, you're going to get it," Chapin said.

Behind the doors that Chapin could not penetrate was a circle of traditional men with traditional views. Giuliani was raised in Catholic schools, as was Lhota. Campaign manager Bruce Teitelbaum had been raised in a conservative Jewish household. Rudy Washington was a devout member of the African Methodist Episcopal Zionist Church. All were offended by the museum exhibit and agreed with the mayor that a considerable amount of Catholic-bashing was at play. What if a picture of the Torah had been treated the way Ofili treated the Virgin Mary, one aide suggested to the group. Would the Jews stand for it?

Giuliani posited other examples: How about if the Koran had been treated as sacrilegiously as the Virgin Mary, he asked the group—could they imagine how the black community would feel? What if it were a picture of Matthew Shepard, the Wyoming student who'd been beaten to death for being gay—would the gay community permit such treatment? Only Catholics, he said, were expected to stand for this.

Predictably, the museum refused to withdraw the exhibit. The stodgy old institution had labored in the shadow of Manhattan's museums for years and had agreed to host "Sensation" to gain the kind of hip cachet that comes with a good controversy. The mayor was doing the place a favor.

Giuliani raised the stakes, threatening to terminate the city's lease with the museum and seize control of the building if its board of directors didn't capitulate to his demands. The museum had banned children under seventeen from seeing "Sensation" unless accompanied by adults—a publicity stunt—and the city's lawyers charged that violated the law. "Last time I checked, I'm the mayor, and I don't find closing down access to a public museum consistent with the use of taxpayer dollars," Giuliani said.

Both sides marched enthusiastically into a full-fledged culture war, and the predictable antagonists lined up behind them. The arts community charged the mayor with trampling on artistic freedom and freedom of expression. The *Times* deplored the administration's "authoritarian overreaction" to the exhibit and warned that Giuliani's conduct, "promis[ed] to begin a new Ice Age in New York's cultural affairs." But the Catholic community, led by Cardinal O'Connor, praised the mayor and urged Catholics to protest the exhibit.

Giuliani was evoking Jesse Helms's epic battle in the 1980s to defund the National Endowment for the Arts for sponsoring objectionable works. It was a curious strategy for the mayor of a liberal city, and an October 1 *New York 1/Daily News* poll showed that city residents backed the museum over the mayor two to one. But Giuliani was a statewide candidate now, and at least one top political adviser was telling him that the crusade would be supported by voters in conservative upstate communities. They were his constituents now, more than the people of New York City, who favored Hillary Clinton by more than two to one. Thus did Mayor Giuliani begin to run against his own city.

Two days before the "Sensation" exhibit opened, the man who endorsed Mario Cuomo for governor traveled to the Ronald Reagan Museum in Simi Valley, California, and hailed the conservative icon as "a force for good in the world." He rhapsodized over Reagan's accomplishments, calling him one of the century's two great presidents, with Franklin D. Roosevelt. A few months later he would push even further to the right, defending the prerogative of teachers to display the Ten Commandments in classrooms.

Giuliani reveled in the Brooklyn Museum fight. When the exhibit opened—drawing 13,000 people, who waited in lines that wrapped around the building—he went on a tear through the television network news shows. On Sunday morning, October 3, he appeared on ABC's *This Week*, NBC's *Meet the Press*, and *Fox News Sunday*. The more attention he received, the more extreme his rhetoric became. "I don't want any money coming out of my pocket to pay for this kind of sick demonstration of clear psychological

problems," he said, speaking about the exhibit at a City Hall press conference. "This should happen in a psychiatric hospital, not in a museum."

Chapin, meanwhile, felt he had held his tongue long enough. "I was hoping it was going to go away," he says, "but as soon as the propaganda began I
had to take a position on it. I was reading in the newspapers that Arnold
Lehman had left behind a trail of anti-Catholic work in Baltimore, which
was bullshit. I thought, 'We're not going to have Joseph Goebbels in 1999.
We're just not going to have it.'" He drafted a letter disagreeing with the
administration's actions and brought it to Giuliani, who had it toned down
and then released. The mayor's aides hinted the commissioner would lose
his job, but Chapin survived.

Eventually the issue ended in court, where the administration was handed
a succession of defeats until it settled the case by basically surrendering. By
then the mayor had enthusiastically planted himself next to Ronald Reagan,
Jesse Helms, and Pat Buchanan in the annals of infamous right-wing attacks
on artistic freedom. Along the way, he probably made some inroads with conservative voters and helped gin up his fund-raising appeals to that audience.

At the same time, he cemented his image with a legion of Americans as a
throwback to the days when American politics was dotted with Nixons,
Daleys, Agnews, and Wallaces. If his crusade seemed anachronistic, the
mayor didn't care. He was standing up for a principle, scoring some political
points with the right wing, and bathing in attention.

Giuliani's behavior was as outrageous as Hillary Clinton's was cautious. His
supporters believed that voters would admire him for his willingness to speak
his mind, as compared with the perpetually calculating First Lady. Giuliani
seemed not to care about the repercussions of his actions leading up to the
big show in 2000. Indeed, some of his decisions seemed downright reckless.

The mayor had long agonized over the city's fate in the event that he won the
Senate seat and had to leave office with a year left to his term. The City Charter
dictated that the public advocate, Mark Green, whom he held in contempt,
would succeed him in office. In the mayor's mind, Green was a liberal carica-
ture, a pawn of unions and black activists who would roll back police enforcement, loosen the reigns of government spending, ease restrictions on welfare
benefits, and generally let the city unravel. Unable to bear the thought of a
Green mayoralty, Giuliani formed a commission to change the City Charter.

It was a preposterous move, made all the more ludicrous when the mayor stacked the Charter Revision Commission with his cronies. Pilloried for his imperious use of executive power, the mayor and his commission, chaired by former deputy mayor Randy Mastro, insisted that they were acting in the long-term interests of the city. But so violent was the reaction from editorial boards, good government groups, and even Green's Democratic rivals for the mayoralty in 2001 that the panel eventually backed down and agreed to recommend that all changes to the charter take effect after the 2001 election. Placed on the ballot as a referendum in November 1999, the commission's proposals were voted down three to one, an embarrassing rebuke to the mayor.

At about the same time that Giuliani launched his charter reform campaign, he sparked yet another furor over his use—or misuse—of power, this time over a party. Tina Brown's *Talk* magazine was to debut in August amid much fanfare. The former *New Yorker* editor, a born showwoman, wanted to launch it with the most talked-about, celebrity-studded party of the year and secured permission from the city to stage the extravaganza at the abandoned site of the Brooklyn Navy Yard.

In June, word leaked out that the magazine had landed an exclusive interview with Hillary Clinton. It was to be her first extended interview since her husband's impeachment trial in the Monica Lewinsky scandal, and the world was waiting to see how she'd weathered the humiliation. The First Lady's face would most likely grace the cover of *Talk*'s first issue.

The mayor's office sprang into action, summarily canceling *Talk*'s permission to use the Navy Yard. Giuliani and his aides were alarmingly candid in admitting that politics played a role in the decision. "A week ago, we heard they were going to put Mrs. Clinton on the cover, and we thought that would lead to an event possibly becoming politicized," Deputy Mayor Randy Levine told the *Daily News*. The next day, the mayor was equally blunt. "People have a right to make their own conclusions about how they want their property used," he told reporters, sounding as if he owned the Navy Yard himself. The national press had a field day with the story of the despotic mayor and his one-man rule.

There were other fiascoes. Schools chancellor Rudy Crew, a onetime ally, resigned after falling out with the mayor over Giuliani's push for school vouchers. At Christmastime, Giuliani ordered an aggressive sweep of the homeless and promised to arrest those who refused shelter. Critics and supporters alike wondered yet again about his lack of compassion.

But if those decisions were curious for a man seeking higher office, they paled in comparison with what Giuliani was doing in his private life.

Judith Nathan started showing up with the mayor a short time after Cristyne Lategano left for South Carolina. One aide remembers him popping up with her at a restaurant without giving his staffers any warning. As the group sat down for dinner and chatted as though nothing unusual were taking place, staffers shot worried looks at one another.

Giuliani brought her into his tight inner circle without a word of explanation. Suddenly this forty-five-year-old divorcée, a drug company executive with stylish clothes, expensive jewelry, and long brown hair, was Giuliani's new confidante. She traveled in the van with him as he raced to events, much as Lategano had. She'd show up at City Hall unannounced and drop into his office. She'd go to town meetings with him and join the crew for dinner afterward. Once again the toughest guy in town had found himself a female companion to lean on.

The mayor's aides soon learned to accept Nathan, and many grew to admire her. Unlike Lategano, she didn't seem to have daggers out for anyone who got too close to Giuliani. She was smart, accomplished, self-assured. Unlike Lategano, she was a grown-up. Like the former communications chief, she seemed to care a great deal for Giuliani and took pleasure in mothering him. "Do you want to try some of this?" she'd ask him at dinner, constantly offering him food. She talked with concern about his health, his moods, and his happiness.

Aides eventually stopped worrying about the fact that Giuliani was still married and that his wife, Donna, was still living with him and their two children at Gracie Mansion. The mayor was so at ease with this new woman in his life and escorted her around in public so frequently that the situation started to seem normal. Watching Giuliani with Lategano all those years, they'd grown accustomed to him spending time with a woman who wasn't his wife. Now that other woman was Judi Nathan.

Donna Hanover Giuliani was as close an adviser as her husband had through his election in 1993. She sat in on his strategy meetings during his two campaigns, helping to decide whom to hire and occasionally chewing out staffers who'd failed him. In public, they held hands, kissed all the time, and seemed genuinely in love. "My husband is the most virile man," she told an interviewer in 1993. "He is so strong and wonderful. . . . He's the most good-looking man in the city as far as I'm concerned." When he was elected mayor, the newspapers ran stories comparing the two to Bill and Hillary Clinton.

But Donna Hanover Giuliani barely survived the transition to City Hall. The blond television anchorwoman was soon supplanted by the mayor's young press secretary as his main confidante, and the news reports about their growing intimacy infuriated the First Lady. Mrs. Giuliani ultimately made it known that Lategano was not welcome at Gracie Mansion. Increasingly, Donna faded from public view, until she disappeared altogether. By 1997 she was so embittered that she refused to tell reporters whom she'd voted for in the mayor's race.

Donna Hanover, as she was now known, stopped functioning as First Lady. She did not appear with the mayor on election night in 1997. She did appear at his inauguration ceremony in January 1998, but that was just about it for their joint appearances. She skipped most of his formal Gracie Mansion events in the evening as well.

The staff at Gracie Mansion divided into two camps—his and hers. Donna's loyalists would keep track of his activities, and the mayor's would keep track of hers. Giuliani and his wife co-existed in a state of estrangement throughout most of his mayoralty, and with the exception of the eruptions that followed the *New York* and *Vanity Fair* stories, the press accepted the unorthodox arrangement as the couple's private business. But by bringing a new woman into his life and ushering her around so brazenly in the middle of a Senate race, Giuliani seemed to be tempting fate.

On February 6, 2000 the political center of gravity shifted to the quiet hamlet of Purchase, New York. A dozen television satellite trucks descended on the State University of New York campus, where a long line of people flocked toward a cavernous gymnasium. Inside, it felt like the electric moment of anticipation before the start of some big game. Every political reporter in New York was there, plus a good segment of the Washington journalistic elite. Hundreds of people began stomping their feet to start the program, creating a booming noise. A Japanese TV crew came late and tried with frustration to find a spot on a riser that already held a hundred cameras. CNN's White House correspondent John King stood on a stepstool, speaking into a camera and a blinding bank of lights.

Politicians like Charlie Rangel and Senator Chuck Schumer served as warm-up acts, revving up the crowd for the main attraction. *"When you have schools that aren't working, you don't blow them up, you build them up!"* Rangel said to cheers, mocking the mayor's recent call to "blow up" the dysfunctional Board of Education. The congressman was defending a terrible status quo against Giuliani's call for reforms, which was exactly why the city's Democrats had been fading from relevance in recent years. But at this moment, the congressman's call to arms sounded exciting.

Then the lights lowered, and for eighteen minutes the audience was treated to a nostalgic film about Hillary Clinton, featuring soft, sweet music and black-and-white pictures of her as a young girl. There was Dorothy Rodham, her mother, recalling that "she was a good child—without being *too* good." There was a friend confiding, "She has a great guffaw of a laugh, to the extent that in a restaurant it's embarrassing." There were home movies of her with Chelsea, a shot of Hillary with Mother Teresa, and interviews with Hillary herself. "I make a mean tossed salad and a great omelet," she confided. Bill flickered in and out so fast a person could easily have missed him. She was the star of this production.

When the lights went up and the crowd finished applauding, Pat Moynihan introduced the First Lady with a benediction of sorts. Noting that she had always admired Eleanor Roosevelt, he turned to her and said in a fatherly voice, "Hillary, Eleanor Roosevelt would have loved you."

The crowd roared as the Democratic candidate to fill Moynihan's seat took center stage in front of a huge blue "Hillary" banner. A sea of "Hillary" signs bobbed up and down in the audience. As the president of the United States remained seated in the background without a speaking role, his wife declared, "I am pleased to announce my candidacy."

She rolled out a litany of reasons for running. "We can bring good jobs to every corner of New York."

"No child should grow up hungry."

"I'll keep fighting until every American has access to health care."

"I'll fight against the divisive politics of revenge and retribution."

It was all fairly standard Clintonian rhetoric, lifted straight from her husband's moderate Democratic playbook. Like her husband, she billed herself as a "New Democrat."

"I don't believe that government is the source of all our problems," she said, "or the solution to them."

If there were no groundbreaking ideas on this day, there was an infectious energy to her announcement, for all its meticulous staging. Mrs. Clinton was not yet an inspiring candidate, but her star power was awesome. The event demonstrated that her campaign had righted itself in the wake of the previous year's disasters. And the candidate was impressive for the sheer effort she was making to prove herself to the residents of her newly adopted state.

Three weeks earlier, Rudy Giuliani had the stage to himself in an altogether different setting. Standing before a large crowd gathered inside the City Council chamber for his State of the City address, he seemed like a man who was reluctant to give up his job. "This could be my last State of the City speech," he noted.

It was a vintage performance, filled with bold proposals and defiant rhetoric. Strolling back and forth in front of the audience with a portable clip-on microphone attached to his lapel, he laughed, grew angry, poked fun at his enemies, and evoked the sense of mission that had brought him to City Hall six years earlier. Criticizing the "job protection system" that locked mediocre teachers into the school system, he proposed that the city cease granting across-the-board salary hikes to all teachers. They should be paid based on their performance, he said, with bigger raises for the best teachers. "The ones that really stink don't get any pay raise at all," he suggested.

"We should be ashamed that we don't have the political courage to take on the unions, the special interests, and everything else," he said.

"It's a tragedy. It's a tragedy! You only get one chance to educate a child, and if you screw it up, then it's very, very hard to redo it later."

Near the end, he held up a blowup of the 1990 *Time* magazine cover pro-
nouncing "The Rotting of the Big Apple." Then he held up the cover of *Time*
magazine from January 2000, showing a million people at a glittering-new
Times Square celebrating the millennium on New Year's Eve. The magazine
covers were his trophies, symbols of how things had changed under his watch.

Looking wistful, Giuliani then admitted what his face betrayed. "I'm
never going to have a better job," he said.

At the end of February, a jury acquitted all four officers who killed Amadou
Diallo. The black community reacted with revulsion, and 2,000 people
staged a demonstration the next day, marching down Fifth Avenue, a number of them chanting "Impeach Giuliani." To many African Americans, the
verdict proved that society considered black lives cheap. Yet the jury's four
blacks concurred with the other eight that the killing of Diallo was an accident. Perhaps the real fault rested with a mayor and police commissioner
who pushed cops to stop and frisk young black men without cause. But they
weren't the ones on trial.

Giuliani responded quietly, almost mournfully, to the news, expressing
"very, very deep, heartfelt sympathy" to Diallo's family. While he praised the
justice system, his tone was far more conciliatory than it had been during
the controversy that followed the shooting the previous year. Now deep in
the middle of his Senate campaign, he seemed to be trying to avoid becoming a lightning rod once more.

Three weeks later, that reticence came to an end. Early in the morning
hours of March 16, he received a police notification while riding in his van.
Standard protocol called for the police to alert the mayor about all major
incidents, and the news this morning was that yet another unarmed black
immigrant had been shot and killed by a plainclothes police officer.

Patrick Dorismond, a twenty-six-year-old Haitian immigrant, worked the
3 to 11 P.M. shift each day as a security guard for the 34th Street Partnership,
patrolling the streets around Macy's in a blue uniform. When work was over
on the night of March 15, he changed back into street clothes and went out
for a drink with his coworker Kevin Kaiser. After knocking back a few at the

Wakamba Cocktail Lounge, situated in a seedy area of Eighth Avenue near the Port Authority bus terminal, they left the bar and went in search of a taxi.

They were soon approached by an undercover narcotics officer named Anderson Moran. Walking twenty feet ahead of him were his partners, Julio Cruz and Anthony Vasquez. The three cops were on a roll this night, having already made eight marijuana busts. Commissioner Safir had launched a massive effort to crack down on drug offenses in January, christening it Operation Condor. The cops were looking to swell their arrest numbers.

Moran approached Dorismond and asked him if he had any drugs to sell him. Insulted, Dorismond started to shout at him, not realizing that the stranger was a cop. Someone threw a punch, and Moran called for help from his partners. As two plainclothes cops ran to his side, two other people came to Dorismond's defense. According to the cops, someone in Dorismond's group yelled, "Get the gun!" perhaps after spotting Vasquez's 9mm Glock in its holster. Alarmed, Vasquez pulled out his gun and, according to the cops, yelled "Police!" Dorismond lunged at Vasquez, the gun went off, and the security guard dropped to the ground. A bullet had ripped through his aorta and lung. He died soon afterward.

"Get me Safir on the phone," the mayor directed an aide. The wheels in his head began to turn.

By daybreak, the administration already had a strategy in place. "Always stay on the offense," the mayor liked to lecture his staff, and this case was no exception. He called for the public to wait for the evidence to emerge. "I would urge everyone not to jump to conclusions," he told reporters, "and to allow the facts to be analyzed and investigated without people trying to let their biases, their prejudices, their emotions, their stereotypes dictate the results."

But at the same time, he launched an intensive campaign to discredit the victim, instructing Safir to release to the press Dorismond's criminal history, including his sealed juvenile file. The records showed that Dorismond had been arrested twice as an adult for assault and gun possession; he had pleaded guilty in each case to reduced charges of disorderly conduct. As a thirteen-year-old, the records showed, he had been arrested on robbery and assault charges, but they were dropped and his record was sealed.

What this proved about Dorismond's killing became a subject of heated debate. Giuliani had no doubt seen the steady stream of family members and friends who'd gone on television and tearfully portrayed Dorismond as a good father and a gentle man. Perhaps the mayor had seen Al Sharpton rise to deplore the police action, succeeded by a bevy of Democratic politicians doing the same.

Whatever his motivations, the mayor proceeded to launch a one-man crusade to tarnish the image of Patrick Dorismond. Each day brought a harsher characterization. Speaking to Fox News from a VFW Hall in upstate New York, the mayor painted a bleak portrait of the security guard.

"If you read the man's background—arrested for robbery, arrested for attempted robbery, arrested for assaulting someone in a driving dispute, arrested for assaulting someone in a marijuana dispute, with calls to his home for other disputes—it is a pretty bad record," he said.

"People do act in conformity very often with their prior behavior," he said, adding that the media, "would not want a picture presented of an altar boy, when in fact maybe it isn't an altar boy, it's some other situation that may justify, more closely, what the police officer did."

He was violating his own admonition not to prejudge the case. Behind the scenes, his aides, particularly his media adviser Adam Goodman, were cautioning him to exhibit some compassion for Dorismond. A growing chorus of black leaders, Democrats, even Republicans were criticizing Giuliani's response. Even the *New York Post* was turning on him, for the first time in his mayoralty ("Rudy Giuliani has screwed up, and screwed up bigtime," wrote columnist John Podhoretz). Dorismond was unarmed and minding his own business when police tried to ensnare him in a drug deal. Why was Giuliani smearing him?

The mayor wouldn't hear his aides' advice. His refusal to be bullied into contrition during the Diallo furor had been vindicated by the jury's verdict, he said. He was right to stand up for the truth then—and now.

Giuliani was on a mission, and there was no one around him with the stature or self-assurance to shake him out of it. After a while his aides gave up trying, even as he ratcheted up his rhetoric. He had the NYPD release newly discovered records showing that Dorismond's girlfriend—the one on

TV calling him a good man—had called police a few weeks earlier to complain that Dorismond had assaulted her while she was holding their small child. "That Mr. Dorismond spent a good deal of his adult life punching people was a fact," Giuliani said.

So over-the-top was Giuliani's one-man jihad that Hillary Clinton, who was loath to be seen as anticop, felt compelled to step forward and criticize the mayor. Speaking in the friendly confines of the Bethel African Methodist Episcopal church in Harlem, she rose to the pulpit on a Monday evening and attacked her rival. "Everyone, whether he is a police officer or a civilian, is entitled to equal protection under the law and a fair investigation before any judgment is rendered," she said, speaking in a stern, sorrowful tone. "That should be the rule, and all of us should abide by it. It is wrong to attack either the character of Patrick Dorismond or the police officer." The church roared with approval. She seemed reasonable and levelheaded compared with the hothead at City Hall.

In the calculus of New York politics, Hillary Clinton was risking a loss of support from the suburban white voters she was trying to lure away from Giuliani. These were people who liked the mayor for his crackdown on the unruly elements of the city and who loathed Sharpton and his causes. But the First Lady and her aides realized that the mayor had gone so far over the edge in this case that she would gain stature by speaking out against him.

On March 25, Dorismond's funeral was held in Brooklyn. Five thousand people massed outside the Holy Cross Church, many chanting "Giuliani Must Go" as Al Sharpton and other activists attended the service. It wasn't long before things turned violent. Rocks and bottles flew through the air at cops in riot gear. Officers fired tear gas to restrain the angry crowd, which smashed up two police cruisers and a telephone booth. Twenty-three cops were injured, some with broken limbs. Giuliani's tough talk had sparked his first riot.

A few weeks later, as the Dorismond furor wound down—Sharpton tried and failed to sustain a Diallo-style civil disobedience campaign—a New York Times poll showed that Giuliani's approval rating had sunk to the lowest point of his mayoralty. A mere 32 percent of city residents approved of the job he was doing as mayor. Hillary Clinton led him by 10 points.

It was a heck of a way to run for senator—presuming that Rudy Giuliani actually cared about being senator. His actions over the previous twelve months had rendered him less popular, reinforced doubts about his temperament, lost him crucial support from moderate Democrats, and turned him into such a racially polarizing figure that the *Times* poll was unable to measure the fraction of the black electorate that still approved of him because it was so microscopically small.

Some outside strategists believed the constant bombast emanating from City Hall could win the Senate race for the mayor. Hillary Clinton was relegated to the sidelines time and again by the controversies her Republican rival was kicking up. She seemed barely able to interest anyone in her proposals to save the Social Security system or shape up Medicare. She was constantly forced to debate on his terms and comment on what were basically New York City issues. The First Lady of the United States, one of the world's most famous women, was staging a historic run for U.S. Senate, yet the mayor was dominating the race. If Giuliani could avoid Dorismond-like fiascoes, he could theoretically continue to overshadow Mrs. Clinton straight through November.

Yet Giuliani had barely deigned to mount a campaign. While Clinton was well on her way to visiting all sixty-two of New York State's counties, he'd hardly traveled outside the city. While she was honing her message, he'd barely issued a position paper. Inside his camp, meetings weren't being held, polls weren't being taken. When an upstate fund-raising event conflicted with Opening Day at Yankee Stadium, Giuliani blew off the fundraiser, burning hundreds of Republicans who'd purchased tickets to see him.

The mayor acted as though he were entitled to the Senate seat, and he didn't seem to want it all that much. His behavior ranged from indifferent to reckless. The growing doubts that Giuliani was displaying, if not admitting, were about to come to a head.

At the end of a mayoral town meeting one spring night, Giuliani started to complain that he wasn't feeling well. It was the first time in six years that his aides had heard the boss complain about his health. He said he felt dizzy and lethargic. More than one person in his entourage noticed that he didn't seem sharp in that evening's performance. Giuliani went home to Gracie Mansion to get some sleep.

On April 26 Giuliani contacted his closest aides: Denny Young, perhaps his closest confidant of all. Tony Carbonetti, his chief of staff. Bruce Teitelbaum, his campaign manager. Elliot Cuker, his good friend. A few others. The mayor told them that he'd been to Mt. Sinai Hospital in Manhattan for three hours that afternoon. Some routine blood tests he'd taken two weeks earlier had revealed some problems. A biopsy performed at the hospital earlier in the day had confirmed that, like his father decades earlier, he had developed prostate cancer.

There is no good time to come down with a serious illness, but Giuliani's diagnosis had serious repercussions. It was six months before Election Day. The State Republican Committee was set to nominate him formally for the Senate in a month; he'd already raised over $20 million for the race. Giuliani went home and broke the news to his wife and kids.

The next morning, after informing a larger circle of staffers about his condition at the regular 8 A.M. meeting, Giuliani called a press conference in the Blue Room. Word had started to leak out already, and television crews and reporters raced down to City Hall.

He stood in front of the room underneath a towering portrait of Thomas Jefferson, facing two banks of cameras and a full house of journalists and worried aides.

"Good morning," he said. "I was diagnosed yesterday with a—with prostate cancer. It's a treatable form of prostate cancer. It was diagnosed at an early stage."

He spoke clearly, deliberately, and without emotion, like a father explaining difficult facts to a worried son. He described how he'd taken a battery of blood tests to gauge the level of the protein called prostate-specific antigen in his blood, how the antibiotics he'd been prescribed hadn't reduced the PSA level, which in turn had led to the biopsy. He would need an operation or radiation treatment, he said—he didn't know which he'd opt for. He talked about how his father had died of the disease at the age of seventy-three, but how that had happened in an age before the PSA test had been invented. "It brings up very painful memories," he said.

"And you know, I miss my father every day of my life. And he's a—he's a very, very important reason for why I'm standing here as the mayor of New York City."

The mayor's willingness to discuss both his condition and his feelings about it was reassuring, even as his news was throwing the race for Senate into chaos. The campaign would have to be put on hold, he said, until he could figure out his course of treatment. Then he'd decide whether he could continue as a candidate.

As the news reverberated through the city, Giuliani became the subject of enormous compassion, and several journalists noted the softening effect that this frightening malady seemed to have on his personality. The sympathy extended into the newsroom of the *Post*, which exhibited its respect for the mayor's plight by delaying publication of some photos that promised to change the course of the Senate race.

Several days of increasingly sympathetic reports went by before a curious item popped up in the middle of Mitchell Fink's gossip column in the *Daily News*:

RUDY & FRIEND DINE & DINE

Rudy Giuliani hasn't let the diagnosis of prostate cancer slow him down. A day after he stunned the city with news of his condition, there he was at 11 p.m. Friday dining on mussels in marinara sauce—but no linguini—with a friend at Cronies on Second Ave.

The pair sat in the back, with much of the mirror and brass-accented restaurant to themselves, as Giuliani's security detail waited up front, two restaurant workers told The News' Richard Weir. Witnesses said the pair talked quietly and sat in a small nook.

Then, Sunday night, he and the same friend reappeared at the restaurant, this time sitting in a more open section of the eatery. Restaurant workers said Giuliani and his companion have been dining regularly at Cronies—a popular hangout for the Yankees, especially Derek Jeter—for several years.

One restaurant staffer opined that the mayor was with his wife, but shown a picture of Donna Hanover, he said it wasn't her.

Giuliani's office had no comment.

The item did not mention his companion's name. But some dam was starting to burst, as became evident in the next day's *Post*. "Here's the first look at the mystery woman who's been spotted dining quietly with Mayor Giuliani," stated a small story that accompanied three photographs at the top of page 7. They showed a fuzzy Rudy Giuliani walking a few steps behind Judith Nathan. The story described her as "an Upper East Side divorcée who's been spending time with the mayor lately.

"The mayor and Nathan have been seen together at restaurants and functions over the past several months," it stated.

Like the Fink story, it was written in code, implying something without explicitly stating it.

On the day the *Post* story was published, a reporter asked the mayor about it at his daily press briefing. "She's a good friend, a very good friend," the mayor replied. "Beyond that, you can ask me questions, and that's exactly what I'm going to say." He too was speaking in code, but that was all the confirmation the tabloids needed.

The next day's papers exploded with coverage of the mayor's relationship with Nathan. "The roller-coaster marriage of Mayor Giuliani and Donna Hanover appeared to take another dip yesterday with the mayor's admission that he is 'a very good friend' of another woman," the *Daily News* reported. It quoted a mayoral "confidant" confirming the story. "They're an item," the confidant stated. "They seem to be very affectionate. They're very open about it."

The spigot was now wide open, gushing details about their summer weekends in the Hamptons and her frequent meals with his staff. Giuliani had brought Nathan to town meetings, to the St. Patrick's Day Parade, even to the annual Inner Circle dinner, the papers reported. The mayor's new "gal pal" was a media star.

The assumption was that the mayor's wife accepted the relationship. On Saturday, May 6, Donna Hanover came forward. She showed up on the southwest corner of 51st Street and Madison Avenue wearing black in honor of Cardinal John O'Connor, who had died the previous week. So removed was she from her husband's life that she'd accepted a role in the *Vagina Monologues*, a scatalogically explicit show, in the midst of his bid for conservative supporters. So estranged were they that she'd responded to the news of his cancer with a one-paragraph statement (though she withdrew from the show because of it). With her back to St. Patrick's Cathedral and her eyes facing Le Cirque 2000, the city's trendiest restaurant, Hanover recited a short speech.

"I will be supportive of Rudy in his fight against his illness, as this marriage and this man have been very precious to me," she said, punching chosen words like the actress she was. "The well-being of Andrew and Caroline will be my primary concern in any decisions that have to be made, as has always been the case."

And then she rushed up a flight of stairs leading to the church, followed by a cloud of aides.

What did she mean?

The story line was changing daily. No longer just the brave cancer patient, Giuliani now was a possible adulterer. One calamity had nothing to do with the other, but they'd become the twin towers of Rudy Giuliani's life. The details of something so drab as a Senate race took a backseat to the unfolding psychodrama the mayor was playing out on the public stage.

The following Tuesday, Giuliani injected a new twist. He stood by his police commissioner, Howard Safir, at One Police Plaza for yet another major announcement: Safir also had prostate cancer. "This is a very strange and ironic thing," the mayor said. "We're both dealing with the same thing at the same time." It was a sad diversion from the main story, which was about to have its denouement.

The front page of the next day's *Post* carried a message for Giuliani from upstate. Joseph Bruno, the Republican majority leader of the State Senate, wasn't amused by the circus taking place down in Sin City. "GOP HONCHO'S ADVICE TO RUDY ON MARRIAGE MESS: WORK IT OUT!" the headline read. Bruno called on Giuliani to resolve his situation and clarify his intentions in the Senate race.

Giuliani, focused as always on remaining on the offensive, took Bruno's advice to heart. At a morning press conference held on the outdoor balcony of the Bryant Park Grill, he took a question about Bruno's comments.

"This is very, very painful," Giuliani replied, looking ashen. "For quite some time it's probably been apparent that Donna and I lead, in many ways, independent and separate lives. It's been a very painful road, and I'm hopeful that we'll be able to formalize that in an agreement that protects our children, gives them all the security and all the protection they deserve, and protects Donna."

As for Judith Nathan, he said, "she's been a very good friend to me before I had to deal with the decisions that I have to make about my illness and what to do about it, and I rely on her, and she helps me a great deal. And I'm going to need her more now than maybe I did before."

It was on one level very sad, and on another fairly disturbing. Why was Giuliani letting the public in on his private turmoil? Was it honest, as he claimed, or narcissistic? Hanover's aides told reporters that the mayor had not bothered to consult his wife before announcing to the world that their marriage was over. Trying always to get the jump on the opposition, Giuliani inadvertently unleashed his most dangerous opponent.

At 4:30 P.M., Hanover held a press conference of her own. Standing outside the gates of Gracie Mansion, shaking with grief, her eyes brimming with tears, she unloaded six years of pent-up anger at her husband before a group of reporters.

"I had hoped that we could keep this marriage together," she said, in another prepared speech. "For several years it was difficult to participate in Rudy's public life because of his relationship with one staff member.

"Beginning last May, I made a major effort to bring us back together, and Rudy and I reestablished some of our personal intimacy through the fall. At that point, he chose another path. Rudy and I will now discuss the possibility of a legal separation."

Long after the city had forgotten about Cristyne Lategano, now married and heading the Convention and Visitors Bureau, Hanover brought back the memory of her husband's relationship with his press secretary, implying that the rumors Giuliani and Lategano had denied for years were true. As televised bathos went, it was a breathtaking performance.

Giuliani's life was in turmoil. He was trying to decide whether to stay in the race for Senate while dealing with a serious illness, a crumbling marriage, and a well-publicized affair with another woman. He had two children to worry about. And he still had to govern a city.

Defiantly, he joined Nathan at Tony's Di Napoli, an Upper East Side restaurant, for a celebration of Sunny Mindel's birthday two days after he announced his separation. Afterward, he took Nathan on a carefree ten-block stroll back to her apartment, bantering all the way with a crush of newspaper photographers, who were delighted to get their first good shots of the mayor together with his new flame. Republican leaders, still praying he'd survive his brush with scandal, were astonished at his arrogance. Governor Pataki and others had swallowed their anger over Giuliani's betrayal in the 1994 governor's race and were counting on him to wage this crucial war against Hillary Clinton. Now the mayor was betraying them yet again by proudly carrying on an adulterous affair in public view, arguing that his private life was no one else's business. The rules for politicians had been established long ago, but Giuliani was acting once again as though he were above politics—and above the rules.

Yet the problems that brought everything to a screeching halt this bizarre week in May were those of an ordinary man, even a weak man. Despite all the bravado he was displaying, Giuliani had little choice but to come to grips with the mess he'd made of things. The pressure to decide whether to continue in the Senate race would force him to confront his hypocrisies, his inadequacies, and, in the case of his cancer, his own mortality.

On the night of Sunday, May 14, as Giuliani agonized, he received a visitor at Gracie Mansion. It was his boyhood pal Peter Powers, who'd come to help him sort out his crisis.

There was something touching about watching Giuliani with his old best friend walking up the stairs to the mansion together. Despite all that had gone wrong for Powers at the end of his stay at City Hall, he was still the person Giuliani turned to in his darkest moment.

In the lushly appointed rooms where generations of mayors had grappled with their greatest crises, Giuliani struggled to make his biggest decision. True to his character, Powers was cautious. He didn't like the Judith Nathan story and feared the fallout from it. "Rudy, there are a lot of sharks in the water," he said. "The smart thing to do is, let's fight another day."

Giuliani's media adviser Adam Goodman came by to offer his advice. The young adman had written a memo to the mayor that strongly advised him to remain in the race unless his health dictated otherwise. It quoted newspaper articles proclaiming George W. Bush's presidential aspirations practically dead after he lost to John McCain in that February's New Hampshire primary. A good campaign carried Bush through that crisis, Goodman argued, just as Giuliani's campaign could help him overcome the events of the past two weeks.

Goodman believed that the stage was set for a historic moment, in which a big-city mayor could rise above his obstacles and defeat the First Lady of the United States. Such a victory, he said, could trigger a national celebration among Republicans so dramatic that it would catapult Giuliani to the position of top Republican contender for the presidency in 2004, if Bush lost to Al Gore in 2000. Even McCain, Goodman argued, would be eclipsed by a victorious Giuliani.

Withdraw now, Goodman warned, and you'll antagonize the Republicans so badly that your political future will be jeopardized.

Displeased with the do-or-die scenario, Giuliani angrily lashed out at Goodman, telling him he was being melodramatic. He didn't like to hear talk of his walking away from the race as if he were a coward. He was a sick man. People would have to understand.

As the days passed, Giuliani found himself increasingly paralyzed by indecision. He told reporters that he was trying to make what was basically a medical judgment—the Judith Nathan story was immaterial, he said. Yet his advisers were worried about Donna Hanover even if he wasn't and they discussed whether his wife would further embarrass him with charges of infidelity if he stayed in the race. As Powers said, there were sharks in the water. Hanover's intentions became an unknown that cast a shadow over the deliberations.

Giuliani was speaking by day to doctors and by night to trusted friends. He had a long dinner with Ray Harding on Monday, May 15, and traveled later in the week to visit Monsignor Alan Placa, who had been a friend to Giuliani and Powers ever since the days of Bishop Loughlin. Tony Carbonetti, the mayor's chief of staff, and Denny Young, his counsel, were with him constantly, and Bruce Teitelbaum, his campaign manager, was speaking to him through the day.

The last member of this circle was Elliot Cuker, who served as an adviser

without portfolio. Like Howard Koeppel, Cuker was an auto dealer who had
bonded with Giuliani over their mutual love of classic cars. But if Koeppel
was the mayor's buddy, Cuker played a more fundamental role in his life.
An unsuccessful actor, Cuker played Lee Strasberg to Giuliani's Marilyn
Monroe, constantly urging him to search his innermost feelings and release
them for the world to see. His influence reached its apotheosis in 1997,
when he literally turned Giuliani into Marilyn, dressing him in drag for the
Inner Circle performance.

A dark, middle-aged Russian immigrant partial to bow ties, Cuker lavished attention on his student and assumed the role of Giuliani's New Age
guru, which gave him extraordinary influence during the mayor's moment
of vulnerability. "Rudy, forget everything else. How do you feel about this?
Do you really want to go through it?" Members of Giuliani's political staff,
who were pulling for him to stay in the race, were infuriated.

The skies turned dark and unleashed a massive thunderstorm Thursday
night, May 18. Giuliani allowed a nationally televised town hall meeting on
MSNBC to come and go without his revealing his intentions, though he
surprised a lot of people by confiding to hostess Andrea Mitchell that he
regretted his behavior during the Patrick Dorismond controversy. He should
have "conveyed the human feeling I have" in the incident, Giuliani said,
sounding very much like a man deep in the throes of introspection.

Later that night, as rain pelted against the roof of Gracie Mansion and
thunder exploded, Giuliani had trouble sleeping. Though his closest advisers felt they had divined his intentions earlier that week, the mayor's
thoughts about the race were still unsettling him. But his indecision would
come to an end by morning.

When he got to City Hall he had his aides call an afternoon press conference. It might have been dramatic to have announced his decision to
Andrea Mitchell on national television, but Giuliani's preference had
always been for the grand press conference with a big crowd, a wall of cameras lined up like a firing squad, and the vast stage to himself. There would
be only one diva at the climax of this opera.

The line of reporters and cameramen waiting to enter the old Board of
Estimate Chamber on City Hall's second floor snaked around the great

rotunda and ended at the mouth of the City Council Chamber halfway across the building. When the doors swung open the audience quickly filled up the extensive room, which, with its high white walls and neat rows of pewlike benches, resembled a New England town hall. The mayor's aides filed into the front row. Ray Harding was on the far left, sitting with Peter Powers, Bruce Teitelbaum, Randy Levine, and Rudy Washington. Adam Goodman and his sidekick Rick Wilson were standing in their Gap-style shirts next to Joe Lhota, dressed in banker blue. All of them seemed nervous.

"Heads up!" a press aide yelled, and moments later Giuliani walked in with that purposeful look he wore when he blew into a room. He was accompanied by Elliot Cuker, Tony Carbonetti, Sunny Mindel, Denny Young, and Guy Molinari, the Staten Island borough president. Giuliani had reportedly told his aides he wouldn't start before the arrival of the two men who were there at the beginning of his political career, Molinari and Harding.

The audience rose and gave him a sustained ovation. The mayor walked to the podium at the front of the room to the left of a towering portrait of former Senator Henry Clay, known to history as the Great Compromiser. Giuliani absorbed the affection for a few moments, then began to speak.

"I'm a very fortunate man. God has given me a lot, and whatever obstacles that are placed in your way, I think the way to deal with it is to try to figure out how to make it make you a better person. The reason I'm such a fortunate man is that I have people that love me and I love them, and they care for me and I care for them. And that's the greatest support that you can have in life."

He seemed older than he'd ever looked before. His temples seemed more gray, his cheeks more sunken, his complexion pale. He seemed nervous and emotional.

When he first learned he had cancer, he said, he thought his treatment decisions would be a lot easier to make. Likewise, he'd found the process of deciding whether to remain in the Senate race similarly vexing. He still hadn't been able to decide how to treat his cancer, he said, and he was almost as paralyzed over the political decision.

He'd found, he said, that "something beautiful happens" when a person is confronted with such problems. "It makes you figure out what you're all about and what's really important to you and what should be important to you—you know, where the core of you really exists," he said. "And I guess because I've been in public life so long and politics, I used to think the core of me was in politics, probably.

"It isn't. I've decided that what I should do is to put my health first and that I should devote the focus and attention that I should to running, to being able to figure out the best treatment, and not running for office.

"This is not the right time for me to run for office. If it were six months ago or it were a year from now or the timing were a little different, maybe it would be different. But it isn't different, and that's the way life is."

New York 1 had already revealed his decision to withdraw from the race earlier in the day, and other news organizations had followed suit. But to hear Rudy Giuliani say it was to freeze in one's seat. This was not so much a political announcement as a description of a life-changing experience. His speech took on the air of a confession.

"There is something good that comes out of this," he said. "A lot of good things come out of it. I think I understand myself a lot better. I think I understand what's important to me better. Maybe I'm not completely there yet. I would be foolish to think that I was in a few weeks. But I think I'm heading in that direction.

"I thank God it gives me, really, another eighteen months to be the mayor of New York City, which I love very, very much," he said. "And I'm going to devote the extra time that I've been given not only to do the things we have done . . . but to overcome maybe some of the barriers that maybe I placed there and figure out how to overcome them. I don't know the answer to that yet. I don't know exactly how you do that. But I'm going to try very hard to do that."

He recalled that on Election Night in 1997 he'd promised to reach out to communities that had felt left out of the city's resurgence, notably the city's minorities. "I'm going to dedicate myself to trying to figure out how we can get them to feel that too," he said, "including, maybe, changes I have to make in the way I approach it, the way I look at it."

This was the mirror image of the man who'd stood on a Bronx street corner two years earlier telling all those friends and enemies who were criticizing him to drop dead. This was a man asking forgiveness for his sins and promising to do better. Councilman Tom Ognibene would later compare him to Ebenezer Scrooge after being visited by the ghost of Christmas future. Others were reminded of a dying Lou Gehrig saying goodbye to his fans at Yankee Stadium.

In one respect, it was a remarkably self-indulgent act. The mayor spent three weeks humiliating his wife and children and betraying his party. Now he was making a play for sympathy with a speech pledging to act more decently to people he'd disregarded for six years. Other candidates had withdrawn from their races by citing larger causes that still needed to be fought. Rudy Giuliani talked only about himself.

The more charitable view was that a series of crises had led this inflexible man to a rare moment of self-doubt, and he'd been smart enough to sense an opportunity in the situation. The resulting speech was an honest—if selective—expression of the pain and soul-searching he'd been experiencing since his odyssey began. Despite all he'd omitted, Giuliani conceded a world more about his true feelings in his graceful talk than most politicians ever offered their constituents.

In either case, Giuliani was removing himself from center stage for the first time in his life, perhaps because of his illness, perhaps because of his marital problems, perhaps because he never wanted to be a senator in the first place. As a younger, more enthusiastic candidate, Rick Lazio, prepared to take his place in the race against Hillary Clinton, Giuliani was left to complete his journey of introspection. He had time to ponder his successes and failures through the years, to reflect upon what had led him to achieve so much on one hand while creating so much misery on the other.

Peter Powers liked to tell the story of how Giuliani once got his classmates at Bishop Loughlin out of a serious jam. On their senior class trip to Washington, D.C., a group of them got into a huge water fight at their hotel. Pitchers of water were thrown from room to room, even under the doors, until the place was flooded.

When the hotel manager got wind of what was going on, he stormed up to their rooms and ordered them to pack their bags and get out in ten minutes.

The students were scared to death, as Powers recalls. If they were evicted, the Brothers would find out and punish them all, perhaps even kick them out of school.

Giuliani thought for a moment, then spoke up. "He's bluffing," he said of the manager. "I'm going to sleep." His classmates nervously followed suit, and that was the last they heard from the hotel.

"He doesn't let fear run his emotions as readily as others would," Powers says of his friend. "He has this uncanny knack to know when he's right and to believe in it."

That certainty of purpose took Rudy Giuliani a long way. But it also turned out to be his fatal flaw.

After Giuliani took a round of questions, the big event wound down and the cable news channels started to wrap up their live coverage. The last question came from Rafael Martinez Alequin, a press corps gadfly who specialized in irritating the mayor. "Do you feel closer to God?" the reporter shouted.

"Do I feel closer to God?" the mayor said. "I hope he's closer to me." The audience laughed and applauded, and Giuliani made his way out of the room. The show was over.

Acknowledgments

I came to realize in the course of writing this book that I'm lucky to be surrounded by a lot of smart people. I'm blessed that they've bothered to expend as much time and energy on me as they have.

Jack Stephenson, my partner, friend, and hero, didn't hesitate for a moment when I told him about my plan to write a book, despite the sacrifices that it inevitably entailed for him. He made this project possible in a million different ways, and I am eternally grateful to him.

Steve Paulus, vice president and general manager of New York 1 News, showed me once again why he is so widely admired and respected by his staff and the television news industry. Without his support and vision, this book might never have been written. He's a great boss.

Flip Brophy, my agent, got this project off the ground. I thank her for her tenacity, wisdom, and awesome intelligence.

Likewise, working with Claire Wachtel of William Morrow was a revelation. Her intellect and warmth in the face of preposterous deadline pressures made this book project one of the best professional and intellectual experiences of my career.

Amanda Mayer began this project with me, and Karen Avrich ended it with me. Both were talented and dedicated research assistants who did so much more, and I thank them for their hard work and good judgment. I was lucky to have found them. Bobby Melton, the transcriber, was phenomenal at his job. Thanks also to Tina Traster and Ashley Heyer for their work on this text.

There was a small circle of friends who were crucial advisers. First and foremost was Claire Brinberg, New York 1's executive political producer, who served as my sounding board every day for over a year and who read my work and criticized it in ways that helped improve it beyond measure. Her help was priceless. Adam Nagourney of the *New York Times*, who is just about the best political reporter I know, and Phil Friedman, the impossibly brilliant political consultant, also gave me important advice and guidance.

Paul Lombardi, the bright and wonderful entertainment reporter for New York 1 and a dear friend, gave me support at an early and critical moment, as did Cathy, Michael, and Elizabeth Stephenson.

Kevin Hayes, a creative marvel at the *Daily News*, and Nancy Hass, a superb reporter, were constant sources of support, ideas, and inspiration, as were my good friends Justin Blake, Michael Willoughby and Mark Halperin.

There were so many people at New York 1 who lent me their time and expertise, particularly Peter Landis, Dan Jacobson, Jamie McShane, Dominic Carter, David Lewis, Kerri Lyon, Taina Hernandez, and—at strange hours of the morning when no one else was left in the newsroom—Colin Miner. Thanks also to former New York 1 colleagues Melissa Russo, Jonathan Dienst, Lisa Reyes, and Hayley Friedman.

Thanks to Fred Siegel, whose book *The Future Once Happened Here* laid out the philosophical underpinnings of Rudy Giuliani's agenda so well. Thanks to *New York* magazine, which provided me a platform during the 1997 mayoral race for some of the reporting reflected in chapter 11.

Thanks to my brothers Jesse and Steven, and my sister, Elissa, who gave me support beyond measure. And finally, I wish to thank my parents, Marvin Friedman and Doris Kirtzman, the smartest ones of them all.

Chronology

May 28, 1944	Rudolph William Louis Giuliani is born to Helen and Harold Giuliani in Brooklyn, New York.
1951	Giuliani moves with his family to Garden City, Long Island.
1957	Giuliani enrolls at Bishop Loughlin Memorial High School in Brooklyn, New York, where he meets life-long friend Peter Powers.
Spring 1961	Giuliani graduates from Bishop Loughlin; named "Class Politician" by senior class.
Spring 1965	Giuliani graduates magna cum laude from Manhattan College.
Spring 1968	Giuliani graduates magna cum laude from New York University Law School.
1968	Giuliani begins clerkship for Judge Lloyd F. MacMahon, district judge in the Southern District of New York.
October 1968	Giuliani marries Regina Peruggi, a childhood friend and second cousin.
1970	Giuliani joins the office of the U.S. Attorney.

1973	Giuliani named chief of Narcotics Unit, U.S. Department of Justice.
1975	Giuliani named associate deputy attorney general and chief of staff to the deputy attorney general.
1977	Giuliani joins the law firm of Patterson, Belknap, Webb & Tyler.
February 20, 1981	Giuliani nominated by Ronald Reagan as associate attorney general in the Department of Justice.
1982	Giuliani and Peruggi have their marriage annulled on grounds they are second cousins.
March 16, 1983	Senator Al D'Amato officially recommends Giuliani as U.S. attorney for the Southern District of New York.
April 12, 1983	Giuliani nominated by President Ronald Reagan as U.S. attorney for the Southern District of New York.
June 3, 1983	Giuliani sworn in as U.S. attorney for the Southern District of New York.
April 15, 1984	Giuliani marries television reporter Donna Ann Kofnovec Hanover.
January 30, 1986	Giuliani and Donna Hanover's son, Andrew Harold Giuliani, is born.
January 13, 1988	*New York Times* reports rift between Giuliani and D'Amato over replacement for U.S. attorney position.
February 8, 1988	Giuliani rules out Senate run.
January 10, 1989	Giuliani announces his resignation as U.S. attorney for the Southern District of New York.
February 3, 1989	Giuliani and Ray Harding meet to discuss his mayoral candidacy.
February 14, 1989	David Dinkins, a Democrat, announces his candidacy for mayor of New York.
February 15, 1989	Giuliani joins the law firm White & Case, bringing with him longtime aide Dennison Young Jr.
May 17, 1989	Giuliani-for-Mayor kickoff ceremony; *Daily News*

front-page story disclosing that White & Case is registered as a foreign agent for Panama, ruled by General
Manuel Noriega.

June 5, 1989	Giuliani takes a leave of absence from White & Case.
August 22, 1989	Giuliani and Donna Hanover's daughter, Caroline, is born.
August 23, 1989	Yusuf Hawkins killed in Bensonhurst.
September 13, 1989	Dinkins beats Ed Koch in Democratic primary.
November 7, 1989	Dinkins wins New York mayoral race by less than 3 percentage points, the slimmest margin in a New York City mayoral race since 1905.
September 10, 1990	*Time* magazine publishes a cover story entitled "The Rotting of the Big Apple."
August 19, 1991	Gavin Cato is killed in Crown Heights, sparking riots.
February 9, 1993	Speaking at Republican fund-raiser Giuliani insists, "Color lines and racial lines and gender lines and ethnic lines and religious lines have nothing to do with what we're about."
May 28, 1993	Giuliani announces his second bid for the mayoralty.
July 1993	Cristyne Lategano hired as press secretary for Giuliani's mayoral campaign.
September 1, 1993	Ramon C. Cortines begins tenure as schools chancellor.
September 9, 1993	Giuliani makes campaign promise to address quality-of-life issues if elected.
November 2, 1993	Giuliani defeats Dinkins in mayoral race and is elected 107th mayor of New York.
December 13, 1993	Mayor-elect Giuliani names longtime friend and campaign manager Peter Powers deputy mayor for operations, the number two position at City Hall.

Cristyne Lategano named press secretary; at
twenty-eight the youngest mayoral press secretary in
New York City history.

Ninfa Segarra named deputy mayor for education

and social services; Paul Crotty named corporation counsel.

December 16, 1993   Liberal Party Chair Fran Reiter named deputy mayor for planning and community relations.

December 24, 1993   Randy Mastro named chief of staff.

January 2, 1994   Giuliani sworn in as mayor of New York.

January 9, 1994   Brawl at Mosque #7 in Harlem injures worshipers and police.

January 16, 1994   The Reverend Al Sharpton and other black leaders criticize Giuliani for racial insensitivity.

           Daily News praises new police commissioner, William Bratton, provoking resentment from Giuliani.

February 2, 1994   Giuliani presents preliminary budget plan, promising drastic cuts and asserting that New York is facing a fiscal emergency.

February 3, 1994   Giuliani prescribes slashing 2,500 workers from the school system's payroll; Cortines objects..

April 8, 1994   Giuliani appoints Herman Badillo as special schools monitor.

April 9, 1994   Governor Mario Cuomo mediates dispute between Giuliani and Cortines.

October 24, 1994   Giuliani endorses Democrat Cuomo for governor over Republican George Pataki, infuriating Republican Party.

November 8, 1994   Pataki defeats Cuomo.

February 1, 1995   Giuliani announces plans to regulate and investigate businesses and workers at Fulton Fish Market, with intent of eradicating domination by organized crime.

February 8, 1995   Giuliani orders dismissal of numerous government officials, including several in the NYPD public relations office.

February 10, 1995   John Miller, deputy commissioner for public information, resigns in protest of Giuliani's mass firings.

March 31, 1995	Lategano promoted to director of communications.
	David Garth relinquishes role as Giuliani adviser to express his disapproval of Lategano's promotion and influence.
June 15, 1995	Cortines announces his intention to resign on October 15.
July 26, 1995	Comptroller Alan Hevesi rejects plan to sell New York City water system.
September 20, 1995	*New York* magazine publishes story about Lategano entitled "The Woman Behind the Mayor."
October 15, 1995	Cortines resigns as schools chancellor.
October 23, 1995	Giuliani has aides tell Yasir Arafat to leave United Nations fiftieth anniversary concert at Lincoln Center, creating an international controversy.
January 15, 1996	Giuliani and Sharpton clash on Martin Luther King Jr.'s birthday.
March 26, 1996	Bratton resigns as police commissioner.
March 28, 1996	Giuliani appoints Howard Safir, fire commissioner and longtime friend, as police commissioner.
April 5, 1996	Giuliani appoints Rudy Washington as his first black deputy mayor.
July 18, 1996	Giuliani consoles families of victims following crash of TWA Flight 800, attacks TWA for incompetence and insensitivity.
July 29, 1996	Marilyn Gelber resigns as head of Department of Environmental Protection.
August 15, 1996	Powers announces his resignation as deputy mayor for operations.
August 20, 1996	Giuliani administration announces it will install managers for the annual Feast of San Gennaro street festival, in an effort to rid it of mob influence.
August 28, 1996	Randy Mastro promoted from chief of staff to deputy mayor for operations.
February 13, 1997	David Dinkins endorses Ruth Messinger for mayor.

March 1, 1997	Giuliani performs in drag at annual Inner Circle press dinner.
August 4, 1997	*Vanity Fair* publishes story alleging affair between Giuliani and Lategano.
August 9, 1997	Abner Louima arrested and tortured by members of the NYPD.
September 10, 1997	Messinger wins Democratic mayoral nomination, yet recount required to rule out runoff with Sharpton.
September 27, 1997	Democrats Rep. Floyd Flake and Rep. Edolphus Towns endorse Giuliani for mayor.
November 4, 1997	Giuliani reelected mayor, defeating Ruth Messinger.
January 1, 1998	Giuliani inaugurated for a second term.
March 26, 1998	Police-Community Relations Task Force releases its report.
June 29, 1998	Randy Mastro announces his resignation as deputy mayor for operations.
July 2, 1998	Budget Director Joseph Lhota promoted to deputy mayor for operations.
January 3, 1999	Senator Robert Torricelli (D-NJ) mentions Hillary Rodham Clinton as possible candidate for 2000 New York Senate race.
February 4, 1999	Amadou Diallo shot at forty-one times and killed by members of NYPD's Street Crime Unit.
March 3, 1999	Hillary Clinton speaks to Women's Leadership Forum at the Plaza Hotel.
March 15, 1999	David Dinkins, Al Sharpton, Rep. Charles Rangel, and Rep. Gregory Meeks among those arrested outside One Police Plaza while protesting the shooting of Amadou Diallo.
June 14, 1999	Lategano takes extended leave from City Hall.
August 24, 1999	Lategano announces she will not return to City Hall but will instead take over as head of New York's Convention and Visitors Bureau.

September 22, 1999	Giuliani threatens to cut off city subsidies to Brooklyn Museum of Art, calling the works exhibited in its "Sensation" show "sick stuff."
February 6, 2000	Hillary Clinton formally declares herself a candidate for the Senate.
February 26, 2000	Cristyne Lategano marries Nicholas Stratis Nicholas.
March 16, 2000	Patrick M. Dorismond, an unarmed security guard, shot and killed by undercover narcotics detectives.
April 27, 2000	Giuliani announces he has prostate cancer.
May 3, 2000	*New York Post* publishes photos of Giuliani and Judith Nathan; at a press briefing he describes her as a "very good friend."
May 6, 2000	Donna Hanover pledges support of her ailing husband, saying "I will be supportive of Rudy in his fight against his illness, as this marriage and this man have been very precious to me."
May 10, 2000	Giuliani announces he and his wife are separating, adding "I don't really care about politics right now." Hanover makes statement to the press regarding the separation plans, saying "Today's turn of events brings me great sadness. I had hoped to keep this marriage together. For several years, it was difficult to participate in Rudy's public life because of his relationship with one staff member."
May 19, 2000	Giuliani drops out of Senate race.

Notes

1: THE RUNNER STUMBLES

Ray Harding provided me with a detailed recollection of the events leading up to Giuliani's race for mayor against David Dinkins in 1989. I interviewed Harding on April 21, 1999, and Rich Bond on July 13, 1999, about the discussions prior to the launch of Giuliani's campaign on May 17, 1989.

A UPI story about Senator D'Amato's attack on Giuliani for being a "publicity hound" prosecutor ran on May 24, 1989.

I have quoted Giuliani's views on politicians Robert Wagner and Barry Goldwater during his college years from *Ars Politica*, Giuliani's column in the school newspaper, the *Quadrangle*. Giuliani's December 3, 1964, column praised John F. Kennedy and a "strong, large government." In an interview I conducted on June 3, 1999, with Giuliani's longtime friend and adviser Peter Powers, he remembered Giuliani as an admirer of Hubert Humphrey and as an opponent of the Vietnam War. He also recalled that Giuliani voted for Democrat George McGovern in the 1972 presidential election.

Giuliani's election as "Class Politician" at Bishop Loughlin Memorial High School can be found in his high school yearbook.

Giuliani's cadre of "Yesrudy's," his loyal deputies at the U.S. Attorney's Office, is described on page 181 of *The Prosecutors* by James B. Stewart, Simon & Schuster, 1987.

A high-level 1989 campaign aide told me in a 1999 interview about John Gross being designated as campaign treasurer while on a restroom break.

Although David Dinkins told me in an August 8, 1999, interview that he does not remember meeting at the Municipal Building with Ray Harding on December 16, 1988, both Harding (on April 21, 1999) and Dinkins's top aide, Bill Lynch (on May 4, 1999), confirmed and recalled details of the contentious encounter. Bill Lynch overheard some of the discussion between Dinkins and Harding as the meeting was ending and remembers talking with Dinkins about what had transpired after Harding left for his home in Riverdale.

Articles in *Newsday* (January 14, 1988) and the *New York Times* (January 13, 1988) chronicle Giuliani's dispute with Senator D'Amato over the selection process of Giuliani's replacement as U.S. attorney. This clash ignited the enduring animosity between the two men.

In an interview I conducted with Rich Bond on July 13, 1999, he recalled his delight at Guy Molinari's suggestion that he head the 1989 Giuliani campaign. Russ Schriefer told me on July 21, 1999, about the campaign team's overall lack of political experience despite its legal expertise, and Ray Harding described on April 21, 1999, the sterile, stolid Giuliani headquarters during the early days of the campaign. Schriefer and another 1989 aide also recounted Giuliani's dearth of personal charm on the campaign trail.

Giuliani received a good deal of negative press during the spring of 1989. A *New York Times* story on March 3, 1989, criticized his comments about Ed Koch and the governor as "harsh," on a day when Giuliani should have been enjoying the endorsement of State Senator Roy Goodman. Giuliani's wavering views on abortion were noted in the *New York Times* story "On Issues for Women, It's a Matter of Nuances," printed August 26, 1989, and in *New York* magazine's August 21, 1989, article "Rudy's Fall from Grace." The unsatisfactory course of the campaign led to a meeting during which it was decided that Rich Bond and Russ Schriefer would be replaced, according to my interviews with three people present. In an interview I conducted with Guy Molinari on April 8, 1999, he described the actual dismissal of Bond by Giuliani. Giuliani then replaced Bond with Peter Powers. Powers detailed Giuliani's offer of the position while traveling to Philadelphia for a fund-raiser and Roger Ailes's subsequent support in an interview on August 3, 1999.

In describing the events surrounding the murder of Yusuf Hawkins in Bensonhurst, I interviewed Yusuf Hawkins's father, Moses Stewart (on June 28, 1999), and his cousin Geraldine Bryant (on September 27, 1999). I spoke with my colleague Dominic Carter (on September 27, 1999), then with WLIB radio, and the Reverend Al Sharpton (on June 28, 1999) regarding the meeting between the Hawkins family, Sharpton, and Dinkins. I also spoke with David Dinkins (on August 8, 1999), who says he doesn't remember the meeting, and with Bill Lynch (on October 2, 1999), who says he doesn't recall Bryant shouting at Dinkins or Sharpton playing peacemaker.

In my research, I consulted the book *The Future Once Happened Here* by Fred Siegel, published in 1997 by The Free Press.

I interviewed Larry Kramer on July 13, 1999, about Tony Lombardi's attempts to gain information regarding Ed Koch's personal life; Lombardi could not be reached. I spoke with Christopher Lyon, an expert in opposition research, on May 19, 1999, about his introduction to the Giuliani campaign by Bond and Schriefer. The Giuliani campaign made use of the controversy surrounding Jitu Weusi, cochair of African-Americans United for David Dinkins, who had made anti-Semitic comments noted in an October 12, 1989, Associated Press story. In a September 27, 1999, interview, Lyon described his pursuit of a variety of damaging information about Dinkins, including the discovery of the love letters purportedly written to Dinkins. Jennifer Raab, the issues director and Lyon's boss at the time, would not comment. I also interviewed a paid adviser to the '89 campaign about the love letters.

2: "WE HAVE A CITY TO SAVE"

I interviewed Al Sharpton on June 28, 1999, to discuss the visit David Dinkins paid while the reverend was in the hospital recovering from a stab wound. Sharpton described Dinkins's plea to "call for peace" regarding the continuous Bensonhurst protests. Dinkins, Commissioner Brown (who later served as mayor of Houston, Texas), and Bill Lynch said in separate interviews that they could not remember the details of the incident, though Lynch noted that it was a mistake to characterize Dinkins's motives as overtly political. Several news accounts at the time have Dinkins saying outside the hospital that Sharpton had called for peace.

Dinkins grappled with a number of racial incidents during his term, including the boycott of a Korean-owned grocery store following an altercation between the managers and a black customer. A *Newsday* story from September 22, 1990, entitled "Dinkins Visits Boycott Store" reported criticism of the mayor from the black community. Dinkins's mayoralty was also hampered by the city's past and current economic travails, as detailed in Fred Siegel's *The Future Once Happened Here.*

I spoke with former Representative Floyd Flake on June 1, 1999, regarding the dangers in New York's minority communities during Dinkins's mayoralty. Ray Harding described the nuisance of squeegee men in an interview on April 28, 1999. Dinkins's inability to control the decline of New York's safety and quality of life was gleaned from my years covering the Dinkins administration for the *Daily News* and was documented in a variety of newspaper and magazine stories, including the September 17, 1990, *Time* magazine cover story "The Rotting of the Big Apple." Dinkins responded to the growing complaints with a speech introducing the Safe Streets, Safe City program; I was present for the speech, and it was reprinted in the October 3, 1990, *New York Times*. Senator Daniel Patrick Moynihan weighed in on April 15, 1993, with his "Class of '43" speech before the Association for a Better New York.

On October 13, 1999 I spoke to Fred Siegel about the impact his work, including a piece in the spring 1992 *City Journal* called "Reclaiming Our Public Spaces," had on Giuliani's 1993 campaign for mayor. Siegel recalled Giuliani's aggressive and fervent interest in quality-of-life issues and his dispute with renowned economist Lawrence Kudlow. I confirmed this altercation with Kudlow on October 15, 1999. The article "Broken Windows" by James Q. Wilson and George L. Kelling in the March 1982 *Atlantic Monthly* also influenced the Giuliani campaign.

On September 16, 1992, Giuliani received a good deal of bad publicity when he attended a rally at City Hall by ten thousand police officers in plain clothes, who were protesting Mayor Dinkins's call for an all-civilian Civilian Complaint Review Board. Two aides who were present with Giuliani at the rally offered their accounts; they and another former campaign aide recounted their concern—and the candidate's reaction—upon viewing coverage of the event on the evening news.

A high-level campaign aide who prefers anonymity described the Giuliani campaign's brief interest in hiring strategist Dick Morris for their 1993 mayoral bid. Morris was rejected for his apparent indiscretion when discussing President Clinton, another client. I interviewed Dick Morris, who did not dispute the story. In an April 28, 1999, interview with Harding, as well as in an interview with another high-level aide, I learned of the strategy to place Powers as a buffer between Garth and Giuliani. Both Harding and Powers described the growing momentum of the campaign, despite such glitches as a problem with the telephone system at campaign HQ. Fran Reiter, a protégée of Harding's, was hired to be deputy campaign manager; I interviewed both Reiter and Harding about her participation. I also spoke with Reiter about the offer, eventually rescinded, to be on the ticket as candidate for public advocate. Reiter and Harding spoke to me about this episode; Dennison Young Jr. would not comment.

Dinkins made race an important part of his campaign, stressing Giuliani's apparent lack of concern for minority voters. Dinkins's deputy campaign manager Jose Torres himself mentioned Giuliani's "racist tendencies." These issues were noted in an April 1993 article in *El Diario de la Prensa* and in an August 3, 1993, *New York Times* piece. The Crown Heights incident in August 1991 had an impact as well. I covered the political fallout for New York 1 News. The details of the riots and the opening of the trial were discussed in a UPI piece on September 23, 1992. My background knowledge of the '93 race was gained from serving as Giuliani campaign reporter for New York 1 that year. I interviewed David Garth on January 30, 2000, and Richard Bryers on October 8, 1999, about the decision to respond to the charges of racism by making competence an issue. I interviewed a number of aides, including Bryers, about the attempt by the Giuliani campaign to encourage the candidate to stay on message. Aides also recalled the influence of aide Ken Frydman and the need, according to Garth, to employ a spokesperson who wasn't intimidated by the liberal-leaning press. In my interview with Bryers, he described the hiring of Cristyne Lategano, who was brought on, in part to minimize the influence of Frydman. David Garth did his best to control the campaign's message, attacking reporter Todd Purdum directly for a story he wrote for the *New York Times Magazine*. Paul Schwartzman of the *Daily News* was attacked by Bryers for being a "racial arsonist" when he published a story about the paucity of black aides working for the Giuliani campaign. I interviewed Purdum, Schwartzman, Bryers, and Garth about these incidents.

Giuliani remained a man with a temper; one aide from the 1993 campaign told me about Giuliani's fierce reaction to the lesbian-themed children's book *Heather Has Two Mommies*. Bryers and Garth recalled the ad campaign to humanize Giuliani. Even so, press coverage often focused on Giuliani's tough side, as was the case after his speech promising to address quality-of-life issues if elected. Stories quoted Dinkins's spokesman Lee Jones attacking Giuliani for a lack of compassion, calling the prosecutor's approach "arrestonomics." *Newsday* ran a story on September 10, 1993, entitled "Mayoral Rivals' Bedtime Debate," and the *New York Times* published the piece "Fight Vowed by Giuliani on Narcotics" on September 19, 1993.

I witnessed Al Sharpton's confrontation with a City Hall guard; I interviewed Sharpton and Dinkins about their relationship. Sources familiar with Rudy Washington's experiences recall that Sharpton made overtures to the Giuliani campaign while officially remaining in the Dinkins camp. I interviewed four people who were present at the meeting between Sharpton and some Giuliani advisers at the Queens diner Carmichael's, including Vincent Roberts (a friend of Washington's), Sharpton, and two others who spoke on condition of anonymity. Washington would not comment.

I interviewed three campaign officials regarding Susan Alter's difficulties during her run for public advocate; she was referred to as a "walking H-bomb." Fran Reiter also spoke on the record about this episode, recalling in an interview on July 26, 1999, how she herself threw Alter's husband, Rabbi Gilbert Klaperman, out of campaign headquarters. I interviewed Alter on May 25, 2000. Klaperman declined to comment. Two senior campaign aides also described how an irate Garth quit after Powers overruled him on the strategy for a last-minute advertising blitz and had to be wooed back with flowers and a phone call from Giuliani. Ray Harding and another campaign aide told me about pollster Frank Luntz's last-minute concerns on Election Day.

3: THE NEW ORDER

The day after Giuliani's inauguration in 1994, which I covered for New York 1, I asked, "Mister Mayor, do you have any message for the press corps?" as he entered City Hall. A former Dinkins and Giuliani commissioner told me that some of Dinkins's aides were notably disloyal and "would have pushed him in front of a bus." Fran Reiter told me in our July 26, 1999, interview about the cluttered, disorganized conditions at City Hall. Another aide to both Dinkins and Giuliani commented in an interview about the offices, about the inappropriately casual dress of the city employees, and about how Giuliani's team entered with the comportment and codes of competent lawyers.

Guy Molinari recounted his efforts to convince Giuliani to rehire Ray Kelly as police commissioner. Ray Harding remembered in our May 5, 1999, interview Giuliani's concern that Bratton would be a prima donna. Bratton's arrival and the incident at the Harlem mosque were reported in a January 16, 1994, *New York Times* article called "Police and the Mosque: Aftermath of a Hoax." The event and its aftermath were also described in various news accounts; in the book *Turnaround* by William Bratton and Peter Knobler, Random House, 1998; in my June 6, 1999, interview with Bratton; in my January 10, 2000, interview with Cristyne Lategano; and in my June 28, 1999, interview with Sharpton. Following the incident, Bratton scheduled a meeting with Don Muhammad and Sharpton but canceled the meeting at the last minute. Lategano told me that City Hall ordered the cancelation of the meeting; Bratton disputes this. While the Dinkins administration attempted to accommodate Sharpton, according to Bill Lynch, the Giuliani administration felt Sharpton would have to fight for publicity, according to Ray Harding in our May 13, 1999, interview. A senior administration aide described Denny Young's request that Washington dine with Sharpton at the Manhattan Ocean Club to keep lines of communication open, although Young and Washington declined to comment. Several participants at the dinner offered me their recollections of the event on condition of anonymity. Arthur Bramwell, the African American leader of the Brooklyn Republican Party, told me in an interview on November 3, 1999, that Sharpton was unquestionably "anti-Dinkins," while a source close to Sharpton acknowledged the reverend's inconspicuous assistance to the 1989 Giuliani effort.

Giuliani's comment that black leaders were "going to have to learn how to discipline themselves in the way in which they speak" was noted in a *New York Times* story on January 18, 1994, called "Black Anger on Mayor's 'Discipline' Remark."

I used Fred Siegel's *The Future Once Happened Here* to glean statistics about New York's economic straits, and I interviewed three senior aides to Giuliani involved in the budget process. I was present during an HHC board meeting on January 27, 1994, and spoke to Fran Reiter on August 25, 1999, about Giuliani's decision on DAS. A former Giuliani administration member who also worked under Dinkins recounted Giuliani's interest in and stamina regarding discussions of budget policy. The same person remembers Giuliani's strong temper, including an incident in which the mayor went "ballistic" at Powers, his best friend. Two former administration members recalled Giuliani's treatment of Denny Young at staff meetings. Kevin McCabe reiterated Giuliani's enormous comprehension of and control over the budget when I interviewed him on June 8, 1999. Peter Vallone declined to be interviewed. Mark Green, in my interview with him on July 8, 1999, emphasized Giuliani's need to control all aspects of his mayoralty, as when the mayor attempted to forbid Green from visiting St. Vincent's Hospital following a shooting. I also interviewed a senior aide to the mayor about that incident.

4: THE BIG SWEEP

I learned about the meeting between New York City advocacy groups and Police Commissioner Bratton from Mary Brosnahan of the Coalition for the Homeless, interviewed on May 6, 1999; Norman Siegel, executive director of the NYCLU, interviewed on May 18, 1999; and Bratton. I used "I.B. Singer's New York: Fading, Yes, but Still Here" by Joseph Berger from the *New York Times* of July 26, 1991, and "The Demonization of the Upper West Side" by Adam Nagourney for the October 19, 1997, *New York Times Magazine* to help describe the Upper West Side. Norman Siegel, too, weighed in on Upper West Side voters in our interview on May 18, 1999. Siegel also commented on Giuliani's stiffness in the 1993 campaign ads that showed him playing catch with his son, Andrew.

In describing the problem of the homeless, I referred to City of New York homeless population statistics and used "Homelessness and Public Shelter Provision in New York City" by Dennis P. Culhane, Stephen Metraux, and Susan M. Wachter, published in the book *Housing and Community Development in New York City—Facing the Future*, edited by Michael H. Schill, SUNY Press, 1999. I also conducted an interview with Culhane on November 18, 1999. The July 11, 1995, *New York Times* cites New York City's allocation of funds from the federal government as $100 million.

I used the book *Turnaround* by William Bratton and Peter Knobler, Random House, 1998, to compile information about Bratton's tenure. On page 218 Jack Maple is dubbed "Rain Man," on page 235 Bratton describes the impact of Compstat, and on page 290 Bratton cites statistics demonstrating the dropping crime rates in New York. I also interviewed Bratton and Maple (at Elaine's) about the high times and the low times.

I spoke with a former commissioner about the aura of machismo surrounding the mayor. I attended the ceremony at which Officer Beckles was commended; the *New*

York Times also reported details of the event on February 8, 1994. On April 30, 1994, the *New York Times* ran a story about police officers who rejected a bribe: "Officers Who Rejected Bribe are Hailed." Giuliani praised the competence and motivation of the police force on March 3, 1994, after an arrest was made in the Brooklyn Bridge shooting and was visibly upset when I observed him at a City Hall press conference recalling his efforts to console the grief-stricken family of a murdered police officer.

On January 16, 1994, the *Daily News* ran a flattering article about Bratton. Bratton and Maple were summoned to City Hall and threatened by Powers, according to *Turnaround*, and my interview with Bratton. Powers refused to comment on the meeting, saying it was confidential. Bratton also recalls, both in his book and in my interview with him, that John Timoney was chastised for failing to thank the mayor on camera for his promotion. Powers refused to comment on this as well, and Timoney did not respond to a request for an interview. When I interviewed Bratton and Maple, they described the torturous feeling of constant scrutiny by Giuliani. And on page 271 of *Turnaround*, Giuliani is quoted as saying, "You know, I have the distinct impression that someone over there is putting someone else's agenda ahead of mine," referring to police headquarters. I also interviewed a senior aide to the mayor and Lategano for the administration's perspective.

5: THE CONTROL MACHINE

I interviewed Lou Carbonetti on May 4, 1999, about his relationship with Giuliani; Tony Carbonetti declined to comment on the patronage issue. Giuliani told the *Village Voice* that patronage was a "municipal plague" on February 20, 1996, and he called for a "dramatic break" from the practice in the *New York Times* on August 8, 1994. That story also detailed various Giuliani family hirings. "From the day that I started exploring running for mayor," he told the *New York Times* on August 6, 1989, "I have made it clear to every political leader almost from the first discussion we have had that there will be no jobs or patronage—only decisions made on merit." An interview with a Giuliani commissioner revealed that the commissioner had refused to hire a candidate sent by City Hall because three of the references furnished by the prospective employee had used the word *scum* to describe him. Interviews with administration sources confirmed that a housing authority worker who received his position because of his ties to the Jewish community had been arrested on the job for exposing himself. Upon his arrest, the man had central booking call Bruce Teitelbaum to bail him out, according to a senior mayoral aide. The record was sealed after the district attorney declined to prosecute, so I have chosen to withhold the name of the person involved.

One former commissioner in the Giuliani administration opined that that the mayor was not troubled if people were being hired for reasons of patronage; he was the one who recalled, "These guys came in with sort of this disdain for government. . . ." Another former high-level city agency official remembers Randy Mastro's calls to demand hires, in which "He would talk to me like I was scum." I interviewed Lilliam Barrios-Paoli on May 22, 2000. Former DEP commissioner Marilyn Gelber, interviewed on May 13, 1999, her former aide Ben Esner, interviewed May 6, 1999, and a senior administration aide recall that when the Department of Environmental Protection tried to hire twenty-five street laborers, the hires were intercepted by Carbonetti, who told the DEP official "You can have five. . . . I'll take the other twenty."

A DEP source told me about City Hall's insistence that the reservoir numbers be inspected by the mayor's press office daily, even if it meant releasing "NA" when no one was available to sign off on them. On February 12, 1995, the *New York Times* ran the story "Firm Grip of a Mayor" regarding Giuliani's new budget and the mass firings. I interviewed Jerry Nachman, the news director at WCBS-TV, on July 28, 1999, about complaints from City Hall to editors following negative coverage in the press. *Newsday* ran a story on July 16, 1994, quoting realtor Nancy Packes about rent breaks for Giuliani staffers. I reference the article "The Times vs. Rudy: It's War" by Hilton Kramer, published in the *New York Post*, July 26, 1994, and "Rent Break for Rudy Pals Rubs Press Wrong" by Jim Sleeper, published in the *Daily News*, same date. Sleeper readily acknowledged to me that he received the information from City Hall and said there was nothing wrong with doing so since the story was legitimate. Kramer told me he couldn't recall where the tip came from. I also reference the book *Prince of the City*, by Robert Daley, Houghton Mifflin, 1978.

I obtained the Tom Michaels letters from a DEP source and learned about Michaels's blasé attitude toward his job interview from a DEP official present in the room. I interviewed Tom Michaels about his heated exchanges with Marilyn Gelber, and I cite directly Gelber's letter to Powers criticizing Michaels. I also interviewed Gelber and Powers on August 3, 1999, regarding this episode. In addition, I spoke to other DEP officials, a high-level administration source involved in the matter, and Vaughan Toney, Councilman Henry's chief of staff at the time, to confirm the events and details of this story. Seth Kaye, an assistant to Powers involved in the dispute, did not respond to numerous interview requests.

In my June 16, 1999, interview with William Bratton, he spoke of an "enemies list." An administration aide recounted how, after Jake Menges informed the mayor that he had heard rumors that Peter Vallone was considering banning Menges from the City Council chamber, Giuliani responded, "I'll tell him to drop dead."

6: THE MAYOR AND HIS LITTLE VICTIM

Although Ramon Cortines declined to be interviewed, I spoke to a number of other people directly involved in the dispute between Giuliani and the schools chancellor. I mention an August 30, 1993, story from the *New York Times*, "Leading Contender for a Schools Job Few Want" by Jane Gross. I interviewed Carol Gresser on May 3, 1999, and Cristyne Lategano on January 10, 2000, about a meeting between Giuliani and Cortines. John Beckman referred to the mayor's "angry reactions" in an April 2, 1994, *New York Times* story "Mayor Derides Cortines' School Cutbacks as Inadequate" by Sam Dillon. A following story in the *New York Times*, called "Giuliani, Still Seeking School Cuts, Gets Personal with Recalcitrant Cortines," printed April 7, 1994, quotes Giuliani as saying that Cortines had "been captured by the school bureaucracy." I interviewed Beckman on April 29, 1999, and Lategano on January 10, 2000, about the dispute over the late-night press release announcing 2,500 cuts from the Board of Education payroll. Beckman also discussed Cortines's desire to resign his position. Gresser described her frantic attempts to patch things up between Giuliani and Cortines. I interviewed Mario Cuomo about his role as mediator in the dispute on June 9, 1999. Gresser also contacted Ed Koch, who does not recall the request but does not dispute her account.

Ed Koch also spoke to me on May 17, 1999, about his birthday party at Gracie Mansion; three other party guests confirmed the details. Koch discussed the events at his brother's funeral, as did two other attendees.

I interviewed Howard Koeppel on April 20, 1999, about Giuliani's intractable stance regarding Cortines; he remembers Giuliani saying that Cortines was "impossible." *New York Times* columnist Joyce Purnick wrote about this issue on December 20, 1994 ("A Man of His Words"). On December 19, 1994, the *New York Times* published the story "A Personality Contest: The Mayor Was Losing," in which the mayor describes himself as "very reasonable." A Quinnipiac College poll taken February 1997 showed that more than 50 percent of the public believed Giuliani didn't have a likable personality, although more than 60 percent felt he was doing a good job.

7: RUDY AND MARIO

I covered the Giuliani endorsement story and was the Pataki campaign reporter for New York 1 in 1994. I interviewed a number of sources who worked on the Cuomo and Pataki campaigns. Giuliani spoke on WABC Radio on September 23, 1994, praising Mario Cuomo. Charisse Jones wrote the story "Campaigning, Pataki Seems to Do Better in Person Than on Camera" for the *New York Times*, October 19, 1994. Pataki aide Rob Ryan told me on January 12, 2000, about Lategano's promise that although Giuliani might not endorse Pataki, he would do nothing to hurt his campaign. Lategano did not return calls to her on this matter, though she cooperated with me on many others. An adviser to Giuliani told me that Randy Levine called a Cuomo endorsement "insanity." According to my interviews with Cuomo and Ray Harding (January 7, 2000), Giuliani was advised to stay neutral, or as Cuomo put it, "aggressively neutral." Senior advisers to Pataki described watching Giuliani's endorsement of Cuomo on the television at campaign headquarters (two campaign aides noted the shocked silence), while an aide to Cuomo described the governor listening to the endorsement on the radio in his car. Joel Benenson recounted the giddy scene at Cuomo headquarters in an interview with me on January 6, 2000. A Pataki campaign aide told me about Kieran Mahoney's swigs from the bottle of scotch at the endorsement news; Mahoney did not dispute this detail.

In an interview with two high-level Pataki campaign aides, I learned about the campaign ad called "The Deal." In interviews with two high-level Cuomo campaign aides and one Giuliani campaign aide, I learned about Giuliani's overreaching involvement in the gubernatorial campaign. David Garth noted in my January 30, 2000, interview with him that Giuliani at least was "ambulatory," whereas "you couldn't get Mario out of the Governor's Mansion." Cuomo, in our June 9, 1999, interview, said, "Rudy was the one who wanted to do it mostly. . . . I just felt, this is wrong." Cristyne Lategano spoke on January 10, 2000, about the gallows humor Giuliani exhibited regarding upstate protestors: "Time to get my head bashed in." Mark Green remembered Giuliani's harsh words linking Pataki and Al D'Amato. D'Amato denied animosity between him and the mayor to the *New York Times* (news analysis, *New York Times*, October 25, 1994). A campaign aide to Pataki noted the mistiming of Giuliani's endorsement (two weeks too early). And Mario Cuomo described in our interview how he assured Giuliani, after his defeat, "I lost this without your help."

8: THE PRESS GAL

I interviewed Cristyne Lategano at length on January 10, 2000. I interviewed several participants at the meeting in which Randy Mastro encouraged staffers to be supportive of Lategano despite their animosity toward her. I interviewed several people who attended Lategano's birthday party and who were in the car with Therese McManus when she sang a hostile "Happy Birthday" to Lategano, then bought her flowers and lottery tickets as a gift. McManus declined to comment.

In my interview with Lategano, she recalled being fired after one day on the 1989 campaign when Russ Schriefer decided she wasn't right for the position. Schriefer said in our July 21, 1999, interview that the issue was money, not qualifications. I interviewed Phil McConkey on January 27, 2000, regarding Lategano's work on his New Jersey congressional race.

Lategano recounted being yelled at by McManus and comforted by the mayor, "Don't let anyone push you around." David Garth told me during our January 30, 2000, interview that he viewed her merely as Richard Bryers's assistant. Her angry response to a *Time* poll—accusing the magazine of bias and demanding "Print the truth"—was reported in "Bush Desperate to Regain State," Times Newspapers Limited, September 14, 1992.

I observed Lategano attending many of the mayor's events herself rather than delegating that duty; this was corroborated by a number of interviews with administration members. During our interview Lategano described traveling with her boss in the white Chevrolet Suburban, planning the mayor's schedule, and discussing his image and goals.

Former commissioners I interviewed described Peter Powers as wise and unruffled, trusted by the mayor, and able to calm him regardless of the situation. Garth likened Powers to Karl Malden's character of the priest in *On the Waterfront*. Yet four senior aides told me that Powers, the firmly entrenched number two, was bothered by Lategano's unusual level of access and by her ability to skirt the chain of command.

When Jackie Barnathan was brought in to City Hall, she was warned by Garth that Lategano was incapable of running her office and needed assistance from someone with a better understanding of the media, according to interviews with Garth and a source close to Barnathan. Barnathan declined to comment. Two aides to the mayor told me that Lategano was threatened by Barnathan, complained to Giuliani that Barnathan was not only inept but disloyal, and warned the mayor and his aides not to trust her. I interviewed a former City Hall official who described how Lategano canceled Barnathan's Christmas vacation, held up her promised $2,000 bonus, and had Barnathan banished from City Hall.

Two administration aides I interviewed acknowledged that Lategano's rough reactions to controversy were learned from Giuliani's own ruthless style of striking back at adversaries, examining his enemies for vulnerabilities and using all available ammunition. Even so, two high-level aides to the mayor recall Powers, usually philosophical about Lategano's influence, occasionally fuming about her machinations and grumbling, "She's driving the rest of us away." Two City Hall officials I interviewed mentioned the Powers-Lategano power struggle in the context of Guy Molinari's criticism of the Cuomo endorsement.

Lategano's yearbook quote from *The Little Prince* can be found in the Lynbrook High School 1983 yearbook. It was researched for me by Tina Traster.

When Lategano was struggling with the media maelstrom surrounding the *Vanity Fair* story, Giuliani encouraged her to ignore the negative press; she told me in our

January 10, 2000, interview, "I would listen to him and just think he was speaking a foreign language." I spoke with Garth and three administration aides about Lategano's belief that Garth had double-crossed and humiliated her when she was angling for the communications director's job. Garth says he recalls the conversation but not what was said. Lategano would not comment about the call. When Lategano was named communications director, she admitted to nervousness and an awkward relationship with the press, as cited in the *New York Times* story "Giuliani Gives Press Secretary a Promotion," April 1, 1995. That same day David Garth ceased communication with the administration, as he told me in our interview.

A high-level City Hall official witnessed Lategano urging the mayor to skip the J&R jazz festival because the audience would be mainly black and therefore hostile to him. Indeed, five senior administration officials confirmed to me that Lategano advised Giuliani to avoid events attended largely by black people. She was not a racist, they said; rather, she was concerned about the reception the mayor would receive from such audiences.

A senior aide I interviewed told me about the mayor saying, "Peter's driving me crazy insisting he must be first deputy mayor." Fran Reiter told me of Powers's grudge against her when she was named deputy mayor for economic development over Richard Schwartz. Powers told me she was cool to him. In our August 3, 1999, interview, Powers said of Giuliani only "we were as close the day I left as . . . the day I arrived."

Concerning Koch's clash with Giuliani over the appointment of two Brooklyn judges, the *New York Times* published "Giuliani Judicial Selection Passed the Bar Exam Despite Lacking a Law Degree" (January 2, 1996) and the *Daily News* printed "Judge Pick Blasted; Koch Gives Rudy An 'F' for Flunkout" (January 3, 1996). A senior aide heard Lategano suggest "exposing" Koch's purported relationship with former aide Herb Rickman. Another senior aide heard her mention the subject on several occasions.

Lategano clashed with William Bratton, who told me on June 16, 1999, "She did everybody in. . . ."

9: RAGIN' RUDY

In gathering facts about Giuliani's insistence that Yasir Arafat be ejected from Lincoln Center, I interviewed Bruce Teitelbaum on June 21, 1999, a second senior aide close to the mayor, a witness to the aides' conversation with Arafat, and a UN official who witnessed the mayor issuing his orders. The *Daily News* published "City Diplo Drama Leaves 'Em Un-impressed" by Jim Dwyer on October 26, 1995. Teitelbaum and another senior aide to the mayor also recalled Arafat's initial enraged reaction to the insult. The *New York Post* wrote about the "Ara-flap. . . ." on

October 26, 1995, quoting Giuliani's explanation that Arafat was a murderer (according to an old Koch description) and uninvited to boot. The following day the *Post* reported the back-and-forth between Giuliani and Koch in "Clash of the Mayoral Maulers," recording Giuliani's apparent pride in his actions. A senior aide to the mayor remembers his boss declaring "My only regret . . . was that I didn't throw Arafat out myself."

The mayor was often volatile; one former mayoral aide with direct knowledge of the incident told me about the time the mayor started throwing telephones inside his van.

After Giuliani created a trade waste commission, trash bills were dramatically lowered, according to a January 29, 1997, story in the *Daily News* headlined "Carting Away the Mob." When he took pains to remove Mafia influence from the Feast of San Gennaro festival, local residents scowled as he paraded down the streets of Little Italy, according to one senior aide to the mayor and the September 13, 1996, *New York Times* story "Rudy Returns to Sanitized Gennaro Festival Opening." The *New York Times* called him "bold" in "The Fulton Fish Market Battle," October 18, 1995, and the *Daily News* on July 5, 1996, raved "now that is reinventing government," in "Good Riddance to Bad Garbage."

The *Daily News* chronicled Giuliani's concern for the families of the victims of TWA Flight 800 in the July 18, 1996, story "Agony of Kin's Airport Vigil." His subsequent attacks on the incompetence of TWA were described in the *Daily News* on July 20, 1996 ("Rudy Pounds TWA Again on Delay"), and in the *New York Times* the same day ("Politicians Provide Comfort and Criticism After Crash"). Giuliani responded to TWA's defense by declaring himself not "outside the process" and by mentioning his own close friend who was on the doomed flight (CBS transcripts). I also interviewed an aide who was with the mayor at the airport.

Giuliani's contest with Alan Hevesi over the water supply issue was reported in "Hevesi Bars Sale of Water System," *Daily News*, June 28, 1995. Hevesi's accusing the administration of "labeling as political anyone who disagrees with them" was covered in "Comptroller Blocks Water System's Sale, and City Hall Plans Suit," *New York Times*, July 27, 1995. I covered the dispute for New York 1.

The statistic that in 1970, 445,000 of the 600,000 children on welfare were living in homes without fathers comes from Fred Siegel's *The Future Once Happened Here*. I learned that Giuliani threatened to abandon the Home Relief program when I interviewed a former senior adviser to Giuliani involved in the budget. Liz Krueger, a well-known advocate for the poor, complained to the *New York Times*, "They've made it so complex to apply that it's sort of like setting up a New York City marathon. . . ." in "New Policy Cuts Numbers On Relief in New York City," April 19, 1995.

Fernando Ferrer's warning that Giuliani's budget proposals "endanger(ed) the social fabric of the city" was reported in "Ferrer: Giuliani Budget Takes City Down, Backward," *Amsterdam News*, July 1, 1995.

Bratton's struggles with Giuliani worsened as *Time* magazine called the police commissioner "One Good Apple" on January 15, 1996. Bratton told the *Daily News*, "I'm at the top of my game . . ." in "Bratton Set to Carry On," January 14, 1996. A former aide to the mayor told me that Lategano fanned the mayor's agitation over Bratton. Giuliani rejected some personnel moves that Bratton was planning for the NYPD; the story leaked into the *New York Times* the next day. Bratton commented to the *Times* on March 10, 1996, "I don't profess that the two of us skip down the lane hand in hand" ("Giuliani and Bratton: The Ties that Chafe"). After Bratton spent a weekend "in high style" with Henry Kravis, described in the *Daily News* on March 13, 1996 ("Commish Escaped to Lap of Luxury"), Giuliani's lawyers launched a review into all the police commissioner's travels. In Bratton's book *Turnaround*, on page 301 he recalls the ousting of Ramon Cortines: "I had seen them hound Schools Chancellor Ramon Cortines out of office." I also covered the Giuliani-Bratton feud for New York 1.

10: "HAPPY KING DAY!" GIULIANI
AND THE BLACK COMMUNITY

The events of January 15, 1996, Martin Luther King Jr.'s birthday, were detailed by Al Sharpton in my June 28, 1999, interview with him and by New York 1's coverage. I witnessed Giuliani's 1993 meeting with David Dinkins; it was reported in the November 4, 1993, *New York Times* ("In 5-Borough Journey, Giuliani Calls for New Unity").

Giuliani insisted he believed everyone was equal under the law, that "Everybody will be dealt with in precisely the same way . . ." ("Testing Giuliani's Single Standard," *New York Times*, January 21, 1994). I learned about Giuliani's early years from a May 11, 1999, interview with Bishop Loughlin classmate Joseph Ciangiola and with other Bishop Loughlin schoolmates of Giuliani's.

A senior aide to the mayor told me that Deputy Mayors Ninfa Segarra and Rudy Washington felt uncomfortable seeing the boss without a meeting. Carl McCall told me in an interview on July 27, 1999, that he believed Giuliani deliberately disregarded the black community since "this community hadn't done anything for him politically. . . .

Giuliani reminded the *Washington Post* on May 27, 1997, about the dramatic drop in crime in minority neighborhoods: "They are alive, how about we start with that?" ("Manhattan Floats on Tide of Money and Migration; Ebbing Crime Rate Energizes Population").

I interviewed Representative Gregory Meeks (March 6, 2000) and Al Sharpton (June 28, 1999) about Meeks's summit meeting of the city's black leadership.

I was present when Al Sharpton announced his intention to run for mayor on Martin Luther King Day, 1997.

11: THE GANG CRACKS UP

The *New York Times* wrote about Ruth Messinger's liberal past in an October 31, 1997, story, "Messinger Has Moved Right, But Not Sufficiently for Some." I interviewed Messinger on March 27, 2000; she told me her friends had warned her about running against Giuliani given his high poll numbers and ruthless tactics, but that she believed someone had to stand against him. The field of Democratic opponents was weak; Ed Koch commented that Messinger, Councilman Sal Albanese, and Al Sharpton offered "a miserable choice" (*New York Times*, March 22, 1997). I covered the '97 mayor's race for New York 1 and *New York* magazine.

Peter Powers said in an April 26, 2000, interview that Fran Reiter "indicated a coolness after she got" the new deputy mayor's job over Powers's protest. High-level aides to the mayor say that by the time Powers left the administration, he and Reiter were no longer on speaking terms. Reiter complained in an August 25, 1999, interview with me of the "nonexistent campaign organization" left behind when Powers "disappeared." Powers noted in an April 26, 2000, interview that there was "plenty of time" to get a campaign up and running without unnecessary spending. Both recounted their dinner to me.

The administration's problems over dealings with Fischbein Badillo Wagner Harding were described in reporter Clifford Levy's articles for the *New York Times* ("2 Giuliani Advisers Prosper from City Lobbying," February 9, 1997; "After Lobbying, Light Penalties in 2 Building Cases," March 6, 1997).

Giuliani refused to address the rumors about his relationship with Cristyne Lategano. Both Adam Goodman, in a May 24, 2000, interview, and Fran Reiter, in a July 20, 1999, interview, described Giuliani's flat reluctance to discuss the issue. After the *Vanity Fair* story made a splash in the local media, I interviewed editors at the *Daily News* and the *New York Post* for New York 1, who conceded that they had no idea whether the *Vanity Fair* story was true. Lategano pulled me aside at a mayoral press conference the following day and thanked me. *Newsday* ran an August 7, 1997, story called "Rudy Raps Reporters," quoting Giuliani's "It's like a broken record." Donna Hanover reacted icily yet acknowledged to the *Daily News* on August 10, 1997: "I've said what I mean when I said we're a family, and we're going to stay together" ("First Lady's No. 1 Worry: The Kids").

The details of Abner Louima's experience during the squad car trip were taken from news accounts and trial testimony. None of the officers were convicted on those assault charges. The account of Louima's torture by Justin Volpe was drawn from Volpe's confession in court, after previously pleading guilty in the case and receiving a thirty-year jail term, and other testimony from his trial. I interviewed Harold Nicolas, Louima's cousin, and his attorney Sanford Rubenstein, who also represented Louima, on March 31, 2000. I interviewed police reporter Aram Roston on March 25, 2000. I spoke to Sharpton on June 28, 1999, about the Louima case; he described his conversation with columnist Mike McAlary, who urged Sharpton to get involved. McAlary passed away in 1999 and was not interviewed about Sharpton's account. Ray Harding told me on May 1, 1999, that he advised Denny Young to tell the mayor and Safir to get ahead of the curve on the Louima attack. Neither Young nor Safir would agree to be interviewed. The *New York Times* detailed the shake-up of the 70th Precinct in the August 15, 1997, story "Leaders of Precinct Are Swept Out in Torture Inquiry." *USA Today*, in "Giuliani Holding Cops Accountable in Sex Assault," recounted Giuliani's pledge to fire any police officer who held back information about the assault. A *Washington Post* story from August 15, 1997, quoted Louima's assertion that Volpe told him: "This is Giuliani time. It is not Dinkins time."

The Campaign by Evan J. Mandery, Westview Press, 1999, discusses the Messinger campaign's reaction to the Louima incident and the complexities of the political ramifications for the Democrat. Messinger told me on March 27, 2000, about her meeting with Louima and with members of the Haitian community. Both Giuliani and Sharpton attacked her for pandering when she addressed the Louima debacle (*Daily News*, August 25, 1997, "Ruth Speech Hit"). Messinger was struggling, but Giuliani meanwhile had built up a vast war chest for his campaign, aided by wealthy New Yorkers who did business with the city, according to my reporting for New York 1 at the time and a January 16, 1997, story in the *New York Times*, "Corporations and Lobbyists Raised Funds for Giuliani."

I interviewed Howard Koeppel on April 20, 1999, about Giuliani's relatively progressive stance on gay issues; he described the mayor's trepidation before the Empire State Pride Agenda fund-raiser began. I also spoke with Jeff Soref on May 22, 2000, about the event and was myself present as the mayor gave his speech.

During the Giuliani/Messinger campaign, I covered the clash over the zoning issue; Giuliani's campaign put out an ad painting her as a liberal extremist, and the *New York Times* ran "Mayor Removes the Gloves and Laces into Messinger" on September 19, 1997.

Adam Goodman and another mayoral adviser confirmed the "Morning in Bay Ridge" story. Cristyne Lategano declined to respond to queries on the subject.

I interviewed Fran Reiter on August 25, 1999, and Peter Powers on April 26, 2000, as well as three other senior aides to the mayor about the tensions in the Giuliani inner circle regarding campaign operations. When Reiter balked at making room for Tony Carbonetti and Rudy Washington at campaign headquarters, Giuliani was livid and ordered her to comply, according to interviews with Reiter and other high-level aides to the mayor. I also interviewed Reiter and several aides who were present at the Gracie Mansion coup attempt.

12: DEMON

I interviewed two senior aides regarding Cristyne Lategano's insistence that Giuliani give his 1998 inaugural address before a giant American flag in an effort to make him appear presidential. She did not respond to a request to speak about this issue. *The Hotline*, on December 5, 1997, ran a Field poll of California Republican voters that ranked Giuliani ahead of John McCain, William Bennett, Lamar Alexander, and Pat Buchanan. A *Daily News* story called "Big Dreams, Big Roadblocks Ahead" on January 2, 1998, quoted Helen Giuliani's presidential aspirations for her son and described the "Rudy for President" buttons. On January 12, 1998, the *Daily News* noted Giuliani's high approval ratings, even among black New Yorkers, in "Big Apple Shines on Giuliani, But Not as Prez: Poll." I covered the inaugural and Giuliani's presidential aspirations for New York 1 and *New York* magazine.

In his second term Giuliani began to focus on issues of civility, saying, "In most cities, there is a better understanding of respect of the rights of other people," as quoted in the *New York Times*, January 13, 1998, "With Higher Fines, Giuliani Hopes to Hobble Jaywalkers."

Information about the Amadou Diallo killing was gleaned from autopsy findings, as reported by New York 1 News, February 5, 1999, as well as from the officers' court testimony. I also interviewed Mohammed Jalloh and Kyle Watters on April 10, 2000, about the Diallo case. I interviewed Al Sharpton, who became so involved with the Diallo killing at the height of its coverage that one senior administration official I spoke to said the administration had tagged New York 1 the "All Sharpton, All the Time" channel.

Statistics regarding police shootings in New York and other cities came from the NYPD, either directly or as reprinted in the *Daily News* on April 9, 2000. It was Jalloh who told me that the Guinean Association agreed to hold a meeting with Giuliani—but only when Diallo's parents were in New York to join it. In my May 13, 1999, interview with Ray Harding, I was told about Giuliani's refusal to denounce the police before the facts of the Diallo case were in.

I interviewed Watters, Jalloh, and Sharpton about Kadiatou Diallo's experiences in New York following the death of her son; Sharpton told me about his interaction with Saikou Diallo at the airport. I interviewed Kadiatou Diallo on May 23, 2000.

Hillary Clinton's actions during the final moments of her husband's trial and her subsequent consideration of the New York Senate seat were reported in the *New York Times*, May 30, 1999 ("The Next Clinton"); *Newsweek*, March 1, 1999 ("Hillary's Day in the Sun"); and *Time* magazine, March 1, 1999 ("A Race of Her

Own"). The comments of Tim Russert and Senator Robert Torricelli on *Meet the Press* were recorded by NBC News Transcripts, January 3, 1999.

I interviewed Sharpton on June 28, 1999, Charles Barron and Michael Hardy on May 3, 2000, and Dinkins about the organization and details of the Diallo protests. I interviewed several aides to Giuliani and had conversations with Representative Charles Rangel on May 26, 1999, about his rancorous relationship with the mayor. I also referred to "Prelude to an Election: Sharpton's Diallo March Builds Anti-Rudy Troop," from the April 26, 1999, *New York Observer.* The *New York Times* covered the story of David Dinkins's arrest in "Dinkins Among 14 Arrested in Protest of Police Shooting," March 16, 1999.

I interviewed Representative Floyd Flake on June 1, 1999, and May 4, 2000, about his disappointing meeting with, and changing views of, Giuliani. A senior aide to Giuliani told me about sneaking Representative Edolphus Towns into the mayor's office. Towns did not respond to an interview request. Three senior aides to Giuliani told me about Rudy Washington's wrenching descriptions of his own experiences with NYPD harassment and about Giuliani's consent to meet with black leaders upon hearing Washington's stories. Two aides told me about the ID he was given.

I interviewed four advisers to the mayor about the focus group that criticized Giuliani's handling of race relations and overall sensitivity, and Giuliani's frustration and subsequent explosion at Frank Luntz.

13: THE RELUCTANT CANDIDATE

I was present at the Sheraton Hotel's Imperial Ballroom for the mayor's May 1999 fund-raiser/fifty-fifth birthday celebration and spoke with Cristyne Lategano there myself. I interviewed Herman Badillo on June 2, 1999, about Lategano's demeanor later that night as he and his wife drove her home.

I interviewed a senior aide to the mayor who told me about Giuliani's derisive response to the prospect of Fran Reiter running for mayor: "Fran, how can you expect to win New Yorkers' support when you can't even get a single colleague who worked with you to support you?" he allegedly said. Reiter denies he said this.

Hillary Clinton's disastrous event with Suha Arafat was covered in the *New York Times,* November 12, 1999 ("While Mrs. Clinton Looks on, Palestinian Officials Criticize Israel"), and in the *Daily News* from the same day ("Hil's Caught in Crossfire"). Giuliani's mockery of Clinton's New York State "listening tour" was described by the *Daily News* on July 27, 1999 ("Giuliani Spoofs Hillary Clinton with Arkansas 'Listening Tour' "), and New York 1.

The *Daily News* published a description of the "Sensation" exhibit at the Brooklyn museum on September 16, 1999 ("B'klyn Gallery of Horror"). I interviewed reporter Douglas Feiden on May 8, 2000, about his exchange with Sunny Mindel. Mindel, interviewed on May 7, 2000, insisted "your account is wrong" but refused to say any more. "I don't want to cooperate with you for this book," she said. A senior aide to the mayor described Giuliani's disgusted reaction to the "Sensation" catalog ("This is not art"). Giuliani's ultimatum to the museum and the accompanying rhetoric were discussed in the October 5, 1999, *New York Times* ("Museum Says Giuliani Knew of Show in July and Was Silent"). Two senior aides to the mayor told me about Chapin's futile efforts to soften Giuliani's stance. I interviewed Chapin on June 2, 2000. A *New York Times* editorial on September 29, 1999, praised the museum and deplored the administration's "authoritarian overreaction" ("The Museum's Courageous Stand"). Despite the negative reaction from New York City voters, at least one political adviser informed Giuliani that the crusade would be supported by voters in conservative upstate communities, according to a senior aide to the mayor. Giuliani enjoyed the Brooklyn Museum fight, and his rhetoric became extreme: "This should happen in a psychiatric hospital, not in a museum" ("New Yorkers Back Exhibit Over Mayor, Polls Find," the *Times Union*, October 2, 1999).

Giuliani's reaction to Tina Brown's proposed *Talk* magazine party at the Brooklyn Navy Yards was described to me at the time by a senior aide. It was also written about in the *Daily News* on June 23 and 24, 1999 ("Giuliani's Party Politics Crushes Mag Fete in Move vs. Hil," "KO of Bash Justified, Says Rudy"), and covered on New York 1.

I interviewed two sources who spent extensive time with the mayor and Judith Nathan. The *New York Post* recalled Donna Hanover's 1993 comments about her husband on May 11, 2000: "My husband is the most virile man . . ." ("Their Love Story Had Problems from Start"). A senior aide to the mayor told me in an interview that Hanover made it clear Lategano was not welcome at Gracie Mansion. A senior aide to the mayor also told me that Gracie Mansion eventually became divided into two camps. Giuliani's eventual admission of his friendship with Nathan was covered extensively in the press, including the May 4, 2000, *Daily News* ("Rudy: She's 'Good Friend' Admits Relationship with East Side Mom"). Donna Hanover did not respond to several requests for an interview.

I covered Hillary Clinton's announcement on February 6, 2000; the observations are my own. Giuliani's 2000 State of the City address was broadcast live on New York 1 and covered in the *New York Times* on January 14, 2000 ("A Theatrical Giuliani Speaks. But is it Goodbye or Hello?").

Events surrounding the killing of Patrick Dorismond were covered in the *New York Times* ("Undercover Police in Manhattan Kill an Unarmed Man in a Scuffle," March 17, 2000; "Fatal Shot an Accident, Officer's Lawyer Says," March 18, 2000;

"Accounts Diverge on What Led to Killing Outside Bar," March 22, 2000). The *New York Times* also noted Giuliani's controversial decision to release Dorismond's juvenile records ("Giuliani Cites Criminal Past of Slain Man," March 20, 2000). A senior aide to the mayor recounted the pleas from aides, including media adviser Adam Goodman, to exhibit some compassion for Dorismond, as even the usually sympathetic *New York Post* was turning on him ("Rudy and His Enemies" by columnist John Podhoretz, March 24, 2000). The *New York Times* reported on March 23, 2000, that "Giuliani's Tone Over Shooting Worries Republican Strategists" and on April 7, 2000, noted "Giuliani's Ratings Drop Over Actions in Dorismond Case." Details of Dorismond's funeral were printed in the *New York Post* on March 26, 2000 ("Dorismond Funeral Melee").

A mayoral adviser described to me Giuliani's seeming weak after a town meeting. I was present at City Hall for his announcement that he had prostate cancer. I was also present when Donna Hanover held her press conference outside St. Patrick's. I interviewed several close advisers to the mayor about the discussions he held inside Gracie Mansion about whether to pull out of the Senate race, including his strong reaction to Adam Goodman's arguments. Finally, I was present at City Hall when Giuliani pulled out of the Senate race.

Index

DiBrienza, Stephen, 109
Dicker, Fred, 29–30
Dinkins, David, 63, 99, 162, 183, 190,
    197, 258
  Diallo killing and, 241–46, 248, 253
  in election of 1989, 8–9, 11, 17, 19–31,
    46, 132
  in election of 1993, 43, 46–50, 55–62,
    182, 183
  love letters of, 28–30
  as mayor, xiv, 32–38, 40, 41, 47–48, 57,
    58, 66, 67, 71, 73, 74, 78, 79, 80, 89,
    114, 130, 147, 170, 211, 233, 234,
    253
  RG's joint press conference with, 180
  taxes of, 9, 27
Division of AIDS Services (DAS), 78, 79
Dorismond, Patrick, xiv, 272–75, 284
Drexel Burnham Lambert, 4
drug dealing, xiii, 1–3, 34, 88, 94, 183,
    214, 273
Dukakis, Michael, 15, 25
Duke, David, 46
Duvalier, Jean-Claude (Baby Doc), 186
Dyson, John, 67, 155, 181, 199

East Flatbush, 108, 208
East Harlem, 33, 97
education, 113–19, 121–26, 181, 209–10,
    212, 223, 267, 270, 271
  cuts in, 76, 77–78, 210, 215
  see also Board of Education
Elaine's, 90–92, 140
election of 1960, 12
election of 1972, 12–13
election of 1980, 13
election of 1988, 15
election of 1989, xiii, 6–31, 46, 48, 72, 98,
    106, 131, 132, 151
  abortion issue in, 12, 17, 19, 24, 28
  Dinkins's small margin in, 30-31
  Giuliani-for-Mayor kickoff ceremony
    in, 1–3
  Hawkins's murder and, 19–22
  Jews in, 24–25, 26

  planning of, 6, 15–16
  press in, 1–3, 11, 16–17, 24–25
  reassessment in, 17–19
election of 1992, 23, 131
election of 1993, 37–62, 98, 106, 131,
    151, 197–98, 269
  blacks in, 8–9, 11, 19–22, 26–27, 46, 72
  commercials in, 53–54, 55
  effects of Clinton's speech on, 58, 60
  Election Day in, 59-61
  fusion ticket in, 45–46
  illegal campaign contributions in, 104
  Lategano in, 50, 143–44
  modern management in, 43–44
  Moynihan's speech and, 37–38
  polls in, 48, 58, 60-61, 144
  press in, 41, 42, 49–53, 60, 103-4, 144
  RG's warmer side in, 53–54
election of 1994, 128–39, 149, 187
election of 1997, 184, 187–90, 192,
    196–222, 269
  commercials in, 214–16
  extramarital affair allegations in, 201–3
  Louima incident and, 204–8, 210
election of 2000, 218, 221–22, 239–40,
    254–61, 265–71, 275–76
election of 2001, 267
Emergency Medical Service, 76, 170
Empire State Pride Agenda, 210–13
Environmental Protection Department,
    U.S. (DEP), 101, 102, 105–11
Erickson, Jeffrey, 168
Esner, Ben, 108–9

FALN, 259–60
Fama, Joey, 20
Farrakhan, Louis, 68, 70
FBI (Federal Bureau of Investigation), x,
    57, 259
Feast of San Gennaro, 166–67
Feiden, Douglas, 262, 263
Feinstein, Barry, 9
Felder, Raoul, 24
Feldman, Sandra, 124
Feliciano, Gina, 20

Felissaint, Giselaine, 33
Fernandez, Joseph, 114
Ferraro, Geraldine, 197
Ferrer, Fernando, 173, 197
Fields, Virginia, 245, 251
Finance Department, 107
Financial Control Board, New York State, 184
Financial Times, 4
Fink, Mitchell, 278, 279
Finkelstein, Arthur, 1, 4, 129, 134–35, 138
fire alarm boxes, 170, 171
Fire Department, 76, 170
Fischbein Badillo Wagner Harding, 200–201, 206
Flake, Floyd, 34, 214, 246–48, 251
Flatbush, 33, 108, 185, 204, 208
food vendors, 225–26
Ford, Gerald, 23
Foreman, Jonathan, 223–24
Fort Greene, 185
Fox, Darryl, 44
France, Dinkins's trip to, 30
Friedberg, Rick, 113
Friedman, Stanley, 4, 98
Frucher, Sandy, 137
Frydman, Ken, 44, 49–50, 143
Fulton Fish Market, 164–65

Gabel, Hortense, 4
Gaebler, Ted, 40
Gambino family, 4, 165
gangs, 34, 35, 185, 247
garbage collection, 40, 41, 165–66
Garcia, Kiko, 41
Garth, David, 103, 120, 146–49
  in election of 1993, 43, 45, 48–54, 57, 60–61, 62, 144, 197, 251
  in election of 1994, 129, 136–37
  Lategano problem and, 147–49, 153, 154, 157, 197
Gelber, Marilyn, 105–11, 149–56
Genovese family, 4, 165–67
Geto, Ethan, 212

"Ghost and Mr. Giuliani, The" (Conant), 202, 203
Gingrich, Newt, 139, 251
Giuliani, Andrew (son), 2, 54, 63, 64, 87, 280, 281
Giuliani, Caroline (daughter), 280, 281
Giuliani, Catherine (cousin), 99
Giuliani, Donna Hanover, *see* Hanover, Donna
Giuliani, Harold (father), 97, 177, 277, 278
Giuliani, Helen (mother), 64, 142, 163, 222
Giuliani, Regina (first wife), 28
Giuliani, Rudy:
  ambition of, 5, 14, 177, 240
  arrogance of, 120, 121, 122, 145, 226–27
  as Catholic, 4, 5, 28, 81, 94, 185, 186, 264
  childhood of, 54, 97, 185
  coldness and lack of sympathy in, x, xiv, 5, 55, 268
  combativeness of, 159–77
  controlling behavior of, xii, 66, 92, 101, 164
  decline in popularity of, ix, 251, 275
  defiance of, xii, 78–79, 162–63
  distrust of, xii, 95, 149
  economic policy of, 74–82, 102–3, 105, 122, 170–74, 181, 184
  education of, 5, 12, 81, 87, 185–86
  egotism of, 176–77, 226
  energy of, 13, 163, 223
  evolution of political philosophy of, 12–13
  extramarital affairs of, xiv, 151–52, 154, 201–3, 267–69, 278–83
  fascism attributed to, xii, 40–41, 72, 101, 244
  first marriage of, 28, 29
  government shrunk by, 74–79, 101, 169–74
  as hero, xii, 4, 6, 14, 163
  inaugurations of, 63–65, 94, 151, 221, 222

Upper West Side, 86–87, 120, 121, 185, 196, 215, 219
U.S. Attorney's Office, 3–6, 8, 13, 14, 25–26, 97, 104, 105, 176, 186
    RG's resignation from, 3–4
    "Yesrudy's" in, 6

Vallone, Peter, 78, 80–81, 82, 110, 171
Vanity Fair, 202, 203, 269
Vasquez, Anthony, 273
Velella, Guy, 99
Village Voice, xii, 24
Volpe, Justin, 204–7

WABC-TV, 104, 132
Wagner, Robert, 5, 23
Wagner, Robert, Jr., 43, 57, 198n
Wai, Sidique, 77
Walker, Wyatt Tee, 188, 241–42
Wallwork, James, 131
Washington, Rudy, 56–57, 71–72, 164, 182, 216–19, 246–51, 264, 285
Washington Heights, 41, 232
Washington Post, 186
water bill problem, 107–8, 110
water supply, 170, 171
Watkins, Brian, 35
Watters, Kyle, 229–30, 231, 235–38

Weingarten, Randi, 261
Weir, Richard, 278
welfare, x, xiii, 13, 34, 74, 76, 82, 171–74, 181, 253
West Bank, 260-61
Weusi, Jitu (Leslie Campbell), 26, 27
What Will You Be? (book commissioned by Giuliani), 210
White & Case, 1–3
Whitman, Christie, 130
Williams, Enoch, 76
Wilson, Howard, 66
Wilson, James Q., 39
Wilson, Rick, 285
Wolf, Dan, 120
Women's Leadership Forum, 239
Wooten, Priscilla, 213
workfare program, 172, 174, 194

Yeltsin, Boris, 159
Young, Denny, 8, 10, 71, 285
    in election of 1989, 6, 16, 17, 28–29
    in election of 1993, 45, 56
    as mayor's counsel, 66, 80, 82, 206, 246, 250, 283
Youth Services, 147

Zimmer, Dick, 143